Regionalisation

SCHOOL OF ORIENTA'

HOOL OF ORIENTAL AND AFRICAN STUDIES

University of London

Regionalisation in Africa

Integration & Disintegration

Edited by
DANIEL C. BACH

JAMES CURREY
OXFORD

INDIANA UNIVERSITY PRESS
BLOOMINGTON & INDIANAPOLIS

First published in Europe
and the Commonwealth by
James Currey Ltd
73 Botley Road
Oxford OX2 0BS

and in North America by
Indiana University Press
601 North Morton Street
Bloomington
Indiana 47404

1 2 3 4 5 03 02 01 00 99
ISBN 0–85255–826–0 (James Currey paper)
ISBN 0–85255–831–7 (James Currey cloth)
ISBN 0–253–21340–1 (Indiana paper)
ISBN 0–253–33598–1 (Indiana cloth)

This volume is published with the support of the European Commission. The views
expressed by the authors do not necessarily represent the views of the Commission.

British Cataloguing in Publication Data
Regionalisation in Africa: integration and disintegration
   1. Regional economics 2. Africa – Economic integration
   3. Africa – Economic conditions – 1960–
   I. Bach, Daniel C.
   337.1'6

   ISBN 0852558317 (cloth)
      0852558260 (paper)

Library of Congress Cataloging-in-Publication Data
A catalog record for this book is available from the Library of Congress.
   ISBN 0–253–33598–1 (cloth)
   ISBN 0–253–21340–1 (paper)

Typeset in 10½/11½ pt Bembo by Saxon Graphics Ltd, Derby
Manufactured in Britain
for Villiers Publications Ltd, London N3

Contents

List of Tables   ix
List of Contributors   xi
List of Acronyms   xiii
Foreword   xvii

I REGIONALISM & GLOBALISATION IN SUB-SAHARAN AFRICA

1 DANIEL C. BACH   1
Revisiting a Paradigm

2 ALICE LANDAU   15
Multilateralism & Regionalism
in International Economic Relations

3 WALTER KENNES   27
African Regional Economic Integration
& the European Union

II STATES & TERRITORIES

4 DOMINIQUE DARBON   41
Crisis of the State & Communalism
New Ideological Stakes in African Integration

5 CHRISTOPHER CLAPHAM   53
Boundaries & States
in the New African Order

6 ABDOULAYE NIANDOU SOULEY   67
Paradoxes & Ambiguities
of Democratisation

Contents

7 CÉLESTIN MONGA   73
Is African Civil Society Civilised?

8 EDOUARD BUSTIN   81
The Collapse of 'Congo/Zaïre'
& its Regional Impact

9 ROTIMI SUBERU   91
Integration & Disintegration
in the Nigerian Federation

10 SIMON BEKKER   103
Territoriality & Institutional Change
in the New South Africa

III REGIONAL ORGANISATIONS

11 OLATUNDE B.J. OJO   119
Integration in ECOWAS
Successes & Difficulties

12 MARC-LOUIS ROPIVIA   125
Failing Institutions & Shattered Space
What Regional Integration in Central Africa?

13 ROLAND POURTIER   129
The Renovation of UDEAC
Sense & Nonsense in Central African Integration

14 MICHEL LELART   139
The Franc Zone
& European Monetary Integration

15 PETER TAKIRAMBUDDE   151
The Rival Strategies of SADC & PTA/COMESA
in Southern Africa

16 COLIN McCARTHY   159
SACU & the Rand Zone

Contents

IV NETWORKS

17 BRUNO STARY 169
Cross-Border Trade in West Africa
The Ghana–Côte d'Ivoire Frontier

18 JANET MACGAFFEY
& RÉMY BAZENGUISSA-GANGA 179
Personal Networks & Trans-Frontier Trade
Zaïrean & Congolese Migrants

19 ALAIN LABROUSSE 189
The Production & Distribution
of Illicit Drugs

Bibliography 201
Index 225

List of Tables

3.1	Basic facts on the main regional organisations	29
3.2	Breakdown of EU regional co-operation funds	35
3.3	Member states of major sub-regional organisations	40
16.1	Distribution of SACU revenue	161
16.2	South Africa's trade with Southern Africa, 1990	166

List of Contributors

Daniel Bach is CNRS Research Fellow and Director of the *Centre d'Etude d'Afrique Noire,* CNRS-Institut d'Etudes Politiques, University Montesquieu-Bordeaux IV, France.

Rémy Bazenguissa is Lecturer in Sociology at the University of Lille I, France.

Simon Bekker is Professor of Sociology at the University of Stellenbosch, South Africa.

Edouard Bustin is Professor of Political Science at the University of Boston, MA, United States, and Director of the *Groupe de Recherches sur l'Afrique Francophone* (GRAF).

Christopher Clapham is Professor of Politics & International Relations at Lancaster University, United Kingdom, and editor of *The Journal of Modern African Studies.*

Dominique Darbon is Senior Lecturer in Political Science at the University Montesquieu-Bordeaux IV, France, and Editor of *Politique africaine.*

Walter Kennes is Head of Section of the Directorate-General for Development of the European Commission, Brussels, Belgium.

Alain Labrousse is Director of Geopolitical Drug Watch (*Observatoire géopolitique des Drogues*), Paris, France.

Alice Landau is Professor of Political Science at the University of Geneva, Switzerland.

Michel Lelart is CNRS Research Fellow attached to the Institut Orléanais de Finance, University of Orléans, France.

Janet MacGaffey is Professor of Anthropology at Bucknell University, Lewisburg, PA, United States.

Colin McCarthy is Professor of Economics at the University of Stellenbosch, South Africa.

Célestin Monga has taught economics and political science at the University of Boston, MA, United States and the University of Bordeaux, France, and is currently a Country Economist at the World Bank.

Abdoulaye Niandou Souley is Lecturer in Political Science at the University Abdou Moumouni Dioffo, Niamey, Niger.

Olatunde Ojo, former Dean of the Faculty of Social Sciences, University of Port Harcourt, Nigeria, is currently a Visiting Professor of Political Science at the University of Montana, Missoula, United States.

Roland Pourtier is Professor of Geography at the University of Paris I (Panthéon-Sorbonne), France.

Marc-Louis Ropivia is Senior Lecturer in Geography and Director of *Centre d'Etude et de Recherche en Géopolitique et Prospective* (CERGEP) at the University Omar Bongo, Libreville, Gabon.

Bruno Stary is Lecturer in Geography at the University of Paris X-Nanterre, France.

Rotimi Suberu is Senior Lecturer in Political Science at the University of Ibadan, Nigeria.

Peter Nanyenya Takirambudde is the Exective Director of Human Rights Watch/Africa, New York, United States.

List of Acronyms

ACP	African, Caribbean and Pacific Countries
ADB	African Development Bank
ADFL	Alliance des Forces Démocratiques de Libération
AEC	African Economic Community
AEF	Afrique Equatoriale Française
AFC	Alliance des Forces du Changement
ANC	African National Congress
AOF	Afrique Occidentale Française
APEC	Asia-Pacific Economic Co-operation
ASEAN	Association of South East Asian Nations
BCEAO	Banque Centrale des Etats d'Afrique de l'Ouest
BEAC	Banque des Etats d'Afrique centrale
BLS	Botswana, Lesotho, Swaziland
BLSN	Botswana, Lesotho, Swaziland, Namibia
CAP	Common Agricultural Policy
CAR	Central African Republic
CARICOM	Caribbean Common Market
CBI	Cross-Border Initiative
CDR	Comité de Défense de la Révolution
CDS	Convention Démocratique et Sociale
CEAO	Communauté Economique d'Afrique de l'Ouest
CEDEAO	Communauté Economique des Etats de l'Afrique de l'Ouest (ECOWAS)
CEEAC	Communauté Economique des Etats de l'Afrique Centrale
CEMAC	Communauté Economique et Monétaire d'Afrique Centrale
CEPGL	Communauté Economique des Pays des Grands Lacs
CFA	Communauté Financière Africaine (Franc Zone)
CILSS	Permanent Inter-state Committe on Drought Control in the Sahel
CIMA	Conférence Inter-Africaine des Marchés d'Assurance
CIPRES	Conférence Inter-Africaine de Prévoyance Sociale

CMA	Common Monetary Area
COMESA	Common Market for Eastern and Southern Africa
CONSAS	Constellation of Southern African States
CUTT	Customs Union Task Team
DBSA	Development Bank of Southern Africa
DRC	Democratic Republic of Congo
EAC	East African Community
EAMA	Etats Africains et Malgache Associés
EC/EU	European Community/European Union
ECB	European Central Bank
ECCAS	Economic Community of Central African States
ECOMOG	ECOWAS Monitoring Group
ECOWAS	Economic Community of West African States (CEDEAO)
ECSC	European Coal and Steel Community
ECU	European Currency Unit
EDF	European Development Fund
EEA	European Economic Area
EFTA	European Free Trade Area
EIB	European Investment Bank
EMCF	European Monetary Compensation Fund
EPLF	Eritrean People's Liberation Front
EPRDF	Ethiopian People's Revolutionary Democratic Front
FCCD	Fund for Co-operation, Compensation and Development
FESAC	Fédération de l'Enseignement Supérieur en Afrique Centrale
FF	Freedom Front
FFC	Financial and Fiscal Commission
GATT	General Agreement on Tariffs and Trade
GCA	Global Coalition for Africa
GDP	Gross Domestic Product
GNP	Gross National Product
GSP	General System of Preferences
IFP	Inkatha Freedom Party
IGADD	Inter-Governmental Agency against Drought and for Development
IGO	Inter-governmental Organisation
IMF	International Monetary Fund
INCB	International Narcotics Control Board
IOC	Indian Ocean Commission
LANTAG	South African Language Board
LGNF	Local Government Negotiating Forum
MERCOSUR	South American Common Market
MMA	Multilateral Monetary Agreement
MOSOP	Movement for the Survival of the Ogoni People
NAFTA	North American Free Trade Area
NDFI	National Development Financing Institutions
NNF	National Negotiation Forum
NP	National Party

NPFL	National Patriotic Front of Liberia
OAU	Organisation of African Unity
OECD	Organisation for Economic and Development Co-operation
OEEC	Organisation for European Economic Co-operation
OHADA	Organisation pour l'Harmonisation du Droit des Affaires
PCTD	Pacific Conference on Trade Development
PECC	Pacific Economic Co-operation Council
PREC	Pacific Rim Economic Council
PTA	Preferential Trade Agreement of Eastern and Southern Africa
RDP	Reconstruction and Development Programme
RMA	Rand Monetary Area
RRP	Regional Reform Programme
SACU	Southern African Custom Union
SACUA	Southern African Customs Union Agreement
SADC	Southern African Development Community
SADCC	Southern African Development Co-ordinating Conference
SAP	Structural Adjustment Programmes
SARB	South Africa Reserve Bank
SDR	Special Drawing Right
TBVC	Transkei, Bophutatswana, Venda et Ciskei
TIPAC	Transit Inter-Etats des Pays de l'Afrique Centrale
TMA	Trilateral Monetary Agreement
UA	Units of Acounts
UDEAC	Union Douanière des Etats d'Afrique Centrale
UDI	Unilateral Declaration of Independence
UEMOA	Union économique et monétaire ouest-africaine (WAEMU)
ULIMO	United Liberation Movement for Democracy in Liberia
UMA	Union du Maghreb Arabe
UMAC	Union Monétaire de l'Afrique Centrale
UMOA	Union Monétaire de l'Afrique de l'Ouest
UNCTAD	United Nations Conference on Trade and Development
UNITA	União Nacional para a Independência Total de Angola
URAC	Union des Républiques d'Afrique Centrale
USSR	Union of Soviet Socialist Republics
USTR	United States Trade Representative
WACH	West African Clearing House
WAEMU	West African Economic and Monetary Union (UEMOA)
WAMA	West African Monetary Agency
WTO	World Trade Organisation

Foreword

Regionalisation is a much discussed topic in North America, in Europe and in Asia. Yet, there is hardly anything written about this subject for Africa because the standard view is that there is no regionalisation process on the continent. This book argues the opposite: there is a regionalisation process in Africa. Throughout the African continent, the effects of globalisation and regionalisation combine with a crisis of the post-colonial states to reshape state-society relations. This is partly attributable to the fungibility of the international, transnational and domestic dimensions of integration in Africa. Equally important, however, is the responsibility of policies and programmes which have proved largely inefficient in stimulating positive interactions between the forces of globalisation, regionalisation and fragmentation.

More than ever before, Africa's regionalisation processes are closely inter-twined with its changing patterns of global insertion. The unremitting margin-alisation of the continent in terms of world trade and investment is compounded by its brutal politico-diplomatic and strategic downgrading, due to the end of bipolarity, and perhaps the return of South Africa to 'normality'. The related decrease of aid flows (euphemistically described as 'aid fatigue') and the new economic, financial and socio-political strings attached to bilateral and multilateral transfers mean increasingly tight prescriptions for the governments of sub-Saharan Africa. Highly dependent on these resources, they are left with fewer opportunites to avoid, formally or *de facto,* external tutelage and conditionality (Wright, 1998). These constraints often reach a scale unprece-dented since decolonisation, but their internalisation remains both limited and largely ineffective. The chains of institutional authority and the political legit-imacy are too weak for externally-induced programmes to be fully imple-mented. Recurrent budgetary constraints, together with the problems of governmental and territorial legitimacy, favour the adoption of escapist strategies by the population concerned. In their own ways, deficient territorial control and alternative forms of allegiance contribute to the reintroduction of margins of autonomy, which are denied to African states in the formal conduct of their external affairs.

The political and developmental failure of Africa's authoritarian regimes was already blatant when the end of the Cold War brought an end to pressures for the preservation of the political *status quo*. Fresh opportunities for the opening up of a democratic space exerted catalytic effects on the expression of identitarian, ethno-regional or religious demands. These challenged incumbent regimes, as much as the concepts of citizenship and territoriality. Single-party and military regimes imposed authoritarian policies in the name of nation-building, and this in turn undermined the perception and values attached to citizenship. Networks based on so-called primordial attachments also emerged as a response to the decay of state capacities, not least with respect to the preservation of civil peace and individual security. Ties between people, and a sense of kinship, sometimes spawning across boundary lines, constitute a potential challenge to the essence of the territoriality principle. In several respects, the multiplicity and diversity of precolonial political formations, as well as the kaleidoscope of primordial identities in perpetual recomposition, create an environment more propitious for deconstruction than for the construction of broader regional spaces.

The extreme fragmentation of the African continent, and the problems of economic survival faced by numerous states, account for the establishment of a large number of inter-governmental organisations (IGOs). Unfortunately, apart from a few cases, large discrepancies exist between the objectives they set out to pursue and their concrete implementation. One of the ambitions of this volume is therefore to clarify the factors responsible for such a trend, so as to move beyond traditional references to state deficiencies and insufficient political will. The vitality of 'illegal' cross-border trade flows may act here as a reminder of the limitations of analytical frameworks based on realist, neo-realist or – for economists – neo-liberal conceptions of the boundaries. The diversity and intensity of the cross-border transactions, their increasing internationalisation, and often their close interaction with state policies, are an invitation to conceptual clarifications. A better understanding of the failure of regional integration programmes based on trade liberalisation is also at stake. One of our working hypotheses here is that, in Africa as in other regions of the world, the 'continentalisation' of trade is a reality, but one that is dependent on the persistence of significant fiscal, tariff and monetary disparities on each side of the borders.

Beyond their diversity, the contributions in this volume reflect a common attempt to question the dominant paradigms in a comparative perspective, taking into account experiences from other regions of the world. The desire to undertake a truly continental treatment of the themes selected resulted in the formation of a group of contributors capable of moving beyond the traditional cleavages between Francophone, Anglophone and Lusophone Africa. Even though such divisions are regularly denounced, they remain all too often implicitly present, and confer a parochial flavour to a number of analyses on African regionalisation processes.

This book is an updated and revised version of the volume published in French under the title *Régionalisation, mondialisation et fragmentation en Afrique subsaharienne* (Paris: Karthala, 1998). It is the outcome of a research programme that was launched following a conference held on 'Integration and Regionalisation in Sub-Saharan Africa' at the *Centre d'Etude d'Afrique Noire* (CEAN), Talence, on 27–29

May 1994. Crucial support for the implementation and completion of this project was received from the European Commission, Brusssels, who made it possible to treat the subject from a broad perspective. Valuable contributions were also received from the Centre National de la Recherche Scientifique (CNRS), the Institut d'Etudes Politiques of Bordeaux University, the French Ministry of Co-operation, the British Council and the French Institutes of South Africa (IFAS) and for Research in Africa (IFRA-Ibadan). As usual, the opinions expressed do not necessarily reflect the views of the organisations which generously agreed to sponsor this project.

Daniel C. Bach
Bordeaux

REGIONALISM & GLOBALISATION IN SUB-SAHARAN AFRICA

1

DANIEL C. BACH
Revisiting a Paradigm

In Africa, as in other parts of the world, regionalisation is a major process and a key factor of evolution in internal and international politics. The time is past when programmes aimed at regional construction were stigmatised as outright utopian, or suspected of harbouring hegemonic ambitions. This was the case when the end of colonial rule in the late 1950s and early '60s raised expectations of the development of cross-border and pan-African solidarities. The newly independent states soon found it difficult to accept restraints on their sovereignty, while the politics of the Cold War encouraged arrangements based on political and ideological considerations. The only notable exception to this overall trend took place in Europe, where regional integration made spectacular progress due to the ability of its French, German and Italian architects to convert the constraints of bipolarity into a source of opportunity (Landau, 1995b).

Outside Europe, the rebirth of regionalism during the late 1980s often had little to do with the numerous international organisations (Smouts, 1995) that were supposed to promote its development. The drive towards the polarisation of international trade on a regional basis (Lafay and Unal-Kesenci, 1991) was primarily associated with the behaviour of micro-actors, in a context energised by the progress of multilateralism, and the generalisation of adjustment and deregulation policies. The main outcome of this powerful trend was the concentration of world trade and investment around three regional areas: North America, the European Union (46% of world trade in 1992) and Asia-Pacific.

Institution-building was then encouraged by fears of the re-emergence of protectionism on a regional basis (Gamble and Payne, 1996). Regional agreements mushroomed, prompted by the uncertain outcome of the GATT/Uruguay Round negotiations, and apprehensions about a possible transformation of the EU into 'fortress Europe'. The collapse of the Soviet Union and the removal of the Iron Curtain gave a renewed impulse to the tendency to emphasise economic interactions at the expense of political and strategic preoccupations.

In a number of cases, the revival of regionalism meant reforming the so-called 'first-generation' regional organisations, which were established in the 1960s to

1

promote integration through import-substitution strategies and 'delinking' from the global market. More frequently, regionalisation involved the creation of new groupings, such as the North American Free Trade Area (NAFTA) and MERCOSUR in the Americas; the Asia-Pacific Economic Conference (APEC) and the Free Trade Agreement of the Association of South East Asian Nations (ASEAN) in Asia. In Europe, the expansion and deepening of EU integration prompted the formation of the European Economic Area (EEA). In Africa, the member states of the Organisation of African Unity (OAU) joined the move and signed in 1991 the Treaty of Abuja towards the establishment of a transcontinental African Economic Community (AEC).

Far from implying the formation of mutually exclusive regional integration groupings, this process was strongly outward-oriented; regionalisation also meant the opening of discussions towards the enlargement of existing institutions and the conclusion of inter-regional agreements. This kaleidoscopic interplay between institutions, identities and socio-political factors accounts for the polymorphous nature of the so-called new regionalisation process. Closely tied to the advancement of globalisation, the regionalisation process often endorsed already existing international economic links between neighbouring states (Hine, 1992: 115). Regionalisation, as in Europe or North America, represented an opportunity to establish a more appropriate framework for absorbing the pressures of multilateralism and globalisation. Elsewhere, as in Asia or Africa, regionalisation was associated with the trade and investment strategies of private agents who operated in the absence of – or, as in Africa, in opposition to – institutionalised regional structures. The specific nature of the regionalisation process in Africa results from this ambivalent relationship between regionalisation, as impelled by private agents, and institutionalised patterns of regionalisation – a distinction which is congruent with that between *de jure* and *de facto* regionalism (Oman, 1996).

Regionalisation reveals itself in sub-Saharan Africa through complex and often conflicting trends of interaction, as the contributions in this volume demonstrate. As an introduction, the following pages discuss the crisis in territorial and governmental legitimacy, and its effects on regional Inter-governmental Organisations (IGOs). We shall then turn to the spectacular development of cross-border regionalisation. It will be argued that, far from contributing to an adjustment of the state to the pressure of globalisation, regionalisation in Africa is primarily the expression of micro-strategies which, unlike what is happening in most other areas of the world, seek to take advantage of the resources of globalisation, with the effect of a further erosion of the states' territorial and governmental legitimacy.

The Diversification of State-Society Relations

Commitments to regional integration in Africa have been constrained by a highly ambivalent critique of the colonial heritage. At independence, the leaders of the new independent states readily acknowledged the disastrous effects of the partition of the continent, but were reluctant, if not totally unwilling, to support policies likely to restrain state sovereignty and, consequently, their power.

Nearly forty years after independence, the boundary-lines inherited from the colonial period remain unchanged despite the intractable problems which they induce. The oft-mentioned issue of their forceful imposition is not so much what may matter here, since this is no less specific to Africa than to most European or Latin American boundaries. Neither should the past replacement of precolonial frontiers by standardised 'linear-borders' (Foucher, 1988) be considered as easily, so long as the post-Westphalian territorial state model remains the international norm. Clearly disastrous, however, are the economic, social and human effects resulting from the lay-out of boundary-lines. This is responsible for severe physical impediments to the unification of the territory of such states as Congo/Zaïre, Congo, Senegal or Namibia, while chronic problems of land-lockedness and poor access to the coast are faced by the Sahelian and Southern African sub-regions. Worse still, in a number of African states, resources are chronically insufficient, due to an unfavourable ecological and human environment. This combination of factors contributes to the description of African states as 'quasi- ' or *'failed'* states owing to their difficulty in meeting the criteria usually associated with international sovereignty (Jackson and Rosberg, 1986; Zartman, 1995; Badie, 1992; Le Roy, 1996).

The break-up of colonial federations at independence suddenly highlighted the negative consequences of the extreme segmentation and the intrinsically problematic viability of the political divisions and economic circuits inherited from the colonial period. Whether violent or negotiated, the dissolution processes meant the disappearance of the fiscal and excise redistribution mechanisms which had been the *raison d'être* of structures like the Afrique Occidentale Française (AOF), the Afrique Equatoriale Française (AEF), the Central African Federation or even, at a later stage, the East African Community. The continent had never been so deeply segmented when the OAU Charter then endorsed and legitimised in 1963 the territorial *status quo* (Kodjo, 1986: 268).

Then came the end of the Cold War and the reduced importance which non-African powers attached to the preservation of African boundary-lines. In sub-Saharan Africa, as in Eastern or Central Europe, superpowers could no longer be considered as unambiguous agents for boundary and regime stability (Herbst, 1992: 107; Wright, 1992: 26–7) at a time when authoritarian regimes were being confronted with renewed demands for autonomy. The OAU-endorsed territorial *status quo* principle appeared seriously undermined when, following the referendum held in May 1993, Eritrea gained independence after several decades of a national war of liberation. Six years later, this remains the only example of a formal reorganisation of the political map of the continent, despite an international environment characterised by a new sensitivity to demands for autonomy and respect for group rights as a whole. The massive transformation of the map of Africa which some analysts predicted following the end of bipolarity (Mazrui, 1993: 34; Makau wa Mutua, 1994) is still awaited.

Secessionist attempts, as witnessed in Nigeria (Biafra), Congo/Zaïre (Katanga) or the Sudan, are the exception in Africa. Civil disobedience, violence and even rebellion remain geared towards the achievement of 'national' objectives, namely, the improvement of access to the state and its resources, not least through the overthrow of the established regimes. Irridentism, as illustrated by pan-Somali nationalism, is equally atypical. The case of the Tuaregs of Niger, Mali or Mauritania is worth noting in this respect: despite ways of life which carry a strong regionalist component, they have always expressed their political demands within their respective national contexts.

The legitimacy of colonial partition-lines has grown to be much stronger than public speeches and the states' problems of territorial control would allow one to imagine. Demands for boundary adjustments have been on the increase since the early 1990s, but they all revolve around the clarification or re-establishment of colonial partition-lines that were once erased or transformed into internal admin- istrative boundaries. The above-mentioned case of Eritrea's independence may be interpreted as the re-establisment of the frontier-line which separated this former Italian colony from Ethiopia until it was invaded by Mussolini's troops in 1936. In the Horn, the Somali conflict has provoked a *de facto* return to the boundary which existed between the ex-British Somaliland and the Italian Somalia until they merged in 1960. The *ex-post* legitimation of this colonial boundary-line is especially surprising if one remembers how the Somali state was commonly described in the 1980s as a 'mono-ethnic' state where people could 'trace their descent to a common ancestor', with the result of 'a powerful web of kinship ties, making them a community of brothers, cousins and kinsmen' (Samatar, 1985: 187). Further to the south, the United Republic of Tanzania – born out of the unification of Tanganyika (a former German colony) and Zanzibar (a former British protectorate) in 1964 – has been confronted with demands for the constitution of a separate government for the mainland. In West Africa, the Saharawi independence movement has been fighting for several decades to secure the international recognition of a boundary-line which has undisputed colonial origins. Elsewhere in the sub-region, agitation in Senegal's Casamance and in the western part of Cameroon is rooted in the assertion of identity claims which draw some of their specificity from distinct colonial and linguistic legacies – Portuguese in the first case, British in the second.

The territorial stability of the post-colonial African states has proved greater than many imagined, yet the future of the pluri-ethnic and strongly territorialised state-model introduced by the colonial rulers remains shrouded in uncertainty. New patterns of state-society interactions are already emerging, shaped by changes in the states' institutional and regulatory capacity, the configuration of ethno-regional interactions, the nature of available resources, and the patterns of territorial control. Attempts to regulate geo-ethnic interests and ensure territorial continuity, through a codification of group rights and equitable access to resources, are few and not without their own problems, as illustrated by the boomerang effects of the Nigerian consociational model (Bach, 1991a: Suberu in Chapter 9 in this volume) and South Africa's more recent, yet equally innovative, approach to post-apartheid reconstruction (Chapter 10). All too often, the decline of available resources enhances the erosion of the states' monopoly of public violence to the benefit of private agents. Circumstantial pressure may then force incumbent leaders to accept compromises which result in an increasingly frag- mented exercise of national sovereignty, due to its outright lease to a trusted clientèle or capture by warlords. In Mobutu's Zaïre, 'the state has opted out and simply ignores much of what is going on' wrote Janet MacGaffey (MacGaffey *et al.,* 1991: 158), with the result of its transformation into an 'archipelago' state (*Etat archipel*) where direct involvement is confined to the economically more attractive areas, the so-called *zones utiles* (Pourtier, 1992). In West Africa, it is the political and economic segmentation resulting from the numerous boundary-lines which is being instrumentalised and transformed into a comparative advantage. Managing frontier disparities on a rent-seeking basis has become a vital component of the policy orientations of Benin, Togo, The Gambia, Niger and, to a lesser extent, Chad. The Béninois 'entrepôt state' ('Etat entrepôt'), as described by Igué and Soulé (1992), epitomises this extensive growth of state-backed 'illegal' transactions.[1] In Southern Africa, the limited territorial control exerted by the Angolan regime contributes to a deterritorialisation of the state, further accentuated by its reliance on off-shore oil production and revenues. In Somalia, pan-Somali nationalism has dissolved into particularly destructive forms of 'segmentary nationalism' (Lewis, 1989), with the resultant disintegration of the state.

Max Weber's classical definition of the state cannot apply in numerous parts of the continent: in Liberia, Sierra Leone, Congo/Zaïre, Angola or Somalia, the state is no longer the sole agency which, within society, possesses the monopoly of legitimate violence. The diversification of state-society relations does not involve any formal challenge to existing boundary-lines, but goes along with the development of new patterns of regional interaction which undermine territorial control and the efficiency of institutional attempts to promote regional integration.

Institutional Crisis as a Reflection of States in Crisis

The results achieved by the numerous IGOs meant to promote regional co-operation or integration are a far cry from the objectives assigned to them in their founding charters. Seven years after the adoption of the Abuja Plan (OAU, 1991), there is no evidence that its programme aimed at the establishment of a continental common market by 2025 has the slightest chance of being implemented.

The break-up of the colonial federations (Nigeria is perhaps the only exception) has had a lasting effect on moves to revive regional co-operation and integration. In West Africa, it was not until 1972 that the Presidents of Côte d'Ivoire and Senegal were able to overcome their past opposition over the preservation of the French West Africa (AOF) Federation, dissolved in 1959 with France's tacit encouragement. Joint concern at Nigeria's growing influence in the sub-region eventually prompted their reconciliation and decision to establish the purely Francophone Economic Community of West Africa (CEAO). In Southern and Eastern Africa, regional co-operation was also adversely affected by bitter memories of the Federation of Rhodesia and Nyasaland and, later, the experience of the East African Community (EAC). It took the pressure generated by South

---

[1] By 1987, the African Development Bank estimated that Gambia's re-export trade amounted to 40% of the country's imports (Sall, 1992: 10). In Benin, the contribution of cross-border trade to the country's recurrent budget fluctuated between 60 and 80% during the 1970s and early '80s (Igué and Soulé, 1992: 26).

Africa's Constellation of South African States (CONSAS) project for the Southern African Development Co-ordination Conference (SADCC) to be established in 1981. SADCC's major concern was initially how to attract international aid towards projects with a regional component, so as to reduce the member states' dependence on South Africa. Hence, the organisation paid lip service to the objective of regional integration until political change in South Africa and the pressure of donors imposed a change of perspective. This resulted in the adoption of the 1992 Windhoek Treaty, whereby the Southern African Development *Co-ordination Conference* (emphasis mine) was transformed into a Development *Community* (SADC). Two years later, in November 1994, Uganda, Kenya and Tanzania agreed to revive the common services which were in operation until the dissolution of the EAC in 1977.

The lack of political and financial internalisation of regional integration commitments has often been denounced, but should not really be considered surprising in a context where a good number of states are confronted with severe 'national' integration difficulties. The overall trend towards a transformation of the ambitious regional integration schemes into more modest functional co-operation programmes is a direct consequence of the member states' reluctance to undertake transfers of sovereignty. The most tangible achievements of regional co-operation are often to be seen in the sectors of infrastructures and telecommunications. In this as in other areas of functional co-operation, programmes have been largely donor-driven, due to limited financial commitments by member states.

The Southern African Customs Union (SACU) and the Franc Zone are the only African regional institutions where integration does exist, as a result of a centralised management of tariffs and revenue distribution, in the first case, and due to joint monetary policies in the second. But these two organisations represent yet another illustration of the weak internalisation of the constraints of regional integration by the member states of regional IGOs. Integration within SACU proceeds from the perpetuation of arrangements that date back to the colonial period. The customs union was still in operation when Botswana, Lesotho and Swaziland (BLS) became independent in the 1960s and decided not to exert their newly acquired international sovereignty in customs and excise policy matters. In Francophone West and Central Africa, a similar decision to preserve the Franc Zone was adopted at independence by all the French colonies but one (Sékou Touré's Guinea). In so doing, the Francophone states did not really have to decide on a transfer of sovereignty, since they had never had the opportunity to exercise it before. As in the case of SACU, the process could more aptly be described as a renunciation of total independence. Within the Franc Zone and within SACU, sectoral integration is guaranteed and controlled by a hegemonic state (France in the Franc Zone and South Africa with regard to SACU), as opposed to a common, supranational entity.

Two chapters in this volume attach special attention to the characteristics and evolution of SACU and the Franc Zone. Suffice it to say here that negotiations to reform (and perhaps dissolve?) the SACU arrangements were launched in late 1994, in the aftermath of the South African general election. The financial, economic and political stakes involved in the negotiations quickly appeared more complex than expected. South Africa and the BLS decided against the dissolution of their union into the far more ambitious, yet uncertain, SADC programmes (Leistner, 1997: 118). The negotiations were initially expected to last only a few months; four and a half years later, their conclusions were still being awaited.

Within the Franc Zone, a programme of reforms was also launched, in 1991, with the initial ambition of avoiding a devaluation of the CFA franc through regionally based adjustment policies. This resulted in the creation of the Conférence Interafricaine des Marchés d'Assurance (CIMA) in 1992, followed a year later by the Conférence Interafricaine de Prévoyance Sociale (CIPRES) and the Organisation pour l'Harmonisation du Droit des Affaires en Afrique (OHADA). These ambitious programmes were launched so as to promote integration through the harmonisation of legal regulations (*'intégration par les règles'*) in the fields of insurance, social welfare and business law. They proved unable to avoid the devaluation of the CFA franc in January 1994, but may well have contributed to avoiding the break-up of the Franc Zone. Indeed, the devaluation of the CFA franc was accompanied by the replacement of existing Francophone regional institutions (CEAO in West Africa, and UDEAC in Central Africa) by the Francophone West African Economic and Monetary Union (UEMOA) and the Central African Economic and Monetary Community (CEMAC). Their treaties were both signed in 1994, but UEMOA is the only one which has so far been ratified. Even in this case, the implementation of the UEMOA treaty has encountered a number of setbacks. The reluctance of member states to internalise integration constraints (including through the convergence of financial and budgetary policicies) is one reason; another is the flawed conception of the CEMAC and UEMOA treaties, both of them born out of an explicit attempt to replicate the dispositions of the Single European Act and the Maastricht Treaty on economic and monetary integration (see Chapter 14 in this volume).

The Franc Zone, CEMAC, UEMOA, SACU and SADC preserve a strong identity within the four sub-regional organisations which are expected to spearhead progress towards a continental common market. These overlapping affiliations are a source of tension and in part contribute to the mixed results achieved by the larger regional IGOs. In the Maghreb and Central African sub-regions, the Arab Maghreb Union (UMA) and the Economic Community of Central African States (CEEAC) have not achieved any tangible results. In West Africa and Southern Africa, the Economic Community of West African States (ECOWAS) and the Common Market for Eastern and Southern Africa (COMESA) – previously known as the Preferential Trade Agreement of Eastern and Southern Africa (PTA) – have managed to identify and implement several important sectoral co-operation programmes. The two organisations have achieved little progress towards market integration through sub-regional trade liberalisation, but this is not surprising.

The assumption that boundary-lines are costly impediments to the free circulation of factors of production, ignores the crucial importance of survival and accumulation strategies associated with the management of frontier disparities in Africa. Large groups of the population – at times whole states – owe their survival to semi-clandestine transactions across boundaries. It is our contention that, due to their failure to address such an issue, Africa's sub-regional trade liberalisation schemes have been doomed to failure.

Cross-border Trade & Trans-state Regionalisation

African boundaries delineate and separate communities, as much as they stimulate the development of cross-frontier transactions (Nugent and Asiwaju, 1996).
In sub-Saharan Africa, the regionalisation process results, far more than in the
case of the Asian economies, from the exploitation of boundary disparities and
distortions on a rent-seeking basis. Transactions are, depending on authors and
circumstances, described as 'informal' or 'unrecorded trade'; as the 'underground', 'second' or even the 'real economy'; and of course as 'smuggling' or 're-
exportation'. This proliferation of loosely overlapping notions reflects the
kaleidoscopic morphology of trans-state regionalisation (*régionalisation transétatique*). The concept refers to processes of cross-border interaction which have
their own distinctive features, although they combine elements of inter-state and
transnational regionalisation. Trans-state regionalisation cannot be associated
with an institutionalised process (Grégoire and Labazée, 1993), although it is
totally dependent on state policies and owes its prosperity to the involvement of
state agents. The diversion of official circuits towards trans-state networks may
result in decriminalising their attitude towards certain sectors of cross-border
trade, but this never leads to their public endorsement since the profits are
realised at the expense of the state(s) on the other side of the boundary-line: the
rent-taking government must avoid at all costs a strict enforcement of its
neighbour's border. Unlike 'regular' cross-border trade, trans-state trade is not
based on ecological complementarities and comparative advantages. Trans-state
trade is dependent on opportunities created by tariff, fiscal and monetary discrepancies between neighbouring economies. This may result in transactions in basic
commodities as much as in sophisticated high-tech products or narcotics.

Access to foreign currency has become an essential component of trans-state
regionalisation under the combined pressure of the states' deepening financial
difficulties and the purely national dimension of most structural adjustment
programmes. Curtailing the costs incurred by trans-state flows between the Franc
Zone and such countries as Nigeria, Ghana or Congo/Zaïre was an essential
component of the decision to suspend, on 2 August 1993, the convertibility of
CFA banknotes outside the Franc Zone banking network. The leverage effect of
the convertibility factor should not be tied exclusively to currency. Trans-state
regional flows may equally develop, though on a lesser scale, on the exclusive
basis of tariff and fiscal discrepancies, as witnessed between the member states of
the Central (CEMAC) and West African (UEMOA) components of the Franc
Zone. Poorer transport facilities through the national outlets, as in Congo/Zaïre,
or political uncertaintly,[2] may also stimulate cross-border transactions.

Precolonial linkages are frequently held responsible for the vitality of trans-
state regionalisation, owing to its heavy reliance on 'primordial' ties, and a high
visibility in the borderland. This perception requires a brief presentation of the

---

[2] During the Sankara regime, capital flight to Togo contributed to the country's consolidation as a
major financial centre for trans-state trade and currency transactions (Igué and Soulé, 1992: 112–13).

circumstances which prompted the development of trans-state flows during the colonial period. As the colonised territories were progressively integrated into the metropolitan economies, competing communications systems and market centres developed. Distinct currency zones also emerged, while restrictive tariff policies attempted to discourage the entry of goods from rival colonial blocs. During the early phase of the partition process, European rulers also competed to establish their territorial claims, with the resulting effect that the populations established on the fringes of the imperial spheres of influence were particularly prone to intimidation and reprisal measures.

Once the boundary-lines were demarcated, the colonial administrations tried to restrict contacts, including with respect to rotating pasture or cultivation habits. Caravan trade underwent an irresistible decline as a result of the imposition of new trade routes and the introduction of tariff policies designed to promote integration among the various component parts of the empire (Bayili, 1976: 62 ff; Grégoire, 1986: 51–62).

Real as it was, the segregative and alienating impact of the partition had strong inbuilt limitations. The colonial rulers soon discovered that patrolling and ensuring the effective enforcement of inter-imperial boundary-lines was impossible because of their sheer length. Competition and mutual suspicion among colonial powers prevented the adoption of harmonised policies against 'illegal' cross-border trade and migrations. As a result, boundary-lines never proved much of a physical obstacle. Whenever attempts to control cross-border trade and migrations were made, they remained limited in duration, due to their cost as much as to their ineffectiveness.

Inter-imperial partition-lines were porous, but they also materialised distinct administrative systems, with different pricing, monetary and tariff regimes. This prompted the development of 'illicit' trade which came to represent 'large profits . . . or at least small profits by quite a large number of people' living in the borderland (Southall, 1985: 99). Illicit transactions developed to the extent that, on each side of the boundary-line between Nigeria and former Benin/Dahomey, entire villages came to abandon traditional agriculture (Mondjannagni, 1963). Pre-existing patterns of social interaction underwent significant changes as profits drawn from trans-frontier trade dwarfed previous sources of income. By 1945 '. . . nearly all young men living in frontier villages were in the business [of smuggling] and in both areas smuggling had given rise to a class of wealthy men and women whose position could no longer be ignored in the affairs of their localities' (Asiwaju, 1976: 199).

The composition and direction of this emerging trans-state trade varied in accordance with such factors as import duties on manufactured goods, transport costs or cash crop producer prices. By the late 1950s, a fairly stable pattern existed in West Africa. The *surprix* (higher-than-world-market prices) system implemented in the French colonies prompted farmers and middlemen from The Gambia, Ghana or Nigeria to sell their cash crops across the boundary-line; in the British colonies, the imperial preference system meant cheaper imports of manufactured products and this created an incentive to clandestine re-exportation to the neighbouring French and Belgian territories. Accordingly, industrial and electronic equipment, liquor, tobacco and paraffin lamps were imported into Senegal through the frontier with The Gambia, while French wines, agricultural implements and fertilisers were clandestinely exported to the neighbouring British territory (Renner, 1985: 79–80).

Similarly, alcoholic drinks, tobacco and printed cloth stood foremost among the goods smuggled from Dahomey into Nigeria, while guns and gunpowder, as well as British-manufactured bicycles, were acquired from Nigeria (Mondjannagni, 1963; Lallement, 1960).

With the end of colonial rule, trans-state trade entered a new phase. The dissolution of colonial federations gave birth to an unprecedented array of customs, fiscal and monetary regimes. Pre-existing customs or monetary arrangements sometimes survived (e.g. SACU and the Franc Zone), but more often disappeared under the pressure of emerging national interests. This meant increasingly diverging tariff, fiscal and monetary policies which created a fertile ground for trans-state regionalisation when the financial difficulties encountered by a growing number of African states, following the oil boom of 1973, brought a collapse of official circuits in large parts of the continent. Population groups which had come to rely on state circuits for health, housing, education, transport and marketing were compelled to seek alternatives (Mbembe, 1992). Entire sectors of society redeployed into the parallel economy, with the effect of an unprecedented boost to trans-state regionalisation.

Today, parallel and 'illegal' circuits contribute to a vital diversification of urban income sources and exert a buffer function when salaries undergo a sharp decline in real terms or, as in the public sector, remain unpaid during substantial periods. The parallel circuits supply consumers with food, fuel and manufactured goods, while creating earning opportunities for women who make up their husbands' salaries to a living wage through unlicensed trade. Farmers living in areas where the state circuits are no longer operational can also find in the 'second economy' vital outlets for their production, as well as pre-harvest cash advances essential to the maintenance of their families and the purchase of tools, seeds and other inputs (MacGaffey *et al.*, 1991: 31).

The second economy and its trans-state regional networks are also vectors of a dispossession of the weaker to the benefit of the stronger, of the poorer to the benefit of the richer, of internal actors to the benefit of international networks. The expansion of trans-state networks beyond the borderland areas is associated with the capacity of powerful patrons, motivated by accumulation strategies, to take advantage of farmers and urban dwellers confronted with severe situations of disposession or hardship. The thesis of a 'communal redistribution' through trans-state regional flows and the 'second economy' relies on a populist myth (Meagher, 1997: 168 ff). Access to the resources necessary to participate in the networks is extremely uneven and intensely competitive: 'the rich and powerful, and those who have jobs, have greater access than do the unemployed, the urban poor, and rural producers' (MacGaffey, 1991: 154). Most importantly, farmers participate in the second economy 'out of desperation rather than choice'. If there is an element of 'social security' in the patron-client relationship between traders and producers, concludes MacGaffey with respect to Congo/Zaïre, it is a very crude one (*ibid.*: 31).

Trans-state Regionalisation as an Obstacle to Institution-building

Far from being an incentive to the disappearance of existing boundary-lines, trans-state regionalisation contributes to their preservation. Trans-state regional lobbies have a strong interest in the preservation of good relations between neighbouring states, but are equally active in preventing the implementation of sub-regional programmes aimed at the liberalisation of customs and tariff barriers.

This paradox is clearly illustrated by the circumstances which surrounded the dissolution of the Senegambian Confederation (1982–9), Africa's only post-independence political integration experiment. The decision to establish the Confederation was based on an agreement whereby Senegal was to guarantee the security of the Gambian regime (recently threatened by a *coup d'état*), in exchange for their progressive evolution towards an economic union. Since the 1970s, the Gambian government actively encouraged the development of imports which were 'illegally' re-exported to Senegal and Guinea. Trans-state trade as it was, took advantage of fiscal, excise and customs disparities which the rent-seeking policy of the Gambian government carefully preserved. From Dakar's point of view, the Senegambian Confederation opened up a perfect opportunity for the disappearance of these 'illegal' transactions. For that very reason, during the subsequent negotiations, no compensation was planned for the loss of revenue which Gambia could expect due to its loss of autonomy with respect to tariff and fiscal policy (Hughes and Lewis, 1993; Sall, 1992). Since 're-exportation' was based on illegal cross-border trade with Senegal, the Gambian authorities were themselves in no real position to raise the issue of compensation. It was at this stage that strong representations were made by the Gambian trade lobby, pointing out the economic and financial costs which the customs union would entail. These appeared overwhelmingly high since Gambian resources were scarce and substantial employment opportunities in Banjul were tied to the harbour's activity. The Gambian government therefore rejected the first set of trade liberalisation measures in August 1989, and this led to the break-up of the Confederation. By the early 1990s, 85% of Gambia's imports were still 'illegally' re-exported (Sall and Sallah, 1994). From this experience, it should not be considered surprising that similar trade liberalisation programmes face severe implementation problems within the larger regional IGOs.

The Gambia also illustrates how attempts to rehabilitate depleted or unviable national economies through the 'domestication' of trans-state flows carry debilitating boomerang effects for state policies. Throughout the 1970s, managing frontier disparities on a rent-seeking basis was a vital component of the policy orientations of Benin, Togo, The Gambia, Niger and, to a lesser extent, Chad. State revenues as well as the prosperity of the population came to depend on the states' capacity to derive resources from the articulation between formal import trade and 'illicit' re-exportation (Egg and Igué, 1993: 39–45). For the national administration, boosting trans-state trade became considered as a development strategy. In Benin, customs and fiscal legislation as well as infrastructure developments were conceived so as to maximise the development of trans-state import and transit activities. Trans-state regionalism, far from being seen as antagonistic to state interests, was treated as an external shock-absorber and an agent of social regulation (Igué and Soulé, 1992: 45).

Such attempts to graft the economic prosperity of Benin, Togo or Niger on to trans-state flows with Nigeria carry their own limitations. From 1982 onwards, the benefits drawn from trans-state trade patterns were increasingly eroded by a phase of recession linked to the decline of Nigeria's oil revenues and, after 1986, the implementation of a structural adjustment policy. Nigerian initiatives towards a reduction of macroeconomic imbalances induced a steady reduction of the scope for manoeuvre left to the Beninois administration. For the state, the loss of fiscal and tariff resources generated by the decline of re-export trade to Nigeria was accompanied by the unwanted growth of 'illegal' (e.g. disruptive) imports of manufactured goods, petroleum products and staple food from Nigeria (Igué and Soulé, 1992: 154–62). Benin's years of prosperity, as Igué and Soulé reflected afterwards, neither favoured 'the consolidation of public institutions' nor enabled the setting of 'lasting economic bases. On the contrary, the 17 years concerned witnessed the establishment of mechanisms of economic and societal destruction' (*ibid.*: 44). In the early 1990s, the attitude of Beninois officials towards trans-state regionalism had clearly become ambivalent, due to its deleterious impact on the country's overall economic situation. Yet, in Benin as elsewhere, the state remains largely powerless to implement any policy of borderland control because of the powerful impact of the flows on interest groups and state revenues.

The swift progress of trans-state regionalisation may be considered as a by-product of the decline of the post-colonial states' financial capacities and terri-torial control. The prosperity of trans-state networks also depends on their capacity to evade state control or negotiate support from their functionaries. For this very reason trans-state regionalism contributes to accentuating the de-institu-tionalisation (*désinstitutionalisation*) and the (formal and informal) privatisation of state agencies (Médard, 1991a: 355–66).

Trans-state regionalisation expands far beyond the original borderland areas to cover entire regions. Since the mid-1980s, it has adapted to the spread and rein-forcement of structural adjustment programmes which tend to reduce the fiscal, excise and monetary disparities among African states. The re-exportation of consumer goods is supplemented by transactions in gold, diamond, ivory, arms and narcotics, as shown in the contributions to this volume of Alain Labrousse, Janet MacGaffey and Rémy Bazenguissa. These transactions provide a highly lucrative access to the world market. They also reflect a new and important reality: trans-state regionalisation no longer thrives exclusively on the exploitation of intra-continental frontier disparities; strategies also, and perhaps increasingly, relate to opportunities offered by internationalised circuits geared towards the economically more prosperous European, Asian and American economies. The reduction of the opportunities associated with the exploitation of intra-African border resources is being increasingly compensated by the internationalisation, and at times criminalisation, (Bayart *et al.,* 1999) of the transactions.

In several regions of the world, the regionalisation process goes hand in hand with institutional strategies which constitute a political response of the member states to the globalisation of economies (Boas and Hveem, 1997). In sub-Saharan Africa, regionalisation proceeds mostly from interactions initiated by non-state actors and inter-personal networks, faced with decaying states unable or unwilling to assert their sovereignty. The continentalisation of trade and financial flows is happening, but as a paradoxical outcome of the preservation of market segmen-tation and inter-state disparities. Trans-state integration is stimulated by market distortions as opposed to trade liberalisation, a situation which accounts for the overall failure of the IGOs' programmes towards market integration. Globalisation becomes a source of renewed opportunities for inter-personal networks which contribute to the deconstruction of state affiliations without seeking to promote the emergence of alternative territorial arrangements.

2

ALICE LANDAU
Multilateralism & Regionalism
in International Economic Relations

The successful completion of the GATT Uruguay Round negotiations and the creation of the World Trade Organisation in 1994 has not put an end to one of the most heated controversies triggered off in the late 1980s. Brought to a head by the confrontation between the United States and the European Community, the debate on compatibility between regionalism and multilateralism is still going on.

The revival of interest in regionalism is due not least to its spectacular development, which has affected all continents. Even the United States was finally won over to the virtues of regionalism when it initiated a series of free trade agreements in 1988. Today's regionalism differs from the previous wave in the 1960s by its being embedded in a different international economic and political context, characterised by the end of the Cold War and its bipolarity, a strengthened multilateral trading system epitomised by the WTO, and the globalisation of the world economy.

Regionalism is also innovative in the diversity of its manifestations; it subscribes to a logic of trade liberalisation, in contrast to the logic of import substitution which prevailed at the time of the first regional agreements. When it first appeared in the late 1950s, under the impetus of the European Community, multilateralism had reigned supreme since the end of the Second World War.[1] At that time, regionalism did not infringe the rules of non-discrimination and reciprocity that make it possible for international trade to expand. Forty years later, harmony has now been outweighed by confrontation, co-existence by threat. Three rival blocs appear to be ultimately splitting up the international economy, marginalising the countries excluded from this tripolarity, and invalidating the rules that once ensured economic stability.

[1] There are several definitions of multilateralism, depending on the negotiating framework and the number of actors required before the term multilateralism can be applied. The most widespread conception, in the context of the international system, is that of a structure of regulations and agreements, whereby the activities of state entities are co-ordinated in such a way as to become the collective rule, see Ruggie (1985: 3; 1992: 567). Regionalism is defined, above all, as 'the creation by governments of international economic links between adjacent countries' (Hine, 1992: 115); it also makes possible an increase in the bargaining powers of the member countries vis-à-vis third countries (Schott, 1991: 1–2).

In fact, we have two interpretations of one and the same phenomenon. According to one, trading blocs threaten the spirit of multilateral trade. Countries committed to regional integration may lose interest in the multilateral system, stalling its evolution. Also, regionalism is likely to divert resources away from the multilateral process. Moreover, regional arrangements may contribute to political clashes among nations.

Another school of thought takes the opposite view on each of these arguments. Regional agreements help the liberalisation of trade, by creating trade rather than diverting it, and by encouraging the development of instruments that would not have been sufficiently envisaged or implemented by the GATT (Bergsten, 1997: 97). Some regional integration arrangements provided models for the Uruguay Round of GATT negotiations. A case in point is the European Union's treatment of trade in services (World Bank, 1997: 136). Another is NAFTA's rules on the settlement of disputes. William Davey claims that 'The FTA dispute settlement provisions were, by and large, the same as the WTO/GATT procedures as they emerged from the Uruguay Round. Indeed some of the Uruguay Round innovations in the GATT/WTO procedures were first implemented in the Canada-US Free trade agreement' (as quoted in Marceau, 1997: 25). Although, it might well be 'NAFTA that has borrowed from the GATT experience and from what was to become the dispute settlement rules of the WTO', there is no doubt that some regional integration arrangements have addressed new issues (Marceau, 1997: 80).

Regional integration has a demonstration effect, increasing the probability that countries will move to similar actions, and devote themselves to similar endeavours. Also, to counterweigh the propensity to conflict of regional integration, the supporters of regionalism contend that regional integration manages conflicts rather than creates new ones, and overcomes traditional rivalries among neighbouring nations. The security concerns of regional integration have a positive effect. Finally, and of considerable importance for developing countries, regional agreements lock in domestic reforms against potential reverse policies. Thus, regional integration and global liberalisation 'simultaneously keep the bicycle moving' (Bergsten, 1996: 7).

However, there is no clear answer. As a matter of fact, many countries devote their energies to concluding regional integration agreements whatever the gains or losses that may be expected (Fernandez, 1997).

For those who refer to regional integration agreements as a second-best choice after complete trade liberalisation by multilateral agreement, liberalising trade within a regional integration agreement would be the best way of helping member countries to open up their protected national economies and eventually to meet world market conditions. Thus, regional agreements would be a stepping-stone for integrating the world market, helping member countries to gain competitiveness in some manufacturing sectors. Even though regional integration 'is not the first-choice, it may still be optimal policy for the countries in the region' (Srinivasan *et al.*, 1995: 54).

Regional Agreements & GATT

General Agreement on Tariffs and Trade (GATT) is no stranger to the ambiguity that characterises relations between multilateralism and regionalism. Established in 1947, the Agreement reflects the economic supremacy of the United States at the end of the Second World War; but it also attests to a compromise with Britain, which managed to retain its preferential advantages within the Commonwealth. GATT is based on two essential principles of international trade (Kaiser, 1980): non-discrimination and reciprocity between the contracting parties, epitomised by the most-favoured-nation clause (Article I of GATT) and national treatment (Article III).[2]

One of the main underlying principles of the GATT regulations is the most-favoured-nation clause, whereby the advantages granted to any one contracting party are to be extended to all other contracting parties. Free trade areas, customs unions and preferential agreements infringe this clause, as they grant to their members concessions which are not necessarily extended to third countries. One of the primary aims of the Treaty of Rome, which established the European Economic Community, was the removal of all obstacles to the free movement of goods, labour, capital and services between the member states. The European Community has introduced a common external tariff as an incentive to harmonisation between the economies of the member countries. It has also moved in the direction of a free trade area in its relations with EFTA; this, in as much as it gives preference to the six countries concerned, is discriminatory in respect of third countries.

Despite this fact, article XXIV of GATT allows regional agreements to co-exist with the General Agreement under certain conditions: customs duties and restrictive trade regulations must be eliminated on virtually all trade between the constituent territories in products originating in such territories (Article XXIV, para 8b); the arrangements must not result in increased obstacles to trade with third countries, by producing a diversionary effect on trade; moreover, the member countries are required to supply information to the contracting parties (Article XXIV, para 7a). GATT thus recognises the role of regionalism, which makes it possible to increase freedom of trade through a closer integration of the member countries' economies. It is not opposed to regional agreements where 'customs duties are not higher or other trade regulations more restrictive than they were prior to the adoption of such agreements' (paras 5a and 5b). GATT has not abandoned this wait-and-see policy, even though it was to admit many years later that it might 'perhaps be expedient to revise the supervisory activities conducted by the working groups responsible for regional issues, so that their efforts are transparent and to the point' (GATT, 1993: 13 and 97).

GATT has never formally objected to regional agreements that have been submitted for its approval, but this is not to say that it has made clear-cut statements on their compatibility with its own basic regulations. It created a precedent in deciding not to give a ruling on the compatibility of the Treaty of Rome with the provisions of the General Agreement but to 'concentrate on specific practical problems of the Treaty' (Schott, 1989: 36). To understand why it acted in this manner, we should call to mind the characteristics of the international system at

---

[2] Internal taxes and other internal charges, laws, regulations and requirements and internal quantitative regulations were not to be applied so as to afford protection to domestic production (GATT, Article III: 1).

the time the Agreement came into effect in 1947. The United States was converted to regionalism out of political necessity; it considered European construction to be indispensable to the stability of Europe, which was in keeping with a multilateral logic to which it was determined to lend active support. The European Economic Community was born out of the Organisation for European Economic Co-operation (OEEC), which had been responsible for the distribution of Marshall Aid. It sealed Franco-German reconciliation, while, at the same time, protecting Europe from Germany's militaristic proclivities. It provided a political and economic counterweight to Soviet domination (Hufbauer, 1992: 2–3). The EEC remained subject to the Atlantic Alliance, with its integration process confined within political, economic and strategic parameters which constituted no manner of threat to American supremacy (Buzan *et al.*, 1992: 138). Changes were not to occur until the late 1960s, when the EEC gained more independence and its integration process took on greater consistency. Hitherto characterised by tolerance, US policy turned to scepticism and reservations with regard to the increasing number of agreements between the EEC and its former colonies (Jackson, 1987: 381).

Flexible Regional Agreements

Today's manifestations of regionalism no longer correspond to those that prevailed in 1947. Today's regional agreements differ in their treatment of issues. Some concern aspects other than the traditional goods sector, shifting from 'shallow integration', that focuses on trade restrictions like tariffs and quotas on manufactures to 'deep integration', covering governmental practices like services and intellectual property, which are far more complex to handle, or investments and capital mobility (Lawrence, 1996: XVIII).

Since the establishment of the European Community, regional integration has continued to win new adherents, especially in the developing countries. There are many reasons for this popularity. Despite its shortcomings, the EC is a model of integration that has managed to ensure the economic prosperity of countries which were, at the time of their accession, still weakened by the effects of the war. This model naturally inspired countries that found themselves in economic difficulties once they had achieved independence. This was especially true in the 1960s, when the EC image was that of an organisation receptive to the needs of developing countries. It was innovative in respect of aid, granting the system of preferences demanded by those countries at the first meeting of UNCTAD in 1964; in 1975, the First Lomé Convention between the EC and the African, Caribbean and Pacific (ACP) countries established a scheme to stabilise the export earnings of the latter group of countries. While it has not been the direct instigator of the ever-growing number of experiments in regionalism in the Third World, the European Community has, by its example, contributed to the expression of a more assertive form of regionalism (Nuttall, 1990: 153).

However, this 'first-generation' regionalism has remained intrinsically different from the European model, as it pursues a strategy of import substitution developed by Raul Prebisch and the Economic Commission for Latin America (ECLA); this was enthusiastically adopted by developing countries anxious to obtain preferential agreements and protect their infant industries against aggression from the international system (Preeg, 1970; Das, 1990: 21–65). These strategies of withdrawal from the international economic system were to fail as a result of rapidly declining growth rates and a loss of competitiveness in industrial structures increasingly cut off from foreign technology.

Moreover, regional agreements are out of keeping with policies that generate income that is not likely to be distributed. In Africa or Latin America, economic disparities between the member countries, exaggerated political sensibilities and a regional structure which is attempting to graft itself on to national construction processes, difficult in themselves, must lead to deadlock; moreover, the urge to withdraw is scarcely compatible with the heavy dependence of national economies on international markets (Landau, 1983; Robson, 1993b: 334). In 1989, the African states were still conducting almost half of their trade with the countries of the European Community, despite a general contraction in trade (Bach, 1992: 118–19). The dominance of trade movements geared towards external markets could not easily be reconciled with the protectionist and essentially inward-looking economic structures that characterised the Andean Pact. Added to this were the often conflicting economic options at national level, which tended to cripple tariff reduction programmes, especially in the case of the Economic Community of West African States (Fieleke, 1992: 3).

Second-generation regionalism pursues a strategy of economic reintegration. Many developing countries, especially Latin American countries, have unilaterally embarked on policies of trade liberalisation, dictated by the debt crisis, the conditions imposed by the IMF and the World Bank, and a growing awareness that they have a certain room for manoeuvre that can be exploited by a more active involvement in GATT (De la Torre and Kelly, 1992: 25–40; Landau, 1996).

Mexico joined GATT in 1986 and embarked on a substantial policy of liberalisation. In 1992, it concluded the North American Free Trade Agreement with the United States and Canada. NAFTA is considered a test case for other regional agreements, especially in Latin America, as it involves countries of both the North and the South. In the southern hemisphere, a similar liberalisation policy led to a reactivation of regional arrangements. In the mid-1980s, Argentina and Brazil adopted liberalisation policies, and not long after signed the declaration of Iguaçu. In 1988, the Treaty of Integration, Co-operation and Development set the stage for a common market between the two countries, with the gradual elimination of all tariff barriers and the harmonisation of macroeconomic policies. MERCOSUR (the South American Common Market) admitted two new members, Paraguay and Uruguay.

This trend is likely to be extended. In the Caribbean area, CARICOM was reactivated and member countries outlined a new schedule for a common external tariff. In Africa, the Union Economique et Monétaire Ouest Africaine (UEMOA), the Common Market for Eastern and Southern Africa (COMESA), and the Southern African Development Community (SADC) have adopted new strategies to deepen regional integration.

Regional Agreements as Incentives to Trade Creation or Trade Diversion?

It is not easy to evaluate the impact of a regional agreement on trade liberalisation. Such an evaluation is none the less necessary in order to substantiate the thesis of a tripolar structure in the world economy, based on the European Union, North America and Asia-Pacific. According to Viner (1975), the establishment of a preferential zone necessarily gives rise to a reorientation of trade flows. Trade creation resulting from tariff cuts within the region is desirable and beneficial for the member countries as well as for third countries; conversely, classical economics considers that the trade diversion which results from the imposition of an external tariff driving the member countries to concentrate on regional trade to the exclusion of trade outside the zone, can incur greater losses. Viner completes his analysis by remarking that states subscribing to a regional agreement have greater bargaining power than they would have if they acted separately. This is a considerable advantage to small countries with limited bargaining options. This strategy of alliance to protect interests plays an undoubted role in NAFTA, giving Canada or Mexico greater room to manoeuvre in multilateral negotiations, thanks to their association with the United States.

Instruments of analysis & regional realities: withdrawal or integration?

Viner's analysis has lost none of its cogency in the present context of a revival of regionalism. A regional agreement produces reactions directly linked to the trade benefits that it generates. As far as the European Union is concerned, it has certainly had 'beneficial effects on the efficient allocation of world resources', but a closer examination suggests that the benefits are unequally distributed among the trading partners, and that the Union, with its political consequences, has also had an effect on multilateralism (Lloyd, 1992: 26).

Between 1958 and 1986 intra-Community trade increased more rapidly than the Community's external trade and now represents almost two-thirds of the latter (Milner, 1992: 132). During the same period, the Community still turned towards the exterior, with imports amounting to 9.3% of its GNP, compared with 7.8% for the United States and 6.2% for Japan (Hufbauer, 1992: 22). The construction of the Community has generated considerable trade benefits for the United States. In 1988, the EC absorbed 24% of US exports, 45% of which were in high technology goods. The Community has also enlarged its sphere of influence through the affiliation of some members of EFTA, its principal trading partner, which supplies 9.5% of its total imports and with which it has a trade surplus. Economic proximity, which has been steadily intensifying since 1960, was to lead in January 1995 to the accession of Sweden, Finland and Austria to the European Union, bringing with it a *de facto* increase in intra-union trade.

The trade benefits generated by the European construction have been perceived differently according to country. The Community has put together a complex pyramid-like system of preferential arrangements, ranging from free trade agreements with the EFTA, Mediterranean and ACP countries (the latter within the framework of the Lomé Conventions) to a system of general preferences extended to a number of developing countries. The benefits produced are dependent on the economic and commercial structures of the various trading partners. These preferential trade arrangements have brought only marginal benefits to countries whose commercial structure enters into competition with that of the EU member states. This has been the case with Central and East European countries, against which the EU has provided itself with safety devices defined in the European Agreements concluded in 1991. A complex web of quantitative restrictions thus regulates the export of sensitive goods (steel, textiles, farm produce and chemicals) to the EU (Landau, 1995a). To this may be added total liberalisation of trade within the internal market, which could eventually marginalise the preferential partners of the EU, while reducing to nothing the benefits accruing to them from association (Pomfret, 1986: 107; Kostrzewa and Schmiedling, 1989: 502).

Among the consequences of the internal market have been the removal of all technical constraints and the harmonisation of the standards and regulations in force in the member states. This was the result of the application of the principle of reciprocal recognition, supplemented by sanitary and veterinary directives. It was the impossibility of ignoring this 'Community asset' that moved EFTA to negotiate a European Economic Area (Krugman, 1988: 2–3; Landau, 1994: 324). Henceforth a partner in the initial stages of the decision-making process, the EFTA countries are still excluded from the subsequent stages: voting in committees and debates at EU institutional level. The refusal of the EU to grant EFTA powers of co-decision finally put an end to the existence of the EEA, which was no more than a transitional stage in the process of accession to the EU (Landau, 1994: 325). The other trading partners of the EU are even more powerless in the face of the constant changes in Community legislation, and are likely to be further marginalised.

Various elements tend to qualify somewhat the role of the European Union in the liberalisation of trade, allocation of government contracts, services and import quotas (Hufbauer and Schmitt, 1992: 315; Balassa, 1992: 302–9). It is also important not to underestimate the strength of national resistance, which further confirms the need to pursue multilateral solutions that might palliate the ambiguities of regional integration policies. The Common Agricultural Policy (CAP) is a good example of this. By protecting European agriculture, it has produced distortions in world agricultural trade, by applying price support, export subsidies and grants which lead to over-production in agriculture and the quest for external markets. This policy gives rise to serious losses in earnings for other agricultural product-exporting countries and to acrimonious relations between the United States and the European Union.[3]

Agriculture undoubtedly occupies a special place in multilateral negotiations. The EU member states do not share a homogenous position with regard to

---

[3] Especially when the accession of Portugal and Spain in 1986 deprived US producers of their virtual monopoly in these markets (Hufbauer, 1992: 356).

agriculture, and they use these negotiations to put pressure on their partners: the Commission used the Uruguay Round to define Community policy, but also to obtain CAP reforms.[4] Thus, after long years of negotiation, the result was a compromise between the United States and the EU on import levels, transformed into fixed tariffs before their final abolition, and the reduction of subsidies and protection measures.

Viner's analysis is also applicable to the North American Free Trade Area (NAFTA). Is it an alternative to multilateralism in that it further promotes regionalism? The rapprochement between Mexico and the United States has awakened fears of an increase in the US deficit and job losses. However, NAFTA is not free of elements that infringe basic GATT regulations. The conditions of accession for third countries are stipulated in the vaguest of terms, while exports from a number of Latin American countries already come up against an assortment of American protectionist measures. Moreover, the question of accession (Whalley, 1993: 9) is further complicated by the mosaic of regional agreements predating NAFTA, such as the Caribbean Basin Initiative, MERCOSUR, the Andean Pact and the Central American Common Market.

For the moment, Mexico's membership of NAFTA encourages Latin American countries, especially Venezuela, Brazil and Argentina, in their efforts at integration for the purpose of increasing their bargaining power and mitigating the effects of NAFTA on their trade (Hurrell, 1992). The parallel search for solutions that could combine continental and regional integration is proving delicate owing to the risk of accumulating obligations that are often irreconcilable. Adaptation is not easy as far as NAFTA is concerned, which, as Vinod Aggarwal (1993) points out, subscribes to a logic of 'protectionist liberalism', as illustrated by its originally restrictive regulations, diffuse reciprocity and the exclusion of agriculture.[5]

The regional configuration of the Pacific region presents a patchwork of agreements: ASEAN, in the process of becoming a free trade area (the AFTA project), co-exists with the Pacific Economic Co-operation Council (PECC), the Pacific Rim Economic Council (PREC), the Pacific Conference on Trade Development (PCTD) and the Asia-Pacific Economic Co-operation (APEC).[6] Several elements combine to make the Pacific region one of the regional areas that comply most faithfully with GATT regulations: it is made up of countries that are firmly anchored to the international economic system by an earlier practice of trade liberalisation. Despite recent controversies concerning its degree of economic liberalism, APEC operates in accordance with the principle that 'co-operation should consolidate the free trade system; it should not imply the creation of a

[4] Robert Putnam refers to diplomatic double-dealing. Governments use international negotiations as an instrument of internal policy, much as they use their internal policy to influence the course of international negotiations.

[5] Restrictions are particularly stringent in the field of textiles and car manufacturing. They should drive foreign firms to establish themselves in Mexico or Canada as import duties are low in the US and high in Canada and Mexico. For manufactured agricultural goods to qualify, less than 7% of their value must come from a third country (Aggarwal, 1993: 28).

[6] APEC comprises the ASEAN countries (Bruneï, Indonesia, Malaysia, Thailand, the Philippines and Singapore) and the United States, Japan, China, South Korea, Australia, New Zealand, Canada, Hong Kong and Taiwan.

regional bloc'. As a result, all countries are eligible for the most-favoured-nation clause, which is the cornerstone of APEC. The safety clauses contained in the GATT agreements do not appear in APEC, which allows independent bilateral negotiations, insofar as they are not incompatible with the agreement (Aggarwal, 1993: 12–14; Hawes and Hong Liu, 1993).

Integration in Asia is less the result of a genuine will to construct a regional area than a reaction by countries, moved by considerations of vulnerability, in the face of the dynamic of European integration and the emergence of NAFTA. The Asian countries rely as much on multilateralism as on bilateralism to maintain their trading positions and settle their political or economic differences, aggravated by the end of the Cold War.

Complementarity between Regionalism & Multilateralism

This tentative analysis of regionalism does not permit the conclusion that it is incompatible with multilateralism, though certain elements suggest this danger. Regionalism is not necessarily synonymous with the emergence of regional blocs or trading strongholds. However, perfunctory debates on regionalism and multi-lateralism frequently lead to this association. There is need for clarification in the light of an analysis of trade flows and an examination of the strategies of the actors involved.

Regionalism & trade flows

Regionalism reflects trends in trade, whether towards the extension of the European Union to include the EFTA countries, the accession of Mexico to NAFTA or the establishment of APEC. These affiliations follow a commercial logic, that of negotiating agreements that can ensure reliable sources of supply and reduce the risk of the closure of export markets: Canada and Mexico are far more dependent on the United States than the latter is on them; in 1990, their exports to the US represented 73.1 and 75.5% respectively of their total exports, compared with 28.3% of US exports. As for the rest of Latin America, commercial dependence on the United States is greater in Central America than it is in the southern portion of the hemisphere, where Japan and the European Union are the main trading partners of Argentina, Brazil and Chile. In 1992 the EU's share of total MERCOSUR exports came to 27%, compared with 21% for the United States and Canada. Trade diversification remains one of the dominant features of Latin American economies. Admittedly, this diversification is scarcely conducive to an incorporation of the different South American regional components into NAFTA. While, in Mexico, NAFTA has consolidated a process of rapprochement already begun, its extension to include the Latin American countries would imply a far more stringent adaptation, which few of them are prepared to undertake (Gerstin and Rugman, 1994: 573). However, their wait-and-see attitude towards NAFTA does not prevent them from cultivating privileged relations with Mexico or from seeking alternative solutions, such as a free trade area with the European Union and a rapprochement with the Pacific Rim.

In Asia, Japan doubled its exports to the European Union between 1967 and 1988 (from 8.8 to 17.1%), while exports to the newly industrialised countries rose from 12.1 to 19.2%). However, the United States is still its main outlet (CEPII, 1992). Japanese investments in South-East Asia increased steadily, from $ 2 milliard in 1985 to $ 8.2 milliard in 1988. The newly industrialised countries are consolidating their breakthrough on to the international market, in the direction of neighbouring Japan or the United States. Japan's two peripheral neighbours, Australia and New Zealand, are also asserting themselves on the Asian market, at the expense of Western markets, with which they used to conduct the bulk of their trade.

The game of interdependence

The regional agreements that have emerged since the late 1980s are the result of a complex chain of reactions, in which the dynamic of the European Community has undoubtedly played the role of catalyst, inducing a mobilisation of political decision-makers, though reactions have not been identical in all regions. In Japan, the United States and the EFTA countries, the initial response to the establishment of the European internal market was to set up within the Community in order to benefit from the Single Market and circumvent the protectionist barriers likely to be raised against third countries. Subsequently, strategies were diversified. Japan relies on GATT to denounce protectionist practices and the dangers of 'Fortress Europe', anti-dumping policy, voluntary import restrictions or financial policy. It showed reluctance, at least at the outset, in respect of encouraging regionalisation in Asia, which would have been perceived as a retaliatory measure vis-à-vis the Single Market (Ostergaard, 1993: 175–9). The free trade agreement between the United States and Canada or NAFTA represents another attempt to limit the negative consequences of the internal market.

Regionalism, multilateralism & protectionism

The difficulties of GATT have encouraged political decision-makers to consolidate areas which are managing to bring about conditions at regional level that were taking a long time to develop at multilateral level. The United States has had ample recourse to this strategy. It is based on the creation of coalitions between countries which use their bargaining power to influence the GATT agenda. The regional agreement supplements the measures not covered, or insufficiently covered, by GATT. John Zysman maintained that 'GATT is simply obsolete. The main issues must be negotiated bilaterally between the three blocs. We must find a means of multilateralising the bilateral negotiations between the three' (IMF, 1991: 94). Services, investment and the environment were included in NAFTA before they were dealt with by GATT. The procedures for settling trade disputes, which are modelled on the free trade agreements between Canada and the United States, are stricter than those applied in the GATT panels, which do not have the power to impose their decisions. This strategy is as much a signal sent by the

United States to GATT as a manifestation of its will to impose its own world vision.[7]

James Baker thus stated that 'liberalisation may be brought about by the Uruguay Round. If that were not to be, we should seek to form a market liberalisation club using a unilateral or bilateral approach. We subscribe to the liberal system with the multilateralism, bilateralism or minilateralism that can promote a more open system' (quoted in Aggarwal, 1993: 12).[8] The United States made free trade a priority in the post-war period, for geopolitical, structural or ideological reasons. But, as with regionalism, bilateralism, protectionism or minilateralism, it used it to influence negotiations; it threatened its trading partners with retaliatory measures more frequently than before, Section 301 providing the means of doing so.[9] The United States has departed from the principles that it once defended, by negotiating bilateral agreements with its trading partners. The aim is to exert pressure and to retain its hegemony by placing its partners on the defensive. The conclusion of the GATT Uruguay Round negotiations and the transformation of GATT into the World Trade Organisation (WTO) has not put a stop to protectionist measures. One wonders whether it is not precisely these practices that are weakening multilateralism, demonstrating that the principal champion of the liberal system doubts its effectiveness and is resorting to methods which it condemns in others. There is thus a tendency to blame regionalism for wrongs that it has not committed. It would also be a mistake to forget that regionalism makes it possible to promote an area from which free trade can spread. The Uruguay Round negotiations were certainly frustrated by the European subsidies policy. But, as Gary Hufbauer remarked on the Kennedy Round negotiations, France and Italy would have refused to grant any tariff concessions had it not been for the intervention of Germany, which could not itself have offered any if it had had to isolate itself from its European Community partners (Lawrence and Litan, 1990: 259). Once again, in the Uruguay Round, Germany stepped out of the coalition of hard-line Agricultural Ministers, led by France, thus solving the CAP reform and helping to end the Uruguay Round.

For endangered sectors which have to be protected from foreign competition, the industrialised countries have repeatedly applied protectionist practices to

[7] The most striking example is the inclusion of services in NAFTA on the basis of national treatment, a subject of fierce debate in the GATT negotiations, not only among developing countries such as Brazil, but also between the United States and the European Community (Fried, 1990: 232–3).

[8] Minilateralism can be defined as collaboration between a limited number of actors within the multilateral institutions. According to Miles Kahler (1992: 682–6), minilateral co-operation was at the core of the multilateralism established after the Second World War. Various obstacles to the construction of multilateralism have been circumvented by minilateralism, and not thanks to the United States.

[9] Since 1974, this has allowed the US President to take steps against a trading partner's discriminatory practices that infringe the rights and obligations of GATT. Section 301 is part of the American rhetoric on 'fair trade'. Since 1988, a series of amendments, the 'Super and the Special 301' have been added to the system of trade retaliatory measures. The 'Special 301' is specifically directed against discriminatory practices in respect of intellectual property, in which case the President delegates his powers to the US Trade Representative (USTR), who is responsible for trade policy, especially with regard to GATT. However, its effects have been limited. Section 301 has led to liberalisation in 1/3 of cases and to retaliation in 1/10, the effects of Super 301 being even more disappointing. However, these measures have been successful in the case of Japan and South Korea (Sjolander, 1991: 16–19).

spare themselves the constraints of structural adjustment. They have themselves caused the erosion of a system which they had previously supported and which had brought them many advantages. The fears awakened by regionalism are exaggerated in view of the scale of the phenomenon, which is indeed large, but which is due rather to the fact that multilateralism has lost credibility for lack of commercial rigour on the part of its principal advocates. The crisis of multilateralism affects not only GATT, but all international bargaining forums and financial institutions. The end of the Cold War may have given some of these forums a new lease of life, but multilateralism has emerged weakened from the crisis.

Which of the two will triumph, multilateralism or regionalism? If multilateralism is to limit regionalism, a more powerful commercial authority must exist. GATT performed outstandingly in the field of tariff reductions. From the 1947 Geneva conference to the Tokyo Round in 1979, protection levels on industrial goods fell from about 60% to 5%. But the results have been less convincing with regard to non-tariff barriers. The main cause can be attributed to GATT, which allowed the developing countries to elude its discipline, and the developed countries to break its rules. The Multi-Fibre Arrangements were thus legalised by GATT. The conclusion of the Uruguay Round, the inclusion of new sectors and the transformation of GATT into a World Trade Organisation (WTO), whose decisions are more binding on governments, suggest that there may be a return to multilateralism. The new WTO is indeed a universal institution with regulatory powers sufficient to control the evolution of the international economic system. Further negotiations have resulted, dealing with the unfinished business of the Uruguay Round. Some agreements have been concluded in financial services and telecommunications. More negotiations are to start in 1999. These trends help to restore the confidence of the partisans of multilateralism. This should not lead to the rash conclusion that regionalism is no more than an epiphenomenon, which will disappear as quickly as it appeared. Regionalism will probably co-exist with multilateralism, aware that it certainly cannot pose a threat to the European Union, a model that can be neither imitated nor replicated (Ricupero, 1993: 7).

In this context of bloc policy, developing countries are forced to form regional alliances, in order to increase their bargaining power vis-à-vis the industrialised countries in the event that the latter should renege on their commitments to GATT. With a few exceptions, regional agreements involve either industrialised countries or developing countries, but seldom both categories at once. It is to be feared that regionalism may further marginalise the developing countries within the international economic system unless it is coupled with the use of multilateralism. For the developing countries, GATT remains the chief option if they are to preserve their export markets. They depend on it all the more as they are doubly exposed to the effects of protectionism and globalism. In their case, regionalism is a two-track process conducted in combination with multilateralism rather than an alternative strategy.

3 WALTER KENNES
African Regional Economic Integration & the European Union*

Ever since the independence era, African leaders have recognised the importance of regional integration to help overcome some of the structural weaknesses of their countries. The small economic size of the new states prevented the operation of many industrial activities on an efficient scale. Exports within Africa were hampered by the fragmentation of the economies, and by the lack of transport and communications infrastructure. Exports to the rest of the world, except for traditional raw materials, faced a competitive disadvantage. *2 waves.*

The drive towards regional integration in Africa can be divided into two waves: the first took place during the post-independence period, i.e. in the 1960s and early 1970s, with an extension for Southern Africa to around 1980. The second wave is quite recent; its start might be put around the time of the signing of the Abuja Treaty on the African Economic Community in 1991. Both waves have been influenced by the views and ideology of their respective periods and by events outside the African continent.

In its co-operation policy with Africa, the European Union (EU) has always paid special attention to regional integration and co-operation. The main reason for this is its own character as a regional body with a relatively long and successful experience. This implies that it has a unique expertise as regards the technical and practical aspects of regional integration.

After reviewing the two integration waves mentioned above, this chapter describes some recent initiatives to promote regional integration in Africa in which the EU is involved. In addition, a few observations are made on the role of donor policies in relation to the revival of regional integration and on some issues that figure prominently in the integration debate. This contribution deals with sub-Saharan Africa, though some reference is made to North Africa. Acronyms are used to shorten the text. In cases where an organisation is mostly referred to in French, the French acronym is used with an English translation provided where it is mentioned for the first time.

*The views expressed are those of the author and do not necessarily represent those of the European Commission. The author would like to thank Emma Achilli and Bernard Petit for comments on an earlier version.

Overview of Regional Integration in Africa

The creation of integration bodies reflects two successive waves. The formation of the regional integration groupings belonging to the first wave is well documented and will be described only briefly here. A more thorough account can be found in Faroutan (1993), Hess (1994), OECD (1993) or Chapter 2 of this volume. Our focus will be on the integration bodies with a broad economic mandate in the field of trade and factor markets. There are also other regional organisations with a more specific sectoral or thematic focus, which can be said to deal with functional co-operation rather than economic integration. An example of such an organisation is the Permanent Inter-state Committee on Drought Control in the Sahel (CILSS), which covers nine countries in the Sahel and concentrates on food, agricultural and environmental issues.

In *West Africa,* the main economic integration organisations are the Economic Community of West African States (ECOWAS) and the West African Economic and Monetary Union (UEMOA). The main regional bodies in *Central Africa* are the Economic Community of Central African States (CEEAC), the Economic and Customs Union of Central Africa (UDEAC), and the Economic Community of the Great Lakes States (CEPGL). The Central African countries that are members of the Franc Zone have established the Bank of Central African States (BEAC). For *Eastern and Southern Africa and the Indian Ocean*, the main organisations are the Common Market for Eastern and Southern Africa (COMESA), the Southern African Development Community (SADC), the Southern African Customs Union (SACU), the Common Monetary Area (CMA or Rand zone) and the Indian Ocean Commission (IOC). There is also a revival of East African Co-operation (EAC). In North Africa, the Maghreb countries have established the Arab Maghreb Union.

The membership of several organisations has changed significantly over the past few years. Some recent changes are as follows: South Africa and Mauritius joined SADC in 1994 and 1995 respectively, while the Democratic Republic of Congo and Seychelles did so in 1997. Guinea Bissau adhered to UEMOA in 1997. Egypt became a member of COMESA in 1998. In 1997, Lesotho and Mozambique indicated their intention to withdraw from COMESA. Some key data on the main integration organisations are contained in Table 3.1, while Table 3.3 at the end of this chapter indicates their present membership.

There is a broad consensus that the African integration groupings have not, on the whole, been successful. While there have been achievements in some areas, the results in terms of progress towards the aim of creating larger and more efficient markets have been limited. Two important and related questions arise: why are the results of the African groupings limited and what can be learnt about the approach towards regional integration in Africa? The rest of this section contains some reflections on these questions.

A striking feature of Table 3.1 is the low share of intra-regional trade for the African groupings. Furthermore, even though not shown in the table, these shares have not increased much since the formation of the groupings. Only for

Table 3.1: Basic facts on the main regional organisations

Organisation	Year of formation	Location of Secretariat	No. of members[a]	Total exports[b]	Intra-trade share[c]
UMA	1989	Rabat	5	26.8	3.2
ECOWAS	1975	Lagos	16	19.2	8.6
UEMOA[d]	1994	Ouagadougou	8	4.3	10.4
CEEAC	1983	Libreville	10	5.6	2.5
UDEAC	1964	Bangui	6	5.1	2.3
CEPGL	1976	Gisenyi	3	0.5	1.1
COMESA	1981	Lusaka	22	13.0	7.0
SADC	1980	Gaborone	14	10.9	5.1

[a]In 1997, for a list of members see Table 3.3;
[b]In billions of dollars (f.o.b.), 1993, source UNCTAD;
[c]as % of total exports, 1993, source UNCTAD;
[d]its predecessor CEAO was created in 1974 and dissolved in January 1994.

UEMOA is the share above 10% while in the case of such groupings as UDEAC and CEPGL intra-regional trade is very low indeed. As a comparison, the share of intra-regional trade currently exceeds 60% in the EU, and when European integration began in the 1950s, it was already around 30%. A rising or high share of intra-regional trade has been considered a simple measure of the success of an integration grouping. A low share of intra-trade is thought to be evidence of failure.

A possible explanation of the lack of success of the African groupings that is frequently mentioned is the *lack of potential* for increased trade within Africa. However, there is an important qualification to be made here and there is evidence that the potential for intra-African trade is greater than is usually thought. The calculated shares refer to *recorded or official* trade. It is known that for many African countries there is a sizeable volume of unrecorded or unofficial trade. Even though the evidence is very incomplete, it is thought that in several cases the volume of unofficial trade exceeds that of official trade. As regards the potential for intra-trade in sub-Saharan Africa, an interesting analysis was outlined in the World Bank's Long-Term Perspective Study on Africa (1989). Official trade among sub-Saharan African countries was estimated at around US$ 4 billion or 6% of the total, which amounted to US$ 65 billion (exports plus imports). By looking at similar goods imported and exported by different African countries, it can be inferred that an additional US$ 5 billion of African imports could be supplied from within Africa. If this amount were supplied from within Africa, intra-African trade (exports plus imports) would increase by US$ 10 billion and its share in total trade would rise to around 20%. It should be kept in mind that the above figure is derived in a purely static way. Taking into account the possibility of dynamic gains from integration (for example, by exploiting economies of scale and through greater competition), the potential for increased intra-African trade must be much larger.

A more plausible explanation for the low level of intra-African trade is that the integration groupings have not (yet) been able to abolish customs duties or more generally the barriers on doing business across borders (including roadblocks, and constraints on payments, investment and movement of persons). To the extent that the measures to abolish barriers have not (yet) been adequately implemented, one should not expect a rise in intra-regional trade. The question then arises: why has implementation so far not been adequate? Explanations can be considered both at the national and the regional level. At the national level one can mention: inappropriate economic polices; inward-looking development strategies emphasising import substitution behind high barriers; lack of political will; local conflicts and civil strife; insufficient knowledge and capacity to implement integration measures (the subject matter is often technical); and lack of involvement of crucial actors (private sector, civil society). At the regional level, the lack of implementation of regional integration can be explained by insufficient co-ordination of national policies; overlapping and inadequate institutional arrangements (see Table 3.3 for overlapping memberships); unrealistic, over-ambitious agendas and lack of resources of the integration organisations.

Some reference should be made to the issue of inadequate cross-border transport and communications infrastructure in sub-Saharan Africa. It is often stated that regional integration cannot be successful because the transport and communications infrastructure is insufficient. The reasoning goes that the infrastructure should be improved before implementing regional integration. Lack of transport and communications infrastructure certainly constitutes a formidable constraint on economic activity in sub-Saharan Africa, virtually as much within as between countries. Nevertheless, it is not the main reason for the integration organisations' lack of results. In many cases, cross-border infrastructure has been badly maintained. In addition, there have been disruptions because of civil strife or conflicts. The border formalities are often lengthy and costly and business across borders is risky. A more effective use of the existing infrastructure will be a consequence of successful integration. Progress with market integration will help to generate the financial resources necessary to upgrade and maintain infrastructures. However, this should not in any sense be interpreted as downplaying the importance of investment to improve cross-border infrastructure. Successful integration and improvements in infrastructure are mutually reinforcing.

Turning to the question of what to conclude from the lack of success so far about the prospects for integration in Africa, the view is sometimes expressed that regional integration within Africa is not a useful strategy. African countries should rather concentrate on liberalisation towards the world market, as there are no prospects in the regional market. The above reasoning on the lack of success, however, leads to another view: regional integration in Africa is worthwhile, but for a variety of reasons, it has not yet been successfully implemented. Attention should be focused on putting in place the conditions for regional integration to be adequately implemented.

The origin of the second wave of regional integration in Africa can be traced to a number of developments outside the continent during the second half of the 1980s (see Chapter 2). There is no clear definition of the 'new regionalism', but some of its most typical characteristics are: outward-oriented trade strategy with low external tariffs, rather than regional import substitution behind high protective tariff walls; harmonisation of macro-economic policies (monetary and fiscal); standardisation of technical norms and procedures and environmental regulations; liberalisation of trade in financial and other services; facilitation of cross-border investment flows; attention given to the credibility of government policies (the involvement of regional partners diminishes the weight of national pressure groups and may help to avoid policy reversals).

The renewed worldwide drive towards regional integration, together with the long delay before the Uruguay Round agreement could be reached, have stimulated a second integration wave in Africa. In 1991 African Heads of State signed the Abuja Treaty on the establishment of a Pan-African Economic Community (AEC). According to the treaty the AEC should be established over a period of 34 years and should build upon the existing sub-regional communities. Even though the formidable practical issues and constraints are not addressed in detail, the treaty can be interpreted as a strong expression of general political desire for more integration in Africa, in view of the increased regionalism in the rest of the world.

In 1992, SADCC was transformed into the Southern African Development Community (SADC). The new SADC explicitly added a market integration agenda to the sectoral co-ordination role that had been the focus of the old SADCC. In 1993, the member states of the Preferential Trade Agreement signed a new treaty to establish the Common Market of Eastern and Southern Africa (COMESA). The objectives of COMESA go beyond the creation of a customs union and include free movement of capital and persons and formation of a monetary union. COMESA includes the possibility of supranational elements in decision-making. Also in 1993 the ECOWAS Treaty was revised.

Other striking developments took place at the beginning of 1994, following the devaluation of the CFA franc. The West African Monetary Union has been transformed into the West African Economic and Monetary Union (UEMOA), taking on board the responsibilities of the West African Economic Community (Communauté Economique Ouest Africaine, CEAO). In a parallel move, the Central African countries that are part of the Franc Zone also embarked on an Economic and Monetary Union (Communauté Economique et Monétaire d'Afrique Centrale, CEMAC). It is interesting to observe that the founding of UEMOA was followed by disbanding CEAO. It was the first time such a decision had been taken in Africa.

Recent Issues in the Integration Debate

In order to put the discussion on the role of donors in perspective, this section will deal briefly with some issues of recent debate.

Economic versus political aspects of integration: In supporting regional integration, donors are almost exclusively concerned about the effectiveness of integration in economic terms. Nevertheless, integration is often motivated by important political or other non-economic considerations. This clearly applied to the formation of the European Community. At the same time, economic integration can have important political consequences (for example, it can help to stabilise the political regime in some countries). The chances of success for regional integration increase when the political and economic benefits complement each other. Regional integration can contribute to regional peace and security. However, there has not yet been much analysis of this issue in the African context.

Integration, the rule of law and good governance: Successful integration requires that joint or common decisions are implemented in a transparent way by the different member states. The type of governance should be comparable and compatible across member states. There should also be clarity on budgetary procedures, both on the revenue and expenditure sides. If the legal systems of member states are not sufficiently comparable and compatible, there will be frequent conflicts between private or public sector agents, which will be hard to resolve. In such cases, agreed measures will usually not be implemented. Again, this is an issue outside the scope of this contribution, and one on which there has not been much analysis concerning the African region.

Intergovernmentalism versus supranationalism: The distinction between intergovernmentalism and supranationalism can be traced at least to the origins of European integration and has always remained controversial. Supranationalism implies putting in place regional institutions that have certain powers of their own. More specifically, it is linked to a system of regional legislation that prevails over national legislation. Under supranationalism, member states or companies can be taken to court if they do not comply with regional legislation. Supranationalism is often seen as a step in the direction of a confederation or even a federation of states. With supranationalism, the member states agree to exercise some of their sovereignty jointly. With intergovernmentalism, on the other hand, there is no regional legislation and each member state fully exercises its own sovereignty. Intergovernmentalism requires close co-ordination of national policies, and intergovernmental bodies typically have a secretariat that has no independent power, its main function being to facilitate co-ordination among the member states which retain their full sovereignty. Under intergovernmentalism, governments must decide separately on the application of regional agreements.

Economic integration can be pursued with supranationalism as well as in an intergovernmental way. However, the two approaches imply important practical differences. The European Union, from its beginning with the European Coal and Steel Community, has chosen a supranational approach towards economic integration. (It should be mentioned that the more recent responsibilities of the EU in foreign policy, justice and home affairs remain intergovernmental.) It is remarkable that Benelux always remained intergovernmental, even though still today there are matters regulated by Benelux that are not (yet) dealt with by the EU. It seems that the intergovernmental nature of Benelux did not prevent deepening because of the small number of partners (only three) which share a lot of history and have similar social, economic and legal systems. Integration bodies in Africa are virtually all intergovernmental. There are only a few elements of supranationalism in the sphere of monetary management; for example, the countries that are members of the Franc Zone cannot change monetary policy on their own. Either they all agree among themselves and with France or they each leave the zone. With intergovernmentalism, it is difficult to agree and implement policies when the number of member states is relatively large. Intergovernmentalism requires unanimity for decisions, whereas supranationalism can introduce majority decisions.

Variable geometry and variable speed: A number of approaches have been developed to facilitate the coherence of regional organisations, as well as to deal with the accession of new member states and the introduction of new policy areas. These include 'variable speed' and 'variable geometry'. Both concepts are sometimes used interchangeably, but a useful distinction can be made. Under variable speed, a set of common objectives is agreed, but some member states are able to move more rapidly towards implementation. Rather than let the pace of integration be determined by the slowest member state, some member states can move ahead on a common policy while the others can catch up when they are ready. Variable geometry allows a situation where a sub-group of member states moves towards deeper integration than the others, on a more or less permanent basis. The application of variable speed can be traced to the enlargement of the European Community in the 1970s from six to nine member states. With a larger number of member states, the views on many issues became more diversified. Furthermore, the capacity to implement policies, or to implement them within a certain time period, differs across member states. The transitional arrangements for the accession of new member states are a form of variable speed. Variable geometry is practised in the EU in the social field and in the area of movement of persons. It is also a characteristic of the European Monetary Union. The continued existence of smaller groupings within a larger one can also be considered as variable geometry.

Variable geometry and variable speed are now widely accepted as important principles to be applied to economic integration among developing countries to help in avoiding costly duplication and rivalries. Variable geometry and variable speed can help to consolidate integration where and when it is possible. In the African situation there has always been an amount of *de facto* variable geometry, for example because of the existence of monetary unions. The application of variable geometry in Africa may help to overcome some of the current institutional rivalries and overlap of competencies. For the Southern African sub-region, the idea of variable geometry is widely accepted. The comprehensive African Development Bank (1993) report on Southern Africa recommends such an approach, which could maintain the SACU and the Rand zone within the wider SADC framework. At an even broader level, one could imagine that several sub-groups within COMESA, i.e. SADC, IOC and the revived East African Co-operation (Kenya, Tanzania and Uganda) would make faster progress or would aim at a deeper form of integration than is undertaken at the COMESA-wide level. Similarly, in West Africa, the new economic and monetary union (UEMOA) could aim for a deeper integration agenda, while complying with the agreements reached under ECOWAS. One could imagine that UEMOA might become a positive stimulus for integration at the ECOWAS level. If an integration agenda cannot be implemented at the level of the UEMOA members which share a common currency and part of their recent history, then it is unlikely that it can be put to work in the much wider ECOWAS context.

Regional dimension of adjustment: Since the mid-1980s, structural adjustment programmes (SAPs) have been applied in most African countries. By and large these SAPs were designed within the national context, even though often with an objective of liberalising the economy towards the rest of the world. The unco-ordinated pace and sequence of national SAPs have profoundly affected regional (especially unrecorded) trade. The EU has drawn attention to the negative spill-over effects of unco-ordinated SAPs and has promoted approaches which take into account the regional dimension in the formulation of adjustment programmes. Regional integration and SAPs can be complementary. The EU view is that outward-oriented regional integration is a logical step in the direction of integration into the world economy. The regional market provides a training ground for the world market.

The EU & Regional Integration in Africa

The Lomé Conventions: The development policy of the European Community has always paid special attention to regional co-operation. This has been concretised by setting up a separate budget for such co-operation under the Lomé Conventions. The financial protocol for the first five-year period of the fourth Lomé Convention (1991–5) earmarked ECU 1,250 million for regional co-oper-ation among the 70 ACP member states. For the second five-year period (1996–2000) the funds for regional co-operation amount to ECU 1,300 million. This represents around 10% of the total financial package.

The standard requirement for a 'regional project' is that it should involve at least two ACP states. Regional projects can also involve a regional organisation that has been *duly mandated* by its member states. Regional co-operation is organised in seven programmes, five of which cover sub-Saharan Africa (West Africa, Central Africa, East Africa and the Horn of Africa, Southern Africa and the Indian Ocean). The remaining two programmes are for the Caribbean and the Pacific. Outside these geographical programmes there are also special regional programmes, for example on trade promotion, industrial development, agri-culture and education. An overview of Lomé funding can be found in Table 3.2.

The process of identification and implementation of regional projects involves all the countries and duly mandated regional organisations. The involvement of the regional organisations differs across Africa, depending on specific circum-stances. The largest expenditures for regional projects have been made in the areas of transport and communications, rural and agricultural development (especially the control of cattle diseases), and education and training. The fourth Lomé Convention puts explicit emphasis on the promotion of regional economic inte-gration, which has been retained as a priority in all the current regional programmes. However, this does not imply large expenditures for regional economic integration in the strict sense, because its promotion often takes the form of training or technical assistance. The actual expenditures will remain dominated by infrastructure investments. The rest of this section outlines some recent initiatives to promote regional integration involving the EU.

UEMOA and CEMAC: In 1990, the Heads of State of the members of the West African Monetary Union decided to build on the existing monetary framework and to establish economic market integration. A new Treaty was signed to this effect in January 1994. It includes the following main objectives: (i) rationali-sation and convergence of macroeconomic policies through a system of multi-lateral economic surveillance; (ii) harmonisation of legal and regulatory

Table 3.2: Breakdown of EU regional co-operation funds (ECU million)

Region	Lomé II[a] (1981–85)	Lomé III[a] (1986–90)	Lomé IV[b] (1991–95)	Lomé IV[b] (1996–2000)
Central Africa	60	80	84	84
Eastern Africa	140	185	194	194
Indian Ocean	20	26	30	30
Southern Africa	70	110	121	121
Western Africa	160	210	228	228
Caribbean Region	55.6	73	90[f]	90
Pacific region	30.4	34	35	35
CDI[c]	25	40	60	73
CTA[d]	1.3	20	42	52
Trade promotion	40	60	70	85
Sub-total	**602.3**	**838**	**954**	**992**
Miscellaneous[e]	29.2	162	296	308
TOTAL	**631.5**	**1000**	**1250**	**1300**

[a]Allocations by region include funds managed by the European Investment Bank (EIB) which represent approximately 8% of the total.
[b]Allocations by region do not include EIB-managed resources.
[c]Centre for the Development of Industry.
[d]Centre for Agricultural and Rural Technology
[e]This covers 'intra-ACP' allocations, i.e. schemes involving all or a large number of ACP states, in particular funds for the ACP-EU Joint Assembly, the ACP Secretariat, cultural co-operation, publication of the ACP-EU *Courier*. Under Lomé IV, it includes a system of regional co-operation among the five Portuguese-speaking countries of Africa and a reserve fund. For the second financial protocol of Lomé IV it also contains ECU 80 million for actions in the area of democracy, the rule of law and human rights.
[f]This amount was increased to ECU 105 million following the accession of the Dominican Republic and Haiti to the ACP group.

frameworks; (iii) creation of a customs union and a single market with free movement of goods, services, persons and capital; (iv) establishment of common sectoral policies.

The arrangements put in place are in principle open to new member states, and are formulated so as to be consistent with the wider ECOWAS framework. The main target is to establish a common external tariff and to eliminate intra-regional tariffs by 2000. Work is also progressing on other key areas including the practical implementation of the macroeconomic surveillance mechanism, and the harmonisation of other indirect taxes and company legislation. The EU specifically supports the formulation and implementation of macro-economic surveillance, to some extent drawing on its own experience. In collaboration with the French Ministry of Co-operation, the World Bank and the IMF, the EU also supports the construction of a customs union and other themes. An interesting feature of UEMOA is that its functioning is financed by means of a share of the customs duties levied on imports from third countries.

As regards the Central African region, it should be borne in mind that the UDEAC has not been successful in increasing regional economic integration despite the existence of a common currency. In 1990, the Heads of State of the UDEAC called for the formulation of a regional reform programme. This was one of the first times that an attempt was made to deal explicitly with the regional dimension of adjustment. The regional reform programme has been supported by the IMF, the World Bank, the French Ministry of Co-operation and the EU and includes the following two central components: (i) reform of indirect taxation, with the objective of restoring a common external tariff and a regional preference; tariffs within the zone should be progressively reduced to zero; (ii) reform of transit transport regulations.

In addition, a new treaty on an Economic and Monetary Union (CEMAC) was signed at the beginning of 1994. This treaty has not yet been ratified by all the member states.

The Cross-Border Initiative (CBI): This initiative focuses on countries in Eastern and Southern Africa and the Indian Ocean, which are members of the Common Market for Eastern and Southern Africa (COMESA), the Southern African Development Community (SADC) or the Indian Ocean Commission (IOC). Fourteen countries are participating in the initiative on a self-selecting basis. The CBI resulted from the desire to formulate a pragmatic way to promote more effective regional integration, and has been co-sponsored by the African Development Bank, the EU, the IMF and the World Bank. Its development has involved the sub-regional organisations mentioned above, as well as the Organisation of African Unity (OAU), the United Nations Economic Commission for Africa (ECA) and the Global Coalition for Africa (GCA).

The participating countries set up 'Technical Working Groups' consisting of participants from the public and private sectors. These working groups drew up an inventory of the most important obstacles to cross-border business (trade, investment and payments). They also made recommendations on how to remove the obstacles, and act as an advisory body to the governments on regional integration matters. The emphasis has been on the regulatory constraints that increase the cost of private sector cross-border business. Examples of such constraints are import licensing and duties, complex procedures for the allocation of foreign exchange and time-consuming arrangements for approving investments. The country-level recommendations were synthesised in a common programme of action that was subsequently endorsed at the first ministerial meeting in August 1993, in Kampala, Uganda. A timetable for removing intra-regional tariffs as well as harmonising external tariffs was agreed at the second ministerial meeting in Mauritius in March 1995. A third ministerial meeting in Harare, in February 1998, agreed to continue and to broaden the CBI.

Many of the recommendations on removing the obstacles to cross-border business dealt with issues that were already on the agenda of the above-mentioned organisations. However, practical implementation lagged behind. The initiative therefore supports these organisations in carrying out their work programmes. The emphasis on removing regulatory constraints does not mean overlooking the importance of diminishing physical obstacles (for example, in the area of transport and communications infrastructure). Progress should be made in both areas. However, removing regulatory constraints can lead to rapid results at a low cost and should not be postponed. The CBI calls for the acceleration and deepening of reforms in the following five areas: (i) trade liberalisation and facilitation; (ii) deregulation and clarification of the investment regime; (iii) facilitation of the movement of persons; (iv) liberalisation of the exchange system (current account convertibility); (v) strengthening of financial intermediation.

The co-sponsors jointly assume responsibility for helping the participating countries to implement CBI-supported reforms effectively, with each individual institution focusing on its respective area of competence. In countries that are under adjustment, the general policy provisions related to the CBI reform agenda are incorporated as appropriate into the Policy Framework Paper (PFP), as the 'regional dimension of adjustment'.

The external support provided to the countries participating in the CBI can be divided into three categories: (i) technical assistance for capacity-building at national and regional level; (ii) balance of payments or budget support to contribute to covering the transitional costs for governments implementing the policy package; and (iii) assistance to the private sector to help with restructuring so as to enable it to take advantage of the wider regional and world markets.

Effective regional integration is generally recognised as a component of a strategy to improve economic growth in Africa. The initiative addresses some of the weaknesses of previous regional initiatives by emphasising outward orientation, national and regional policy complementarity, and direct involvement of the private sector. It promotes a strategy of integration into the world economy combining, where appropriate, unilateral reform, regional reform and multilateral reforms under the World Trade Organisation.

Research and training: Not much research is carried out on the costs and benefits of different types of co-operation and integration in Africa. It is unfortunate that sweeping statements on regional integration in Africa are sometimes based only on casual observation. There is a specific need for more endogenous research to take place within Africa and outside official circles. The capacity to carry out such research should be strengthened. The EU is contributing to a collaborative research programme of the African Economic Research Consortium (AERC), based in Nairobi. This involves several researchers from different parts of Africa as well as a few European research institutes.

Slow progress on integration cannot be attributed to a mere 'lack of political will'. Even if this will is present, there is often insufficient capacity or human resources at the national level to implement measures agreed at the regional level. Integrating regional agreements into national legislation is not at all straightforward. There is thus a need for more training on the 'technology' of regional integration. This also applies to the multilateral agreements reached under the WTO. A better understanding of the subject matter could help to put forward more realistic objectives and avoid disappointment with the results.

At the request of the EU, some pilot training workshops have been organised involving the European Institute of Public Administration (EIPA), the European Centre for Development Policy Management (ECDPM) and the University of Aix en Provence. The workshops involved around twenty-five participants from national and regional administrations. The programme focused on elements of the European experience, not at all with a view to proposing a similar approach in Africa, but to enhance practical understanding and to study how problems were overcome. The workshops were evaluated positively by the participants, and a regular training programme along those lines is envisaged.

The Role of Donors in the Revival of Integration

Regional integration is not worthwhile for its own sake; it is part of a strategy to increase the prospects for equitable economic growth. Most of the general analysis on regional integration outside Africa concludes that regional integration can make a positive contribution to welfare, even though it remains a matter of debate as to how important this contribution is and especially how quickly the results will show. Any transition in economic policy will also have some costs, at least in the short run, and these costs may be concentrated within particular groups in society. As observed above there is a lack of thorough analysis of these issues with regard to the African situation.

It is not yet clear what the results of the recent new wave of integration initiatives in Africa will be. Their success will mainly depend on the will of the governments and civil society in general. Nevertheless, external support can play a useful role. This support can take a variety of forms, including: a contribution to cover transitional costs for the government, technical assistance and training, and investments that reduce the cost of cross-border operations.

Donors can also provide support in the form of trade or monetary agreements with a group of countries. These should preferably not be unilateral concessions, but agreements with obligations on both sides. Such agreements may help to increase the credibility of policy measures in African countries. This point has been elaborated by Collier and Gunning (1993). If policy reforms are really considered credible, new direct foreign investment and repatriation of capital can be expected. Experience in Latin America has demonstrated the validity of this point.

In the past, several donors, including the EU, demonstrated a positive bias towards regional ventures, many of which have been formulated or implemented in collaboration with regional organisations, and not necessarily those with a broad economic mandate discussed here. Evaluation studies of these operations have sometimes been highly critical, pointing out the lack of positive results. To some extent, this is understandable, because regional operations usually involve several countries and/or institutions. Procedures are more complex and thus more costly than when there is only one country involved. Delays are very frequent. The positive bias of donors towards regional operations has also probably contributed to the costly and unsustainable proliferation of regional institutions in Africa.

Regional operations have also been badly co-ordinated among donors. There have been contradictions in external support. Sometimes donors have maintained a special relation with a specific regional organisation, disregarding its effectiveness. By and large, the Bretton Woods institutions have taken a negative view of regional operations and have stayed away from them, although there are recent exceptions, as illustrated by the initiatives mentioned above. The Bretton Woods institutions have emphasised unilateral economic liberalisation towards the rest of the world rather than within a region. The EU view is to favour regional liberalisation as a step towards wider liberalisation and integration into the world economy. The regional market provides a training ground to build up experience before the world market can be effectively handled. However, regional arrangements should be outward-oriented without excessive protective tariff walls.

It is too early to say whether the new wave of regional integration across Africa will produce more positive results than the earlier wave. Integration can only be part of a wider strategy to reverse the economic and political crises that confront many African states. The view taken here is not that the lack of results of the first wave of integration has come about because regional integration in sub-Saharan Africa is a mistaken strategy, but rather that for a variety of reasons regional integration has not yet been properly managed and effectively implemented. Because of progress towards openness and sound macroeconomic management, it is fair to say that the chances of its success have improved.

In Africa, there is a positive attitude towards regional integration at the political level and at the level of civil society. It is important that the agenda for the new wave of regional integration should be realistic. Great care should be taken that the objectives set can actually be attained and can produce visible results. To this end there should be a more thorough analysis of the practical aspects of regional integration, together with training to develop the skills required to deal with the subject matter. Even though the secretariats of the regional institutions should not be forgotten, there is a specific need to develop and upgrade these skills at the national level. Whether or not integration will succeed in the future will be determined in the first place at the national level.

There also remains a positive attitude among donors towards regional initiatives. However, given the past record, donors should be very careful in deciding where they put the weight of their resources. Donors can make a positive contribution, but they should set up genuine co-ordination mechanisms and develop a consistent approach to supporting realistic regional integration strategies.

Table 3.3: Member states of major sub-regional organisations in Africa

	UMA	ECOWAS	UEMOA	CEEAC	CEMAC	CEPGL	COMESA	SADC	IOC	SACU	CMA
Algeria	*										
Angola							*	*			
Benin		*	*								
Botswana								*		*	
Burkina Faso		*	*								
Burundi				*		*	*				
Cameroon				*	*						
Cape Verde		*									
Chad				*	*						
Comoros							*		*		
Congo				*	*						
Côte d'Ivoire		*	*								
Djibouti							*				
Egypt											
Eritrea							*				
Ethiopia							*				
Gabon				*	*						
Gambia		*									
Ghana		*									
Guinea		*									
Guinea Bissau		*									
Equatorial Guinea				*	*						
Kenya							*				
Lesotho							*	*		*	*
Liberia		*									
Libya	*										
Madagascar							*		*		
Malawi							*	*			
Mali		*	*								
Mauritania	*	*									
Mauritius							*	*	*		
Mozambique							*	*		*	*
Namibia							*	*			
Niger		*	*								
Nigeria		*									
Uganda							*				
Central African Rep.				*	*						
Dem. Rep. of Congo				*		*	*	*			
Rwanda				*		*	*				
São Tomé				*							
Senegal		*	*								
Seychelles							*	*	*		
Sierra Leone		*									
Somalia							*				
South Africa								*		*	*
Sudan							*				
Swaziland							*	*		*	*
Tanzania							*	*			
Togo		*	*								
Tunisia	*										
Zambia							*	*			
Zimbabwe							*	*			

II STATES & TERRITORIES

4 DOMINIQUE DARBON
Crisis of the State & Communalism
New Ideological Stakes in African Integration

In this last stretch of the XX th century, we should be equally wary of class struggles, in the Marxist sense, as of ethnic conflicts which may be predominantly socially, politically or racially oriented. (Aron, 1967: 105)

The increasing inability of African states to meet their obligations and international responsibilities, and to manage and lead their own societies, coupled with the financial bankruptcy and socio-economic collapse of most of them, makes it necessary to re-examine the relevance of the nation-state model in Africa[1] and to reformulate the apparently 'hackneyed' theories of regionalism (Tredano, 1989; Cornevin, 1978: 17–22).

A major aspect of the crisis of the state in Africa is its inability to make progress with the integration of its people and to ensure their compliance with strategies designed within a specific territorial framework. Historically, the principle of territoriality was one of the fundamental dynamics of state construction in North-Western Europe. This principle, which is recognised in international law as the constitutive basis of the state, is employed in most scientific analyses of the state, but appears to be very weak in Africa. Doubtless this weakness confirms the analyses of Lacroix (in Grawitz and Leca, 1985: 472) and Badie (1992: 82–99), which identify the state as a largely differentiated historical product that cannot in any way be reduced to the European model or its idealistic image.

What we have become accustomed to defining, for the sake of simplicity, as the African state is a mode of domination accepted as legitimate and resulting from the formal imitation of the historical model developed by certain Western countries. Since its foundation during the colonial period, this state has been bedevilled by a serious territorial deficit which in turn has yielded a deficit of integration. Historians and geographers have clearly shown that the colonial partition of spaces which were to metamorphose into the constitutive territories of African nation-states was but the unforeseen consequence of an 'accidental hypothesis' marked by the 'contingent and the unforeseen' (Hargreaves, 1985: 19

---

[1] For a a brief survey of some of the most striking contributions which herald the end of the state in Africa, see Ibrahim (1991: 142).

and 26). Chance and necessity imposed the territorial boundaries as *faits accomplis,* with no consideration for either pre-existing local movements or integration structures.

The space allocated to each colonial power through demarcation agreements did not become a territory, that is, a space permanently subjected to the monopolist domination of a state. The colonial and, more importantly, the post-colonial state never succeeded in bringing about the structural transformation of these spaces into territories. The principle of territoriality, which in European history materialised the ability of one method of constraint over other modes of dominance, has not met with similar success in Africa, except in cases associated with conditions of natural isolation. Political integration may be strongly desired by the local people, but is only partially and selectively coterminous with its territorial dimension as witnessed in Western state systems.

The concept of the *soft state* suggested by Gunnar Myrdal to describe African modes of state domination thus remains very pertinent in that it implies both a form of concentrated potential power that is selectively applicable and a generally impotent power. It can be linked with the notion of the *rhizomous state* (Bayart, 1989) which related to the logic of the *soft state*. It also allows one to grasp the paradox inherent in the ability of this form of domination to project itself beyond its formal territory, while at the same time being often incapable of creating a permanent, stable network of domination within its own sovereign space.

The main problem of integration arises from the permanent inability of these states to valorise territorial law at the expense of what are supposed to be residual individual rights. The failure of African states to administer their spaces and transform them into territories affects their foundational basis as much as new modes of thinking about development. This undermines, if not the nature of the state itself, at least the relevance of its undisputed domination. The communalist ideology, the renewal of regionalist theories and recent developments in the theory of international relations carry a potential challenge to the classic link between state, territory and integration. This further weakens African states and boosts the idea of individual rights at the expense of territorial law.

Contrasting Stakes in the Spread of the Communalist Ideology

The formidable expansion of the communalist ideology produced in the countries of the North is gradually spreading into countries at the periphery of the world system, particularly on the African continent. The spread of debates cannot but have profoundly different effects in the North and the South, bearing in mind the weak institutionalisation of Southern states and the weakness of structures of horizontal mobilisation.

Since the end of the 1970s, a new concept of the respective place of the individual and of social groups has steadily developed (Darbon, 1994; Ceylan, 1994) at the expense of the revolutionary principle carried by the Enlightenment movement, as enshrined in the 1776 American Constitution and the 1789 French Declaration of Human Rights and Citizenship, both of which postulated that the individual, completely free of all social ties, was the foundation and the very core of human societies. This principle no longer seems capable of responding to the conflicting, if not contradictory, demands of equality and respect for differences. The idea of group rights, particularly powerful in the United States (Schlesinger, 1991; Grofman and Davidson, 1992) and Canada (Knopf, 1990), has gradually spread in Britain (Neveu, 1993) and on the European continent, benefiting paradoxically from the convergence of theories of political correctness and postmodernism and from the effects of dependency generated by the gradual closing up of the world system.

These potentially revolutionary principles are now spreading across the totality of Western social and judicial space. Equality based on the obligation of means is replaced with equality based on the obligation of results through a differentiation of the judicial treatment of citizens based on their place in the community. These theories, often described as communitarian, frequently flirt with the idea of group rights, as in the case of South Africa (Darbon, 1995; Bekker, Chapter 10 of this volume). This confers an unexpected legitimacy on calls made by communitarian groups in the name of difference. Those groups which consider that the social markers identifying them place them in a situation of 'systemic discrimination' and 'minority' in the legal sense of the term (which is irreducible to a purely quantitative meaning) can demand for their members differentiated methods of social and legal treatment, the best-known expression of which is Affirmative Action (Klug, 1994). Accordingly, visible cultural minorities, Afro- and Latin Americans, sexual and linguistic minorities, ethnic and religious groups, multiply their demands for differentiation, confirming the demise of the developmentalist belief in the inevitable transition from vertical community allegiances to horizontal trans-community allegiances. With the works of Charles Taylor, Alasdair MacIntyre and Amitai Etzioni, and, to a certain extent, those of Norbert Rouland or Susan Millns, communitarianism is changing into 'practically a new ideology' (Ceylan, 1994: 169) which attempts to rediscover sources of historical legitimacy in pre-Enlightenment writings (Marsile of Padua, and even Rousseau for some). For these authors, the model of society is a 'mechanical society' based on the association of different groups, and no longer an 'organic' society based on the interdependence of individuals.

Drawing on these attempts at the reconceptualisation of social relationships and the place of the individual in social interactions, communitarian theories are becoming more visible in political debates *in* and especially *on* the countries of the South, notably in Africa. This phenomenon reflects the institutional and ideological dependency in which the periphery finds itself in its relationship with the centre. The expression *world system* cannot in fact be reduced to the economic and financial sectors alone. It denotes in a broader sense the increasing interaction of political systems in unequal relationships, as illustrated by the transfer and spread of the ideas of group and communitarian rights in so far as social dependency is concerned.

The dynamics of globalisation portend an ever-increasing dependency of the different states regarding institutional and legal innovations. This dependency is the product of the indisputable domination of a very small number of political systems from the North which are themselves hierarchised among themselves; it is also the result of the increasing interaction of political and judicial systems which tend towards a harmonisation of the different legal solutions suggested as well as much less nationalistic training of the élite groups than before. Institutional innovations are mostly carried out in the North, more precisely in its dominant pole, the United States. This location is solely able to ensure that innovation also acquires legitimacy. Group rights, although they were practised long ago in the Ottoman Empire or more recently in the Indian and Lebanese constitutions, have never become a model. Quite the contrary. Similarly, legal techniques for the management of social pluralism have existed in such modern states as The Netherlands – where the notion of *verzuiling* was invented – or later in Alto Adige (Italy), where the idea took the form of the *Proporzpaket* in 1969 and 1972, and in Belgium in the case of Brussels. These innovations were never elaborated into a theory, and remained temporary palliative management methods for temporary situations. The current communitarian ideology is much more universal because it is produced at the centre, and is carried by its legitimising power and by the belief in the premonitory value of innovations arising from it. For the most part, barring some scattered, highly differentiated and poorly constituted experiences in the countries of the South, the debate on group rights and their concrete organisation is most pertinent in the developed countries in the North, even though countries in the South are increasingly concerned.

Innovation only becomes a model when it addresses issues considered as legitimate in the countries of the North-West. To describe this process of international legitimation modestly attributed to the 'international Community', the South African Law Commission argues that:

> The parallel with the history of the protection of individual rights, where the legal opinion of the international Community played such an important role, is striking. It is therefore possible to predict with a reasonable measure of confidence that in the eyes of the international Community the protection of minorities and communities within a nation will become increasingly legitimate and will come to be seen as indeed worthy of protection in the foreseeable future. It may, therefore, also be confidently asserted that those who simply ignore minorities and communities within our nation and would make no provision for them are out of step with international Community sentiment and development of the law (South African Law Commission, 1991: 110).

The unequal imbrication of political systems in the world system results in a transfer of stakes and solutions proposed in the dominant poles towards the peripheries. The institutional innovations carried out by the dominant pole become quasi-automatic stakes in the periphery due to the activities of hitherto marginalised lobbies which utilise the institutional novelties legitimised at the centre to push forward their strategies for power enhancement. In the margins of the South, this dependency is welcomed by local elites who find an opportunity to legitimise their local domination and their authoritarian power on account of a self-assigned modernising mission – namely, the importation of modern technologies into so-called traditional societies. Thus, for them, it is a strategy of legitimation through formal dependency. By identifying with the modernity of core states, they immunise themselves against external attacks as well as from critics in their local society who, from then on, can only reveal their own 'barbarity'. As the South African Law Commission remarked in a telling phrase, 'the Commission regards the need for protection of communities and minorities within a nation as legitimate, the only question being how it should be addressed in the constitution so as to be fair to all and therefore to be accepted as legitimate' (South African Law Commission, 1991: 115).

In developed countries with a stabilised pluralist political system, the institutionalisation of the political game, the legitimacy of control mechanisms and the power of the judicial machinery enable a relatively easy management of the contradictions generated by this development of the group idea within a framework designed on the model of the abstract individual. In all the states of the North-West facing this problem, the judge is in fact the key factor in the group's rehabilitation (Grofman and Davidson, 1992; Knopf, 1990; Lochack, 1989; Neveu, 1993; Jackson and McGoldrick, 1993: 225–48). He regulates the conflicting interpretations not in a general abstract manner but case by case, so that the group is never reified directly as such, through recourse to such metaphorical expressions as 'systemic discrimination' or 'private interests'. It is symptomatic that authors such as Marinus Wiechers (1994), or the South African Law Commission, after very lengthy work foresaw the need to guarantee the protection of minorities through a strengthening of the legal protection of individual human rights, particularly by granting *locus standi* to anyone acting in his own name or '… on behalf of a particular group or class of persons without having to prove actual injury' (South African Law Commission, 1991: 183).

The development of these communitarian claims can contribute to a significant weakening of the degree of social cohesion, not to mention the preservation of communitarian stereotypes, leading to ignorance or even outright rejection (Elbaz, *et al.,* 1993: 119–46). Scholars like Arthur Schlesinger (1991) or Thomas E. Mann emphasise the negative effects of these claims and their legal repercussions: accentuation of community resentments, persistence or even reinforcement of minority stereotypes and, most importantly, the freezing of all desires for bi- or multi-racial political alliances. As Elbaz and Morin put it, '… Essentialisation and categorisation of holders of rights to positive equality result in the creation of communities soldered together by marks reputed to be somatic' (Elbaz, *et al.,* 1993: 9). Even if these effects are always discussed and can occasionally be understood as promoting the stabilisation of national integration processes (Gluckman, 1967; Coset, 1964), the recognition of effective advantages for some groups and not others can, according to this logic, contribute to a significant strengthening of violent and symbolic global conflicts, e.g. the Hutu/Tutsi conflict in Rwanda and Burundi; 'black-on-black violence' in South Africa up until 1994; the military repression in Matabeleland during the 1983–5 period in Zimbabwe, or the Casamance conflict since 1980.

The strong plurality of social divisions and their marked interconnectedness and possibilities of interaction can also help to prevent the polarisation of conflicts in terms of groups, while minimal agreement on the rules of the game allows for a systematic recourse to negotiation and compromise. Alliances between individuals of varied identities exist and contribute both to avoiding polarisation and to establishing the unity of the entire state-based society. In the United States, the strength of the communitarian movement does not exclude other forms of identity, notably transversal differentiation associating interests of different communities in common social struggles. In Canada or similarly in Belgium, there is an 'ethnic or linguistic' specialisation of some parties which are essentially confined to a specific area corresponding to a particular community. This is the case for the *Parti Québecois* in Quebec, the *Vlaams block* in the Dutch-speaking part of Belgium or the *Parti Démocratique Francophone* in the Francophone part. However, this specialisation is never carried out fully, since many other parties are formed at the same time, on the basis of ideas held by a majority which extends beyond identity divisions, nor is it permanent, because of the rhythm of politics. In addition, institutionalisation of politics guarantees 'democratic' treatment of current conflicts. In all cases, specificities are always associated with confusion of interests and opportunities for multiple alliances.

The states of the South, and particularly those of sub-Saharan Africa, do not have a well-established legal tradition. Constitutional and public jurisprudence is practically non-existent (Conac and de Gaudusson, 1990). Thus, the establishment of special rights for certain minorities cannot have the finesse, the circumspection and the feel for specific cases found in the decisions of the American, English or French courts or those of the European Court of Justice. South Africa is the only state that can claim to have comparable legal capacity because of the existence of true expertise and a relatively sophisticated political system favourable to the development of transversal modalities of integration – now used to promote democracy. Elsewhere in Africa, Acts of Parliament have to be relied upon, and they can only describe general situations. As a result, a decision cannot be made for each case on its own merit, but in an abstract, general fashion. In short, the law itself is called upon to verify or challenge the direct existence of groups, and this provides the possibility of global confrontation of interests and strategies of communitarian confrontation. Yalden endorses this analysis when making the following comments about the Canadian situation:

> No doubt there are pitfalls in endorsing collective rights and group action, not the least of which is the prospect of their prevailing on the basis of lobbying muscle rather than intrinsic merit. Critical checks against that prospect nonetheless are present in the continued validity of the individual rights, and of judicial independence in mediating the balance with collective norms and interests (Yalden, 1993: 25).

The states of the South, weakly institutionalised and scarcely concerned with the rule of law and the judiciary, will not be able to assume this task.

Communitarian Ideology versus Integration

The impact of this new conceptualisation of groups in the functioning of societies takes place through both the transformation of national legislation and the ever-increasing international recognition of the rights of minorities. Whether one likes it or not, the communitarian revolution associated with current regionalist theories will have a decisive impact on the strategies of African political professionals towards states that have always been afflicted by a deficit of territoriality.

The classic deficit of the principle of territoriality in Africa

There is no need to elaborate on a well-known subject. The semantic inventiveness of authors would in itself suffice to express this deficit. The expressions 'soft state', 'rhizomous state', 'state in upheaval', 'bouncing state', 'centrifugal state', 'state with variable polarisation', 'predator state', to mention but a few, undoubtedly reveal the vitality of the construction of the state but also, in particular, the constant deficit in the imposition of sovereignty on the territorial space.

The crisis of integration in Africa is merely a reflection of the more general inability of the principle of national territoriality to make itself felt as a universal social reality inherent in the dynamics of state creation (Badie, 1989). The crisis of the principle of territoriality is reflected in the failure to get the monopoly of state domination accepted within the territory and also the failure to control the territorial boundaries and to separate clearly the *inside* from the *outside*.

There is a crisis of allegiance because African states have proved incapable of retaining the monopoly of domination over their people, who remain largely enmeshed in vertical mobilisation systems which maintain communitarian modes of identification in competition with statist modes. In Africa, the principle of territoriality has never been able to guarantee the monopoly of allegiance nor has it stopped escapism and the classic exit option characteristic of pre-colonial African societies. Just like the debilitating fiscal constraint, the multiplication of refugee camps throughout the continent and the permanence of international migratory flows constantly demonstrate the porosity of boundaries (Chapters 1 and 5 of this volume) and the state's inability to exercise sovereignty over its territory.

The formally demarcated territory of the state most often appears divided between different rival groups, each of which maintains its domination over a specific area. The case of the former Zaïre, in which entire provinces fell into the hands of warlords who contented themselves with paying tribute to the great central chief as the only form of allegiance, is particularly striking, as are the cases of Angola, Sudan, Mozambique and Somalia or even, in a more institutionalised form, Nigeria.

Boundary disputes occur because the border is not merely a demarcation line. It is also an area of resource exploitation which notably allows the state to extract important resources from commercial activities through systems of indirect imposition. This control is all the more important in Africa, as Jean-Claude Gautron recalls, since most of the state's resources are derived from indirect taxation (Gautron, 1981: 51–8). Thus, the border appears more and more to be an area for profit-making from resources for private and government actors who utilise it to maximise the potential profits to be made from differences in the exchange rate and the prices of goods and services between different states or to enrich themselves through the systematic diversion of state taxation. The informal cross-border trade between Cameroon, Nigeria, Chad, Niger, and Togo is particularly notorious, as is that between The Gambia and Senegal. The border is no longer a line of separation, of de-standardisation over which the state reserves for itself the interface monopoly. Rather, it is a totally wild and deregulated market area, a place of escape from state control (Chapter 1 in this volume). This dual dimension of the crisis of integration provides the communitarian ideology with a leverage effect which transforms the very concept of the state.

Towards an end of the integrationist monopoly of the state?

The legitimation of these new communitarian theories in the North-West represents a direct challenge to the present structuring of countries where the political regime is unstable, weakly institutionalised and composed of people often coming from different and plural identity backgrounds – namely, practically all African countries and the great majority of all states in the South The absence, in most cases, of a real institutionalisation of power, of forms of trans-community mobilisation and quite simply of a coherent 'civil society', transforms the power struggle into a race for access to wealth, forcing political leaders (the political entrepreneurs) to create for themselves faithful clienteles. This systematic clientelism, analysed by Jean-François Médard under the term 'neo-patrimonial system', and corresponding to the now classic classification of 'clientelist state' as opposed to 'administration state' (Lapierre, 1977: 135), invites the more active groups to mobilise around regional leaders on the basis of a reconstructed identity. For lack of an alternative form of mobilisation, this vertical social structuring causes antagonisms between several clientelist groups with exclusive identities. There is no shortage of examples, from Rwanda to Burundi, from Kenya to Zimbabwe, from Niger to Sudan, or from Nigeria to Senegal.

This effect is all the more strengthened in that the competing elite groups who are excluded or who must share power acquire, by means of communitarian reha-bilitation, a 'historical' opportunity to create fiefdoms in which they are able to secure a monopoly of the management of political resources. The elite groups can also appeal for international solidarity and invoke the 'right of humanitarian inter-ference' or the right of minorities, no longer objectively, but as a means of legit-imising a particular political struggle. This practice, common to all liberation movements, is being amplified, since calls for the re-invention of the nation-state, for the constitution of potentially supranational regional integration organisa-tions, for the promotion of informal modes of integration (particularly by the World Bank and the European Union through their experts and their working documents) cannot but enhance these new interests.

The recognition of groups carries with it *ipso facto* the complete rehabilitation of minorities of all sorts. Up to the present time, these communities were supposed to be integrated, at best by association and at worst by physical constraint, into a binding national unity. Acknowledgement of groups results in acknowledging that minorities have an autonomous life, particularly ethnic groups in Africa and in places like ex-Yugoslavia, Canada and the United States. Such a trend is perhaps likely to improve the lot of minority peoples (this remains to be seen), but it may also reduce the political life of these countries to global conflicts, no longer about ideas, which permit all possible alliances, but among groups, confining the choice of the individual to a narrow predetermined field. The confrontation of this communitarian vision with the weak institutionalisation of these regimes can only result in preventing the formation of political movements at country level and in the effective ethnicisation of all political forces.

This situation has already in fact been in existence for a long time in many countries. In the countries of the South, the issue is particularly complex. Numerous countries are going through this ethnic and identification explosion of political management of the state. Some of them have even drawn the consequences at certain periods in terms of group rights. Thus, without even mentioning the issue of the 1965 Unilateral Declaration of Independence in Rhodesia, the Lancaster House Agreement of 1979 established for a period of 10 years a quota system in the Zimbabwe Parliament, along with separate elections granting the whites a specific representation. This system prevented the formation of trans-identity and national alliances, which only began to come into being and emerge as a challenge to the existing power after the end of the transition period in 1990 (Darbon, 1992: 1–23).

Strengthened by this experience, and on the basis notably of renewed understanding of the idea of democracy in so-called plural societies, the different parties associated with drawing up the independent Namibian Constitution have carefully avoided this system in favour of open consultation, thus allowing the 'nationalisation' of political movements. Nigeria, with its system of infinite dilution of its territory into new States and increasingly numerous local governments based on the automatic territorialisation of groups, has increased the phenomenon of the automatic rejection and marginalisation of citizens considered as strangers (non-indigenous) outside their state of origin. And, as Bach concludes, 'the fact is all the more worrying in that, as long as the political-financial stakes involved in the creation of new States remain what they are at present, the legislator cannot hope to stabilise the internal morphology of Nigeria' (Bach, 1991a: 128). It is undoubtedly in South Africa that reflexion about group rights has developed most extensively. One cannot help noting, however, that the solutions opted for rely on a major institutionalisation of South African political life. The protection of minorities in the Constitution has been organised without recourse to particular electoral quotas or rights (Chapter 10 in this volume). The very principle of group rights was rejected by the South African Law Commission, and by the main parties in the ruling government alliance: respect for individual rights was perceived as the best guarantee for the protection of minority rights, which imply respect for the legal system and the independence of the judiciary.

The political and quasi-legal rebirth of groups incites minorities in the process of integrating to demand the acknowledgement of their differences. The stock of sympathy which every minority, particularly small ethnic minorities, benefits from, becomes an important argument in *irredentist* strategies. These 'progressist' sympathies are piled on top of the most conservative vision of African political life which reduces everything to 'tribal' issues, resulting in strengthening not only the respect by the ruling power of differences but the affirmation of these differences, or even, in the end, their autonomisation. In Namibia, a relatively minor case in point provides an astonishing example. The Reoboth Community, undoubtedly very cleverly advised by some members of the South African judiciary in search of opportunities for institutional experimentation, demanded to be recognised at the

United Nations as an indigenous community in order to be able to benefit notably from considerable autonomy and to strengthen its chances of obtaining an autonomous government – all, of course, to the severe displeasure of the Namibian government.

The rapid transformation of international law now makes it possible to legitimise every kind of minority demand more easily, as Cloete (1990) and Blaauw (1988) demonstrate very well. The many texts and international agreements on the protection of minority rights are not directly mobilisable either politically or legally to found claims for autonomy or even independence. Indeed, these texts aim at the protection of all sorts of communities and minorities (while at the same time leaving the subject of rights – individual or group – highly ambiguous), but always within the framework of a nation-state which still manages this Wilsonian legacy. The right of secession or partition is never recognised, but the minorities, although they may not be recognised as a legal person – this remains very uncertain (Svensson, 1979: 421) – do have the right to demand protection within the framework of the state.

This system of protection under the compulsory and indisputable guardianship of the state has functioned efficiently since the legitimation processes were entirely subjected to the nation-state. The new balkanisation of Eastern Europe so as to take account of 'national minorities' (as defined by Article 27 of the Final Helsinki Act or the CSCE Resolutions of June 1990 in Copenhagen) and the collapse of African states in constant deficit of territoriality tend to shift progressively the locus of expression of minorities, and to marginalise the hitherto indisputable place of a state now in competition with the communitarian legitimacies, whether territorialised or not, that are being recognised.

Badie has drawn attention to a decision of the International Court of Justice which went largely unnoticed among authors interested in Africa (Badie, 1992: 90–91). Set with the task of dealing with the delicate question of the sovereignty of the former Spanish colony of Western Sahara, the Court seemed ready to challenge the classic principle of territorial allegiance when evoking, in 1995, the principle of political and communitarian affiliation.

These shifts in state/minorities relationships still contribute to endangering the material and especially the symbolic resources which the African state struggles to control in a territory which it has never succeeded in possessing. The impact of communitarian movements is reinforced by the emergence of well-organised lobbies geared towards the protection of 'necessary' groups (such as Survival International or Tribal Act) or towards the advancement of the rights of 'voluntary' minorities (feminists, homosexuals, etc.). Small human communities, particularly those which according to Western mythology should be close to the 'noble savage', are the subject of articulate supporting movements demanding their recognition as specific social entities endowed with special rights, implying, notably, recognition of the supremacy of individual over territorial rights. The political construction of the communitarian stake is under way.

In this context, the renewal of debates on regional integration very often brings an explicit or implicit condemnation of the nation-state. This cannot but strengthen the potential legitimacy of demands for autonomy, if not independence. Two options emerge for the state: either it continues to be part of the classic concept of regional integration, which will remain practically useless, apart from increasing the number of regional and international organisations for Africa (Constantin, 1991: 239); or alternatively, it can opt for the new path of a re-examination of the principle of territoriality, involving *ipso facto* a re-shaping of the spheres of state sovereignty and, in this case, supported objectively by the new communitarian ideology intent on strengthening the territorial network. This could lead to a thorough recomposition of the morphology of the state in Africa. The stakes are clear, it is simply a matter of accepting them.

5

CHRISTOPHER CLAPHAM
Boundaries & States
in the New African Order

The peculiar dynamics of integration and disintegration in sub-Saharan Africa at the end of the millennium result from a combination of the upheavals in the international system since the end of the Cold War and the crisis of the state within Africa itself. As other contributions to this volume show, the model of inter-state integration through formal institutional frameworks, which has hitherto dominated the analysis of integration in Africa and elsewhere, has increasingly been challenged by the declining control of states over their own territories, the proliferation of informal networks, and the incorporation of Africa (on a highly subordinate basis) into the emerging global order. This chapter examines state boundaries in Africa, as the critical lines of demarcation which define both the states that lie within those boundaries and the relationship between the entities on either side of them. It seeks to show how our conceptions of integration have been determined by a particular idea of boundaries, and how changes in the nature of African statehood in turn affect conceptions of frontier, territory and integration both within states and between them.

Our conception of integration in Africa, as elsewhere, has been determined by our idea of the state and its boundaries. The international rules of boundary maintenance, laid down initially by the League of Nations, taken over by the United Nations, and enthusiastically adopted by African states and incorporated into the Charter of the Organisation of African Unity (OAU), reinforced an ideology of state sovereignty which in turn pushed the quest for integration into a particular political form: the creation of inter-state organisations, the intended function of which was to seek increasing levels of co-operation between states but the fate of which was at every turn to raise the implicit tension between the states which belonged to the organisation, and the softening of boundaries between those states which integration was expected to bring about. Once the nature of boundaries is called into question, as has increasingly happened under the impact of changes in the international order, the concept of integration must be called into question with them.

This contribution will therefore examine the factors which have, since independence, led to a particular conception of state boundaries in Africa; the factors which have in recent years increasingly threatened and undermined that conception of boundaries; and the new kinds of boundary, and the consequently different forms of integration and disintegration, which – at least in parts of the continent – are thus emerging.

The Conventions on the Maintenance of African Boundaries

At the time of African independence, there was at least some speculation that the displacement of colonial regimes by indigenous governments might lead to the redrawing of the state boundaries which had been imposed on the continent in such an apparently arbitrary manner by the colonial rulers. There were, of course, a small number of adjustments: British Somaliland and ex-Italian Somalia united to form the Somali Republic; the peoples of the Northern and Southern Cameroons were allowed to decide whether they should form part of Nigeria, on the one hand, or Cameroon, on the other, one region opting for each of the possible outcomes; more controversially, the former Italian colony of Eritrea was in 1952 federated with Ethiopia, following a process of consultation with its inhabitants but without any vote. Elsewhere, existing colonial administrative divisions – even where, as in parts of French colonial Africa, these were both recent and relatively insignificant – hardened into the boundaries between states.

Even though the boundary-lines themselves were often (though not always) artificial and externally created, the determination with which they were maintained after independence was due not so much to continuing colonial influence as to the nature of the states which were created within them, and the nature of the boundaries that African statehood implied. It is possible to distinguish two broad kinds of relationship between a state and its boundaries: between boundaries which are created by states, and states which are created by boundaries. In the first case, the state is founded on the association of a group of people (who may or may not constitute a 'nation') within a given territory, and the creation of mechanisms for governing those people which eventually constitute a state; where the jurisdiction of this state comes up against the jurisdiction of other states which control neighbouring territories, a boundary is formed. These boundaries may be adjusted in one direction or the other – as the boundaries of France have been over many centuries – without affecting the identity of the state which lies within them.

In the second case, which has been the common (but not universal) experience of African peoples in the modern era, the boundaries come first, and the state is then created within them. The Ghanaian or Ivorian state is the organisation created in order to govern the territory which has already been identified as Ghana or Côte d'Ivoire. In this second case, the boundaries may well be more 'artificial' than in the first, but they are for that very reason more, and not less, central to the identity of the state that lies within them. If Côte d'Ivoire, say, is defined by its boundaries, then any change in those boundaries raises basic questions about what Côte d'Ivoire is, and what right it has to exist. The familiar conventions of African boundary maintenance are imposed by the mutual recognition of the rulers of African states that their boundaries constitute the *raison d'être* for their own right to rule.

The point may be illustrated by looking at the boundaries between African states formed in this way, and those of the minority of African states whose identity as states conceptually precedes the boundaries that enclose them. Kenya, for example, was formed by British colonialism, and its boundaries – with Tanzania, Uganda, Sudan, Ethiopia and the Somali Republic – were, from the Kenyan point of view, formed in much the same way, through demarcation between the British colonial administration and those – the German administration of Tanganyika, the British protectorate of Uganda and the Anglo-Egyptian condominium of Sudan, the Ethiopian empire, and the Italian government of Somalia – who controlled the neighbouring territories. After independence, however, the boundary with the Somali Republic constituted a problem, in a way that the others did not, because the Somali state defined itself in terms of a conception of Somali ethnicity which both preceded (conceptually if not historically) and challenged its boundaries. Ethiopia and Sudan likewise defined their statehood independently of their boundaries, but since the core communities through whom statehood was defined were far distant from the Kenyan border, this did not create the same problems as in the Somali case. Some other African states, such as Rwanda and Burundi, Swaziland and Lesotho, also had conceptions of statehood that preceded their boundaries, but since they were either broadly satisfied with the boundaries which colonialism had allocated to them, or else at least recognised the imprudence of challenging their boundaries with states much more powerful than themselves, this did not give rise to major problems.

African state boundaries, in short, were so rigorously maintained because – rather than in spite – of their artificiality. These boundaries defined and legitimated the particular kind of power structure which grew up within post-colonial African states, and provided the framework for the politics of patronage and allocation through which those who controlled these states sought to survive. One of their most important functions was to define the revenue base of the state, and hence the access of state elites to financial resources. In Katanga and Biafra, dissident rulers of territorial subdivisions – which were themselves demarcated by the former colonial power, and no less artificial than the territory of the state itself – threatened to abscond with a major portion of the revenues. In states which derived a high proportion of their income from customs duties, and from state manipulation of markets for agricultural produce, control over the boundaries was essential to provide the financial underpinning of the state itself; the creation of national currencies, through which governments sought to establish their control over domestic economic transactions, can in turn be seen as a form of boundary maintenance.

Once the conventions of boundary maintenance were established by African states themselves – in the Charter of the OAU, reinforced by the resolution on respect for existing frontiers approved at the Cairo summit of 1964 – they were sustained by alliances between African states and their external patrons. Regardless of the artificiality of these boundaries, and the feebleness of the states which lay within them, it was much easier for external powers to work within the rules upheld by the continental consensus than against them. The first and for many purposes the most important of independent Africa's external patrons, the former colonial powers, generally had an interest in boundary maintenance which derived from the fact that they had themselves created the boundaries concerned. These boundaries corresponded to the usage of their own national languages, to the scope of administrative, educational and legal systems established on metropolitan models, and to an economy which generally enjoyed particularly close relations with the former metropole. Only in the former Belgian Congo, where the attempted Katangan secession offered the Belgians the prospect of retaining control over the most valuable part of a state which was otherwise eluding it, am I aware of any subversion of African boundaries by their European creators. Tacit French support for the Biafran secession provides a rare instance of a major colonial power undermining the boundaries even of an African state outside its post-colonial aegis.

The protection of African state boundaries by the two Cold War superpowers illustrates the support of the post-1945 global order for the principles of 'juridical statehood' (Jackson and Rosberg, 1982; 1986). Even though neither the Soviet Union nor the United States had any commitment to the particular boundary-lines drawn between African states, it was much easier for them to seek clients through the recruitment of state administrations rather than by challenging principles of state sovereignty which they needed to uphold in other cases. Both the Soviet Union and the United States tacitly subverted the principles of state sovereignty by supporting opposition movements within states controlled by their rival, but neither of them called into question the boundaries of the state itself.

It must obviously be recognised that, in at least some African states, a concept of the state and its boundaries, which rests neither on pre-colonial identities nor on external protection, has come to be shared by a substantial section of the population; and even if the internal politics of these states draws to a large extent on ethnic and regional rivalries, they have achieved at least the first stage of the progression towards an indigenous sense of nationhood. These are correspondingly the states which are likely to control the whole of their national territory, and whose boundaries are most effectively maintained. If, in much of this chapter, little attention is paid to these 'normal' states, this is not because they have been forgotten, but because the chapter concentrates on the significant number of states in which this norm does not apply, and which illustrate important developments in African statehood and boundary maintenance which have easily been overlooked because they do not readily fit into the idea of statehood approved by the ideologies of state sovereignty and post-colonial nationalism. The resulting challenge to African state boundaries, and indeed to the states themselves, now calls for urgent attention.

The Challenge to African State Boundaries

African state boundaries have in recent years been challenged in many ways and at many levels, and the upheaval in the global geopolitical order represents only one source of the threat which they currently face, and by no means the most important one. It is indeed most appropriate to begin by looking at the declining capacity of African states to control their own territories, before going on to examine the effects of changes in the international setting.

The most basic source of the challenge to African boundaries derives from the failure of African economies. The reasons for this failure, which is so strikingly at variance with the successful economic development of many regions of the Third World, are of course the subject of intense controversy, and lie beyond the scope of this chapter. It has, however, had a number of important effects. One of these has been the 'shrinking' of the state away from the peripheries of its formal national territory, and its concentration in the capital and major cities, and in the most important areas of export production. This shrinking evidently varies between states, and also takes different forms. In some cases, it is demonstrated by the simple disappearance of government services, as state revenues decline and are increasingly concentrated in those places where political patronage and hence regime survival most require them. Local bureaucrats – starting with the more dispensable ones, such as schoolteachers, and working up to administrative officials – do not get paid, or find that their salaries have been reduced by inflation to a level at which they no longer support subsistence. They then have to keep themselves going by finding alternative employment, using (or abusing) their official positions in order to exact funds from the local population, or disappearing for long periods to the capital or the provincial headquarters in search of their salary cheques.

In other cases, when the weakening of government on the spot is accompanied by local grievances, counterproductive central retaliation, and support from across the frontiers, state control is contested by insurgent movements, which may either seek to attack the national capital or else simply maintain an autonomous government within the region itself. A substantial number of African states now do not in any way, even the most nominal, control the whole of their national territories, and their formal frontiers have ceased to hold any meaning except on official maps. Whereas once the challenge of insurgents and warlords was limited to certain fairly well-defined zones of regional conflict, notably the Horn of Africa and the southern African 'front line', it subsequently spread to encompass states which could previously be regarded as 'safe'. From the Horn, a continuous band of states without effective government control over all of the national territory extends from Djibouti and Somalia through Ethiopia and Sudan to Uganda, Rwanda and ex-Zaïre, and then Angola. The Liberian catastrophe has affected Sierra Leone, while serious fighting has been reported even from northern Ghana.[1]

At another level, Africa's economic decline has led to attempts at rehabilitation, largely orchestrated and indeed enforced from outside the continent, the effect of which has been to reduce still further the control which African states have been able to maintain over their formal territories. One mechanism of control, the national currency, has been removed from contention by drastic devaluation or imposed convertibility under externally imposed structural adjustment programmes. The purchasing agencies through which states sought to extract a surplus from their peasantries have been dismantled. The capacity of state elites to operate neopatrimonial patronage systems has been undercut by the removal of many of the mechanisms which they used for the purpose. In the eyes of their

---

[1] See *Keesings Record of World Events 1994*, p. 39848.

supporters, these policies would, if successful, eventually create the basis for a stronger state by restoring the economy on which any successful political order must ultimately rely. Regardless of the arguments over whether these policies will actually lead to economic betterment, however, their immediate effect has been to accelerate the process of state decay.

A similar process has been taking place in the political sphere, through the attempt to enforce mechanisms for democratic accountability, which form the precise analogue to programmes of economic restructuring. As in the case of economic management, the means previously used to maintain political control were ultimately self-defeating, and often resulted in abuses of power which were difficult to justify on the most basic moral grounds. It can likewise plausibly be argued that an increased level of accountability provides the essential precondition for the rehabilitation of states which have displayed none of the features of the developmental autocracies identified in Eastern Asia or even in parts of Latin America.[2] In some cases, such as Zambia, the experience of fair elections may have helped to restore a sense of political community, and (despite the problems of the Chiluba government) to reinforce the identity of a state whose boundaries are among the most bizarre even in Africa. In Nigeria, too, the aborted presidential elections of 1993 showed a pattern of support for the winning candidate which, for the first time in the country's chequered electoral history, was not evidently dependent on ethnic and regional affiliation. The demand for multiparty democratisation may nonetheless weaken or destroy the state rather than strengthen it, since a system of government which depends on popular election must ultimately be prepared to recognise the right to secession of any community which does not wish to remain within the existing frontiers of the state – as has been clearly shown by the distintegration of the former Soviet Union, and even of Czechoslovakia.

At the same time as the boundaries of African states have come under challenge from within, they have also been affected by the decline of the international consensus which had previously supported them. Moreover, despite the formal adherence of African states to the principles laid down by the OAU, this consensus has declined as much within the continent as outside it. Respect for the principles of boundary maintenance and non-interference in the internal affairs of other states has never been complete: the Somali Republic challenged its inherited boundaries from the outset, while Nkrumah was charged by several other African states with seeking to subvert them. The militarisation of African politics which became evident from the mid-1970s nonetheless internationalised African state security in a way that had not previously been the case, even during the Nigerian civil war. Much of this militarisation reflected the tacit support of African governments for insurgent movements fighting in neighbouring states – a support which was sometimes, as in the south of the continent, legitimised by the canons of liberation from colonial or settler rule. During the Mobutu period in

---

[2] The failure to create 'developmental states' in Africa which in any way correspond to the experience of other regions of the Third World is emerging as a critical issue, not just for African economic development but for comparative development studies as a whole (Berger, 1994; Clapham, 1996b).

Zaïre, assistance to the opposition in Angola, and corresponding Angolan acquies-
cence in the Shaba incursions of 1977 and 1978, was matched elsewhere in the
continent by the mutual toleration of or support for neighbouring insurgencies
by Ethiopia, on the one hand, and Sudan and Somalia, on the other, and by the
frequent interventions in Chad. Still more corrosively, as the availability of
weapons increased, and their use 'escaped' from the control of states, conflicts
were no longer contained within state boundaries, but spread from one state into
another. In military as in economic terms, the idea of a 'boundary' which marked
a reasonably clear line between states was replaced by that of a 'borderland', a tract
of territory in which one state gradually gave way to another, or in which semi-
independent warlords were able to maintain themselves against official governments on either side.

The politics of the borderland represents a relatively new and insufficiently
studied phenomenon in Africa's international relations, and points the way
towards ideas of integration and disintegration which are very far from those
embodied in the formal inter-state organisations with which Africa abounds
(Nugent and Asiwaju, 1996). The cases I have in mind include those between
Ethiopia, Eritrea, Djibouti, Somalia and Sudan; between Libya, Chad and Sudan;
between ex-Zaïre, Uganda, Rwanda and Burundi; between Liberia, Guinea and
Sierra Leone; and between Angola and Mozambique, and most of their neighbours. These are not, certainly, the only boundaries in Africa, nor do they
encompass more than a minority of African states; but they include a substantial
number of states, several of them very significant ones, spread over a large part of
the continent, and they draw attention to developments which have often been
overlooked. In many of these cases, the 'boundary', as a line policed by the forces
of the states on either side, has effectively disappeared; sometimes one state
controls the territory up to its frontier, sometimes neither. Insurgent movements
may exercise effective control over the territory on either side, in the way the
EPLF did in the Sudanese-Eritrean borderlands prior to 1991. Armaments pass
freely across, by capture or exchange between groups on either side as often as by
official transfer. Massive movements of refugees take place, sometimes in both
directions, sometimes in only one.

In a few cases, of which Jonas Savimbi's UNITA and Charles Taylor's National
Patriotic Front of Liberia (NPFL) provide the best examples, it may now be plausible to identify a 'shadow state', which performs many of the functions of
statehood without taking on its obligations (Reno, 1995, 1998). These movements
have, over a number of years, maintained control over a substantial part of the
territory of the state within which they operate, and to some extent that of neighbouring states as well. They have little evident desire to seize national capitals and
assume the responsibilities of formal statehood, with its constitutions, ministries,
currencies, structural adjustment programmes, human rights commitments, and
membership of the OAU, the United Nations, or other international bodies. What
they do seek to acquire is the surplus to be extracted from control over important
zones of export production, especially when these can be exploited in a reasonably
discreet manner through contacts with international middlemen. Diamonds are
the perfect commodity for this purpose, but Charles Taylor has evidently been able
to export even bulky items such as timber and iron ore.

The relationship between this softening or even disappearance of some state boundaries in Africa and the recent changes in the global geopolitical setting, is only indirect. Developments in Africa ultimately derive more from long-term evolutions in the structure of African statehood, which represent in some sense a merging of precolonial and post-colonial patterns, than from the upheavals in Europe. They have nonetheless been affected by the global scene, as it has evolved both during the Cold War and after it.

The confrontation between the superpowers first seriously affected Africa during the period that has been called the 'Second Cold War' from the mid-1970s onwards, when the apparent decline in American strength, symbolised by the ejection of the United States from Indo-China, coincided with a resurgence of Soviet interest in the Third World, from Nicaragua to Afghanistan (Halliday, 1986). This coincided, largely fortuitously, with demands on the part of a number of African states for greatly increased military resources to meet the challenges arising from the contested decolonisation in Angola and the subsequent destabilisation in both Angola and Mozambique, from domestic revolution, regional insurgency and external invasion in Ethiopia, and from sheer misgovernment in ex-Zaïre and Chad. In each case, African regimes were able to profit from the intensified global conflict to gain access to a level of armaments which easily outweighed anything that had previously been available. Most of these arms came from the Soviet Union, although Western states such as the United States and France were also prepared to support their own clients against opposition associated with the Soviet Union, Cuba or Libya.

In the event, these armaments proved to be not merely useless, but often disastrously counterproductive. Rather than strengthening the state, they actually destroyed it. At its most basic, this was because the state structure was not strong enough to control the means of repression donated to it by its external patrons. In some cases, like Siyad Barre's Somali Republic, weapons were distributed to clan militias which – though judged at the time to be 'loyal' to the central government – rapidly set themselves up as independent factions amid the wreckage of the collapsing Somali state. In others, like Ethiopia, the declining morale of the Mengistu government forces led to desertion and the capture of vast stocks of weapons by its opponents. Ultimately, the instruments of physical control, however technologically sophisticated, have to depend on the mechanisms of social control at the disposal of the regime which tries to use them.

In the aftermath of the Cold War, the willingness of external patrons to supply arms with which to maintain African states has virtually evaporated. Only very few states, such as Sudan, are able to obtain weapons through alternative patronage networks – in this case through the Islamicist connection with Iran. More important, the international conventions of support for state sovereignty have also disappeared. There is no evident rationale for industrial states to support existing frontiers in Africa, when states such as the mighty Soviet Union itself have shattered into pieces. The first generally recognised secession of any part of an African state to form a separate state of its own – the independence of Eritrea from Ethiopia, which was effectively achieved in May 1991 and formally confirmed two years later – passed virtually unnoticed in a world where such events had become commonplace. In the new world order, the boundaries of African states will have to be those which they can maintain for themselves.

The New Politics of African Boundaries

Scholars in international relations have persistently sought guidance on the possible development of the international system in the post-Cold War era by looking to the patterns which characterised previous historical epochs. I have lost count of the papers and lectures called 'Back to the Future', though a more precise description would be 'Forward to the Past'. A similar approach, however unoriginal, may be appropriate to speculation about the redefinition of state boundaries in Africa, and the forms of integration and disintegration which are likely to accompany it.

The kinds of boundary inherited by African states from the colonial period have certainly been very different from those which characterised Africa in the pre-colonial era. Pre-colonial Africa did feature separate political jurisdictions, with boundaries between them, and in some societies – such as those of highland Ethiopia – boundaries acquired a considerable cultural as well as political signifi-cance (Clapham, 1994: 27–40). These boundaries by no means necessarily corre-sponded to the differences between African ethnicities in the way that the popular stereotype implies. Many pre-colonial African political structures were multi-ethnic in nature, while many if not most ethnic groups were divided between different political jurisdictions. The frontiers between them were generally fluid and shifting, and encompassed zones of contested or sometimes uncontested territory, depending on the density of the population or the value of the economic resources to be found in border areas. The perennial movements of African peoples, extending into the period of colonial conquest, led to corresponding changes in territorial control and to constant wars between advancing and retreating peoples. Great warriors established personal empires, which sometimes – like Shaka's Zululand – survived them, but more often decayed after their death.

Despite the level of variation amongst pre-colonial African political arrange-ments, ranging from centralised states through a variety of federal and confederal arrangements to societies in which specialised political authorities were scarcely detectable, one can, however, conclude – in terms of the distinction outlined earlier in this chapter – that boundaries were determined by the structure of political authorities, rather than vice versa. This pattern must eventually be re-established; the system under which, in the colonial and post-colonial eras, political jurisdictions were created within an arbitrarily demarcated territory, can only be temporary. Where the state is unable to create an effective political authority within the frontiers it has inherited, then whatever authority does emerge must eventually create its own frontiers, no matter how long it takes the publishers of maps or the allocators of seats in the United Nations General Assembly to recognise them.

This process will certainly include a place for many of the boundaries estab-lished by colonial rule. In the same way that the Austrian and Ottoman empires, and even the Roman empire, have left lasting residues on the map of Europe, so the European empires have left a mark on Africa which will not be easily erased. The language differences which instantly signal the crossing of any border between Francophone, Anglophone and Lusophone Africa are likely to remain in place, because they have become the medium for communication between indigenous peoples, quite as much as a means for communicating with the outside world. In some areas, notably in Anglophone West Africa, the development of an indigenous English-based lingua franca has already marked off communities which are linguistically distinct from the metropolitan tongue. In other parts of the continent, languages such as Hausa, Xhosa or Swahili may serve a similar function.

In addition, as already noted, the demarcations between peoples left in the wake of colonialism are no longer altogether artificial. Ghanaians and Ivorians are distinguished not simply by the side of a colonially created dividing line on which they happen to find themselves, but by differences of historical experience and personal identity which may well deepen as they are transmitted to subsequent generations. One paradox of state creation in post-Cold War Africa is indeed that the two 'new' states which have so far made their appearance, with a greater or lesser appearance of solidity – Eritrea and Somaliland – have boundaries explicitly based on colonial demarcations which had earlier been erased as part of a process of 'unification'. One reason for this, at any event in the case of Somaliland, is that any existing boundary retains a residual international legitimacy, and is not so threatening to the international order as an attempt to redraw boundaries from a new situation: the same rationale accounts for the independence of Estonia, Latvia and Lithuania within the boundaries ascribed to them as Union Republics of the USSR, rather than those in place before their forcible incorporation into the Soviet Union in 1940. But in addition, Eritreans have clearly developed some sense of common identity within the entirely artificial lines established by Italian colonialism, which links people of different language and religion and at the same time separates them from other people with the same language and religion as their own, across the border in Ethiopia or Sudan (Pool, 1993). Analogous identities will continue to link other peoples who have suffered a less traumatic transition to independence.

The two major factors determining the redefinition of African boundaries and borderlands must, however, be authority and resources. Often these will coincide with existing frontiers, but often they will not. Authority, for a start, may derive from a variety of potentially conflicting elements. In some cases, it may still be defined by the boundaries of the post-colonial state; in others, it may be created by commonalities of language, ethnicity or religion; elsewhere, it may be imposed by warlords who, like Charles Taylor or Jonas Savimbi, succeed in carving out a stretch of territory which they are able to control, and which may in turn give rise to an embryonic state that may well survive them.

One implication of the idea of conflicting sources of authority is, moreover, that authority may – and often must – be shared. The post-colonial African state, whose rulers have been obsessed with the importance of maintaining their own monopoly of power within the inherited frontiers, has been intensely inimical to the prospect of shared authority, and to the mechanisms – federal systems, separation of powers, the acceptance of legitimate opposition – through which this has been institutionalised elsewhere. Given that the monopoly state has failed, however, the price to be paid by a ruler for undisputed control over a territory must be the reduction of the size of that territory to often ludicrously minuscule proportions. It must eventually make sense to return to a system, of which many examples can be found in the experience of pre-colonial Africa, in which local rulers are accorded a high level of autonomy, in exchange for recognition of the ultimate authority of a national ruler. Once rulers are no longer able to impose their authority, the acceptance of some division of power becomes the sole basis on which stable political structures can be maintained at all. The attempt by the EPRDF government in Ethiopia to create a confederation of ethnically based regions, in place of the centralised state which collapsed in May 1991, represents one testing ground for such a system, though one marked by considerable uncertainties and ambiguities (Clapham, 1996c: 27–40; Abbink, 1995, 1997).

Any effective African state system must likewise take account of the extremely uneven distribution of resources in the continent, in just the same way as the pre-colonial system did. Areas of relatively dense population, with a reliable resource base, were for the most part able to maintain stable and effective political authorities; areas with slight and uncertain resources, difficult communications, and sparse populations, had correspondingly weak and fragmented political structures. Some such system must return, since it is implausible to suppose that states which are entirely incapable of maintaining themselves from their own resources will indefinitely be enabled to subsist on the largesse of external patrons. The case of a state such as Mozambique, where some 55% of gross domestic product is derived from foreign aid, makes the point with dramatic force.[3] The end of the Cold War, by removing much of the incentive for outside patrons to maintain derelict client states in Africa, has helped to promote a crisis of state survival which would eventually have taken place in the normal course of events.

The resource base on which African state structures have to be built will, however, differ appreciably from that which supported the political authorities of the pre-colonial era, since the creation of wealth has been irreversibly affected by the incorporation of Africa into a global market economy. In most of pre-colonial Africa, wealth depended largely on production for the domestic economy – though even then, political authorities from Dahomey to Zanzibar were maintained by an export trade in slaves, and to some extent in other commodities such as gold and ivory.[4] Any revitalised African state system is likely to depend on export production, the density and skills of its population, and the effectiveness of its government. The uncertainty of the last of these – and post-independence Africa has already demonstrated that really bad government will destroy societies faster than almost anything else – means that much of its shape must be unpredictable; but the extreme differentials that Africa exhibits, between areas with substantial resources and areas with virtually none, must

---

[3] Calculated from 1991 figures for GDP and unrequited transfers at current rates of exchange (*Africa South of the Sahara 1994*, 1993: 608–9). Estimates that aid accounts for 75% of Mozambican GDP are widely cited.

[4] Jean-Francois Bayart (1993: 20–32) has argued that 'extraversion', or the utilisation of external resources in order to maintain domestic authority, has been a consistent feature of politics in Africa over a long period.

result in some concentrations of relatively viable states, interspersed with zones where government is very slight indeed. In Somalia as in Mozambique, the major resource available to those who seek to build a power base for themselves already consists of humanitarian aid provided by industrial states; and since such aid is unlikely to keep coming indefinitely, its withdrawal can only prompt a crisis in political authority, as well as in human need. It is likewise difficult to envisage a future for structures of authority which, like Charles Taylor's Greater Liberia, appear to depend on selling for ready cash whatever local sources of wealth (such as diamonds or forest trees) can most easily be carried away. Similarly a retreat into subsistence has nothing to offer. Only regular and expanding production, in collaboration with the world market, provides any plausible prospect for maintaining effective African states.

In the confusing order which has been left behind by the end of the Cold War, two apparently contradictory tendencies clearly stand out. The first is a process of political disintegration and fragmentation, which in Africa has merely accentuated a decline in state power and authority that was already becoming evident as a result of the decay of post-colonial institutions, the decline of African economies, and the frequent failure of government. The second is an intensifying process of economic globalisation, reinforced by the collapse of the socialist alternative and the growing power of international financial institutions. For the moment, these twin tendencies appear to be heading in contradictory directions; eventually, however, they must converge to produce some new synthesis, within which Africa will have to find its inevitably subordinate place. That synthesis in turn will determine the form of new patterns of political and economic integration.

Past attempts at integration, through formalised inter-state institutions, have all too evidently failed. In economic terms, such would-be economic communities made very little sense from the start, because there was so little that they could usefully trade with one another. Politically, they were doomed to impotence, because governing elites within each state depended on the control of national economies which attempts at integration could only undermine. Eventually, the whole system of state regulation of the economy on which inter-state integration depended became self-defeating, and in quite a number of cases, the state itself crumbled.

In regions where a single state enjoys both an effective domestic political order and a size and economic weight which dwarf those of its neighbours, it is possible to envisage a new pattern of integration through regional hegemony. The regional dynamic is already being manifested in the development of structures of co-operation which, in effect, provide a mechanism to regulate the role of the leading state within each region. In essence, these concede the primacy of the dominant state, and its right to concern itself with the domestic as well as the international politics of its neighbours, in exchange for regulation and legitimation through an appropriate regional organisation. The role of Nigeria within ECOWAS, and notably the role of ECOWAS in regulating the Nigerian-led ECOMOG intervention in Liberia, provides the classic case. Even though the economic impact of this ostensibly economic community is negligible, its political influence has been significant. Within southern Africa, the predominance of South Africa makes a similar system almost inevitable, despite the considerable difficulties that the new

South African government has experienced in its regional diplomacy. In Central and Eastern Africa, on the other hand, structures of regional political management have failed to emerge, because no single state has a size and strength which would enable it to secure a position of leadership recognised by the others. This failure has in turn been reflected in levels of conflict in the region.

The creation of effective systems of regional integration nonetheless depends on the success with which potential regional leaders are able to secure political stability, and a reasonably working economy, within their own territories. Regional leadership in Africa has been undermined, not only by connections between individual African states and their external patrons, but also by the divisions within any state large enough to aspire to a position of leadership. All of Africa's larger states – South Africa, Angola, ex-Zaïre, Nigeria, Ethiopia, Sudan – have endured some form of civil war. Both South Africa and Nigeria face considerable problems in establishing viable domestic political structures, and Nigeria's potential hegemonic role is being eroded by the failure of the domestic political order in the present, just as South Africa's was in the recent past. Ex-Zaïre, with its perennial political problems, has been quite unable to assume the role in Central Africa which its size and location might have indicated.

Furthermore, any effective structure of integration must depend on those mechanisms for transnational economic management in Africa which have been shown to work, and which must therefore operate in compliance with international markets, while avoiding those mechanisms – and notably attempted regulation by ineffectual states – which do not work. The first effective mechanism, however resented it may be by governmental elites within Africa, is the imposition of common macroeconomic conditions from outside the continent. It is only, indeed, with considerable external aid – and hence, inevitably, external control – that the macroeconomic requirements for integration can be met at all. One of these is the effective destruction of individual state currencies, which served to control economic transactions in the interest of state elites, and their displacement by convertible means of exchange which are accepted across state boundaries; there is no reason why domestic as well as intra-African trade should not be conducted in internationally acceptable currencies such as dollars, Euros, or yen. Another is the creation of externally guaranteed trading regimes, capable of stabilising import and export markets, as well as prices and credit, not merely across African boundaries but between Africa and the industrial world. A third is the imposition of structures of domestic economic management.

The other mechanism which clearly works is the microeconomic efficiency and flexibility of informal African trading systems, which have proved capable of surviving, and indeed flourishing, amidst the failure of state-managed economies. In the statist economies of post-independence Africa, smuggling has helped to maintain the trading networks which developed in the pre-colonial era, and which can only benefit from the breakdown of control by states over their own boundaries. The most lively markets I have encountered in Africa have been in places like Koindu, near the frontiers of Liberia, Guinée and Sierra Leone, or Dire Dawa, close to those of Ethiopia, Djibouti and Somalia, where one can see a process of economic integration dramatically different from that promoted by organisations such as ECOWAS. The declining control by African states over their own economies may well be an essential precondition for more effective forms of economic integration, which are driven by common needs and managed by indigenous traders, in place of ineffectual inter-state structures managed by national and international bureaucracies.

The major difficulties lie in the area of political control, since no effective process of integration can take place without states capable of maintaining a level of political order which has disappeared in much of Africa, and providing stable conditions for the enforcement of contracts and other essential economic services. This in turn calls for a reversal of that process by which, after independence, control of state power became a mechanism for appropriating economic resources, and its replacement by one in which control of economic resources becomes the basis for building up political authority. This remains, however, the critical area in which the reintegration of Africa is at its most fragile.

6

ABDOULAYE NIANDOU SOULEY[1]
Paradoxes & Ambiguities
of Democratisation

Since the collapse of the ideological models in Eastern Europe, democratisation has been the burning issue of the hour in Africa. Everyone agrees that the institution of democracy in this continent is a requirement of our time, if only to free people from the yoke of an asphyxiating and economically unproductive authoritarian state. There are, however, divergent opinions, indeed arguments, concerning the meaning and content of the democratisation process to be pursued. These days, as the facts show, there is no doubt that the process of democratising Africa's political systems poses huge problems. Here and there, citizens are wondering what tomorrow holds. Most frequently they ask: Where are we headed? Towards chaos? Civil war? Ethnic war? Revolution? Anarchy? Or towards a better tomorrow? So many teleological questions, which no one can answer, short of being a visionary or a seer.

One thing is certain, though. Africans do know where they have come from; they know they are emerging from a long period of autocracy, whether civil or military. They also know that they are coming out of a prison state typified by the vicious circle of censorship, repression, imprisonment and physical elimination. At present, Africans are discovering democracy. They are discovering that history is not static and that things can change. It can no longer be said that everything is just as it used to be in Africa.

No sooner had Africans discovered democracy than many of them began to wonder whether they ought to be happy about it or not. Was it not as a result of this very democracy that they had come to know so many of the world's ills? In the past, people say, there was social peace, and wages were paid regularly and on time. This is no longer the case in many African countries. For want of better solutions, it is easiest to blame all of today's difficulties on democratisation, to such an extent that the word is now associated with an increasing number of paradoxes and ambiguities. Hence people can no longer distinguish between 'bread-and-butter democracy' (*démocratie alimentaire*) and true democracy, in a context in which, it must be admitted, the state has not changed at all (Médard, 1990).

---

[1] The author wishes to express his sincere thanks to Souley Adji, lecturer at the Faculty of Arts and Human Sciences, Abdou Moumouni Dioffo University, Niamey, for his invaluable co-operation.

Differentiated Conceptions of Democracy

One of the ambiguities of democratisation in Africa is that there is no agreement on the actual notion of democracy, and this gives rise to doubts, anxieties and uncertainties. This may be explained by the fact that the implementation of democracy is occurring against a background of economic crisis. In almost all cases, the beginning of the democratic process coincided with a period when the African states were already ruined, in debt, sucked dry. Since that time, for some, democratisation has meant solutions to all their daily problems, while for others it has been a springboard for gaining control of the state. Finally, for a third group, it has simply been a way of conforming, for the sake of form alone, to Western discourse and pressure.

Bread-and-butter democracy

The question here is: What type of democracy does one build? There is no single answer to this question. All we know is that, for many, democracy is synonymous with a better future, reminding us of Denis-Constant Martin's question as to what, in the end, can really transform and improve the daily life of the largest number of people (Martin, 1991: 22).

Those who demand democracy – students, workers, young people looking for work – have taken action, and continue to take action, to improve their living conditions. The basic problem therefore is to discover how a democratisation process that gives rise to the expression of more political demands can be reconciled with the scarcity of state resources. The link between the economic context and democratisation in Africa rests on a dilemma, namely, how and where to find adequate or necessary material resources to meet the numerous and sometimes contradictory demands expressed by social leaders. They fail to understand that democracy has no miraculous solutions for the scarcity of state resources in the short term. Democracy can, however, provide relief if it is exercised as a new social contract based on the principle of equitable distribution of resources (Niandou Souley, 1991: 265). We realise today that it is easier to proclaim multi-party elections and to organise them than it is to create jobs and increase wages, scholarships and retirement pensions.

The danger is that the bread-and-butter concept of democracy may lead Africans away from genuine democracy and even make them wish they had the authoritarian regimes of the past back again. Communication and civic education efforts are therefore required. In particular, people must understand that democracy is a political system that is desirable not simply because it entails fewer political nuisances than authoritarianism and imposed single-party systems (Médard, 1991b).

Democratisation as a springboard

Many African intellectuals have rallied to the democratic movement, not because they have really been won over to democracy as a political ideal, but because they see it as an opportunity to attain power by overthrowing those in power now. This gives rise to ambiguity since one does not know whether the social movements of 1990 corresponded to the imperative of democratising African political systems, or whether they were a response to the manipulation of elite groups competing with those in power, in a desire to replace them. For many activists, democratisation was more a means of getting rid of the leaders of the day than a political ideal to be achieved. During the past few years, the evidence shows that even the formal freedoms provided for in the new constitutions – for instance, press freedom – have become increasingly flouted.

Moreover, in some countries, one has the impression of a return to imposed unanimity, as in the days of single-party politics. Hence, in Niger, for example, the Democratic and Social Convention (DSC), one of the nine political bodies constituting the Alliance of Forces for Change (AFC), made it known through its national political office that all administrators not in full support of change should be dismissed from their positions of responsibility.

This is not an isolated case, since everywhere the problem is posed in terms of a democracy of exclusion and humiliation. Those who came to power by means of free competitive elections (implicit in democracy) give the impression of refusing to observe certain democratic principles, such as the political neutrality of administrators. Now the question is: Are they convinced democrats, or did they use the democratic movement simply as a springboard to seize control of the state, conceived as a privileged avenue for accumulation? (Joseph, 1987)

Complacency democracy

Complacency democracy could also be called 'opportunism democracy' or 'seduction democracy'. It refers to the way authoritarian regimes rallied the movement, as a means of political survival, to the demands that swept across the continent during 1990. So it was in order to yield to pressure from the street or to comply with the international discourse on the necessity of democratisation and respect for human rights that the African states opted for 'glasnost', however timid. International forces certainly played a role, but there were also internal political conditions that forced leaders like Kérékou, Mobutu or Eyadéma to agree to a process of democratisation in their respective countries.

Still with regard to 'opportunism democracy', one should recall the revealing words of a Nigerian Minister of Foreign Affairs, who, while on a tour of Western capitals in March 1994, adopted as his leitmotiv 'no money, no democracy'.[2] Such a conception was far from innocent, since Nigeria was then seeking to have its foreign debt rescheduled. Behind this type of statement one may detect an attempt to seduce Western countries and lenders, in an attempt to squeeze a few more subsidies out of them. Democratisation thus becomes a subject of reverse blackmail, since while extra-African powers use democratisation to apply pressure on poorer countries, the latter can also instrumentalise the democratic process to get the most out of donors. In this regard, Jean François Bayart (1993) rightly points out that the behaviour of African leaders falls perfectly in line with the

[2] *Jeune Afrique,* 9 March 1994.

perpetuation of opportunistic practices of mobilising international aid to fund national conferences and election procedures. Those involved in the democratisation process – governments, donors, new African leaders, political parties – have their strategies, their expectations and their requirements, and these are sometimes diametrically opposed. Building democracy in Africa is clearly taking place against a background of ambiguities and paradoxes.

Clearly, the economic cost of democratisation is hard to bear for states whose own resources are quite limited. While foreign partners, notably Western democracies, may help or facilitate the transition to democracy in Africa, they can neither impose it nor take the place of Africans to provide indefinite funding. External financial and technical contributions cannot replace African commitments; they also have their limits, since donors have their own domestic problems to cope with.

Even when foreign aid is both necessary and useful, its volume remains limited. So it would be more realistic if it were not seen as the main source of funding for democracy in Africa (Niandou Souley, 1992). Given that such aid seldom matches the hopes invested in it, it should not be counted on to meet the political demands generated by democratisation; these require the mobilisation of domestic economic potential, however weak it may be (Mbembe, 1992c).

The Paradoxical Behaviour of the Major Actors Involved

Paradoxical trends affect both the attitude of donors and Western countries, and the behaviour of the ruling classes and political parties born out of democratisation in Africa.

Donors & Western democracies

In the past, these actors have been much criticised mainly for their encouragement and support of authoritarian, single-party regimes in Africa (Bayart, 1984). Today, the major role played by these external actors in the expansion of democratic freedoms in Africa is acknowledged, but debates about the dual agenda of Western countries have resurfaced. Thus, some scholars and analysts of African politics insist that 'capitalist imperatives are ever present and override democratic imperatives' (Adji: 1992).

The debate is concerned with the weak reactions of Western democracies to the infringement of, non-compliance with, and attacks on the basic principles of democracy in some African states. This was best illustrated by the largely symbolic sanctions imposed on Nigeria, following the decision of General Ibrahim Babangida to annul the results of the presidential election of 12 June 1993 (Sklar, 1997). As a result, M.K.O. Abiola was first robbed of his victory and a year later, sent to prison without trial where he died on 7 July 1998. This was a hard blow for democracy and a situation in which donors and Western democracies could have demonstrated much more firmness, so as to show that their prevailing imperative was no longer one of so-called stability, but rather of respect for fundamental democratic principles, notably respect for the African voters' choice. Clearly, Nigeria should not be treated as an isolated instance, as reflected by the pursuit or restoration of authoritarian practices in Togo, Cameroon, Kenya, Algeria and elsewhere.

The new African leaders

Empirical observation of the attitude of the new African leaders reveals that a trend towards the restoration of authoritarianism often prevails over genuine democratisation. This is a major paradox since democratisation is the very process that brought these leaders to power. With regard to respect for basic freedoms, their behaviour is not very different from that of their predecessors. It is paradoxical indeed to want to muzzle the press, when the press, particularly the independent media of the private sector, contributed significantly to the critique and demise of the single-party authoritarian systems. Those who currently hold the reins of state power often resorted to the press to spread their ideas and express their opinions on the previous regimes' management of public affairs; the initial connection between President Alpha Oumar Konaré of Mali and the independent newspaper *Les Echos* provides an illustration of this.

Nowadays, it is acknowledged that press freedom is under threat in a number of African states. The new repressive arsenal is built on such catch phrases as 'defamation', 'incitement to violence', 'invitation to ethnic hatred' or 'incitement to civil disobedience'. In addition, the use of violence, which once used to be resisted, is increasingly being invoked as a method of governance, chiefly to dissuade students and workers from organising meetings and protest marches against government measures. In Niger, a student died on 10 March 1994, following a confrontation with law enforcement agents during a demonstration.

Finally, ethnocentrist discourse, albeit broadly decried at national conferences, still prevails, as was seen in Niger in November 1993, when there was open conflict between the President and the Senior Vice-President of the National Assembly. Similarly, what Jean-François Médard would term 'the logic of patrimonialism' lives on. In short, everything occurs as if, despite democratisation, the form and content of political measures had not changed at all (Kaptinde, 1994).

Political parties

Through their pronouncements and deeds, political parties run the risk of ruining the democratic system which guarantees their very existence and without which single-party regimes would still prevail in many cases. First of all, in many countries, political parties seem to have lost sight of the fact that political change is a fundamental dimension of democracy. This translates into a refusal to accept the role of opposition parties and to play according to the established rules: hence, such reactions as the refusal to sit in the National Assembly, the recourse to violent street demonstrations, the development of 'stay-at-home' practices or the calls for civil disobedience. Such behaviour may incite democratically chosen regimes to drift towards authoritarianism, particularly when the temptation is already inbuilt.

In addition, political parties make practically no effort to discipline, train and educate their militants. This could constitute a threat to democracy since, without any ideological preparation, the parties' composition may reflect purely ethno-regionalist or parochial concerns. And in turn this may give rise to the creation of a government reflecting such concerns, at the expense of rational criteria for qualifications, technical skills and know-how.

Democratisation and Territorial Delegitimisation

Insufficient emphasis is given to the fact that the democratisation of African political systems is coinciding with an acute financial crisis. This situation renders the state incapable of performing its most elementary tasks, including those inherent in the exercise of sovereignty. Inadequate control by governments over their territories is accompanied by a lack of protection offered to the people living in them. One of the crucial issues raised by democratisation in Africa resides 'in the inability of African states to control their own territories. Unlike the colonial states, the post-colonies are not endowed with the spirit of conquest, the pioneer spirit that would enable them to extend state power right up to the boundaries of its territory' (Toulabor, 1994).

Democratisation within a financially exhausted state is an empty word for populations daily confronted with enormous difficulties. All that matters is survival, which people are prepared to seek on the other side of the border. This context accounts for the massive exodus from such Sahel countries as Burkina Faso, Mali or Niger towards the supposedly more clement coastal countries, like Côte d'Ivoire, Ghana and Nigeria. As the economic crisis deepens, bringing its share of misery and suffering, the states' spaces are gradually being deterritorialised. The increase of cross-border exchanges is a good illustration of this, as is the tendency of the populations themselves not to submit to the exclusive authority and jurisdiction of a single state.

As a result, the state, for want of resources to redistribute, has lost all legitimacy (Niandou Souley, 1991); it has hardly any authority any longer over the people or the territory, and still less over the flow of populations across its borders. The state framework is no longer regarded as the sole area of reference, since, on the other side of the border, one can find, through bartering and smuggling, the minimum one requires to survive or to speculate, as the case may be. Rwanda, Burundi, Somalia and Liberia are so many tragic examples showing that the authoritarian state is undergoing a crisis of legitimacy, the corollary of which is a delegitimisation of the state and its territorial framework. In this context, one can argue that, with time, processes of reconfiguration of the present state territories can no longer be excluded.

The paradoxes and ambiguities associated with the democratisation of African political systems give the impression that democracy poses more problems than it solves. This may be true, but one should not conclude from this that democracy is doomed to failure. Even though past experience invites caution, only time will tell.

7

CÉLESTIN MONGA
Is African Civil Society Civilised?

'What is irritating in despair is its cogency, its obviousness and its documentation …'
Cioran, *Syllogismes de l'amertume*

The study of civil societies is one of the recurrent themes of the political literature on Africa (Diamond, 1993; Mbembe, 1992b; Bakary, 1993). This interest is justified by the argument that the nature and functioning of these entities constitute the main determinants of the success of democratic regimes. It is more and more frequently admitted that the viability of a democratic system depends on the quality of the consensus on the configuration of institutions, which are themselves being shaped by the history, culture and political practices of each nation. All these factors are themselves dependent on the activities of the political parties, the socio-professional organisations and the civic associations. Putnam summarises this vision, when stating that

> Social context and history profoundly condition the effectiveness of institutions. Where the regional soil is fertile, the regions draw sustenance from traditions, but where the soil is poor, the new institutions are stunted. Effective and responsive institutions depend, in the language of civic humanism, on republican virtues and practices. Tocqueville was right : Democratic government is strengthened, not weakened, when it faces a vigorous civil society. (Putnam, 1993: 182).

The success of the notion of civil society among academics is accompanied by a certain scepticism concerning its transferability to Africa, and the degree of 'civilisation' that such a concept may convey to an environment where 'barbarity' is supposed to characterise the prince's as much as the people's behaviour. A writer like Revel argues accordingly that

> In Africa, be it in the Maghreb or South of the Sahara, the fight for democracy does not oppose authoritarian regimes to people imbued with liberty. For the moment, the people do not seem to be more in love with liberty than their dictators, that is to say, not capable of accepting diversity. (Revel, 1992: 339)

The themes of integration and regionalism offer an interesting framework of analysis for such problematics. The first section of this chapter describes the silent chaos that we can observe in numerous countries where the state has not succeeded in positioning itself as a federating core *vis-à-vis* centrifugal forces, or with respect to the production of symbolic order. Some objective reasons for anxiety will be listed before turning to the interpretation grids used by researchers to decipher these motives for anxiety, and to emphasise the inconsistency of a tele-ological perception of disintegration. The conclusion of the chapter will state the necessity of toning down such judgements, while suggesting that integration is at work, although it is taking place in accordance with lines of rupture created by the present dynamics of disintegration.

Democratisation versus Disintegration?

Researchers are prompted to study the diverse and mysterious structures that have animated African societies since the enunciation of participation as an 'official' principle and a new framework for the validation of development policies.[1] Their motivation has increased with the current political changes; the emergence of incomprehensible social dynamics (outside, and in the absence of, political parties or other listed organisations) has ended up convincing the most sceptical 'experts' that a civil society did exist and was active as well as powerful despite its low profile.

The first question which comes to mind is obviously that of knowing whether we can Africanise the concept popularised by Antonio Gramsci. Applying the notion of civil society to African societies implies a risky approach, just like any other transfer of sociological concepts from one geographical area to another (Monga, 1994a). In this chapter, I shall define civil society in sub-Saharan Africa as the forces whose actions aim at amplifying the assertion of social identity and the promotion of rights and duties attached to citizenship, in opposition to public authority and political parties, whose natural tendency is to ignore or ridicule these attributes.

The epithet 'civilised' is equally fraught with ambiguity. I shall use it in its common, most naive and most provocative sense, the one which nevertheless served as the title of a prestigious anthropology chair at the *Ecole des Hautes Etudes en Sciences Sociales* of Paris:[2] 'civilised' will refer to a state radically distinct from those characterised by the epithets 'primitive', 'barbaric' or 'savage', when referring to social groups which share as a main characteristic the propensity to violence and conflict.

In so far as integration is concerned, questioning the degree of 'civilisation' of African civil societies should consist of evaluating the nature of the relations between the state and society and, in the present context of political reform, observing the degree of synergy and the level of ethical ambition which governs

---

[1] The adoption of the African Charter for Popular Participation in Development in February 1990 in Arusha, Tanzania, marked the official recognition by the Heads of State of the role that the society must play in the construction of each country (OUA, 1990).

[2] The title of the chair held by Marcel Mauss was '*Religions of uncivilised people*'. His successor, Claude Lévi-Strauss, decided to change this title, after he was challenged by a black listener during a conference: 'One could hardly say that people who would come and talk to you at the Sorbonne were 'uncivilised'!' (Lévi-Strauss and Eribon, 1990: 81–2).

the new actors in the political field. How do civil societies position themselves in the political reconfigurations South of the Sahara? Do their organisers (association leaders, trade unionists, religious authorities, intellectuals, journalists, businessmen, etc.) subscribe to the national or regional integration projects proclaimed by the governments?

In a number of countries, the current social restructuring process reveals *a priori* a logic of disaggregation, as civil society seems to oppose national integration. Civil economic society's most influential components – which include employers, socio-professional associations, trade unions and representatives of the informal sector – impose a kind of veto on national integration and, more generally, public policies. Without modifying anything to their own objectives or discourse, states react by displaying new strategies aimed at conquering new territories within civil society; but in doing this, they rather tend to aggravate the cacophony.

The political game of national integration

Since independence, national integration has only been a protective sophism, serving as a pretext for the construction of political systems based on the domination of the majority through unstable coalitions of interests. It has thus served to validate the access to power, by means of co-optation, of urban elites claiming to represent the populations with which they episodically share social labels (profession, tribe, etc.). Sometimes, a handful of selected farmers, village heads, religious leaders or former directors of professional associations became ministers 'without party affiliation'. In return for financial hand-outs and minor roles, they agreed to toe the official line; this permitted the proclamation that civil society was integrated into the politics of the country, and that the incumbent authorities enjoyed popular support. Hence, the former Ivorian Head of State never missed an opportunity to present himself as a 'farmer'.

In Cameroon, former president Ahmadou Ahidjo even claimed to have established a 'science' of national integration, making it a point of honour to constitute his government on the basis of an ethno-regional alchemy guaranteeing the equilibrium and stability of his power (Ngayap, 1982). Before leaving office in 1982, he had his formula made official by means of a law instituting written quotas for the civil service entrance examinations. These quotas were designed in accordance with the ethnic origin of the candidates, without taking into account demographic criteria or the spatial allocation of the population.[3] His successor Paul Biya continued along the same track and increased the 'legal' foundations of a policy of national integration consisting precisely of disintegrating the country: the legislation adopted by Ahidjo was up-dated and completed by new criteria of political and administrative exclusion. Ministerial texts were thus adopted, in 1991, so as to determine, according to ethnic origins, spatial boundaries for the settlement of individuals; a ministerial circular accordingly forbade the sale of plots to 'non indigenes' (*allogènes*) in the vicinity of the country's capital.

---

[3] Presidential decree No. 82–407 of 7 September 1982, and the decree of 4 October 1982 (Monga, 1986 : 227).

This conception of national integration as a dupes' deal is observable in many other countries, where it expresses itself in various ways (see Chapters 4, 9 and 10 in this volume). In Congo-Brazzaville as in Gabon, it is customary for the most senior state representatives to proudly proclaim that the source of their 'legitimacy' lies in their ethnic origins, and not in just any field of competence. Claiming to speak in the name of their tribe, they identify themselves not with the nation but with a group, whose boundaries are ill-defined. At election time, ministers and senior civil servants are required to campaign 'in their villages of origin', as the stock official phrase puts it, where, in actual fact, they have never been. They travel to the bush by helicopter or at the wheel of a powerful Japanese car; dressed in fine suits, they raise their sun-glasses to ask for the votes of the people with whom they claim to share ethnic origin ... This absurd play-acting generally occurs in front of the cameras of national television which can broadcast every evening news of the exploits of 'senior state officials' 'who went out into the field' to 'sensitise and mobilise the people'.[4]

The efficiency of these intermittent games of representation is limited, however. In almost all sub-Saharan countries, recent events indicate that the people are far from being fooled, as evidenced by the behaviour of civil economic society.

Civil economic society against 'integration'

National integration therefore does not coincide with the desire to extend participation in the conception, implementation and follow-up of public affairs. The authorities always claim to act in such a way that no social group is being marginalised, but these are mere slogans. Promises and government commitments are never kept, since power South of the Sahara is not subjected to any domestic constraint.[5]

The institutions are captured by a handful of urban and village elites who use them as career springboards and opportunities for enrichment. In the economic field, for example, reforms and strategies as well as commercial and monetary choices are decided within secret networks, without the representation of the civil society directly concerned (employers, private financial institutions, trade unions, community development associations, etc.). S. Kondo, Chairman of the Cameroonian industrial workers' union SYNDUSTRICAM, states a point of view widely shared by the community of company directors in sub-Saharan Francophone Africa when he says on this issue: 'The authorities [in our countries] do nothing. Paradoxically, I receive more support from my French friends ... The *Conseil des investisseurs français en Afrique* has undertaken to intercede with our governments in favour of private African enterprises' (Kondo, 1994). Since the man who is speaking in this manner is a member of the central committee of

[4] On the integration of the urban elite in official circuits, on the worship of luxury and ostentatious displays of power see Mbembe (1992a).
[5] One of the weaknesses of African political systems lies in the incapacity of existing institutions to respect their commitments and their own rules of functioning because of the absence of 'agencies of restraint' (Collier, 1991).

Cameroon's former single party and, as such, is close to the principal decision-makers including the Head of State, one can easily imagine the type of exclusion felt by the ordinary company director in the private sector who does not have any special political affiliation. One can also understand why, throughout sub-Saharan Africa, numerous small and medium-scale entrepreneurs, association and trade union leaders as well as businessmen joined the ranks of the opposition parties during the popular uprisings of 1990–92.

In spite of being forgotten, neglected or deliberately excluded from decision-making, civil society is developing; it is extending its field of competence every day. This involves the defence of peasant interests, permanent education, the training of young people, rural communications, the retraining of those made redundent (the so-called *'compressés')* by the structural adjustment programmes, responsibility for abandoned children, mobilisation of funds for the sick and disabled, etc. The success of the *tontines* and credit associations is well known (Monga, 1997); in several countries, they are the only institutions for the mobili-sation of savings and the allocation of credits to families as well as to small and medium-scale enterprises. However, the achievements of development associa-tions like the Naam groups, created in Burkina Faso in 1967, are less well-known. The pertinence of their objective – 'to develop without damaging, to motivate and to mobilise the peasant on the basis of what he is and what he can do, to help him to progress in accordance with his cultural values' (Braekman, 1993) – fully justifies their success: 5.7 million people are active in these associations, based in Burkina Faso, Senegal, Guinea-Bissau, Togo, Niger, Mali and The Gambia.

Because it feels excluded, civil economic society tends to oppose both national integration, as conceived by the incumbent authorities, and public policies as a whole. Structural adjustment programmes fail in black Africa primarily because of the way they are perceived by those active in civil economic society (Monga, 1994b). More generally, economic reforms yield few results South of the Sahara because of their lack of legitimacy, which prompts certain actors in the economic system to use their informal right of veto (Brinkerhoff *et al.,* 1994).

This cursory reading of current events tends to substantiate the idea of a not very 'civilised' civil society, bringing together centrifugal forces working in favour of specific interests. However, such objective reasons for anxiety should not justify hasty judgements since, everywhere, the disintegration of the totalitarian state is generating new dynamics.

The Structuring Role of Disintegration

The failure of integration policies which were conceived solely as plans of elite co-optation indeed provoked a larger social disorder, but it also favoured the emergence of social groups independent of political power. These groups are structuring new areas of contestation, while being vehicles of citizenship.

The level of political culture achieved by African civil societies has been the subject of a rich literature since the late 1980s (Lemarchand, 1991 and 1992; Woods, 1992; Lewis, 1992; Bratton, 1989). The conclusions of the various authors boil down to the idea of there being a 'rate of political illiteracy per citizen' in each country, and that, on average, such an indicator would still be too high South of the Sahara for one to be able to form stable democracies. Some Africanists use models developed on this theme by Robert Dahl (1992) to draw out definitive lessons, and build theories based on opinion polls, statistical inquiries and mathematical equations. Elementary prudence required by the use of statistics in the field of the social sciences does not prevent them from engaging in adventurous extrapolations.

The basic idea is simple: democracy only functions if it is supported by a general high level of political culture within the population, and by the active participation of the citizens. This principle takes us back to the period of the French Revolution, when the influence of Montesquieu's followers was so strong that the 1791 constitution restricted voting rights to citizens who were over twenty-five years of age and capable of paying at least three days' taxation. During the nineteenth century, Stuart Mill, Alexis de Tocqueville and others pursued the idea that the existence of a democratic system presupposed well-informed citizens, attached to pluralism and anxious to commit themselves.

Since the works of Berelson et al. (1954) followed by Almond and Verba (1963 and 1980), we know, however, that this postulate is utopian. As emphasised by Mayer and Perrineau:

> The paradox is sizeable: since democracies often have several decades or even several centuries of existence they can accommodate the passivity and indifference of the great mass of citizens (Mayer and Perrineau, 1992: 7).

It is therefore an illusion to try to establish a positive correlation between political culture (as measured by the level of participation) and the quality of a democracy. Unless we are prepared to consider that the levels of political culture in the United States and in Zambia may be identical, and this is precisely the idea which the defenders of this notion reject.

The excessive use of different models constructed by American political scientists to analyse the political action of groups of the civil society in Africa leads equally to erroneous results. Most of the so-called ecological or psycho-sociological models capture in an incomplete and biased way the rationality of trade unionists in Dakar, of members of corporatist associations in Abidjan, of religious groups in Kinshasa or of students in Nairobi.

The idea of connecting the behaviour of people with the geographical, social or historical characteristics of the territorial units in which they live (as is suggested by the so-called ecological models) is not systematically verified in Africa. The regularly proclaimed lines of cleavage between town and country or Sahelian regions and forest areas are far less evident than one would like to think. The organisations of the civil society in Mali tend to function like those operating in Gabon. The behaviours observed tend to indicate an increasing homogenisation of objectives and modes of action, as well as a distinct erosion of contrasts linked to geography.

Similarly, historical traumas do not seem significant enough to justifiy specific group behaviours. In certain countries, the so-called cultural associations aspiring to influence the political game may try to base their action on the memory of particularly painful experiences in a tribe or region. In a number of states, democratisation has given birth to a blossoming of small insignificant groups which identify themselves with an ethnic group whose rights they claim to want to defend – as in the case of the *Laakam* of the Bamilekes in Cameroon, or the *Essigan Beti* (*Collectif 'Changer le Cameroun'*, 1992). The press has often amplified such initiatives which corroborate institutional speeches as well as current intellectual fashions on tribalism. Yet, nowhere have we observed such movements having a determinant influence on the results of political competition. Everywhere, these associations have been weakened by their intrinsic superficiality, by the opportunism of their leaders and by the lack of historical depth of the events to which they refer. They have neither had any real impact over time nor been able to 'build durable mentalities'.[6]

Patterns of opinion formation and validation within the African civil society are more closely connected with the so-called psycho-sociological models. Yet, we are far from the homogeneity of the social groups described by Lazarsfeld and regularly reiterated by his interpreters. Social determinism, according to which 'a person thinks politically like he/she is socially' (Lazarsfeld *et al.*, 1994: 27), cannot be considered as an axiom of reference in black Africa. Clearly, specific individual choices may be governed by collective standards such as socio-economic status, religion, family or clan/ethnic considerations; yet, it would be over-hasty to conclude that these criteria alone determine adherence to such a particular association or organisation. No combination of these different variables allows for the elaboration of a reliable indicator of the political predisposition of citizens who join trade unions, co-operatives, religious movements or intellectual circles.

The individual who belongs to the most rigid corporate, professional or religious structures tends to preserve his margin of action and, therefore, a minimal freedom of choice. If we exclude the famous cases of sects and religious brotherhoods (essentially Senegalese and Nigerian), we can affirm that the indoctrination of minds is not (yet) an unavoidable sociological feature of sub-Saharan politics. This explains these organisations' inability to mobilise the masses strongly in one direction or another, as witnessed with the fundamentalist groups in North Africa. On the other hand, political traditions, which should be derived from professional orientations and religious convictions, are subject to the pressure of new ideas, and are redefined and readjusted to a changing world. In most African countries, the recent success of the intellectuals and the private press can be understood as a reflection of this collective desire to know more, not to mention the desire of each citizen to challenge his own convictions and predispositions.

Whenever it is mismanaged, this need to give a political aspect to social structures can lead to the crystallisation of opinions. Some politicians have found out how to reap advantage from the emotional and passionate character of relations within civil society; they are clearly successful in controlling and provisionally domesticating collective mechanisms of perception. Alpha Oumar Konaré thus came to power democratically in Mali, through the formation of a subtle coalition

---

[6] Leroy-Ladurie (1973: 179) uses this phrase to account for the traumatic events which radically transformed the peasant populations of the French West and converted them to the ideals of the Revolution between 1793 and 1798. The result was the formation of 'mental structures' that were to reproduce themselves over more than a hundred years.

of cultural associations, representing different trends of opinion, and underground political parties, some of which had been banned since the 1968 military coup d'etat of Moussa Traoré (Vengroff, 1993). Paul Biya remained in power in Cameroon – despite the rigged elections denounced by the international community – thanks to a thorough adjustment of mystification and incorporation methods *vis à vis* civil society (National Democratic Institute for Internal Affairs, 1992). The magnitude of the social conflicts which they both had to confront subsequently confirmed that, in spite of their 'abilities', they could not reckon on any captive votes.

Far from justifying pessimism, the failure of national integration policies in Africa should be taken as evidence of the dynamism and 'civilised' character of societies which some authors have been inclined to regard as chloroformed. This in turn suggests the necessity of working out new ways of decoding the current socio-political changes. One of the essential conditions for the success of public policies in Africa relates to the ability to take account of the influence of civil society. Good 'governance', which is one of the indicators of the quality of institutions depends on four main factors, all of which rely on the degree of organisation and the power of civil society, namely: the efficiency of the current laws and regulations (effectiveness and coherence of texts with respect to the objectives of public policies); the efficiency of the private sector (degree of influence on decisions adopted and weight in their implementation); the reactions of the social body to public policies (acceptance/rejection of decisions by the people, whose blocking power can no longer be rejected); the efficiency of the communication systems in the country (freedom of expression, access to different social actors on the news networks, fluidity of information networks from one region to the other). Only the efficiency of civil society can contribute to fruitful interactions among these four related processes.

8

EDOUARD BUSTIN
The Collapse of 'Congo/Zaïre'
& its Regional Impact

One can hardly resist the temptation of thinking of Congo/Zaïre as the most para-digmatic instance of the dynamics which not only hamstring the 'federating' role that large African states might be expected to play, but also seem to condemn them to some form of internal balkanisation. Much of this reading undoubtedly traces its roots to the 1960 Congo crisis and its sequels, possibly because the oversim-plified summation of that period has been uncritically accepted.

The only two genuine secession attempts since 1960 were those of Katanga and its more tentative counterpart in Southern Kasai. They owed as much to the strategy of Western business circles as to some inchoate aspirations to 'national' self-determination. Contrarily, the formation in Stanleyville (Kisangani) of a counter-government led by members of the embattled Lumumbist coalition tried to affirm the continuity of Lumumba's unitarist vision in the face of the dubious 'legitimacy' claimed by the regime sitting in Kinshasa. This position was essen-tially re-affirmed in the late 1990s by the uprising of Laurent Désiré Kabila's *Alliance des Forces Démocratiques de Libération* (AFDL), as well as by those dissidents who subsequently launched a rebellion against his new regime.

The process of *de facto* federalisation which emerged by default during the Congo crisis (and received qualified endorsement in the 1964 Constitution) soon proved to be nothing more than a temporary expedient, fraught with an endless outpouring of insoluble claims, counterclaims and boundary disputes. In conse-quence, the country's fragmentation into some two dozen would-be 'provincettes' was promptly reversed after Mobutu's 1965 takeover, and left no visible traces of nostalgia. The only declared objective of the 'Tshombist' mutinies of 1966 and 1967 was the overthrow of the regime based in Kinshasa, and the seizure of power at the national level. This was also true of the 'Mulelist' or 'Lumumbist' uprisings of 1963–5, or the two 'Shaba wars' of 1977 and 1978. The only movement which, starting in the pre-independence period, had articulated an implicitly secessionist (and irredentist) programme – the ABAKO – soon opted in favour of a federalised structure(Monnier, 1973: 303 ff).

Does this mean that the crystallisation of Congolese identity or the 'nation-building' process which the erstwhile Mobutu regime claimed as one of its (few) achievements can be taken for granted? To answer that question in the affirmative would require boundless optimism, but one should equally beware of the superficial oversimplification which, in 1963, led a French commentator to conclude, somewhat prematurely, that the Congo should be dismantled and merged into the [French-inspired] Union Africaine et Malgache.

Factors of National Cohesiveness & Integration

A number of factors that allow the viability of the former Zaïre to be put in doubt may be listed (Pourtier,1994: 281–6). They begin with the country's sheer size, and the peripheral character of its population concentrations, whether rural (with the highest densities occurring in the Kongo-Kwilu-Kasai and Great Lakes belts) or, more tellingly, urban (with most major cities being located at or near the borders), in a ring-like pattern circling the relatively empty inland basin known as the *cuvette centrale*. It should be noted, however, that instead of being drawn into the orbit of adjacent countries (Congo-Brazzaville, Angola, Rwanda, Burundi, Zambia), most of these urban centres (and some of the rural areas as well) have long drained inputs from their neighbours' border regions – somewhat like Basel with respect to Upper Alsace in Europe.

Regarding other commonly mentioned factors (such as the artificial nature of the imperial boundaries, the diversity of the populations, or the inadequacy of the transportation infrastructure), one hardly needs to stress the fact that they apply with equal or greater validity to nearly every African state, whatever its size. Conversely, one might consider the deep similarities between the Bantu languages used by some 90% of Congolese, between the traditional material cultures of the forest and savanna environments, largely unaffected by pastoralism, or between the pre-colonial patterns of social or political organisation – far less diverse than those encountered in Nigeria or Cameroon.

Nor should one overlook the importance of the human interactions resulting from socio-economic change and migration flows, or of those 'contact zones' studied by Deutsch (1961) or Weinstein (1966) in which diverse populations, none of them truly autochtonous, come to rub elbows with one another. Such urban or peri-urban zones are especially significant in the case of Congo/Zaïre where the rate of urbanisation is currently estimated at 40%, although no 'cities' in the full sense of that term existed before this century.

While Belgium offered only a diffuse civilisational 'model' (reflecting its own ambiguous cultural identity), such was not the case where the bureaucratic and institutional legacy of colonial rule is concerned. In Zaïre as in other parts of Africa 'many political institutions created during the colonial period have become, in the eyes of living men, part of the natural order of things' (Zolberg, 1966: 144).

When it comes to the integrating effects of colonial or post-colonial 'development' (including that of major infrastructures), it is fair to say that the purpose of such policies was not to create integrated or self-sufficient economic areas – except, possibly, within an autarchic 'imperial' project linking colonies to the metropole. Thus, few horizontal linkages were created between the various regions, whereas they were all linked to the outside world by routes designed to carry their exportable products to the nearest or most convenient shipping outlet. Nor was complementarity a major consideration, except in the indirect form of the diversification of exportable products. This was an obvious improvement as far as the achievement of a stable trade balance was concerned, but one that carried few integrative sequels, since each production sector (coffee, copper, cotton, palm products) operated as an export-oriented enclave, with no links to the other sectors.

One of the first preoccupations of the Belgian colonial administration was to dam, or to redirect into its own circuits, the flow of the ancient commercial networks; these, along the old caravan routes, channelled exportable commodities (ivory, native rubber, wax, copper ingots, or – earlier – slaves) into Portuguese, Swahili or Sudanese trading posts in exchange for consumer goods. (Bustin, 1975: 43–4). Once such flows were halted and customs barriers tightened, however, the development of a 'modern' transportation system (notably rail) tended to follow the pattern of these very same older routes, to which was added the southward axis running through the Rhodesias to provide the first outlet for the Katanga copperbelt. The deliberately non-traditional *'voie nationale'* was subsequently developed by combining rail and river segments to link Katanga with the hard-won Atlantic outlet at Matadi. This route reflected a blend of imperial autarky and hubris rather than strictly logical economic considerations. Such was not the case, on the other hand, with the imposing set of natural waterways represented by the Congo River and its major tributaries. These effectively linked the Atlantic hinterland to the Great Lakes region; to serve their common trading needs, their traditional users had also developed a *lingua franca* (Lingala) which was to grow into one of the country's four major languages.

The development of a truly 'national' domestic transportation system was always considered from a political, rather than from an economic, perspective: this was the case with the all-rail version of the *voie nationale*. It was time and again postponed, but its completion remained throughout the 1980s one of the Mobutu regime's pet projects. This was also the case with the grandiose post-war road project which gathered dust in the Belgian administration's files. The construction of several major axial roads intersecting the heart of the country, in Northern Sankuru, was also considered. Political, rather than strictly economic, considerations were again largely responsible, during Mobutu's final 'fat years', for the construction of the absurdly exorbitant high-voltage power line linking the Inga hydroelectric dam near Kinshasa to the Shaba mining region at the opposite end of the country. (Willame, 1986).

Political Instability & the Erosion of National Infrastructures

Not much remains of those projects today. The rail, river and road infrastructures have reached an advanced state of decrepitude which includes the badly deteriorated Kinshasa-Kwilu motorway, one of the Mobutu regime's few achievements. This trend has reduced many regions to the condition of isolated enclaves, precariously linked by air. In the course of a study conducted in 1991, one of my two colleagues was told by a Sankuru village head that the 40 kilometres separating him from district headquarters, once passable by trucks, then by motorcycles, and more recently still by bicycles, could now be negotiated only on foot, as the road had returned to the condition of a footpath.

This erosion of basic infrastructures, along with the breakdown of economic and administrative institutions, accounts largely for the creation or re-creation (especially in the peripheral regions which are also the most productive) of exchange, barter or contraband networks with adjacent countries for commodities as diverse as coffee, gold, foodstuffs, textile articles, motor vehicles, spare parts – and, naturally, gold and diamonds.[1] The growing irrelevance of porous national borders might have carried political repercussions. If they have not materialised thus far, it is largely due to the lack of strong irredentist currents and the fact that the country's neighbours do not, for their part, represent credible polar points of stability or prosperity: Angola, Rwanda, Burundi, Uganda and the Sudan are torn by internal dissensions, Zambia is mired in the sequels of its 'readjustment' crisis, while Congo-Brazzaville and the Central African Republic have foundered into civil war.

More ominous, on the other hand, is the fact that the country's own instability has made it highly susceptible to forms of unrest communicated by its neighbours – notably from Rwanda, Uganda, Burundi, Angola and Sudan. Mobutu's cynical yet unwise manipulation of the ethnic conflicts spilling over from the Great Lakes region paved the way for his demise at the hands of a rebel movement activated, in turn, from Kampala and Kigali. Angola's involvement on the side of Kabila in 1997 was similarly motivated by Mobutu's record of support for UNITA – a support increasingly rewarded in the tangible form of diamonds. Fifteen months later, Kabila proved unable to rid his Eastern borderlands of their adversaries, and unwilling to let them do it directly. Uganda and Rwanda therefore decided to throw their weight behind another rebellion improbably spawned by a combination of ex-Kabila followers and unreconstructed Mobutists. The role of this latter group, by contrast, convinced Angola to come to the assistance of the Kabila government, despite the fact that the new Kinshasa regime had been almost equally ineffective in stopping the arms-for-diamonds flows to Savimbi's followers. Together with Zimbabwe and Namibia, Angola brought the Southern Africa Development Community (SADC) in line behind Kabila, notwithstanding South Africa's misgivings.

But then again, South Africa's posture and interests follow a different logic. When the moribund Mobutu regime, in its desperate need for ready cash, seemed ready to sacrifice all national assets, a number of multinational mining groups had

---

[1] The diamond prospecting and smuggling network was increasingly controlled by the Mobutu presidential clique and its military associates, for whom it represented a substantial source of income unrecorded in the national accounts. More significantly, diamonds are also the lifeblood of UNITA, a fact which largely accounts for the Angolan Government's decision to intervene militarily in the two Congos, as well as for the unofficial collusion between Jonas Savimbi and the DRC with its Ugandan and Rwandan backers. For the role of diamonds in the Angola civil war, see Global Witness (1998).

shown unmistakable interest in the crippled, yet eminently 'salvageable', mineral resources of the Zaïre-Zambia copperbelt. The same mining groups then turned their attention to the anti-Mobutu rebels when these appeared to be on their way to victory. How (or why) such economic prospects might tie in with plans for political integration remains unclear, however – especially in view of the fact that the 'new' South Africa has more pressing issues of that sort on its own doorstep (Chapter 10 of this volume). The old idea of a vaguely confederal 'constellation' of Southern African states may well re-surface through the re-vamping of SADC (from which Zaïre had been excluded, but to which Kabila's 'new Congo' was promptly admitted). It seems unclear whether, from the perspective of South Africa's business circles, the integration of Katanga or, conceivably, Kasai (subject to some as yet unresolved variables, such as the fate of Angola) may be worth the cost of being sucked into the Central African vortex.

Whether plausible or not, such a scenario (together with those revolving around the alleged need by Rwanda, Uganda or Angola for 'security zones' along Congo/Zaïre's borders) would almost inevitably postulate the breakup of the country, following a process of which its 1961–5 fragmentation into 'provincettes' can offer a preview. The fact that this process had, at the time, generated more problems than it had solved is not *per se* a sufficient reason to discard that hypothesis, especially after the outbreak of the anti-Kabila rebellion. To gain a clearer view, we must analyse the meaning and the dimensions of the country's ongoing turmoil, while keeping in mind that, in many respects, it merely represents the most recent installment in what, at an early stage Young (1978) characterised as its 'unending crisis'.

The Legitimacy Deficit

What does the record show? First of all, a state in which the thread of political legitimacy that was brutally ruptured in 1960–61 has never been effectively repaired. The Mobutu regime only managed, by default, to capture briefly a makeshift form of legitimacy derived from the exhaustion of competing forces, from sheer opportunism, or from the fear of continued anarchy. This legitimacy was later nurtured by the slogans of a populist discourse (*authenticité*), by the effects of a temporary spell of relative prosperity, and by the systematic use of prebendal co-optation (see, *inter alia,* Gould, 1980; Schatzberg, 1988; Callaghy, 1984; Willame, 1980; Young and Turner, 1985).

More recently, attempts by the Kabila government to reach back to the Lumumbist fonts of popular legitimacy soon proved hollow. This was partly because of Kabila's own dubious credentials; Lumumba's elusive ideological legacy could also be claimed by many power seekers, only a handful of whom had not eaten out of Mobutu's hand over the years. Until 1998, Kabila was also saddled with a disproportionate number of ethnic Tutsi (some of uncertain nationality), with more than a few opportunists, and even with several presumably reconverted ex-Mobutists. The new regime was still reluctant to co-opt leaders of the pre-1997 domestic opposition or of civil society, and failed to convert its initial popularity into a lasting form of legitimacy. Then came the 1998 uprising, which was perceived as a case of foreign aggression (possibly with Western collusion) and providentially gave Kabila a refurbished patriotic image as the champion of national integrity.

Mounting voices of opposition to the Mobutu regime developed over the last twenty years of its existence, but this opposition was not necessarily homogeneous, nor was it unanimously agreed on an alternative programme. As the magnitude and the specifics of the country's economic bankruptcy were brought into the open, the opposition could find common ground only in a vague 'need for change' that did not even automatically rule out a possible 'recycling' of the system, and of Mobutu himself. The catchword of 'democratisation' offered a conveniently imprecise point of mutual agreement for these opponents, as well as for some of Mobutu's henchmen, anxious to re-position themselves as the 'winds of change'. This common ground was sufficiently vague for Mobutu himself to exploit it: on 24 April 1990, he decreed the demise of his own regime and the introduction of a limited form of political pluralism. Political pluralism was soon transformed into a free-for-all *multipartisme intégral* which he promptly proceeded to manipulate by surreptitiously funding a flock of pseudo-parties, soon derided as *'particules alimentaires'* (Gbadendu Engunduka and Etolo Ngobaasu, 1991: 101 ff).

Having laboriously managed to weld their different tendencies into a seemingly united front (later formalised under the name of *Union Sacrée*), the opposition leaders were now in a position to force the convening of a National Conference. They were then faced with Mobutu's obstructionist tactics, and failed to secure firmly the 'sovereignty' and the constituent powers which had been successfully claimed by the National Conferences in Congo-Brazzaville or Benin. Meanwhile, in Kinshasa and other cities, military units loyal to Mobutu indulged in allegedly 'uncontrolled' bouts of looting and physical intimidation, selectively targeted against known opposition leaders. The National Conference (whose numbers, in the absence of agreed membership criteria, had swollen to some 4,000, later to be whittled down to a 'mere' 2,750) promptly sank into a morass of smouldering disputes. Artfully fanned by presidential agents, these disputes revolved around the premature sharing of an illusory cake along increasingly ethnic or parochial lines.

These were familiar waters for Mobutu who, in the meantime, rescinded his ostensible resignation and resumed his position as head of the former single party. Mobutu now went on to drive further wedges into the opposition's somewhat ragged ranks by handpicking those 'moderate' elements inclined to leave him in charge of the system during the 'transition' period (a scenario favoured by the US State Department), or by naming as an alternative to Etienne Tshisekedi (whose appointment to the Premiership had been forced on him by the National Conference) the unsinkable Nguz Karl-i-Bond; the latter's sinuous career had lately led him to be re-born (once again) as an 'opponent' technically affiliated with the *Union Sacrée*. Once Nguz' credibility had worn thin, Mobutu promptly replaced him with the equally implausible Mungul Diaka. Then, after feigning to yield by again re-appointing the ineluctable Tshisekedi, Mobutu co-opted yet another substitute Premier, Faustin Birindwa, from the ranks of Tshisekedi's own party.

As for Nguz, now excommunicated by the opposition, he shifted his sights to his home region of Shaba which he promptly turned into a personal satrapy with Mobutu's tacit agreement. As in the days of the Katanga secession, Nguz rekindled a campaign of 'ethnic cleansing' directed against 'non-indigenous' communities – notably the Luba, the group to which Tshisekedi belongs. By December 1993, Nguz even upped the ante by declaring the 'autonomy' of his fiefdom, a move which Mobutu was unwilling or unable to challenge.

The rest of the story is only too well known. Zaïre sank deeper into stagnation as the remnants of the regime and of the opposition held each other in a deadlock grip; meanwhile, Western pressure (always relative at best) drifted into divergent stances. For some two years (1992–4), the country had two national assemblies whose representativeness could be challenged for different reasons: the High Council of the Republic had been invested by the now prorogued National Conference; and the rump of the single-party parliament had been elected under an officially abolished system, but never formally disbanded. Two competing cabinets also co-existed; both equally shadowy and frustrated by the *de facto* grip which the presidency managed to retain over the military and security apparatus and the national exchequer.[2] The same deadlock was repeated, in different forms, at the regional and even municipal or local government levels. And, serving as a backdrop to this sorry scene, were the military and police forces whose so-called 'elites' were the only ones trusted with effective firepower. They had temporarily chosen to remain loyal to Mobutu because of ethnic affinities, or due to such perks as the tacit *carte blanche* they had been awarded to help themselves by looting or ransoming or by stripping gold and diamond deposits.

Such activities, in their caricatural form, could be said to blend into the mythology of the 'informal sector' which, along with its socio-political counterpart, 'civil society', has been at the centre of the deliberately optimistic discourse spun by some Western agencies and scholars.[3] It is true that the return to a subsistence agrarian economy limited the worst ravages of malnutrition in the rural areas. This was not the case, however, for urban centres where the 'informal sector' was always articulated with the formal economic and monetary system which had collapsed. In that perspective, as noted by J. C. Willame, the so-called 'Bindo syndrome' (named after the best known of the various pyramid schemes which multiplied in Kinshasa in 1990–1) and the collapse, for lack of maintenance, of the country's largest underground copper mine at Kamoto were linked in more than a symbolic way (Willame, 1994: 139–41; Jewsiewicki, 1992; Bomsel, 1991).

The paralysis of state institutions and the collapse of Zaïre's economy and public finance resulted more from the ineluctable decay of a system long rooted in pillage, than from some Machiavellian 'scorched earth' policy deliberately concocted by Mobutu. Two key state functions (at least in a *Raubwirtschaft* perspective) continued to operate under the President's watchful control: coercion and (through the national Bank) the direct uncontrolled appropriation of foreign-exchange earnings by the President, or by selected warlords in his entourage.

[2] See: 'A Three-Headed Monster', in The Economist, 17 April 1993, p. 42.
[3] For a balanced analysis of this informal sector in Zaïre, see: MacGaffey *et al.* (1991), de Villers (1992), Mafikiri Tsongo (1996) and de Boeck (1996). For a critique of the 'state-society' debate, see Ferguson (1995).

With regard to the 'transition process', on the other hand, there is little doubt that its decay was encouraged and even willed by Mobutu. While it may be excessive to claim (in a paraphrase of André Malraux's quip on Gaullism) that all who matter in Zaïre 'are, have been, or shall be Mobutists', the fact remains that few among the country's assorted 'notables' could pride themselves on having kept their hands clean, or never having supped with the devil. The longer the wait for the rewards of 'change', the sharper the appetites, and the cynical or opportunistic obsession with grasping what could still be salvaged. Such is the context of the much-stimulated resurgence of 'tribalism' which was often insidiously explained as the inevitable price paid for the repudiation of the single party, of the 'strong' state, and of its patrimonialist, yet supposedly effective, 'nation-building' record. In actual fact, even if the regime's well-oiled policies of 'ethnic balancing' had ostensibly been designed to produce a thin, oligarchic 'national' veneer, such policies were, first and foremost, co-optative by nature, and (governed as they were by an open concern for ethnicity) bound to exacerbate an issue which they purported to exorcise.[4]

By early 1994, the transition process had come full circle since its initial phase. The High Council of the Republic, which had been entrusted by the National Conference with the task of orchestrating that transition process, yielded to increasingly insistent Western entreaties. It agreed to take steps toward a form of 'national reconciliation' and convened into a joint body the members of the High Council itself, together with the Mobutu-dominated ex-parliament, a vestigial remnant of the Second Republic. This expanded assembly, now enlarged to 730 members, faced the task of choosing yet another Prime Minister who, under the ritually reiterated terms of the April 1994 compromise agreement, had to be an 'opposition figure'.

This necessity was easily circumvented with the opportunistic candidacy of Kengo wa Dondo, a technocrat held in high regard in Western capitals. Kengo had been intimately linked to the Second Republic and to its President. After serving him faithfully throughout the 1980s, and more recently in 1990 as Prime Minister, he had deftly distanced himself from the system by sponsoring, in 1991, a small paper formation made up of his personal clients and protégés. This so-called *Union des Démocrates Indépendants* had carefully abstained from siding with the main opposition groups.[5] Kengo's appointment was ratified through a

---

[4] Whether they were technocrats or former dissidents, the regime had consistently co-opted (though not truly integrated into its Equatorian 'inner core') a number of key individuals originating from marginal groups (Rwandans, mulattos) or from constituencies affected by successive uprisings (natives of Kwilu, Upper Zaïre, Kivu, members of the Tetela or Luba ethnic groups – the latter being, in fact, far from homogeneous). From the start of the National Conference, however, Etienne Tshisekedi's uncompromising stance, along with his proclivity to assume a quasi-messianic leadership stance among his fellow-members of the opposition, contributed to reviving dormant anti-Luba stereotypes promptly exploited by the regime and by its covert allies in Shaba. A special study is needed of the ethnic tensions of Kivu, fuelled by the voluntary or involuntary migration flows from neighbouring Rwanda and Burundi, and exploited (like those in Shaba) for political ends.

[5] Kengo, a mulatto raised by his European father under the name of Léon Lobitsch – and thus lacking an 'indigenous' ethnic base – had the added distinction of being ineligible for the presidency, under Zaïre's constitutional laws. This precluded him from ever being a direct rival to Mobutu and ensured his loyalty, since his fortune depended entirely on the ruler's favour. This, added to his close links with Western banking circles, made him an obvious 'transitional candidate'. The acronym of the party launched – but not formally chaired – by Kengo (UDI) was at once maliciously translated as *Union des Détourneurs Impunis* (Union of Unindicted Embezzlers).

procedural gimmick, and by a relative majority (332 out of 730). Although the vote was boycotted by the opposition, this appointment was welcomed with obvious relief in Western circles. It now became Kengo wa Dondo's task to organise the 'second act' of the increasingly hypothetical transition process by taking steps to prepare presidential and legislative elections in an increasingly confused and fragmented political landscape.

The creation of a government based on compromise shifted the struggle for power to a different ground, despite the suspicion it inevitably bred and its inability genuinely to fill the gaping political vacuum. The country was being led, willy-nilly, into a pre-electoral phase riddled with ambiguities, renewed tensions and confrontations. A resort to the automated reflexes of 'ethnic voting' seemed inevitably programmed in preparation for the hurdles which regime supporters and adversaries now prepared to face, with vastly unequal means at their disposal. Yet, the real stakes in this power struggle were indeed 'national', and the use of regional or ethnic particularism by rival power seekers actually represented the means rather than the end of their aspirations.[6] As it turned out, the Rwanda crisis, followed by the sweeping campaign waged by the AFDL and its allies, put the plans for elections on indefinite hold.[7]

Towards a New Congolese Identity

Upon seizing power in May 1997, Kabila was immediately confronted by a host of problems, most of which reflected the contradictions that tainted his victory. On the one hand, he enjoyed considerable popularity as the man who was seen as Mobutu's nemesis. On the other hand, he had no ready-made domestic constituency, and no organised civilian or military cadres other than those seconded by his East African allies. The sense of his own vulnerability combined with his fear of being outmanoeuvred or upstaged, either by those who had monopolised the political discourse (for the regime, against it, or both) during the Mobutu era, or by those who had helped him to power. This largely explains his subsequent defensive decision to ban all political organisations, and to reject outright any resumption of the flawed 'transition process'. Kabila also showed a growing determination to silence those who accused him of being a puppet in the hands of Kagame, Museveni or the BanyaMulenge. This he achieved by shedding the awkward tutelage of his former allies, and by shifting power to members of his own kin and native region (North Katanga).

That very same sense of the new regime's precarious hold on power probably also accounts for Kabila's diffident dealings with the 'troika' of Western powers most consistently associated with the country (Belgium, France and the United States), with foreign multinationals and with the Bretton Woods institutions. Ironically, the early erosion of whatever measure of Western goodwill was initially

[6] In different perspectives, the political careers of a Tshombe, or a Buthelezi, amply illustrate the use of particularism as a stepping-stone.

[7] Among the many accounts of the final days of the Mobutu regime, see Braeckman (1997), Reno (1997), Turner (1997) and Kennes (1998: 175–204).

extended to the 'New Congo' regime was due in some substantial part to the stubborn resistance on the part of its influential Tutsi members to allowing the international community to investigate the indiscriminate hunting down of Hutu refugees as well as *génocidaires* by the same forces that had brought it to power (and later turned against Kabila).

The anti-Kabila rebellion had a disturbingly ambiguous character: legitimate grievances were evidently swamped by considerations of *Realpolitik*, naked greed, opportunism and Mobutist revanchism. This makes it unlikely that it could ever achieve any enduring form of legitimacy, unless it comes in the externally imposed form of a compromise for which Mozambique offers a dubious precedent. Nor is it clear that such a settlement would necessarily insulate the country from the fallout of unresolved conflicts in neighbouring states. The sense of Congolese patriotism or aggrieved national pride triggered by the rebellion and its perception as a foreign invasion was surprisingly strong. This may be its only positive legacy. Even if it involves an unsavoury dose of scapegoating, a populist sense of national identity has been built up in the country over the past forty years at least. A general election held shortly after Mobutu's overthrow would almost certainly have invested Kabila with a populist form of legitimacy. As long as the current conflict remains unresolved, however, the elections which both the Kinshasa authorities and the DRC vehemently claim they are prepared to hold at short notice are unlikely to provide any more satisfactory outcomes than those held in Angola in 1992, or Mozambique in 1994.

The scenario of an ever deeper plunge into anarchy cannot be ruled out, however, and one might indeed argue that it is already being played out in the real-life conditions of the 1990s. It remains to be seen in what ways this slide into anarchy might be aggravated, and what spillovers it might entail. The 'warlord mentality' increasingly apparent throughout the country is all too real. Regions, whether by choice or by default, have been taking advantage of their own resources, while outside contacts will probably retain for some time the option of ignoring directives issued by convalescing or unpredictable central authorities. This, of course, does not mean that such latitude will remain viable, or even rewarding over the long term, nor that it must necessarily lead to the emergence of centrifugal trends corresponding to specific local aspirations or to some forms of sub- or trans-national consciousness.

9

ROTIMI SUBERU
Integration & Disintegration
in the Nigerian Federation

Nigeria has emerged as the outstanding example in Africa of the use of federal-local institutions to contain disintegrative tendencies and to promote integrative processes at the national level. The commitment to federalist accommodation and integration in Nigeria has survived the turbulent contours of nearly four decades of independent statehood during which the country has witnessed the breakdown of two Constitutional Republics, the eventual abortion of a protracted transition to a Third Republic, a damaging 30-month civil war, periodic military coups and other forms of political violence, and a crushing, ongoing economic crisis. Indeed, the seeming viability or durability of the Nigerian federal experiment in the face of severe odds has turned the country into an important reference point of constitutional efforts to engineer unity and peace in deeply divided societies elsewhere on the African continent.

However, today, perhaps more than during any other period in the country's history since the 1967–70 civil war, the nature of Nigerian federalism has become precarious and contentious. Recent debates about the 'national question' in Nigeria would tend to suggest that a useful way of accounting for this federalist crisis is to examine the dialectics between the policies of political centralisation that have been mounted to promote integration in the country and the centrifugal backlash which these policies have generally tended to induce. This, in essence, is what this chapter will attempt to do. It is, however, useful to begin by identifying the general structural context of Nigerian federalism.

The Nature of Nigerian Federalism

Nigeria is a federation of enormous sociological complexity and cultural diversity which comprises 36 states, 744 local government areas and the federal capital territory (mayoralty) of Abuja. The federation's peculiarly volatile character derives from its vortex of combustible regional, ethnic and religious cleavages. The most explosive of these divisions include the broad cleavages between the North and the South, among the Hausa/Fulani, Yoruba and Igbo majority nationalities,

91

between majority and minority ethnic groups, and between the adherents of the two world religions of Christianity and Islam.

This extraordinary cultural dissonance should, however, be considered alongside a number of centripetal influences and tendencies in the Nigerian Federation, deriving mainly from the structural evolution and material conditions of the Federation. For instance, the Nigerian Federation has its basis in 'an amalgam of unitary colonial structures' (Oyovbaire, 1979: 83), and its internal territorial configuration has been shaped by a process of disaggregation rather than aggregation. Indeed, prior to the inauguration of a federal constitution in 1954, Nigeria was administered by the British as a decentralised unitary state. The Federation is, therefore, not the product of a political compact among previously autonomous territorial units, but the result of the devolution of constitutional authority by a central government to designated territorial sub-units of the country. More importantly, the shape, number and distribution of these units have been determined largely by the Federal Government which has relied on their periodic fragmentation as a strategy of structural centralisation and consolidation.

Powerful centripetal pressures are also inherent in the political economy of the Federation. The sense of regional economic self-sufficiency which gave impetus to the pressures for a federal constitution in 1954 began to dissipate from the late 1950s onwards as the prices for regionally controlled commodity exports suffered a sharp decline in the world market, and as the Federal Government began to assume the leadership role in national development planning (Dudley, 1966).

The process of economic centralisation was consummated during the 1970s when the oil boom dramatically expanded the volume of revenues available for appropriation and redistribution by the Federal Government. Since that period, federally collected mineral rents, royalties and taxes have accounted for some 80% of public revenues at federal, state and local levels. Furthermore, the revenue-sharing arrangements that have been instituted since the 1970s have enabled the Federal Government to retain and spend a disproportionate share of mineral revenues, while leaving the states and local authorities in a state of financial dependence or subservience vis-à-vis the centre.

To all these forces of centripetalism in the Nigerian Federation must be added the overwhelming impact of military rule in the country: 'Centralist by organisation and outlook, relatively unimpeded by local or regional claims and pressures, frequently guided by the ideals of nationalism or national greatness, and standing to advance their own careers considerably', successive military rulers in Nigeria have sought to promote integration '... by means of far-reaching and comprehensive – but not revolutionary – programmes of consolidation and centralisation' (Graf, 1988: 49). Thus, one of the hallmarks of military rule in Nigeria has been the institution of a pragmatic and pyramidal federal system which has entrenched the 'centre at the apex and the states and localities at the base' (Aikhomu, 1993: 1–2) of the federal power structure. This centralisation has been achieved by, among other measures, the imposition of the military's unitary command structure on the federal administrative system, the institution of a variety of centralist decrees and constitutional provisions, the fragmentation of the sub-federal entities into smaller and weaker constituent units, and the institutionalisation of revenue-sharing arrangements which have enhanced the relative financial position of the Federal Government.

Thus, virtually all the major policies of centralisation that have been developed to promote integration in Nigeria bear the imprint of military rule. The rest of this chapter is devoted mainly to an examination of the nature and impact of two of these policies, namely, revenue allocation and the reorganisation of state and local governments.

Redistributive & Reorganisational Policies Towards Integration

Nigeria's current revenue-sharing system revolves around the redistribution to other parts of the country of wealth obtained from a few oil-rich, predominantly ethnic minority states in Southern Nigeria. This centralised redistribution of economic resources has been achieved by the elaboration of specific vertical and horizontal rules for intergovernmental revenue-sharing.

The vertical rules for revenue allocation in Nigeria prescribe the formula for distributing national financial resources in general, and federally collected revenues in particular, among the three tiers of government administration in the country. Succinctly, these rules have been guided largely by the following centralist principles or features:

(i)   The collection or administration by the Federal Government of the most lucrative financial resources and tax revenues, including the petroleum profits tax, mining rents and royalties, company income tax and export and import duties.

(ii) The allocation to the Federal Government of federally collected revenues exceeding the combined shares of the state and local authorities. (This asymmetrical sharing of revenues is regarded as necessary to enable the Federal Government to manage the national economy as well as undertaking its extensive responsibilities under the 1979 and 1989 Constitutions.)

(iii) The direct administration by the Federal Government of all funds set aside under the national revenue-sharing scheme for special purposes or programmes, including the amelioration of national ecological problems, the development of the new federal capital territory and the rehabilitation of mineral-producing areas.

(iv) The progressive institutionalisation of direct financial relationships between the federal and local governments, and of the rights of the localities to participate directly in the national revenue-sharing scheme.

(v)   The progressive reduction in the proportions of federal statutory financial allocations to the states simultaneously with an expansion of the local authorities' shares of these allocations (Danjuma, 1993).

Under the current revenue-sharing arrangements, for instance, 48.5% of federally collected revenues are retained by the Federal Government, against 24 and 20% for the states and local authorities respectively. The balance of 7.5% of the Federation Account is devoted to federally administered funds for the rehabilitation of mineral-producing areas, the amelioration of ecological problems and other related purposes. In essence, over 55% of the Federation Account is retained and/or directly administered by the Federal Government.

Admittedly, recent revenue arrangements have sought to enhance the relative financial position of the local authorities vis-à-vis the Federal and state governments. It is, however, the states that have suffered more directly from these arrangements, which have occurred in tandem with the expansion of the Federal Government's intervention in local government affairs and a contraction in the scope of politico-legal controls hitherto exercised by the states over the localities. Indeed, it can be said that recent local government reforms in Nigeria have probably done more to bring the local authorities within the purview of the federal governmental machinery than to strengthen such authorities.

The rules for distributing revenues among the states and the local authorities – the horizontal revenue-sharing rules – have reinforced the tendency towards the centralisation of intergovernmental financial relationships. Basically, these rules emphasise the principles of equality, demography and equity rather than efficiency or derivation. For instance, the current formula for distributing federal revenues among the states and localities is based on the following criteria and accompanying weights: equality (40%), population (30%), social development factor (10%), internal revenue generation effort (10%), land mass and terrain (10%).

It must be conceded that the revenue-sharing formula described above gives greater recognition to efficiency principles than some of the revenue-sharing arrangements adopted in the past.[1] Nevertheless, the allocation of only a 10% weight to the criterion of internal revenue generation effort, instead of the 20% recommended by the Danjuma Revenue Mobilisation and Allocation Commission (Danjuma, 1993: 32–6), reflects the intense political opposition that has developed in Nigeria to the notion that the sub-federal units can be induced to become relatively autonomous financially.

However, the growing emphasis on centralised redistribution, rather than on sub-unit financial autonomy, has been most glaring in the progressive diminution of the importance attached to the derivation principle in the elaboration of revenue-sharing arrangements in Nigeria. Whereas as much as 50% of mining rents and royalties were allocated to the region of derivation in 1960, by 1975 the proportion had been reduced to 20% (Oyovbaire, 1985: 167–71). Furthermore, in 1979, in accordance with the recommendations of the Aboyade Technical Committee Report, all federally collected revenues were consolidated in a Federation Account. As a result, the derivation principle was completely extinguished from the revenue-sharing scheme; the Aboyade Commission merely

---

[1]For instance, only a 5% weight was assigned to the criterion of internal revenue generation effort under the revenue-sharing scheme implemented and bequeathed by the Shehu Shagari Administration of the Second Republic (1979–93).

proposed the use of 3% of the Federation Account for the benefit of mineral-producing areas and other parts of the country in need of ecological rehabilitation or special attention (*ibid.*: 192).

With the inauguration of the Second Republic, however, some modest effort was made to reintroduce the derivation principle into Nigeria's revenue-sharing system. Thus, the scheme instituted during 1981–2 assigned 2% of the Federation Account to the mineral-producing states on the basis of derivation, and 1.5% of the same account for the development and ecological rehabilitation of mineral-producing areas (Federal Republic of Nigeria, 1982: A1–5). Following the collapse of the Second Republic at the end of 1983, however, the Buhari-Idiagbon Administration (1984–5) decided that these proportions should apply to federally collected mineral revenues only, rather than to the totality of the Federation Account.[2] This, in effect, meant some reduction in the proportion of the Federation Account allocated to the mineral-producing states and areas on a derivation basis.

Similarly, despite intensive pressures for fairer treatment by the mineral-producing states and communities, the Ibrahim Babangida Administration (1985–93) was able to implement only modest, and somewhat ambivalent, changes in the rules for reallocating mineral revenues to these areas. For instance, the proportion of federally collected mineral revenues transferred to the mineral-rich states on the basis of derivation was reduced from 2 to 1%, while the allocation for the rehabilitation and development of mineral-producing areas was increased from 1.5 to 3% of mineral revenues (Danjuma, 1993: 23).

In sum, current revenue-sharing practices in Nigeria have encouraged the financial hegemony of the centre, the chronic dependence of constituent states and localities on the centralised redistribution of resources, the massive transfer of revenues from the oil-producing areas to the other parts of the Federation and, in general, the development of a highly integrated and unified public financial system.

Like the revenue-sharing arrangements, successive reforms of the internal territorial configuration of the Nigerian Federation have operated to augment the ascendancy of the Federal Government or to create a more centralised federation. Among the objectives of the state creation exercises undertaken since 1967 can be numbered the following centrist goals:

(i)   The fragmentation and relegation of the former regional ethnic majority groups (Hausa/Fulani, Yoruba and Igbo) into smaller constituent units.

(ii)   The creation of a federal system of multiple states(as distinct from the four-region Federation of the pre-1967 era) in which no one state or region would be able to dominate the Federation, threaten the corporate existence of the country, or hold the nation to ransom.

(iii)   The use of the states as instruments of federally co-ordinated development and as outlets for federally collected oil revenues (Osaghae, 1992).

[2]See *Daily Times* (Lagos), 3 January 1985, p. 1.

(iv) The integration of the minorities into the mainstream of the federal political process by constituting them into separate states and liberating them from regional domination by the ethnic majority groups.

(v) The promotion of administrative convenience, political security and national unity.

It must be added that, with the exception of the establishment of the Midwest Region in 1963, all state creation exercises in Nigeria have been undertaken by the military in typically centrist fashion, with little or no consultation with the communities involved. Thus, the replacement of the four-region arrangement with a 12-state structure in 1967 was put into effect by a hasty military Decree. Although the Justice Ayo Irikefe Commission was appointed to advise on the 1976 state creation exercise, the attendant replacement of the 12-state structure with a 19-state system did not follow fully the recommendations of the Commission (Federal Republic of Nigeria, 1976). Babangida's promulgations of a 21-state system and a 30-state structure in 1987 and 1991, respectively, were similarly characterised by very limited investigation or consultation. A major consequence of this arbitrariness has been to contribute to the contentiousness and self-perpetuating character of the state creation process, with each reorganisation exercise inducing fresh statehood agitation from marginalised, disadvantaged or inequitably incorporated groups.

In recent years, local governments have been subjected to the same kind of centrally co-ordinated fragmentation and reorganisation as the states. The effort to entrench a uniform structure of local government under the 1976 local government reforms provided the initial historical basis for federal intervention in the definition of local government boundaries. Those reforms included the stipulation by the Federal Military Government of regulations that were explicitly designed to discourage the state governments from creating extremely small or unviable local authorities. Thus, a general population range of 150,000–800,000 was prescribed for local authorities (Gboyega, 1987: 134–57). Although local governments in very large metropolitan areas were allowed to exceed the upper limit in order to avoid undue fragmentation, no local authority whose population fell below 150,000 people could be established without the approval of the Federal Military Government. In the end some 301 local authorities were established throughout the Federation. Under the Second Republic (1979–83), however, the local governments became the victims of politically inspired fragmentation and proliferation, leading to the creation of over 400 new local government areas in the country by the end of 1981 (Graf, 1988: 180).

As is well known, one of the initial acts of the Buhari-Idiagbon Administration was to revert to the pre-1979 301-local authority structure. Yet, in what were perhaps the most extensive and arbitrary local government reorganisations ever undertaken directly by the Federal Government in Nigeria's post-independence history, the Babangida Administration increased the number of local government areas in the country to 449 and 589 during May 1989 and August – September 1991 respectively. These reorganisations have predictably provoked unprecedented strictures regarding the distribution, configuration, designation, headquarters and boundaries of the local government areas. The reorganisations have been rendered even more sensitive and explosive by the new roles of local authorities as state and national legislative constituencies, as relatively autonomous expressions of presidential government at the local level, and as direct recipients of 20% of federally collected revenues (Suberu, 1994).

In essence, reflecting its commitment to a programme of integration through centralisation, the Federal Government in Nigeria has sought to establish a uniform national scheme of local government, often in violation of local preferences and initiatives. As we shall now attempt to demonstrate in more detail, however, the centralising project of the Federal state has produced contestable and contradictory results.

Integration or Disintegration?

An important feature of current agitation about the 'national question' in Nigeria is the crystallisation of opposition to the centralising features of the Federal system. This opposition is evident in comments by major opinion leaders and in the agendas of most of the associations that have been formed in response to the crises of governance and democratic transition in the country. Chief Anthony Enahoro's Movement for National Reformation (MNR), for instance, was committed to the establishment of a truly federal or confederal structure, the full reintroduction of derivation as a principle of revenue-sharing, the 'Zoning' or rotation of key political offices among designated sections of the country, the recasting of the presidential constitution into a parliamentary or 'presidential-parliamentary' system, and the convening of a sovereign national conference to deliberate on the modalities for the reorganisation of the Federation along ethno-confederal lines (Movement for National Reformation, 1993).

Other contributors to the debate on the national question have recommended the decentralisation of resource control, the institution of a collegiate presidency and/or a multiple vice-presidential system, and the establishment of an all-embracing national government as possible solutions to the country's deepening problems of ethnic accommodation and national integration (see, for instance, Obasanjo, 1992; Ekwueme, 1992). The underlying theme in these and related recommendations is the quest for a formula to reduce overcentralisation of political control or ensure a more equitable access to centralised federal power. The alternative to such a reform strategy is seen as the continued hegemonic domination of the country by a section and the possible violent disintegration of the Federation. The sensitivity of the issue of political control at the centre is underscored by the tension which enveloped the country in the wake of the June 1993 presidential election and the abrogation of the victory of the first Southern politician to be elected Head of State since independence.

Partly in an attempt to contain the growing ferment over the national question, the country's seventh military ruler, General Sani Abacha, unfolded plans in November 1993 for a national constitutional conference to debate the political future. The 369 delegates to the conference, including 96 nominees of the government, met during July–December 1994 to discuss such issues as federal, confederal and unitary constitutional options; the relative merits of presidentialism and parliamentarism; the value of zoning, a rotational presidency and other strategies for power-sharing; the relationship among ethnic nationalities, national identity and citizenship; and problems of revenue distribution and generation, including compensation for the ecological problems of oil- and mineral-producing areas.

Indeed, the most potent threat to the nation's corporate existence lies in the autonomist agitations and distributive pressures emanating from the oil-producing ethnic minority communities in and around the Niger Delta area. It is in these parts of the country that accumulated grievances over the centrist appropriation of oil rents, royalties and profits, and the neglect and ecological devastation of the oil-bearing areas, have resulted in violent communal agitations and protests directed mainly against the state-backed oil prospecting multinational companies and the Federal Government. In April 1994, for instance, the Shell Petroleum Development Corporation, one of Nigeria's leading oil companies, lost millions of dollars when its operations were paralysed for 18 consecutive days by protesting oil communities.[3]

These agitations have not been arrested by the decision of the Babangida Administration to increase statutory allocations to the mineral-producing areas and to establish a fully-fledged federal agency – the Oil Mineral Producing Areas Development Commission (OMPADEC) – to administer the expanded allocation. On the contrary, the representatives of the oil-bearing areas are demanding the allocation of not less than 10% (as opposed to the present 3%) of mineral revenues for the development of these areas, as well as the more effective representation of these communities in OMPADEC.[4]

Since the publication of the Ogoni Bill of Rights in August 1990, the Ogoni community has come to symbolise the travails and struggles of Nigeria's oil-producing communities. Under the auspices of the Movement for the Survival of the Ogoni People (MOSOP), and the leadership of the noted Nigerian writer and publisher, the late Ken Saro-Wiwa, the Ogoni community demanded:

(i)   The transfer of the proceeds of mineral rents and royalties from the Federal Government to the oil-producing communities who own the land from which oil is derived.

(ii)   The payment of reparations by the Federal Government and the oil prospecting companies to the Ogoni community for past and continuing expropriation and neglect of the community.

(iii) The abrogation of section 42 (3) of the Constitution of the Federal Republic of Nigeria, 1989, which vests in the Federal Government ownership and control of 'all minerals, mineral oils and natural gas' in the country and its territorial waters.

[3]*Newswatch* (Lagos), 11 July 1994: 15.
[4]The Guardian (Lagos), 9 March 1993: 28.

(iv) The demonstration by the oil prospecting companies of a greater degree of sensitivity to the ecological, developmental, educational and employment problems or needs of the Ogoni and other oil-bearing communities.

(v) The establishment of adequate institutional, financial and legal arrangements and regulations to protect the mineral-producing areas from the ecological risks of oil exploration.

(vi) The revision of the federal structure, presumably along confederal lines, in order to give the Ogoni full political and economic autonomy (Saro-Wiwa, 1993).

In seeking to advance these demands, the Ogoni have circulated the Ogoni Bill of Rights within and outside Nigeria, launched an Ogoni Survival Fund, staged mass rallies and demonstrations, threatened secession from the Federation and made representations to a variety of international agencies such as the United Nations, the Unrepresented Nations and Peoples' Organisation, the British Parliamentary Human Rights Group and the London Rainforest Action Group.[5] These agitations have been sufficiently strident to compel the Federal Government to resort to 'tough tactics,' including the proscription of ethnic and ethno-regional associations, the promulgation of a treasonable offences Decree imposing the death penalty on advocates of ethnic autonomy, and the intimidation, detention and execution of Ken Saro-Wiwa on 9 November 1995.

The Federal Government's repeated reorganisations of the internal territorial structure of the Federation have arguably engendered less direct challenges to the corporate existence of the country than the expropriation of the mineral-producing areas. Nevertheless, the worst cases of intercommunal violence in the country's recent history can be linked, either directly or indirectly, to sectional differences over the configuration and demarcation of the boundaries of some of the states and local authorities.

Apart from competition over land and over the control of traditional governance in Wukari (Taraba State), an additional factor in the ongoing feud between the Tiv and Jukun is the contested demarcation of the boundaries between Taraba and Benue States. This conflict, it should be noted, has led to the sacking of several settlements and the killing of thousands of people, including the sole female member of the Taraba State legislature.[6]

Following the August–September 1991 creation of new states and local government areas, communal agitation and tensions also developed in Sokoto, Jigawa, Delta and Ondo States over the configuration and headquarters of some of the newly created constituent units. The establishment of Delta State, for instance, immediately led to the intensification of the age-old struggle between the Urhobo and Itsekiri for control of Warri, while simultaneously inducing a polarisation of Urhobo-Igbo relationships over the location of the capital of the

[5]See *Newswatch* (Lagos), 25 January 1993: 9–17.
[6]*The Punch* (Lagos), 29 June 1992: 1 and 5.

state in the Igbo town of Asaba rather than in a part of the old Delta province. In essence, the narrower geographical context of Delta has fuelled conflicts and cleavages which had been relatively muted in the more ethnically complex Bendel State, from which Delta was excised in August 1991.

Communal tensions over the Federal Government's allegedly prejudiced location of the headquarters of a number of local government areas have been a prominent feature of politics in Ondo State. These tensions have led to violent communal riots and/or paralysis of governmental and political activities in at least three local government areas of the state, namely Emure-Ise-Orun, Ifedore and Akoko North-West (Suberu, 1994).

But the most devastating communal riots in recent Nigerian history have involved the confrontations between Muslim Hausa/Fulani groups and non-Muslim minority communities in Southern Bauchi, Southern Kaduna, Taraba and Adamawa States. These conflicts have resulted from complex communal struggles over traditional authority, economic control and religious and cultural values. However, they have also been generated by recent reorganisations and reforms in the local government structure which have afforded wider scope for the articulation of ethnic minority opposition to the Fulani emirate system. In this respect, Federal intervention in the redefinition and fragmentation of the local government structure may have advanced the cause of political liberalisation, but at the price of communal instability.

The foregoing consideration of some of the controversial consequences of centrally directed territorial reforms in Nigeria has not mentioned the serious problem of governmental discrimination against non-indigenes at state and local levels. Each exercise in the fragmentation of states and local authorities makes such discrimination even more pervasive and pernicious, since this fragmentation induces a corresponding contraction in the geographical space where a Nigerian citizen can claim indigeneity (Bach, 1989a & 1997a). In the recent past, discriminatory practices by state and local governments in the disposition of employment opportunities have intensified in the wake both of the autonomy granted to the local authorities to recruit their staffs, and pressures for bureaucratic rationalisation arising from mounting financial difficulties. These practices, along with the increasing resort to zoning and related ethno-distributionist formulas in party political affairs, clearly underscore Nigeria's growing segmentation and polarisation along ethno-territorial lines, despite the Federal Government's centrist strategies and integrationist rhetoric.

Over the past twenty years, the Federal Government has relied on systematic policies of centralisation to achieve integration and curb disintegrative tendencies in the country. Although a federal arrangement has been institutionalised as a concession to Nigeria's cultural complexity, the central administration has systematically consolidated its hegemony over the sub-federal authorities through a variety of constitutional, fiscal and territorial arrangements.

The maintenance of Nigeria as a single entity, despite the deep tensions and divisions, may be suggestive of the efficacy of the centralist path to integration in Nigeria. The recent resurgence and intensification of ethnic, regional and religious tensions in the country would, however, tend to belie such a suggestion. One would, in fact, like to argue that the more viable path to integration in

Nigeria lies not in the extremes of centralisation or confederation, but in the promotion of truly federalist institutions and processes. This will entail the reform of the present barely concealed unitary system in order to give freer rein to pressures for decentralisation and local autonomy and initiative. This, in essence, is the underlying theme in much of the current debate about the future of federalism in Nigeria.

10 SIMON BEKKER
Territoriality & Institutional Change in the New South Africa

During the twentieth century, South Africa has passed through a reasonably clearly defined period of change characterised by rapid industrialisation and urbanisation; increasing economic inclusion of black South Africans in these processes; increasing political and residential exclusion of black South Africans from these processes; increasing resistance and struggle by the excluded majority against the Afrikaner Nationalist Government and its apartheid policy; and the establishment of a democratically elected government, the main mission of which is to institute equity, reconciliation and prosperity in the society (Bekker, 1996).

Two key features of this new government will be identified. The first is that of constitutional sovereignty. Under previous constitutions, governance was guided by parliamentary sovereignty which accorded the national executive and legislature supremacy over the judiciary, a constitutional authority which was employed on numerous occasions (Abel, 1995). Today, the Constitutional Court bears this authority. When the South African state, reflecting – as it inevitably will – certain interests, is called upon to be even-handed in constitutional terms, as it surely will often be, it will be the judges of this Court rather than the government who will adjudicate.

The second feature is the particular territorial dispersion of political power which is constituted. Intergovernmental relations between the central government, nine provincial governments, and numerous urban and rural local governments are constitutionally required to be 'distinctive, interdependent and interrelated', thereby constituting 'co-operative government' (Republic of South Africa, 1996: section 40(1)). The provinces have substantial devolved powers, including authority to adopt a provincial constitution, to raise certain taxes, and to legislate on local government affairs. The central government has a wide range of overriding powers which it can exercise when conflicts between national and provincial legislatures emerge. An advisory Fiscal and Finance Commission, comprising nominees of central, provincial and local government, is established to ensure equitable sharing of revenue between these governmental tiers (or 'spheres', to use the new terminology). In short, this division of powers establishes multiple territorial domains of representation and participation without constituting a federal arrangement. Moreover, the nature of this division of power reflects the territorial and cultural diversity in the country by, for example, allowing a provincial constitution to include the institution of a traditional monarch (*ibid.*: section 143(1)(b)), and by enabling each provincial government to select at least two of the eleven official languages as its medium of communication (*ibid.*: section 6(3)(a)).

The general and provincial elections of 1994 took place under the Interim Constitution of 1993. Its prescriptions required the establishment of a national assembly and nine provincial parliaments elected under a simple system of proportional representation. The 400 seats in the general assembly were filled by the first 200 successful party candidates on two separate lists, one national and one provincial. Seats in the Senate – elected by the provincial governments – numbered 90 (10 from each province). This electoral system, distinct from the Westminster system practised under the former Constitution, was designed to improve the minority political parties' chances of representation in the national and provincial governments. National and provincial cabinets were composed proportionately by all parties with at least 5% of the vote – thereby establishing a government-of-national-unity and provincial governments-of-unity. Local government elections took place (in 1995 and 1996) under a mixed proportional representation and ward-based system designed with similar aims in mind. For the first time in South Africa's history, the franchise was universal and no seats were reserved for minorities. Political parties, including a large number of new interest-based parties, competed openly with one another. Expressed in South African metaphor, the political playing field had been levelled. What has been proclaimed to be the South African miracle is due in no small part to the nature and outcome of this multi-party electoral system which clearly identified the winning party, while facilitating the emergence of minority party rule in two provinces and minority party representation in all other governments-of-unity. The new Constitution of 1996 replaces the Senate with a National Council of Provinces which will include the provincial premiers and nine delegates from each province, selected to ensure minority party representation. Regarding legislative matters previously addressed by the Senate, each provincial delegation casts a single vote and decisions are taken on the basis of a majority (of at least five votes). The new Constitution also abolishes the requirement to establish governments-of-unity at central and provincial level; 'Co-operative government' is erected in their place. Elections in 1999 will take place under this modified electoral system.

The purpose of this chapter is to identify the institutional arrangements emerging from this process of fundamental political change in South African society. The focus will be squarely upon new emergent public policies and state institutions, particularly regarding their spatial features. Moreover, since chapters 15 and 16 address regional institutions and policies in Southern Africa, the focus will be restricted to national rather international aspects of this process of institutionalisation.

Accordingly, with a view to introducing this institutional analysis, a number of overarching checks and balances informing the current process of state policy formulation in South Africa will be summarised. Subsequently, emergent state institutions will be identified in three separate domains: first, intergovernmental relations between central, provincial and local tiers of government; secondly, economic and financial institutions, particularly regarding development and intergovernmental relations; and finally, institutions designed to address the multi-cultural nature of South African society. In each case, a brief historical overview of previous institutional arrangements will precede the substantive analysis of current emerging institutions in the new South African state.

Checks & Balances on Public Policy-making

Public policy comprises three dimensions. First, it communicates what a government values. Thereby, in the second place, it provides direction to those who make and take decisions in government. Thirdly, it is a measure against which a government may be held accountable and may be evaluated. Particularly if it is subject to regular democratic elections, no government is wholly free to make and communicate policy at will. Its will is limited by a number of constraints. Five such constraints will be identified, which, taken together, make for a web of divergent, potentially colliding rules of the policy-making game. Or, if one prefers to see it that way, they make for a system of checks and balances in the game of governance. Though not exhaustive – for budgetary constraints are obviously fundamental to policy-making – these five constraints do offer a significant context within which the institutional analyses presented below may better be understood. These constraints are: the new-and-old mix in the policy-making institutional culture; the untested democratic and tested populist rules of the game; the policy imperative to combat inequality and poverty; the culturally diverse society in which South Africans live, and South Africa's role in the new global economy.

The new & the old

The process of political transition in South Africa bears the tag of 'miracle' rather than the weighty identification of 'revolution'. It was miraculous rather than revolutionary in that a distinct shift took place from conflict and violence to compromise and negotiation. This shift took place in the minds and actions of the two main political adversaries of the 1980s – in the mass democratic movement and the apartheid regime; in the African National Congress (ANC) and the National Party (NP), each with its allies; and in the minds and actions of Mandela and de Klerk. The shift enabled a number of unexpected developments. Parties falling outside the ambit of the two main camps, such as the Africanist and Afrikaner separatist groups, were drawn into negotiations through bilateral discussions and public exposure. New governments at national, provincial and local levels were established as governments-of-unity, bringing together both new and old politicians. This combination also took place in state and parastatal organisations where new civil servants today work side by side with functionaries from the previous administration. In short, an important part of the miracle has been the extent to which political transition implied just such a mixture of change and continuity, transforming the foundations of the political system through negotiation rather than by force.

The rules of the game

The making of public policy is governed by a number of rules. There are two new sets which restrict the nature of the game in specific and potentially divergent ways. The first set derives directly from the recently established institutions of democratic governance, including, for instance, the formal responsibilities of constitutional judge, attorney general and public protector, whilst the second set of rules has evolved from what I shall call the forum movement and reflects the expectation that public policy needs to bear the stamp of popular approval. Rules of the first set are still generally found only on paper and take on weight only to the extent that they are tried and tested through contestation and controversy. Rules of the second set have been forged during the decade of the 1990s through wide-ranging advocacy, emotion and experience.

Democratic practice – particularly within the public sector – does not appear fully-grown once formal institutions have been established. Countervailing influences within political parties, and within political cultures that developed before these institutions were established, exist in parallel with this new set of rules. As a political analyst put it a few years ago: 'there are … critical moments in which public watchdogs have to decide whether to take on parts of government – and in which it is not at all certain that government will accept their authority' (Friedman, 1996). The new South African democracy, accordingly, is still mostly theoretical and academic; its rules – spelled out as they are in legal and procedural documents – are typically without precedent or practical example. Though often employed to justify and legitimise government decisions, they have yet to carry the weight of justice and sanction that such rules carry in mature democracies.

Rules about consultation with civil society, on the other hand, are well-entrenched. Inclusivity, participation and transparency, together with deep scepticism towards politicians, are firmly rooted in the game. Fair play requires that the voice of the people, the voice of the community, is called for and listened to. Under these rules, public policy-making becomes a populist game.

The antecedents of this game may be found immediately before and after the 1994 general election when a wide spectrum of South African interest groups, including organised labour and business, non-governmental and community-based organisations, state bodies, political parties and civic associations, entered into a series of meetings with a view to addressing issues of direct concern to them. These activities took place at local, provincial, and national level, and became known as the forum movement. The bodies these interest groups brought into being were known as forums which developed as a result of three factors: (i) acknowledgement by the pre-April 1994 NP Government that its illegitimacy precluded effective unilateral decision-making; (ii) abandonment of the old pattern of struggle politics in which non-participation was elevated to a binding principle; and (iii) a growing understanding – fuelled by constitutional negotiations – that an array of stakeholders needed to be drawn into the decision-making process.

The forums displayed a strong belief in the need for inclusivity of representation, considerable variation in membership, a widely held perception that the role of forums was to formulate policy rather than implement projects, and a desire to address the broader picture rather than issues solely of local concern. A further striking feature of the forums was that, in general, they were not state-initiated but developed each in their own way, rarely following a pre-determined pattern.

Inequality & poverty

In the preamble to the Reconstruction and Development Programme (RDP) White Paper, President Mandela is quoted as declaring that 'at the heart of the Government of National Unity is a commitment to effectively address the problems of poverty and the gross inequality evident in almost all aspects of South African society' (Republic of South Africa, 1994). It is from this conviction that the primary substantive focus of public policy-making in the country derives.

Accordingly, the requirement to be able to motivate proposals in terms of their contribution to the RDP is quite simply a policy imperative, a principle of the game, as it were. Simultaneously, the economic cake can only be distributed fairly and generously if it continues to grow. The presidential quotation from the RDP White Paper continues by arguing that poverty and gross inequality can only be addressed '… if the South African economy can be firmly placed on the path of high and sustainable growth'. Clearly, both business and labour need to be persuaded to remain committed to this game.

Cultural imperatives

South Africa is a culturally diverse society. Its different groups have experienced divisions – shifting though these divisions may well have been – along lines of language, of class, of territory, and of felt racial difference. Today, two related currents in the country are apparent – one promoting a new form of nationhood based on territory rather than on cultural coherence; the other claiming the right to celebrate cultural uniqueness, a right that sometimes tends towards claims for self-determination. The dialectics created by these two potentially divergent currents are inherent in the politics of culturally plural societies. These dialectics, moreover, are complicated even further by the racial consciousness that persists in the country.

In reaction to this predicament, the South African Government is developing a position with regard to these two allied challenges: to build a single nation, on the one hand, and to enable changing cultural forms to express themselves and to flourish, on the other. These emergent policies relate both to nation-building and to language, religion, education, the proposed role of traditional authorities, and land tenure. Simultaneously, non-racialism remains a national goal of high priority to the government.

That these circumstances create constraints for policy-makers is self-evident. First, the rules of the cultural game are anything but clear. Secondly, the game evokes high emotions among players and spectators alike. In particular, the technological and scientific predominance of Eurocentric forms of thought invades and corrodes other systems of knowledge and thereby nourishes resistance to Western ways. Thirdly, policy-making on capacity-building and affirmative action in a non-racial context appears extremely difficult to justify consistently. In short, the game appears fraught with difficulty and many policies simply avoid the issue whenever possible and evade it when it appears. One result is that much development policy is devoid of cultural content, implying that all South Africans share a common view of what is valued most and what least.

Rebuilding a place in the world

Since the end of the Cold War, a new world order has come into being. Global interdependence proliferates and the global economy increases steadily. There is growing international mobility of financial instruments, of information, of investment, and of some kinds of elite labour. International economic organisations gain in influence and authority. Within the European Union, the North American region, and the Pacific Rim region – the Big Three – member nations enjoy special treatment.

This new order takes South African policy-makers into unfamiliar and daunting territory, particularly since this order implies rules over which South Africa has little, if any, say. As a semi-industrialised, medium-sized economy with an inherited industrial strategy of import substitution, the country is struggling both to attract significant volumes of offshore investment and to find niches in the international industrial market. Growth is a prerequisite for the implementation of the policy imperative of addressing inequality and poverty. Conforming to the rules of this global economy places policy-makers addressing trade policy and industrial relations, for example, in exceedingly uncomfortable straitjackets. Populist rules requiring that the people's will be realised, or redistributive rules requiring equity in the short term, collide with the seemingly intractable rules of the global economy and of the Big Three in the northern hemisphere. In particular, the RDP is being challenged – within government – by the more economically orthodox development approach advocated by the Department of Finance (Republic of South Africa, nd).

Intergovernmental Relations between Central, Provincial & Local Tiers of Government

In geopolitical terms, before the 1994 general elections, South Africa differed dramatically from its present form. Reflecting the logic of apartheid philosophy, the central government ruled over four provinces – the Cape, the Orange Free State, Natal and the Transvaal. The powers of these provincial governments had eroded substantially over the previous three decades to the extent that the central government's control over them may be typified as highly centralised. Each of these governments was White, elected by exclusively White electorates. Those classified as Coloureds and Asians living in these provinces voted for separate Coloured and Asian 'national' governments, bodies with severely circumscribed powers which were widely dismissed as institutions collaborating with apartheid.

Apartheid philosophy envisaged separate 'ethnonational' territorial states for each 'ethnonational' black community in the country. Accordingly, ten homelands were constitutionally established, four of which were assigned 'independence' by the South African Government, a status that no state in the international community was prepared to recognise. Each homeland established a government with substantial formal powers which it found difficult to exercise since economic constraints rooted in the peripheral location of the homeland territories and political resistance deriving from widespread rejection of apartheid philosophy and practice created enormous constraints on homeland governance.

Under this system, local government was a provincial matter and, in practice, the responsibility of White city and town councils acting as 'guardians' of local authority matters in urban areas demarcated by statute for other races. The system was structured strictly on racial lines. Accordingly, White municipalities, conforming to an inherited British local authority model, enjoyed considerable autonomy and held sway over Coloured and Indian management and local affairs committees which – though intended to be local governments – were effectively no more than advisory bodies without meaningful decision-making powers.

During this period, Black local authorities can only be understood by reference to developments both within and outside the former homelands. Outside these homelands, Black local authorities were thrust into formal autonomy in 1982, with minimal experience and entirely inadequate financial resources. On paper, they were granted powers equivalent to those of White municipalities and were, accordingly, expected to play a role in meeting the challenge of 'black' urbanisation. Simultaneously, they were strictly controlled by higher-tier state bodies. As a consequence, they found themselves without real local authority and became a primary target, during the turbulent 1980s, of struggle politics. In the former homelands, urban local authorities were closely controlled by their respective homeland governments and were assigned few decision-making powers. Outside the urban areas, traditional authorities had been established and they too operated – at least with regard to service delivery – as little more than agents of these governments.

In short, except for White urban local government, local authorities in apartheid South Africa acted as agents of other, often higher-tier, authorities. Defined on racial lines, they delivered services on behalf of these other authorities when they could, but were generally unresponsive to their publics' needs, and – in the urban-industrial centres of the country – increasingly became institutional targets for popular resistance.

The national multi-party negotiations of the early 1990s fundamentally altered this geopolitical profile of apartheid South Africa. In the first place, the integrity of the entire territory of South Africa is constitutionally guaranteed. This principle is elegantly expressed in the preamble to the new Constitution 'We, the people of South Africa, ... believe that South Africa belongs to all who live in it ...'

(Republic of South Africa, 1996). The spectre of a series of black 'ethnonational' statelets forming a constellation around 'White' South Africa has been laid to rest.

In the second place, nine new provinces have been demarcated. Their boundaries reflect an attempt to establish economically viable units, large enough to develop effective second-tier governments, and explicitly to move away from former homeland 'ethnonational' boundaries. This provincial demarcation process, which was required to be completed before the 1994 elections, was generally successful both in applying such criteria and in eliciting public participation in the process. The number of disputes over boundaries that create, in the opinion of certain groups, both cultural and economic fault-lines is small and these appear to be reaching resolution (Griggs, 1995).

With the exception of the Western Cape province, each new province incorporates the territory (or part of the territory) of at least one former homeland. Four of the nine provinces – the Western Cape, the Free State, KwaZulu-Natal and Gauteng – have inherited the bulk of the former White provincial administrations. The other five provinces are accordingly establishing administrations on the basis of generally inefficient, former homeland and sub-provincial structures. The three primary metropolitan areas of the country which produce a disproportionate amount of the GDP are located in Gauteng, the Western Cape and KwaZulu-Natal. Two of these three provinces, moreover, are governed by minority parties – the Inkatha Freedom Party (IFP) in KwaZulu-Natal and the NP in the Western Cape. All other provinces are governed by the majority ANC party. In short, in terms of administrative and economic capacity, party political control of government and public policy, circumstances in the nine provinces vary widely.

The national multi-party negotiations also resulted in a constitutional definition of intergovernmental relations, in particular with regard to powers exercised at the centre and concurrently at provincial, local and central levels. Powers assigned to provincial governments include education, health and welfare, agriculture, housing, local government, and environmental affairs, but are circumscribed by the principle of 'co-operative government'. In effect, therefore, these powers appear to be concurrent rather than devolved. The portfolios of police, land reform, water and forestry are defined as central powers, together with finance, economic affairs, trade and industry, the military, transport, and foreign affairs. Intergovernmental matters are regularly discussed in the National Council of Provinces (Humphries and Meierhenrich, 1996) and via a series of intergovernmental forums, technical committees and ministerial forums which bring together provincial premiers, national and provincial ministers, and their respective civil servants on a regular basis. One of their primary aims is to resolve conflicts between the centre and the provinces as well as between the provinces themselves (Humphries, 1995; Rapoo, 1995).

In May 1996, the new Constitution eliminated the requirement that the party receiving a majority of the national vote after a national election be obliged to form a government-of-national-unity within its cabinet. Consequently, the NP decided to instruct all its national and provincial cabinet members – other than in the Western Cape where it holds power – to resign. The IFP, on the other hand, decided to retain its current ministerial appointments. By mid-1996, except in the

Western Cape, governments-of-unity at national and provincial level no longer existed.

The issue of local government was treated differently by the national negotiating parties in the early 1990s. First, they agreed to postpone the establishment of a new system of local government until after the 1994 general elections. Local government, in fact, appears to have been of minor and belated concern to them. The framework for a new local government system was negotiated in a body (known as the Local Government Negotiating Forum, LGNF) entirely separate from the National Negotiating Forum, the main body. It was only after constitutional negotiations had been completed that this main body addressed the proposals of the LGNF: to establish a transitional local government framework and to translate it into legislation (Christianson, 1994).

Secondly, the national negotiators proposed that local government, constitutionally, should remain a provincial matter and, accordingly, that the new provincial governments – once elected – should be empowered to monitor and supervise the proposed process and timetable of local government transition. This process comprises three phases: (i) the pre-interim phase, which was to begin with the promulgation of the Local Government Transition Act, would involve processes of local negotiations, and would end once local governments were established by popular franchise; (ii) the interim phase – parallel to the period during which the Interim Constitution was in place – which would begin once local governments were established and would end once the 'final' constitution was in place; and (iii) the final phase under the new Constitution (Bekker *et al.*, 1997; Cloete 1995).

Thirdly, local governments would be established in both rural as well as urban areas, and, in the case of metropolitan regions, a two-tier system of metropolitan and sub-metropolitan government would be put in place. Local elections took place late in 1995, except in the cases of KwaZulu-Natal and the metropolitan and rural regions of the Western Cape where conflicts between provincial and central governments could not be resolved in time. After deliberations in the Constitutional Court, local elections were held in these regions in May 1996.

Local governments and their municipalities are responsible for the delivery of locality-bound services. These include potable water and sewerage, electricity and housing delivery, transport in metropolitan areas, refuse removal, and allied services. Service delivery during the apartheid period was characterised by deep fragmentation – caused by the compartmentalisation of South African urban areas into racial group-areas, each with a separate local authority – and pervasive inequality – caused by the highly unequal budgets that these racially separated local authorities were required to administer. The areas of jurisdiction of the newly elected local authorities conform to 'economically and historically bounded' criteria rather than racial ones. Accordingly, all cities, towns and rural areas have been re-defined administratively and, as in the case of the provinces, reflect wide-ranging differences in administrative and economic capacity, party political government and public policy (Bekker *et al.*, 1997; Götz, 1995; Govender, 1996; Johnson, A., 1996; Johnson, R. W., 1996; Seekings, 1995 and 1996). Simultaneously, the local government ministries of the new provinces are on a steep learning curve regarding their local government responsibilities.

Some two years after their establishment, a *White Paper on Local Government* (Republic of South Africa, 1998a) was published. It confirms the national government's intention to decentralise powers within the three spheres of co-operative government and to promote integrated development planning within these spheres (Pycroft, 1998). The chief criticism of this intention relates to the over-optimistic allocation of responsibilities and duties to the third tier, which – in many cases – has neither the administrative nor the financial capacity to undertake sustainable basic service delivery (Special Forum, 1998).

Economic & Financial State Institutions, Particularly Regarding Development & Intergovernmental Relations

In the early 1980s, the apartheid government had recognised the challenge of 'development' in South Africa, a middle-income country experiencing economic stagnation, increasing unemployment and poverty, declining living standards, high population growth, growing basic socio-economic needs, rapid urbanisation and environmentally unsound development patterns. 'Development', accordingly, was conceptualised as the delivery of shelter, infrastructure, services, training and jobs. The government's development policy, however, was intimately connected to apartheid philosophy and suffered both from economically irrational spatial criteria – to support 'separate development' – and from administratively defective and fiscally unsound strategies of implementation – via a series of fragmented racially defined state and parastatal 'development' institutions both within the homelands and outside.

As illustrations, two parastatal development institutions created during the 1980s have been selected: the Development Bank of Southern Africa (DBSA) and the Regional Industrial Development Programme. Both institutions evolved from central government initiatives. The former was established as a banking institution to enable development in the homelands, but rapidly extended its activities to South Africa in general. The latter represented a shift from the earlier 1970s government view of promoting homeland development by stimulating homeland industrial growth and restricting such growth in metropolitan areas. Regional industrial policy in the 1980s was based on more economically rational criteria, which led to the demarcation of the country into nine Development Regions which cut across homeland boundaries. Once these nine Regions had been ranked in accordance with their relative basic needs, central government subsidies were made available to industrialists in designated industrial points within them. The regional ranking played an important role in the allocation of these subsidies. It is significant to note that the boundaries of South Africa's nine new provinces and the boundaries of these nine Development Regions coincide to a high degree.

In short, state development policy in the 1980s, conceptualised and financed by the central government, tended increasingly to address development challenges in terms of socio-economic and rural-urban criteria – market-related criteria – rather than in terms of apartheid criteria. Simultaneously, state development institutions, which rarely enjoyed legitimacy in the eyes of their target communities, tended to deliver development products 'on the ground' rather than sustainable development processes. This shift towards market principles took place within the context of, and was facilitated by, the highly centralised taxation powers of the apartheid central state, which collected about 90% of all tax revenue and about 80% of total revenue (taxes and user charges). The regional authorities (provinces and homelands) themselves collected less than 5% of the total revenue, while local authorities collected 4–5% of the tax revenue, and 30–35% of the non-tax revenue. The central government made more than 90% of the transfers that took place between general government institutions. Regional authorities received almost 70% of the total intergovernmental transfers, and local authorities about 8% (du Pisanie, 1991).

In the new South Africa, this inherited institutional profile has been difficult to change. In the first place, new governments had to be established. The composition and culture of the specialised bureaucracies in the parastatals have proved difficult to replace. Of most importance, the emphasis the new government placed on reconstruction and development – on the RDP as its primary domestic policy initiative – led to over-ambitious short-term goals, which resulted, within eighteen months, in its tacit acknowledgement of institutional failure. Complex as they undoubtedly are, the causes for this failure include the absence of institutional capacity in the RDP office; the failure of the RDP to deliver expected outcomes; populist demands for participative processes of decision-making; and 'an underestimation of the impact of the global economy on South Africa's ability to determine its own development' (Pycroft, 1998: 153). The failure was symbolised by the closure of the RDP office located in the Office of the President, the transfer of its Minister without Portfolio to another ministry, and the effective scrapping of the RDP Fund Act of 1994 which was intended to be the primary instrument for funding integrated reconstruction and development programmes in the country. Currently, the Department of Finance is directly responsible for development finances.

Policy and state institutions addressing the RDP, accordingly, remain work in progress at present. What will be sketched below are themes in current policy debates regarding state development and fiscal initiatives. Institutions identified in this section are all in the process of being established in a new form.

State development funding will be directed by three criteria – fiscal and financial soundness; maximisation of development over time, that is, sustainability; and minimisation of fiscal exposure. Five National Development Finance Institutions (NDFIs), each substantially sector-specific, are being established by reorganising former parastatal development institutions. These are the National Housing Finance Corporation, the Land and Agricultural Bank, the Industrial Development Corporation, a transformed DBSA focused on infrastructural funding, and a finance institution focused on support for small, medium and micro enterprises. A regulatory framework for these institutions is being put in place to ensure that the above policy criteria are met. Three domains of finance for development will be available: government grants for non-cost-recovery welfare activities ('fiscal grants'); market-related funding for development projects based on full cost-recovery ('private capital'), and soft loans made by the government through these national development finance institutions ('development finance'). Though a mix of funds from these domains will be encouraged to finance development projects, separate budgeting and fiscal accountability procedures for funds from each domain are considered essential and will, accordingly, be introduced into policy. Regarding development finance in particular, each NDFI will play a wholesale funding function on the understanding that all government guarantees for such development finance fall away (Republic of South Africa, 1995).

Three aspects of this policy initiative deserve mention. First, it is squarely centralised in conception and in thrust. For example, the following newly established bodies promoting small, medium and micro enterprises are linked to the national Department of Trade and Industry: the Small Business Centre, Ntsika Enterprise Promotion Centre providing non-financial assistance and Khula Enterprise Finance Limited for wholesale loans (Republic of South Africa, 1998b). Secondly, decentralised provincial development institutions have yet to be established – let alone, to function – in this new policy environment. And thirdly, the policy initiative reflects significant central government concern regarding fiscal exposure to rising demands for development funding country-wide, especially since stable fiscal and monetary policies have become a primary requirement for accessing international economic support.

With regard to intergovernmental transfers and fiscal federalism – *inter alia*, the extent to which lower-tier governments are empowered to raise and allocate revenue themselves – the current policy situation is equally fluid. The Constitution has established a new body, the Financial and Fiscal Commission (FFC), the purpose of which is to advise on fiscal transfers and financial arrangements within the system of 'co-operative government'. With regard to centre-provincial financial arrangements, the FFC has negotiated with the provincial governments a formula for annual centre-provincial transfers based on the provincial populations (with a positive rural-weighting factor), and on the ranked basic needs profiles of provinces modelled on the basis of selected socio-economic and welfare indicators. This formula has become the instrument employed to provide a large proportion of central state transfers to the provinces.

With regard to local government, a formula for intergovernmental transfers intended to address backlogs in basic municipal services country-wide was proposed by the FFC in 1997 (Republic of South Africa, 1997). This formula, which combines a capital grant, operating transfers and equalisation components, will be based – for an interim period – on identified backlogs of water and sanitation services in the areas of jurisdiction of each local authority. The FFC has also recommended that an increasing proportion of revenues ought to be raised by the provinces and local governments themselves, thereby avoiding the present situation of ad hoc cuts in central transfers to lower-tier authorities that are typically accompanied by accusations of central government responsibility for retrenchments and cut-backs. Neither intergovernmental transfers to local authorities nor greater powers of taxation for lower-tier authorities had been implemented by 1998.

Institutions Designed to Address the Multicultural Nature of South African Society

Under the NP Government before 1994, the multicultural nature of South African society was concealed by the apartheid state (Bekker, 1993). According to state ideology, South Africans were divided into four races – Black, White, Coloured and Asian – and the Black race in turn was divided into ten 'ethnonational' communities. Politically, these ten communities were on a path of self-determination culminating in sovereign independence. The Republic of South Africa, according to this ideology, was a bilingual – Afrikaans and English – and Christian state in which citizens were obliged to live their lives within one of these state-defined racial and 'ethnonational' domains. The apartheid state was authoritarian and racist and had defined, in effect, for its various subject communities a series of separate nations.

The new South African Government has come to power in a world in which there is far greater awareness of the political force of communal identities (Young, 1994). Simultaneously, the new government has inherited a state that broadcast an authoritarian, racist and multinational ideology which was deeply rejected and resented by a large majority of South Africans. It is within this international and domestic context that the new South African state has launched its dualistic project of nation-building and promoting cultural pluralism. In a highly unequal society with a past of poverty and violence, such a project is formidable, since not only does the spectre of racism in both its overt white and reverse black forms continue to cast shadows across the new state but the need for tolerance, reconciliation and equity is complicated by the politics of identity – exchanges between the nation-building state and citizens in culturally diverse circumstances – particularly since competition for group resources is taking place under circumstances of changing identities (Coughlan and Samarasinghe, 1991).

The nation-building project of the South African state begins with a territorial (rather than ethnonational) definition of the nation. The substance of this nation has been spelled out above – a Bill of Rights, a democratic constitution entrenching the integrity of South African territory, a division of powers between executive, legislative and judicial spheres of government, and a commitment to non-racialism. Beyond these, the South African state has resorted to symbolic action; a new 'rainbow nation' flag, a charismatic President, and various national sporting events have been employed to promote a national identity among its citizens. These citizens, in fact, share neither a common language nor a common religion nor the consciousness of a common history. At present, as reflected in the nation-building project at least, national identity comprises elements of modern democratic constitutionalism together with a number of recently created unifying national symbols. Tolerance and clemency for past state violence and violation of human rights are being pursued through the activities of the Peace and Reconciliation Commission, an organisation committed to uncovering past wrong-doings in a spirit of forgiveness; the slogan 'amnesty, not amnesia' captures its mission.

On the other hand, the institutionalisation of 'respect for the rights of cultural, religious and linguistic communities' (Republic of South Africa, 1996: section 185) is progressing. Eleven national languages have been officially proclaimed and a Pan South African Language Board (LANTAG) was established in 1996. This advisory Board is intended to promote the development and equal use of each official language, as well as multilingualism. In like spirit, religious and cultural practices have been constitutionally safeguarded. A National Arts Council has been established which, in the words of the Deputy-Minister of the responsible national department, will 'ensure that the arts, culture and heritage of all South Africans are, for the first time, protected, promoted and developed ... while ensuring that existing cultural formations are retained and their functions maximised' (Mabandla, 1996).

The multi-cultural dimension of this state project has not, however, been plain sailing for the South African Government. During pre-election multi-party negotiations, a Volkstaat Council was agreed to, in recognition of the threat posed by the Afrikaner separatist parties to demand secession once the new South African state was established. This Council has met on a number of occasions to debate the principle of self-determination under the new constitutional order. Flowing from acrimonious debates between a recalcitrant IFP controlling the provincial government of KwaZulu-Natal and the central government, the status of traditional leadership has been officially recognised and Councils of Traditional Leaders established. Accordingly, the credibility and utility of many of these authorities, particularly in rural areas located within the former homelands, have been constitutionally and financially recognised by the state. The political role they play – with KwaZulu-Natal being the most visible example – has also become apparent to both Government and civil society. Their particular role, and how that role will complement the role of the newly established rural local authorities, is work in progress. Customary law, allied as it is to traditional authority, is currently being tested under the new constitutional system. A division of Traditional Affairs has been established within the central Department of Constitutional Affairs.

With regard to language use and religious instruction and their relationship to state education, moreover, a number of minority political parties are opposing emergent policies. In Gauteng province – the most linguistically diverse province in the country – three minority parties, the NP, the Democratic Party and the Freedom Front, sought to overturn clauses in proposed provincial legislation prohibiting the use of language testing as a basis for admission to provincial schools. Simultaneously, they sought to overturn schoolchildren's rights not to attend religious classes and practices at school. In both cases, the Constitutional Court's unanimous judgement was in favour of the provincial legislation. The Court found that, while every person had the right to establish schools based on common culture, language or religion, it did not follow that the state was obliged to establish such schools (Salgado, 1996).

Four events during 1998 have been selected to illustrate that language in contemporary South Africa cannot be viewed as a simple 'technical' or 'linguistic' issue:

- Dr Neville Alexander, a well-known activist and intellectual who played a significant political role during the 'struggle' years before 1994, was until recently a leading member of LANTAG. Citing the central government's lack of resolution to address the language question as set out in the Constitution, he has recently resigned from the body which he believes is not able to be employed effectively without such resolution.

- During the 1998 central parliamentary session, it was announced that parliamentary proceedings (in Hansard form) would be made available in the future in three languages: English, Afrikaans and one other. This decision follows a *de facto* unilingual (English-language) policy over the previous two years.

- South African Airways, under new management, also introduced more than one language – Afrikaans in particular – on a number of their domestic flights, also a change from a controversial unilingual (English-language) policy applied domestically over the past few years.

- Finally, ensuing from the insistence of Afrikaner separatist minority parties, the new Constitution has institutionalised a Commission for the Promotion and Protection of the Rights of Cultural, Religious and Linguistic Communities, which is empowered to establish or recognise cultural councils for different South African communities (Republic of South Africa, 1996: section 185). While avoiding the politically unacceptable notions of group or minority rights, this new constitutional principle does appear to introduce a 'community' rights balance to individual rights entrenched in the Bill of Rights. The Commission has yet to put this constitutional provision into practice by the establishment of such councils.

Conclusion

The three brief surveys of state institutional change presented above do not claim to be exhaustive. In South Africa at present, policing and prosecution services, economic affairs, education, land reform and agriculture – to list but a few – are state sectors experiencing ongoing policy and institutional change. The three state domains selected, however, are revealing, not only because each is important in its own right but also because they illustrate differences in both the nature and pace of state institutional change.

The instruments of formal democratic government are in place in the country. Forged through multi-party negotiations and informed by Western and Commonwealth models, these institutions are now in daily use and accordingly are taking root in the political activities of governments and their civil societies. Their establishment reflects the South African miracle, their maturation the political test now facing the state. The NP's decision, in 1996, to quit all governments-of-unity in which it was represented as a minority party illustrates this shift from living the miracle to moving beyond it. Secondly, fiscal and financial institutions that the state requires to pursue its primary policy objective – the RDP – as well as effective government at lower tiers, are emerging slowly and with distinct difficulty. Over-ambitious commitment to domestic development reveals the dilemmas the state is experiencing in pursuing state restructuring and state delivery simultaneously, whilst attempting to minimise fiscal exposure. In the third place, the state challenge of managing the politics of identity that has appeared in post-apartheid democratic South Africa, is manifest. There are few tested comparative models in this domain and the basic question regarding whether South African society ought to remain culturally diverse in the long term or only during a transitory period has yet to addressed, if indeed the state is able to address it.

11

OLATUNDE B.J. OJO
Integration in ECOWAS
Successes & Difficulties

The Economic Community of West African States (ECOWAS), founded in May 1975 but effectively operational in 1978, covers the 16 West African states. Its main objective was the acceleration of the economic co-operation and development of its members and of the sub-region as a whole (ECOWAS, 1976a: Article 2). As originally envisaged, during the first two years members were to freeze their tariffs on unprocessed goods or handicraft products and on industrial products which met the definition of originating from within the Community. During the next eight years, members were to eliminate among themselves import and export duties, non-tariff barriers, and taxes of equivalent effect. The free trade area thus created would proceed over the next five years to a customs union in which members were to adopt a common external tariff and a common trade policy vis-à-vis third countries (ibid.: Articles 13 and 14). Full common market status would be achieved during this phase by the removal of all obstacles to the free movement of persons, services and capital, while implementing the right of residence and establishment (CEDEAO, 1979: 3–5). The final stage of economic union was then to follow with the adoption of common macroeconomic and socio-cultural policies, including common investment codes. As the ECOWAS is now more than twenty years old, it is pertinent to ask: what are its achievements? What are its problems? What are its prospects?[1]

Achievements

Strictly in terms of market integration objectives, ECOWAS has achieved relatively little. However, its achievements should not be assessed solely in terms of market integration, given its broader developmental goals. Axline (1980) has suggested broader evaluative criteria which we shall successively utilise.

[1] I am grateful to Monsieur Boubacar Ba, Deputy Executive Secretary (Economic Affairs) of the ECOWAS for supplying recent information on the Community. The views expressed in this chapter remain strictly mine.

The Executive Secretariat has been the main source of ideas and proposals for policies and projects as well as the engine of their implementation at the institutional level. Recent illustrations include:

- By 1997, the agreement on some 450 industrial items produced by more than 150 industrial companies established in 11 member states. In accordance with Community regulations on the rules of origin, these products are eligible for the trade liberalisation scheme;

- The Secretariat's sensitisation missions to the member states, its campaign for a deepening of the integration process instead of a broadening into new areas, and its relentless push for an enabling environment, all of which paved the way for the revision of the ECOWAS treaty adopted by the Heads of State and Government summit of July 1993 in Cotonou.

- The formation of the ECOWAS Monitoring Group (ECOMOG) and its contribution to conflict resolution in the Liberian and Sierra Leone crises (Prkic, 1995: 163–80).

To provide visible and tangible developmental benefits the Secretariat early on pushed for the 'integration of production', entailing the laying of the necessary foundations, including creating a regional infrastructure and ensuring progress toward self-sufficiency in agriculture and adequacy in energy supply. Of the priority projects earmarked for member states' action, the first telecommunications programme (INTELCOM I) was officially completed in 1995, with the automatic interconnection of the capitals of the 16 member states. In August 1997, a second programme (INTELCOM II) was adopted at a cost of about US$ 100 million.

Meanwhile, the three trans-regional highways projects have also made substantial progress. By mid-1997, the trans-sahelian highway, running from Dakar to Ndjamena (2,790 miles), was 87% completed, while 83% of the coastal route between Lagos and Nouakchott (2,850 miles) was tarred. This was also the case for 70% of the highways (4,876 miles) due to connect the trans-sahelian and trans-coastal routes.

Some progress has also been made in respect of self-sufficiency in agriculture and energy. Several pre-feasibility and feasibility studies and workshops have been conducted, with an emphasis on agro-industries. Since 1990 at least 11 states have each received $50,000 under a subvention scheme to purchase equipment, develop improved seeds and train local technicians in seed development technology. Several Community Seed Production and Cattle Development Centres have also been selected for the production and popularisation of selected species (ECOWAS, 1994: 51–2).

ECOWAS also embarked on village and pastoral water schemes involving 200 water points per member state, focusing first on the 10 Sahelian states (ECOWAS, 1994: 53). By late 1996, five of them had secured financial support for their projects. ECOWAS, with the help of a $3.1 million non-refundable grant from the African Development Bank (ADB), was also able to commission a study of the best scientific method to control the floating weeds menace that has caused declines in riverine fishing and untold difficulties in the navigation of the lagoon systems in Benin, Côte d'Ivoire, Ghana and Nigeria (*ibid.*: 54). The study, completed in October 1995, was followed by the identification of six projects to promote biological, mechanical and chemical control. Support was subsequently secured from donors at a conference held in Abidjan in March 1997.

Lessons learnt from the failure of the Community's first industrial development programme (1987–91) have influenced the new regional industrial master plan adopted in 1994. Formally adopted by the Heads of State and Government in November 1996, the new programme should enable the Community to establish an industrial data bank as well as to plan realistically for industrial co-operation, including identification of possible regional industrial enterprises that the organisation could embark upon or help promote. The creation of three trans-frontier industrial areas has been earmarked and funding is currently being sought.

The Fund for Co-operation, Compensation and Development (FCCD) is the main instrument for ensuring equitable distribution of costs and benefits among member states. The Fund is also expected to mobilise resources towards integrating development projects in the member states (Okolo, 1985: 145; Davies, 1983: 174). In 1990, for the first time, FCCD made available the sum of $350,000 as compensation for loss of revenue arising from trade liberalisation. In addition to this kind of compensatory payment, the ECOWAS Treaty (ECOWAS, 1976a: Articles 25, 26 and 52) and the Protocol on Assessment of Loss of Revenue by Member States (ECOWAS, 1976b: Article 2) specifically enjoin the organisation to promote projects in the less developed countries. In this respect, the role of the Fund has been particularly significant in the field of infrastructure, transport and telecommunications. Early beneficiaries included Benin (which received a loan of $3.745 million for the construction of two bridges on the Mono and Sazue rivers) and Liberia (which was granted $365,221 for feasibility studies of the Tappita Tobli-Blay trunk road). Seven member states also received $12.5 million for partial financing of their telecommunication programmes.

Problem Areas

The major problem affecting integration in the ECOWAS is the members' failure to implement fully and faithfully the numerous protocols and decisions of the organisation. We shall now examine the causes and the major areas of deadlock.

The first and second phases of the trade liberalisation scheme were postponed due to institution-building; this involved the adoption of common regulations, the harmonisation of customs nomenclature, and the establishment of common terms for road transport, etc. Yet, later on trade liberalisation continued to stall. One reason is the reluctance of the member states to liberalise trade because of IMF/World Bank-imposed structural adjustment programmes (SAPs) and their effect on industry (Cornia, 1991). Many industries have closed down. Capacity utilisation for those remaining in business has dropped to between 25 and 40% for lack of inputs, spare parts and effective demand. Excess capacity has raised costs by as much as 80%, while currency devaluation, at least in the Anglophone states, further inflated the local currency costs of production and intensified liquidity problems. Imports declined generally by 6% a year between 1980 and 1987, but official imports from within the region were even worse affected (Moseley, 1992: 11–12). In these circumstances, governments, already losing revenue from the SAP-imposed liberalisation of external trade, have been in no mood to implement free trade further even at the regional level, although little revenue loss occurs at that level as the paltry sum of $350,000 allocated for compensation in 1990, and the fact that it had no takers, make evident.[2]

The second and more important reason for the stalling of the ECOWAS liberalisation scheme arises from the rules of origin provision of the Treaty. The provision had been intended to ensure preferential treatment for products from businesses owned primarily by West Africans. However, Nigeria and Ghana, which had indigenised major foreign-owned companies for the purpose, succeeded in pushing for a set of exclusion criteria which have caused problems. Ostensibly aimed at undermining French-owned firms which dominated the Francophone countries, the criteria effectively excluded Côte d'Ivoire and Senegal. But Côte d'Ivoire is the dominant trading partner in the West African sub-region, mainly within the rival CEAO/UEMOA where trade liberalisation has advanced considerably. Unwilling to lose this advantage, Côte d'Ivoire (along with the other CEAO/UEMOA members) resisted phasing the Francophone community into the larger ECOWAS. This has resulted in a deadlock. The CEAO member states have also refused to reduce their tariffs on goods from the other ECOWAS states unless the latter first do the same, whilst the other ECOWAS members insisted on the precise opposite.

The consequence goes beyond mere stalling of the trade liberalisation scheme. The exclusion of the foreign-owned firms which produce most of the region's prime goods in effect created an artificial scarcity. This has provided incentives for massive unofficial trans-border trade in Francophone manufactured products and in re-export of overseas goods imported with the overvalued CFA franc, until it was devalued in January 1994. At the same time, steep devaluations in Nigeria and Ghana subjected the Francophone states to reverse flows of 'Anglophone' products, especially textiles, footwear, cosmetics, detergents, plastics and other petroleum products (Moseley, 1992: 14, 19; ECOWAS, 1979b: 9). Unofficial cross-border transactions were preferred by a host of small-scale to medium distributors and manufacturers now in competition with the traditional women petty traders, the so-called 'market mammies' and 'Nana benz'. Considerations of sheer convenience, the even cheaper black market rates, and substantial assistance by corrupt officials, many of whom have vested interests in smuggling (Adibe, 1994: 210–12; Bach, 1983: 109), made this almost inevitable.

---

[2] The amount was particularly small because official pre-liberalisation trade, the base from which to calculate losses, constituted a small fraction (4–5%) of total foreign trade and an insignificant source of government revenue.

Monetary union has equally been unable to progress significantly. Like the ex-CEAO with respect to trade liberalisation, the West African Monetary Union (UMOA), based on a long-standing, pre-independence Francophone monetary union with a central bank, a common currency, and harmonised credit policies, is pitched against ECOWAS on the latter's Monetary Co-operation Programme. Adopted in 1987 to solve the problems posed to intra-regional transactions by the multiplicity of inconvertible currencies, the ECOWAS programme suggested reforms that should have led to a single monetary zone by the year 2000. In spite of this, however, the Francophone West African States expanded their existing monetary integration arrangement into an Economic and Monetary Union (UEMOA) which superseded both CEAO and UMOA in January 1994. Part of the reason is the continuing fear of Nigerian domination of ECOWAS. The other element is the uncertainty about the prospects of the ECOWAS programmes. For one thing, its interim or transitional institution, the West African Clearing House (WACH), has fared poorly. During the 1990–92 period, its operations declined sharply from 223.3 million West African Units of Account (UA) to between 14.9 and 17.67 million (Momoh, 1991; Cole, 1993). The WACH was also beset by a backlog of arrears in settlement payments which the debtor banks have failed to honour. Not surprisingly, the ratification of the July 1993 protocol transforming WACH into a specialised agency of the Community, the West African Monetary Agency (WAMA), went through a slow process, thus scuttling the intention that it be operational as from January 1994 (ECOWAS, 1994: 44–5). Although the statutes of the WAMA were eventually signed in Banjul on 8 March 1996, the transformation of the WACH was further delayed because of financial considerations (arrears owed by two central banks) and political problems (the crisis in Sierra Leone).

Labour and Rights of Establishment has been another problem area for ECOWAS. Pursuant to the wish that citizens of the member states be regarded as Community citizens with freedom to move, reside and engage in commercial and industrial activities within each others' territories, the Authority adopted a protocol on the Free Movement of Persons, Right of Residence and Establishment in 1979. This did no more than abolish visa requirements for citizens intending to stay for a maximum of ninety days in another member state. The more crucial matter of residence and establishment was to be decided in the light of the effect of this experiment in its first five years. Unfortunately, the Ghanaian closure of its borders in September 1982 and Nigeria's expulsion of an estimated 2 million 'illegal aliens' (mostly Ghanaians) in 1983 created a crisis of confidence (Okolo, 1985: 143–4; Asante, 1986: 154–62). The worsening economic crisis which precipitated these actions soon led to the ubiquitous SAPs and attendant closures of industries and privatisation of parastatals. General streamlining of personnel in the public sector resulted in mass retrenchments. In the circumstances, although a protocol on the right to residence and establishment was signed in 1986, few states ratified it and the matter now appears to be in abeyance.

The failure of some ECOWAS members to meet their financial obligations is a long-standing problem that has worsened under the impact of structural adjustment. By the end of 1993 the accumulation of arrears of member state contributions to finance the Secretariat amounted to $31.69 million. Complaints about the equity of the existing co-efficient of member contributions, given the changes in their economic fortunes, led to proposals for a review. Despite initial reservations by Mauritania and Cape Verde, a new formula was adopted by the Heads of State and Government at the end of July 1994.

In the light of the foregoing problems the ECOWAS Treaty has been reviewed in the hope of securing a better future for the Community. The revised treaty specifically tackles the problems of failure to implement decisions of the organisation and to meet financial obligations towards it. On the first issue it offered a two-pronged indirect solution. First, it sought to create interest and pressure groups supportive of ECOWAS.[3] The new Treaty also established the principle of a West African Parliament that would take binding decisions without the need for prior ratification. A follow-up enabling protocol was ready for adoption by 1994. In addition, the Authority took a more direct line on rationalising sub-regional organisations to put an end to the frictions and conflicts of interest between the ECOWAS and its CEAO or UMOA members. Strengthened by the African Economic Community's call for the creation of a single sub-regional integration scheme, in 1991, the Authority directed that an independent study be commissioned to propose a pragmatic and flexible rationalisation plan. This was completed in July 1994, but its recommendations did not take into account the recent establishment of UEMOA. Revisions were therefore requested from the consultant who took over three years to make them available to the ECOWAS Secretariat.

The revised Treaty also sought a solution to the perennial problem of non-payment of financial dues by providing that ECOWAS institute a Community levy. Details were embodied in a proposed protocol to be considered by the Council of Ministers. Meanwhile the Chairman of the Authority was mandated to persuade Mauritania and Cape Verde to reconsider their position so that a revised coefficient of members' contributions to the organisation might be adopted (ECOWAS, 1994: 38–9). Finally, the revised Treaty reiterated the commitment of the Community as well as the obligation of its members to ensure the removal of obstacles to the free movements of persons, goods, services and capital, and to the right of residence and establishment.

There can be no doubt that the new Treaty was an improvement on the old. Yet, as subsequent developments have shown, the problem of building regional integration within the ECOWAS lay not with the adequacy or inadequacy of treaty provisions but with their implementation. And this, the new Treaty has not been able to guarantee on its own.

[3] 'Highlights of the (New) Treaty', *West Africa*, 19–25 July 1993: 1248; ECOWAS, 1994: 43.

12

MARC-LOUIS ROPIVIA
Failing Institutions & Shattered Space
What Regional Integration in Central Africa?

Africa was still reviewing the disastrous achievements of most of its regional institutions when its most highly placed leaders gleefully advocated at Abuja, in June 1991, the construction of an ambitious pan-African Economic Community by 2035 (OUA, 1991).

There is little doubt that the twenty-first century will be the era of the construction of new regional entities, but how can such an important communitarian enterprise be envisaged in Africa at a time when the evils undermining its development are becoming more prominent? (de Rochebrune, 1994). How can African leaders succeed in establishing at the continental level what they have failed to promote within smaller regions and sub-regions? More specifically, how can Central Africa subscribe to this prospective vision of Africa in 2035, given the deliquescent character of its three major regional institutions: the *Union Douanière des Etats de l'Afrique Centrale* (UDEAC), the *Communauté Economique des Etats de l'Afrique Centrale* (CEEAC), and the *Communauté Economique des Pays des Grands Lacs* (CEPGL)?

Regional integration did not originate in sub-Saharan Africa from an endogenous philosophy, but from an extraneous conception, of which the European Community (EC) was the principal source of inspiration. Nor did regional integration proceed from an internal will shared by all actors; it was decreed, hence its lamentable failure in Central Africa (Ropivia, 1994).

The impetus for a regional integration process in post-colonial sub-Saharan Africa was closely associated with the 1957 Rome Treaty. During the negotiations for the treaty, France successfully secured that its African interests be taken into account. Accordingly, Title IV of the Treaty and, from 1964 onwards, the Yaoundé Convention laid the groundwork for a Euro-African association between the European Community and the 18 African and Malagasy Associated States (EAMA). The UDEAC, also born in 1964, was equally influenced by this philosophy of 'Eurafrique'. Although the genesis of the integration idea in Central Africa went back to the pre-independence period (Dreux-Brézé, 1968), the concept meant little more than that France, its principal architect, was trying to find a formula to reorganise its former Central

African colonies into the grouping that would be most suitable to its own interests. The EAMA associative response was the manifestation of an institutional paternalism that rested on the fundamental idea of indissoluble linkages between a dominant Europe and a dominated Africa. This had the effect of limiting the capacity of African states to define their own autonomous integration strategy.

The subsequent phase of regional integration was marked by the transformation of African regional institutions into subsidiary organisations. Initially, this corresponded to the immediate implementation of European suggestions by African ruling elites: 1973 marked a landmark in this respect, with the enlargement of the EC to include Great Britain and Ireland. A West African response to this was the formation of the Economic Community of West African States (ECOWAS) in 1975. The grouping gathered together the member states of the Francophone *Communauté Economique d'Afrique de l'Ouest* (CEAO), created in 1973, and Britain's former West African colonies. In Central Africa, the emergence of the CEEAC equally reflected the subsidiary nature of African regionalism: the establishment of the CEEAC, in 1985, resulted from the addition of portions of the former colonial empires of France (UDEAC) and Belgium (Zaïre, Rwanda and Burundi), as well as Spain (Equatorial Guinea) and Portugal (Angola and Sao Tomé & Principe) whose forthcoming entry into the EC had been announced. Here again, the EC enlargement corresponded, in sub-Saharan Africa, to the concomitant creation of a new regional organisation, designed to include the former colonies of the European powers now being admitted into the European Community.

Since then, instability and insecurity have emerged as the greatest impediments to regional integration in Central Africa: due not only to the existence of military bases in the vicinity of inter-state borders, but also to chaotic internal political situations or explicit civil wars, as in ex-Zaïre, Congo-Brazzaville, Rwanda and Angola. The fear of a few states' contagious warmongering also hindered the desire to construct a common political and economic space. An awareness of peace and security problems was manifest in the sub-region in the early 1990s. In September 1993, a permanent consultative committee on issues of security in Central Africa held a meeting under the aegis of CEEAC in Libreville; its recommendations included the creation by all member states of specialised units trained for crisis management and the adoption of a non-aggression pact. Unfortunately, these projects subsequently remained on paper only.

Among the centrifugal forces that threaten to disintegrate Central Africa, the impossibility of reconciling the different sub-groupings within the CEEAC figures most prominently. While displaying greater coherence, the UDEAC area has, nevertheless, been undermined by severe dysfunctions and disarticulation problems that have progressively emptied the group of much of its content.

The fiscal and customs reform of the UDEAC (see Chapter 13 in this volume) raises a number of questions with regard to the effects of the deregulatory measures which are involved. What complementarity is there between the Central African economies? These are, for the most part, specialised in the export of primary goods and semi-finished products. They also have a very weak manufacturing sector. The only possible exception is Cameroon. This country may as a result become the new core-state of Central Africa and will feed the vast markets of ex-Zaïre and Angola, as well as the much smaller ones of Gabon, Congo, Equatorial Guinea, and the Central African Republic.

What this implies is not the development of exchange in the sense of reciprocal trade flows, but rather the establishment of unidimensional economic relations between the few countries able to export and the majority of the other member states. As a result, new centres and peripheries will emerge. Under these conditions, the chances are that there will be no sub-regional integration, but disintegration and the accentuation of the already profound disequilibrium between member states. The fiscal and customs reform of the UDEAC should not be considered as a panacea. In effect, it was severely criticised by the employers' organisations in Cameroon, Congo, and Gabon. Reforms cannot be expected magically to intensify intra-regional official trade, which remains almost non-existent, nor will they be able rapidly to modify the structures and orientation of anachronistic national economies. If market integration should aggravate rather than improve the situation, one may ask whether it would not be better to return to a voluntarist approach based on the co-ordination and harmonisation of national development policies. Industrial or sectoral specialisation could then promote the complementarity of economies and stimulate intra-regional trade.

Discussions on the possible effects of the UDEAC reform were still going on when the Heads of State met in Ndjamena on 16 March 1994 and decided to create the Communauté Economique et Monétaire d'Afrique Centrale (CEMAC). One could wonder about the purpose of this new organisation since the UDEAC has failed to achieve what were after all similar objectives. Since then, CEMAC has become yet another episode in the unending quest for regional integration in Central Africa. It also seems highly unrealistic to expect regional integration to be promoted in Central Africa without including ex-Zaïre and Angola in the existing institutions.

To have any chance of success, 'regional integration presupposes that three conditions be met: real political will, comparable levels of development and important intra-regional trade, facilitated by a relatively dense and organised system of communication' (Moundoumba, 1992). In Central Africa, regional institutions have not worked towards achieving these conditions. The integration process is in a phase of involution and it is certainly not the CEMAC that has reversed the trend. The Central African sub-region remains *par excellence* an area of spatial discontinuities and territorial segmentation. The distances are multiplied by underpopulation and dense forests; communications are poor, telecommunication networks are barely interconnected (Verlaque, 1993). Inter-state boundaries remain an obstacle to the mobility of people, capital, and merchandise. All these ills do not favour regional integration; on the contrary, they amplify the segmentation of the economic space. The Central African elites should become aware of the urgency and necessity to rebuild regionalism. Otherwise the sub-region will be condemned to being little more than a playground for the projection of power politics.

13

ROLAND POURTIER
The Renovation of UDEAC
Sense & Nonsense in Central African Integration

Attempts to revive the *Union Douanière des Etats d'Afrique Centrale* (UDEAC) emerged in extremely paradoxical terms. After three decades of a moribund existence, doctors reassembled around its bedside in the early 1990s. Unexpectedly, this was not to address the fact of its death, but instead to give it a new lease of life at a time when the virtues of integration were being rediscovered worldwide. In order to get out of their crises, should not the states of Africa, once victims of partitioning, segmentation and 'balkanisation', quickly regroup, unite, and integrate? But then another question arises: Why has regional integration in Central Africa lost so much ground since the UDEAC was created in 1964? This question quite naturally raises others: Has the revival of policies towards integration any chance whatsoever of achieving their goals? Are conditions more favourable today than in the years immediately after independence?

Nothing is less evident. In effect, recent history has shown that cases of successful economic integration have progressed along with economic growth. Yet, for the past two decades, the economic marginalisation of sub-Saharan Africa has become more accentuated with each passing year. National or regional policies prevail over outward-looking strategies, while the crises encourage short-term visions and territorial confinement.

Far from having been initiated by the member states themselves, projects aimed at reforming the UDEAC resulted from initiatives taken by two external sources: the World Bank, and the French Ministry of Co-operation. Admittedly, African Heads of State affirmed their willingness to promote pan-African economic integration at the Abuja summit in July 1991, but this did not go beyond the stage of a general declaration of intent. It was the French Co-operation Ministry which mobilised and brought forward a series of reforms aimed at promoting regional integration. Its action was then endorsed by the Libreville meeting of UDEAC Heads of State in December 1991. This project, instigated from 'above' by extra-African actors, had yet to be 'internalised'.

Prospects for this internalisation developed under truly inauspicious circumstances: the political tensions affecting most of the states were compounded by the destabilising effects of a devaluation whose social consequences have only just begun to emerge. The shock of the devaluation of January 1994 shook an edifice that was already full of cracks. It is uncertain whether or not this edifice can withstand the shock, as the countries of the Franc Zone have expressed divergent views on the change of parity of a currency which has generally been recognised as the significant trump card in the construction of regional integration. The political and social environment does not really call for sober reflection on integration: the states' priority at this time is survival, and not their coming together.

But states are only one group of actors among many. As they pass through the greatest crisis in their short history, other regional dynamics are developing with other actors. These dynamics come from 'below' and are generative of cross-border networks. They thus tend to superimpose a new geography on that of the states. Hence, they participate in their own way in the integration process, whose ambivalence they reveal.

The realities of trans-state regionalism (Chapter 1 of this volume) based on commercial networks stand in opposition to institutional integration. The declared policies of renovating the UDEAC cannot make an abstraction of those socio-economic forces which are usually categorised as 'informal' for want of proper conceptual tools to grasp them in their full manifestation. The effects of the envisaged reforms would be singularly limited if a large section of the real economy is not included. An analysis of UDEAC renovation therefore implies reckoning with all the actors capable of contributing to the recomposition – or decomposition – of a Central African region, whose configuration is directly inherited from metropolitan France.

The UDEAC as a Colonial Heritage

The UDEAC was instituted by the Brazzaville Treaty of 8 December 1964; it initially comprised the four states born of the *Afrique Equatoriale Française* (AEF) Federation as well as Cameroon. Equatorial Guinea was physically surrounded by this grouping and joined it in 1983, before being integrated into the Franc Zone. The constituent territories of the UDEAC gather together 25 million inhabitants over 3 million square kilometres. They share no other uniting attribute apart from having been colonised by France, with the exception of tiny ex-Spanish Guinea. The creation of the UDEAC was designed to compensate for inconveniences caused by the break-up of the AEF's federal structures and the failure of the *Union des Républiques d'Afriques Centrale* (URAC), a tentative regrouping of the ex-AEF countries suggested at the time of their accession to independence. The UDEAC was expected to maintain a vast ensemble of contiguous Francophone territories in the centre of the continent with privileged connections to their former metropole; in this respect, it represented only one of the possibilities for regional regroupings in Central Africa. This quickly turned out to be fictional as the newly independent member states gave priority to national unity: the embryonic bourgeoisie that was emerging politically preferred to construct its identity within the individual ex-colonial territories. These were more easily controllable than a geographical entity which was extensive, extremely diverse and poorly articulated; only the colonial administration had been able to handle it (Pourtier, 1994).

The UDEAC experienced numerous problems due to its lack of unity and the all too fragile memory of a brief colonial history. In 1968, the two poorest partners, Chad and the Central African Republic (CAR), feeling that the Union was not of benefit to them, left it to join Zaïre in the ephemeral *Union des Etats d'Afrique Centrale* (UEAC). The CAR returned to the bosom after a few months of infidelity, but Chad stayed away from the UDEAC until 1984. This was no accident; Chad has hardly any affinity with the rest of the zone. This results from an ecological frontier which also carries historical, cultural and religious dimensions: the Chadian territory belongs essentially to the Sahara-Sahelian area, except for the country's southern areas, located between the Chari and Logone rivers. Chad's sole attachment with UDEAC results from its enclave position which makes Douala, and eventually Pointe-Noire, its maritime outlet; but Lagos could also fill this function.

Territorial proximity and cultural kinship naturally drew Zaïre into the problematics of integration in Central Africa. Even though the country has been for more than a decade the sick man of the continent (Pourtier, 1992), we cannot gloss over this giant with 40 million inhabitants on the south-eastern flank of the UDEAC (see Chapter 8 of this volume). Moreover, ex-president Mobutu never hid his ambition to lead Francophone Central Africa. In 1981, the creation of the *Communauté Economique des Etats d'Afrique Centrale* (CEEAC)[1] in Libreville heralded a reconciliation between the UDEAC countries and Zaïre. The CEEAC represented a market of 70 million inhabitants spread over a surface area of 5.4 million square kilometres, but it was to remain stillborn. Interestingly, this move brought to the fore the ideals of regional regrouping advocated by Barthélémy Boganda in the late 1950s, at a time when the collapse of the AEF had become predictable. At that time the idea was to constitute an enlarged Central Africa around the nucleus inherited from the French empire, so as to include the former Belgian Congo, Burundi and Rwanda as well as Angola. This project of forming the 'United States of Latin Africa', was expected to counterbalance the influence of the neighbouring Anglophone countries. The creation in 1992 of a permanent consultative committee for questions of security in Central Africa, regrouping member states of the CEEAC and Angola; and the signing of a treaty of non-aggression on 3 September 1993 at Libreville, could have given a semblance of reality to this regional ensemble. Unfortunately, this treaty has never come into existence, as the wars in Rwanda, the DRC and Congo-Brazzaville, as well as the difficulties of installing a lasting peace in Angola, have demonstrated (Pourtier, 1997).

The composite legacy of colonisation is evidenced in the interlocking of the UDEAC, the *Communauté Economique des Pays des Grands Lacs* (GEPGL) and the CEEAC. The scale of these integration schemes is a crucial issue, since extension and deepening are often mutually exclusive.

---

[1] The CEEAC includes the UDEAC states, Sao Tomé & Principe and the *Communauté Economique des Pays des Grands Lacs* (CEPGL) – Burundi, Rwanda and the DRC.

The Challenge of Integration

Nearly four decades after independence, the outcome of integration programmes presents no ambiguity: national policies have nipped all regional co-operation initiatives in the bud. Dispositions in the treaties which instituted and amended the UDEAC were progressively emptied of their substance. The discourse on the necessity of regrouping lived on, but the dynamics of separation kept distending the economic and institutional linkages among states which were very protective of their young sovereignty. Was this the infantile sickness of independence? What was at stake may also have been the need to consolidate first the national states – a more appropriate expression than that of nation-state, which does not apply to any Central African state. The 'rich' territories were also unwilling to share – a situation that allowed the former president of Gabon, Léon Mba, to proclaim on 28 June 1958: 'Before speaking of federation, confederation or unitary state, let us wait until each of our states has proven its capacities within its own territory'.

The consolidation of individual states was effectively given priority for political action and this worked to the detriment of communal enterprises of a broader character. Subsequently, the states of Central Africa positioned themselves in a competitive rather than a complementary mode. In the area of higher education, for example, the *Fédération de l'Enseignement Supérieur en Afrique Centrale* (FESAC) did not resist the will of its member states to create their own establishments. The economic sector offers numerous comparable illustrations in such areas as petroleum refining, solid fats or sugar production. As for transportation infrastructures, these were conceived and implemented in the framework of the states' own territorial spaces, and not as a means of reinforcing regional integration: territorial planning was deliberately put to the service of state building. The most glaring example of this is the Trans-Gabonese railway which brought an end to the most important flow of cross-border exchange between member states of the UDEAC: since the autumn of 1991, Point-Noire is no longer the *de facto* south-eastern port of Gabon,[2] as manganese ore from the Haut-Ogooué region is all being exported through Owendo. As a result, the famous 'trans-equatorial' route linking Central Africa to the Atlantic via the Congo-Oubangui railway has become nothing more than a memory.

Years of 'disintegrative' policies have followed the end of colonialism and its federal structures. The Francophone Central African states deliberately loosened these ties, despite maintaining a common currency; the *Banque des Etats d'Afrique Centrale* (BEAC) was not an instrument of regional action. The dynamics of withdrawal responded to geographical, historical and sociological factors as well as local geopolitical forces. They also satisfied the former metropolitan power, France, whose position in this respect was somewhat ambiguous. Division is, on the whole, favourable to the maintenance of situations of domination and privilege.

[2] A grave accident on the *Congo-Ocean* railroad provided a pretext for COMILOG to accelerate the closure of its transport installation between Mbinda and Pointe-Noire.

African countries and their foreign partners, principally France, the World Bank, and the IMF, were all satisfied with a situation of non-integration. By the end of the 1980s, they were heading for an outright closure of the General Secretariat of the UDEAC whose uselessness had become obvious. The disappearance of this ghost institution would have gone unnoticed except in Bangui. The move would have endorsed the insignificance of its achievements; trade relations represented only 6% of the foreign trade of UDEAC countries.

Contrary to all expectations, high-level conferences multiplied from 1991 onwards. This reflected an effort to get the integration of the UDEAC back on track, and in so doing, bring a breath of fresh air to moribund economies. For that is really what we are talking about here: a vast enterprise to salvage bankrupt countries which structural adjustment programmes (SAPs) had failed to keep afloat. It seems as if integration policies were expected to take over from these failed macroeconomic programmes: 'Integration appears to be one of the strategic options. In the context of the crisis which the sub-continent is undergoing', observed Coussy and Hugon (1991). Edgar Pisani's famous formula, 'Africa will be regional, or it will not be at all', was revived and supported (Schulders, 1990).

A Voluntarist Approach to Integration

The reform of the UDEAC was initiated by the World Bank. In November 1989, the Bank came to an agreement with the Union's Secretary General on a Regional Reform Programme (RRP) which included four components: fiscal and tariff reforms, financial policy, transport and transit (see Chapter 3 of this volume). The impetus for reform came from Washington, but the French Ministry of Co-operation soon embraced the idea and took an active part in its implementation. It did not want an initiative that concerned one of its traditional zones of influence to fall solely into the hands of the Bretton Woods institutions. Initially the French position differed strongly from that of the IMF on one essential point: the usefulness of devaluing the CFA franc. As a result, reform programmes were prepared and adopted under the assumption that no change of parity would occur. It was only after signing the Bangui accords in May–June 1993 that events unfolded rapidly, culminating in the seismic devaluation of January 1994.

The fiscal and tariff aspects of the RRP were the only components which carried truly regional stakes for Central Africa. Most of the discussions bordered on these issue areas, since the reforms were due to undermine a number of established advantages. Over the years, the UDEAC had ended up being emptied of its substance by successive derogations and ad hoc agreements. The blind implementation of economic liberalism, however, carried certain risks: it could lead, for example, to the rapid disappearance of the whole of Gabon's agro-industrial sector. Not surprisingly, therefore, Gabon was highly obstructive during the negotiations on the reform and eventually decided to postpone its implementation from July 1994 until January 1995. Three years after the implementation of the fiscal and customs reforms, their impact remains difficult to assess. The wars in the DRC and Congo-Brazzaville (Pourtier, 1998), the uncertainties concerning the future of the CAR, tensions in Cameroon and instability in Chad mobilise attention towards other fronts. Regional integration policies cannot be a priority in a context dominated by violence and insecurity.

The reformed customs and fiscal policies were meant to introduce greater transparency while improving the collection of fiscal revenues. The programme adopted by the Steering Committee of the UDEAC on 21 June 1993 involved: the restoration of a common external tariff based on four rates (from 5% for basic necessities to 50% for luxury products); a regional preference for locally produced goods and a tax on the companies' turnover. Pre-existing arrangements which discouraged competition within the UDEAC were due to disappear within two years. The petroleum and mining sectors which are of considerable importance to the economies of most UDEAC states were not included in the reform.

Another component of the RRP was the *Transit Inter-Etats des Pays de l'Afrique Centrale* (TIPAC), a programme for the establishment of a regional scheme for the transportation and transit of goods. The guidelines were adopted by the UDEAC Heads of State in December 1991. The ultimate goal of the programme was to contribute to regional integration by rationalising transport policies in Central Africa. Its implementation, supported by the World Bank, France, and the European Union, has been severely hampered by political instability in the sub-region.

The transformation of UDEAC into a truly economic and monetary integration community was prepared in conjunction with the *Banque des Etats d'Afrique Centrale* (BEAC) and discussed by the UDEAC Heads of State in December 1992. Two treaties were drafted to cover the monetary and economic aspects of regional integration. The treaty on the *Union Monétaire de l'Afrique Centrale* (UMAC) was to promote among the member states of BEAC the convergence of macroeconomic policies and the reinforcement of financial and monetary management through a system of multilateral economic surveillance. The second treaty was due to transform the UDEAC into a *Communauté économique et monétaire d'Afrique centrale* (CEMAC) based on the development of common economic and monetary policies. The treaty establishing the CEMAC was signed on 16 March 1994, yet by 1998 it was still awaiting ratification by all the member states. Even were this not the case, the implementation of the treaty is bound to remain ineffective so long as regional security is not re-established.

Retrospectively, the feverish agitation of the early 1990s appears to have been largely sterile. The initiatives and the implementation of the programmes (concerning policies of integration as much as the CFA devaluation itself) were undertaken without any participation of the protagonists most directly concerned, namely the African states. The Heads of State or their representatives were required to sign willy-nilly documents which committed them to unwanted policies; devaluation and integration became engulfed in the same silent reprobation.

Independently of this context, the success of integration presupposes that certain conditions be met: among others, a protection and an efficent control of borders; a management of territory so as to facilitate exchanges and communications between states; compensatory mechanisms capable of ensuring the minimum of 'spatial justice' without which integration remains an empty word; and finally supranational instances of decision-making and control. In short, what is necessary is a determined political will. This does not manifestly exist within the UDEAC/CEMAC schemes; nor will it so long as none of the constituent states is able to guarantee its own national integration. Which architect will construct a building from broken pieces? Regional integration makes no sense unless the component parts are integrable.

The crisis in which the UDEAC/CEMAC countries find themselves does not predispose them to integration. Ex-Zaïre is torn asunder and will have difficulties to recover. In Chad war has continued to prowl for over a quarter of a century, rendering the state increasingly ghostlike. Internal tensions in Cameroon continue to harden. Gabon has not escaped violence as a result of presidential elections tarnished by anomalies. And what does one say of a moribund CAR or an Equatorial Guinea tragically smothered by an obscurantist regime? The prospects for a voluntary policy of integration are certainly not good. To change these, one would need to rehabilitate the states, the rule of law and civil peace. Otherwise integration will be confined to mundane debates between learned men who can extoll its merits in the name of abstract economic rationality, while remaining disconnected from realities on the ground.

Networks, Trans-State Flows, & Integration

Reports of important 'informal' cross-border activity contributed to projects aiming at a consolidation of the UDEAC and designed to promote greater control of economic activity and better fiscal capacity among the member states. Informal activities involve the more or less clandestine commercial networks which feed significant contraband. The nature and scale of cross-border exchanges are largely dependent on fluctuations in monetary parities over time. Goods have not always circulated in the same way (Hallaire, 1989). Before the 1994 devaluation, the CFA franc was particularly attractive to the neighbouring countries of the UDEAC whose non-convertible currencies continued to depreciate. Nigeria became a major supplier of energy and manufactured goods which inundated the nearby border markets of Cameroon. Its artificially strong currency did not favour regional integration; the effect was rather the opposite, since the devastating competition that followed contributed to the collapse of certain sectors of production.

While regional integration by institutional means failed, endogenous dynamics developed along the frontiers of the UDEAC, engendering a truly 'trans-state regionalism' (Bach, 1997b). That borders attract markets is not new: 'differences in potential' created by the juxtaposition of different currency regulations stim-ulate exchanges. The novelty resided in the magnitude of the phenomenon, as illustrated by the commercial ascendancy of Nigeria over Cameroon (Engola Oyep and Harre, 1992). Cross-border trade also reveals the vitality and efficiency of merchant networks, generally constructed on ethnic affinities (the Hausa and Kanuri networks, for example), which represent genuine instruments of inte-gration through the market (Egg and Igué, 1993). This form of integration, resulting from the 'dynamics from below' worked against the official objectives assigned to the revival of the UDEAC/CEMAC.

Such a pattern of integration raises the more general problem of the relationship between the informal and formal sectors. There is a school of thought that is inclined to see in the informalisation of the economy and society a panacea for the African crisis – a model that would replace failed states with something that works. This line of reasoning is somewhat precipitate: the informal is at best a last resort, a response to circumstances in the face of state deficiencies. Although it performs many functions which render it currently irreplaceable, its proliferation may further weaken the states by draining their fiscal resources. Ex-Zaïre provides an example of an informalisation so profound that the state has dissolved in it. This is certainly not the example to follow. It would be wiser to rediscover the ways of the state, of its administrative and territorial frameworks without which no development is possible. Merchant networks do not function without the complicity of public sector actors. Nor do they have the capacity to take the place of the state in the equally vital areas of infrastructural development or socio-educative programmes. Trans-state dynamics act on the peripheries of central power and in a predatary manner since they deprive the state of what it needs to exercise its traditional territorial function (see Chapter 1 of this volume).

Conclusion

Let us be clear about two things concerning the future. First, the UDEAC/CEMAC do not exist any more, except on paper. Secondly, integration cannot be created by decree, but must be constructed. Under these conditions what are the chances that the renovation of the UDEAC/CEMAC will go beyond the stage of good intentions? Is there any probability of constructing a real economic and customs union?

Building integration requires a priority for the improvement of communications so as to 'network' the space. Without this preliminary step, all is but vain discourse. Roads play an irreplaceable role in this regard. The steering committee of the UDEAC was clearly conscious of this when, on 21 June 1993, it decided to give priority to the construction of highways aimed at opening up the CAR and Chad. Their construction should reinforce the strategic importance of Cameroon, which is situated at the centre of this plan of action. Yet, all road construction should be accompanied by a keyword: *laisser-passer*. One does not refer here to customs tariffs, but to the much more illegal levies which burden transport activities and which those who use African roads know all too well. This multiplication of 'toll-points' (*péages*), according to the Cameroonian expression, and constant administrative interferences impede economic activity. The addition of illegal taxes levied by customs agents, policemen, gendarmes and other military men often exceed by far the total amount of legal taxes. To give one example, between Eboro and Libreville 'toll-points' increase the price of transported goods by 20–30% on average. Resolving this kind of problem would surely contribute more to regional integration than endless discussions on the classification of products and tariff rates that will always be only marginally applied.

One must therefore not construct transport mechanisms without first improving behaviour. There are too many serious obstacles ingrained in the society for such practices to be modified at a stroke. Integration will remain an illusion unless it can be applied by an administration deserving of that name.

Telecommunications for their part play an increasingly important role. The UDEAC/CEMAC is unfortunately completely deficient in this respect: radio and television remain essentially nationally oriented. Africa Number One, with its powerful transmitter at Moyabi in Gabon, constitutes a unique case, but its vocation is more continental than regional. Since the production of programmes is divided between Paris and Libreville it does not express any particular interest in Central Africa. The quasi-silence of mass media support vis-à-vis integration results as much from general indifference as from the lack of political will. The public media deliver messages almost purely designed for national audiences. In this still virgin terrain, action is without doubt possible, especially since the general use of the French language constitutes an unquestionable advantage. The preconditions for integration involve language, culture, and communication as much as roads and the movement of people and goods.

Integration must also be a collective project, legitimated by a common memory. Is this still possible after four decades dominated by centrifugal forces and states obsessed with the assertion of their uncertain identity? Can the UDEAC/CEMAC countries draw on their past, notably the legacy of colonialism and memories of their common history, and extract heroes that all will be able to claim? Historians from the region have so far been submerged by demands for 'national' histories at the expense of broader scales of reference. The alchemy of identities, nourished by fragments of collective history, enriched with growing memories, has remained ineffective when confronted with the all too abstract framework of the UDEAC.

Recent history gives us further reasons to be sceptical. Yet, the countries of the sub-region possess a precious capital: their community of language. Francophonie, whatever one may think of it elsewhere, creates ties, instils mental affinities, and entertains complicity. It has its role to play in the syncretism of cultures; but such an asset must be maintained for fear that it will contribute to the forces of dispersion, if left uncherished.

The precondition for potential integration is a capacity to communicate through space and through shared languages. The projects of the UDEAC/CEMAC were piloted by Northern technocrats, often distant from the concerns of Southern populations and largely inattentive to this double requirement. It is therefore not surprising that the train of integration went off track in Central Africa. The UDEAC and CEMAC have been unable to become more than abstract acronyms.

14

MICHEL LELART
The Franc Zone
& European Monetary Integration

In January–February 1944, the Brazzaville Conference, organised by General de Gaulle and the Free French movement to review French colonial policy, laid the foundations for the Franc Zone by deciding 'that the goal of our colonial economic policy should be the development of production potential and the enrichment of the overseas territories with a view to providing Africans with a better life by increasing their buying power and raising their standard of living.' While the French franc was used in all the colonies, where it had been put in circulation by the commercial banks, colonial francs now had to be issued by public agencies (Gérardin, 1989: 63–4). The franc, that is, the franc used in the French African colonies, was quickly unpegged from the French franc, and did not follow it when it was devalued in 1945 and 1948.

The Franc Zone then shrank gradually as Syria and Lebanon, the Maghreb states and Indochina became independent. In 1962, however, the newly independent states of the former West and Equatorial African federations signed two co-operation agreements with France; the Francophone West African states also signed a Monetary Union Treaty among themselves. When these agreements were renegotiated in 1973, Mauritania and Madagascar left the zone. Since then, the Franc Zone has remained stable. In West Africa, Mali even reintegrated its reserve bank into the Central Bank of West African States (BCEAO), which it had left in the early 1960s; while Guinea Bissau became a new member. In Central Africa, the former Spanish colony of Equatorial Guinea joined the Bank of the Central African States (BEAC). These 14 countries, to which the Comoros must be added, maintain close ties with France and constitute the Franc Zone.

From the outset, this monetary union was a basically political undertaking for reasons arising from its history, its constitution and its foundations. First, the Franc Zone consists of former colonies: for this reason the operations accounts (the 'comptes d'opération'), which are the main mechanism of the Zone, are managed by the French Treasury and not the Bank of France. The political dimension of the zone also results from its constitutive elements which equally relate to history: it is a complete monetary union between two groups of countries, each with a single currency and a fixed rate of exchange to the French franc.

139

Finally, the Franc Zone is a political undertaking because of its foundations: it is based on close co-operation among countries which have the same operations account, as well as on co-operation with France which funds this account and grants significant assistance in various forms. This is why the Franc Zone is so different from the Sterling Zone, which is simply a group of countries that maintain a large share of their reserves in Sterling, without Great Britain being bound to them in any way (Lelart, 1986).

The European construction adopted a totally different approach. It was initially conceived, in the early 1950s, as a sectoral project, focused on the production of coal and steel and later nuclear energy. In 1958, European integration acquired a new dimension with the establishment of the Common Market, which, in the beginning, concerned only customs duties. The exchange-rate arrangements between central banks that followed, up to and including the European Monetary System (EMS), were simply a reaction to the evolution of the international monetary system.[1] It was not until 1985 that the decision to create a single European market, including free capital flows, led almost naturally to a plan for a monetary union, based on a single currency to replace the national currencies. The Maastricht Treaty was in this respect primarily a political project.

Such a development did affect the Franc Zone on several counts. On the one hand, African countries do much more business with the European Union (EU) than among themselves. On the other, the CFA franc is pegged to the French franc, which made way for the Euro on 1 January 1999. We shall examine the implications of these developments: after considering the consequences that European integration has already had on the Franc Zone, we shall then discuss the consequences that the creation of a single currency may have on the zone and on other African countries.

The EMS & the Franc Zone

When the EU member states decided to stabilise their currencies, the Franc Zone was indirectly affected since the creation of the EMS included the French franc to which the CFA franc is pegged. The poorer performances of the Francophone African countries also raised fears about a devaluation of the CFA franc.

In March 1979, the European countries decided to reduce the fluctuations of their currencies in relation to one another to 2.25%, and the CFA franc became linked to the Deutsche Mark (DM) or the Belgian franc with identical margins of fluctuation. This is the reason why it could be said that the EMS consisted not of 12, but rather of 26, currencies (Sandretto, 1988). The relationship was certainly looser, owing to the existing margins and realignments agreed: thus, the French franc was devalued four times between 1979 and 1986, and fell by 31% in relation to the DM, but since April 1986 it has not been devalued again.

[1] In technical terms, the EMS aimed at restoring the stability and convertibility of currencies, and it is based on solidarity among its members. These are exactly the principles of the Franc Zone. This is why it is possible to describe it as a 'Franco-African Monetary System' (Lelart, 1985).

It was around this time that difficulties began to arise for the Franc Zone. The drop in the prices of raw materials caused a heavy deterioration in the terms of trade; the dollar, which had strongly increased in value up to 1985, began to decline steadily; finally, the currencies of the neighbouring countries, Ghana and especially Nigeria, suffered a noticeable drop in value. Furthermore, the convergence of European economic policies was not based on the Community average, but rather on the results obtained by the top performing country; the EU member states sought to match the inflation rate of Germany whose monetary rigour is well known.

The combination of this anti-inflationary policy and relatively high interest rates was to turn the EU into a hard currency zone. At the same time, it was a low-growth zone because the stability of the currency did not help economic recovery and because Germany, owing notably to its demography, was not likely to carry its partners along the road to lasting growth. Thus, the EMS came to be perceived as a Mark zone, in which the Deutsche Mark became the anchor for the other EU currencies (Lelart, 1994a: 88–9), and therefore for the Franc Zone.

In addition to currency stability, the European monetary and financial initiatives concerned freedom of circulation for capital. The Treaty of Rome was extensively revised following the implementation of the Single European Act on 1 July 1987. Important changes concerned the mobility of capital, which was to be liberalised in 1987 for long-term capital and three years later for short-term capital. This new European financial zone allowed a better allocation of savings, stimulated investment, improved bank performance and consolidated the importance of the major financial centres.

These measures were not without their consequences for the countries in the Franc Zone. The EU asserted itself as an attractive zone of prosperity at the very time when the Franc Zone's difficulties were accumulating: the economies were beginning to decline and there was less and less incentive to invest savings locally. And since the CFA franc could be freely converted into French francs, the capital available in the Zone took flight, like that of the neighbouring countries – notably Nigeria and Ghana – whose currencies were converted into CFA francs on parallel markets. The phenomenon was not a new one: each year the Bank of France redeemed bills from the Zone, brought out legally or otherwise. But these outflows of capital now increased considerably: in 1987, they accounted for 31% of the bank notes circulating in the BCEAO area; in 1988, 57% of the bank notes circulating in the BEAC area had to be redeemed by the Bank of France. These percentages, however, varied appreciably from year to year, and it would be improper to ascribe them to the impact of the EU reforms, particularly since the increasing likelihood of a CFA devaluation accelerated this movement in 1992 and 1993.

As of 1985, the situation in the countries of the Franc Zone deteriorated noticeably and quickly. The international environment remained unfavourable, even though the dollar began to fall in value; public deficits increased due to the contraction of fiscal revenues, linked largely to customs tariffs and therefore dependent on foreign trade. The banks practised risky credit policies and the central banks did not react vigorously enough. Restructuring, necessarily costly, of certain national banking systems was required. Finally, the states went into debt, having been asked by France, in view of the way the operations accounts were evolving, to borrow on international markets. Servicing the debt quickly became unbearable for some Franc Zone members. The results largely confirmed these difficulties. In the UMOA, the growth of GDP in 1991 and 1992 was only 1.2% and then 0.5%; in the BEAC zone, recession set in with GDP at −1.3% and then −2.6%.

Performances in the Franc Zone declined and the contrast with the results previously achieved was striking. This evolution was also particularly striking in relation to the new prospects offered to the EU member states, with the creation of the large domestic market, with reunification, which generated greater growth in the German economy, and with the tendency of the Eastern European countries towards a market economy which created new opportunities for Europe. Such divergence added to the expectation of an increasingly probable devaluation. This boosted the outflow of capital: 59% of the notes issued by the BEAC for 1992, CFA 230 billion within the UMOA the same year, more than CFA 250 billion during the first six months of 1993 (Hugon, 1993a). Such a drain did not, of course, concern informal savings or the savings of ordinary people; it concerned the savings of the well-off, those aware of the diversity of investments and the pace of financial innovation in the Northern countries, particularly within the EU.

We know how devaluation finally became inevitable. We also know about the role played by the International Monetary Fund and the World Bank in such a crucial decision. But we can ask ourselves whether the evolution of the EU and the prospects of a single currency did not work in favour of devaluation. When, on 1 January 1999, the French franc was replaced by the Euro, the CFA franc was automatically pegged to the new single currency. In this perspective, it would have been unrealistic to imagine that the CFA franc could retain a parity determined in 1948, as if the economies of Niger or Chad had evolved in more or less the same way as the French economy! It would have been equally impossible to await the creation of the European Monetary Union (EMU) to determine, on the eve of the effective date, a change of parity of the CFA franc in relation to the Euro. This would have meant announcing, several years in advance, if not the rate, at least the date, of a devaluation.

The change of parity decided in January 1994 could have been the opportunity for fixing the CFA to the Ecu. This would have reinforced the credibility of the new parity and avoided possible expectations of another future realignment (Hugon, 1994a). But this solution was not without its drawbacks, for four reasons. First, although the Maastricht Treaty was eventually ratified by all the member states, there was a risk of not keeping to the timetable. Secondly, the Ecu was mainly a unit of account, based on a basket of currencies, until its transformation into a single currency, the Euro, on 1 January 1999. Such pegging would therefore have been merely a nominal change in the anchor of the CFA franc. The conversion of the CFA franc to the French franc would then have occurred at a rate liable to vary both in the short term since the value of the basket varies daily, and in the long term since the value of the basket decreases when a currency is devalued. Thirdly, the Ecu was a reserve asset held by the central banks and could be exchanged for CFA francs if the BCEAO and the BEAC were admitted as 'other holders' of Ecus. In such a case, the conversion would result in an exchange risk since it could no longer be guaranteed by the French Treasury, which would not have an account with the European Monetary Compensation Fund (EMCF), but by the Bank of France. Finally, as a settlement currency, the Ecu had a limited role to play, since it was only used by the central banks to settle the balance of their intervention transactions: the African central banks could not use it in this way. Nothing would have prevented the CFA franc from being converted to private Ecus held with commercial banks, but such use, even within the EU, was still in its very early stages.

Long before the devaluation of the CFA franc, France and its partners understood the need for radical reforms to arrest the long-term decline of the Franc Zone. It was not normal for such a complete monetary union to account for more than forty years of existence without the least progress towards economic integration. Intra-regional trade today accounts for only about 5–10% of the region's foreign trade. This observation is all the more surprising since the EU followed exactly the opposite course: first, the establishment of a common market, then co-ordinated policies, and finally a single currency. Its example could only strengthen the will to reform.

The first reflections on this issue occurred at the UMOA Council of Ministers' meetings during 1990. Discussions focused on the mobilisation of savings, the excessive indebtedness of most of the countries, the large amount of capital outflow, the collapse of the banking systems and the preponderance of informal savings. The first measures adopted concerned two specific areas. On the one hand, the creation of a regional financial space was expected to retain and mobilise domestic savings more effectively. In particular, this involved reforming the insurance and social welfare funds, creating new financial products, developing co-operative and common structures, harmonising banking regulations and tax laws for savings, and setting up regional commissions to oversee financial institutions. A regional bank commission replaced the UMOA national commissions in October 1990; in the BEAC area, the Central Africa Bank Commission was officially established in January 1993.

Secondly, unification of business law was undertaken to eliminate the discrepancies between the various national regulations and legislative texts. Since there is no need to change currency at the borders, why should the legislation change? This unification was also designed to promote competition and facilitate investment. This is a vast area for reforms involving corporate law, commercial law, labour law, as much as the auditing of financial statements and help for the recovery of businesses in trouble. Also involved is the creation of a regional jurisdiction with authority to give final decisions.

This original approach to integration by way of financial institutions and the legal environment is fairly similar to the approach adopted in the EU, as reflected by the increasing importance of Community law. It corresponds to the principles of a single market for goods, services, people and capital, which became envisaged in the Franc Zone (Guillaumont and Guillaumont, 1993 a,b). This comparison may be extended to two other, less ambitious, though equally interesting programmes: the creation of regional training centres for economic and financial administration managers and the intention to develop universities on a regional basis – a recall of the EU Erasmus programmes? Another programme launched with the aim of creating a common economic observatory, Afristat, with the goal of producing reliable statistics, naturally reminds us of Eurostat (Lelart, 1994b).

The African Heads of State decided to go further and to undertake quickly an ambitious integration process capable of turning the Franc Zone into an economic union and a single market (Bach, 1997b). A new West African Economic and Monetary Union treaty (UEMOA) was signed on 11 January 1994. A similar treaty, establishing the Central African Economic and Monetary Community (CEMAC), was signed on 16 March 1994. These treaties were negotiated between the African countries and France, as well as with the EU since they also amended the monetary co-operation provisions.

The experience of the EU was used to establish the UEMOA and CEMAC Treaties;[2] these were directly based on the new EU Treaty, which is a revision of the provisions of the Treaty of Rome. Without going into a detailed comparative analysis of the texts here, we shall note several of the key provisions they have in common.

The institution of a common market is defined in both cases as the elimination of internal customs duties and quantitative restrictions; this is accompanied by the establishment of a common external tariff and trade policy, common rules of competition, free movement of workers, the right of establishment and freedom of provision of services (Articles 3 and 76, respectively). There is even mention of the harmonisation and mutual recognition of standards, a principle introduced in the Community by the famous 'Cassis de Dijon' decision.

A second shared feature is economic and monetary union. The Treaties are similar with regard to their area of application: economic policy (respectively Articles 102 and 63), agriculture (Article 38 and protocol no 2, Article 14), industry (Article 130 and protocol, Article 21), transportation (Article 75 and protocol Article 7), teaching and vocational training (article 126 and protocol Article 1), and finally the environment (Article 130 R and protocol Article 10). The UEMOA and CEMAC Treaties also refer to existing monetary agreements, whose provisions – naturally – cannot be compared to those of the EU. Furthermore, the terms and conditions of multilateral supervision in the UEMOA Treaty are strangely similar to those contained in the Maastricht Treaty (Articles 104 C and 64 to 75). In both cases, they refer to convergence indicators and economic policy orientations that the states must respect, such as excessive public deficits which must be avoided. The so-called surveillance procedure is based each time on recommendations, reports, deadlines, the taking into account of special circumstances and even sanctions.

Finally, the institutional organisation of the UEMOA is also modelled on the example of the EU. The conference of Heads of State and the Council of Ministers already existed, but the UEMOA Treaty provides for the creation of a seven-member commission – one member for each country, a Court of Justice and an Audit Office. The CEMAC Treaty provides for an Inter-country committee and an Executive Secretariat, a Judicial Chamber and an Audit Office (Lelart, 1997).

---

[2] We refer below only to the UEMOA Treaty. But the CEMAC Treaty does not differ with regard to the points discussed.

The Consequences of a Single Currency for the Franc Zone & for Africa

The real purpose behind the Maastricht Treaty was the substitution of a single currency, the Euro, for national currencies, and the adoption of a common monetary policy. These changes came into effect on 1 January 1999 when 11 out of the 15 member states of the EU (the exceptions being the United Kingdom, Greece, Denmark and Sweden) adopted the Euro as a single currency. Replacement of the French franc by the Euro will have an effect on the Franc Zone and on Africa.

With regard to the Franc Zone, assets and debts in French francs will be converted and the CFA franc will no longer be quoted in DMs or dollars. This substitution raises difficulties, however. The new parity will not be easy to use, after 45 years of a parity of CFAF 50 for FF1, replaced in January 1994 by CFAF 100 for FF 1. Of course, exchange operations are not carried out by ordinary people, but by well-off Africans and modern sector businesses, but the temptation will be great to round off this new parity, for example, one CFA franc = 0.0015 Euro, which is a devaluation of the CFA franc of 2.1%, or 0.00125 Euro instead of, for example, 0.00115328 Euro, which is a devaluation of 18.5%. Will it be possible to avoid another adjustment if the situation in the zone has not improved and, in such a case, could the percentage be identical for the two subregions, or even within each of them?

The European System of Central Banks will be responsible for defining and implementing monetary policy (Article 105.2); no single national central bank will have any monetary power. This provision will not have any effect on the Franc Zone since the operations accounts are kept with the French Treasury which will continue to supply Euros to the African central banks. The French government budget will still be able to finance the needs of the Franc Zone with taxpayers' money.

The Treasury's means of action, however, will be limited since the EU states will have to avoid 'excessive deficits' (Article 109 E.4), while the Commission will be monitoring the evolution of the budget situation and the public debt of each member state (Article 104 C.2). Will this greater rigour create constraints in financing the operations accounts of the Franc Zone? The issue was raised by Coquet and Daniel (1992), who nevertheless admitted that there should not be much of a problem since 'the volumes concerned are so small and the overall imbalances in the transaction accounts so marginal'. Overall deficits are what are concerned, since the surplus from one operations account can partially compensate for the deficit in another. Even if we take account of other forms of aid, the Treasury's contribution has always been relatively modest.[3] It is difficult to imagine how the Franc Zone could compromise the public finances of France,

---

[3] The money supply (M2) for the entire Franc Zone represents about 1.4% of the French money supply.

particularly since the new UEMOA and CEMAC treaties also require greater budgetary discipline and provide for the African states to ensure command of their foreign indebtedness.

It remains that the coming into effect of the single currency may complicate the functioning of the Franc Zone to the extent that EU monetary policy is oriented towards stability of prices and therefore very rigorous. Will this solution be acceptable to all the countries in the Franc Zone? Is it right for the currency of Niger or Chad to be as strong as the Euro which will circulate within the EU? Some will say that this is already the case, albeit in a less formal way, since France has been giving priority to the stability of its currency in relation to the DM. But we have seen that this had its effects on the devaluation of January 1994. The whole issue is to know whether the situation in the Franc Zone will really improve, and whether the availability of a strong currency will make it possible to return to the good performances of earlier days.

A final criticism sometimes addresses the compatibility of the Franc Zone and the European Economic and Monetary Union. It pertains to the external use of the Euro which will become an issue from the moment the French Treasury begins to transfer the new currency to the BEAC and BCEAO in exchange for CFA francs. This is the reservation expressed notably by the Bundesbank. Although legally permitted, how will this affect the job of the European Central Bank? On the one hand, there is not the slightest reference to the Franc Zone in the Maastricht Treaty, which therefore has no legal reservations with regard to the Zone; a protocol merely stipulates that France will retain the right of issue in its Overseas Territories and Departments and that it will be allowed to determine the parity of the CFA franc. On the other hand, financing the operations accounts does not entail any creation of currency, since the Treasury can transfer only the Euros it has and cannot obtain any from the ECB. Finally, will the Franc Zone countries be the only ones to hold Euros? What will the East European countries do, for instance? The Euro could well become a substitute for the dollar and the yen. As the currency of the Community, it will be definitely held in foreign banks. Will the ECB adopt some sort of policy to monitor these 'Euro-Euros' and if so, what will it be?

The formation of 'Euroland' should also make it possible to envisage a new type of relationship between the EU and the rest of Africa. The idea is based on the kaleidoscopic nature of African currency systems. In addition to the 15 countries of the Franc Zone, two African countries have now linked their currency to the dollar, three to the South African rand, one to the Portuguese escudo, and four to *ad hoc* baskets of currency. Ten currencies float within limits and 17, including the South African rand, float freely; 36 countries have for the time being made their currency officially convertible within the meaning of Article VIII of the IMF statutes (Lelart, 1998).

The EU could help to reduce these drawbacks since it is Africa's main trading partner. In 1990, the EU received 63% of the exports from the Franc Zone and 50% of those from other sub-Saharan countries. EU exports represented 57% of imports into the Franc Zone and 46% of those of sub-Saharan countries (Coquet and Daniel, 1992). The creation of a single European currency may be the opportunity for an original effort by Europe to the advantage of Africa, which in many ways is so close to it. This effort could be made in three directions (Lelart, 1989 and 1994): help with transactions clearing, support for currency stability and contribution to regional integration.

Following the famous Triffin Report, which recommended as early as 1964 the implementation of a clearing house system within an African payments union, several countries did negotiate agreements and created clearing houses, one of which has brought together the BCEAO countries and five other neighbouring countries since 1976, and another the BEAC countries and ex-Zaïre since 1982. A third clearing house is that of the member states of the PTA/COMESA. Instead of being settled one at a time, exchanges between the countries are cleared each month. The transactions are converted into a unit of account, based on the SDR. The balances are settled in foreign currencies: five, including three European currencies, in the first clearing house, six, including three European currencies, in the second, and in dollars in the third. The procedure is purely one of accounting, the accounts with the clearing houses are quickly settled, and no international liquid assets are created (Lelart, 1986; Cerruti, 1991).

The Euro could be useful in three ways. It could become *the unit of account* in which these transactions are denominated. It could also be *the currency* in which balances are periodically settled. It could even become *a reserve asset*, which the creditor countries would keep with the clearing house if the debtor countries were not bound to settle their balances in full monthly. There would then be a creation of international liquidities, in the form of Euro assets.

The activity of clearing houses has remained very limited, particularly in West Africa, where the debtor countries have accumulated unsettled payments, while in Central Africa transactions have almost come to a halt. The reasons are communication difficulties, banking habits, and the limited importance of official trade within each sub-region. But these initiatives are excellent since they tend to facilitate the payment of exchanges between countries. The EU could help with such experiments, by guaranteeing the equilibrium of transactions, by facilitating the proper operation of the system, by providing the institutions with resources so as to transform them into credit agencies participating in the financing of balances. Such a transformation was envisaged by the Triffin Report thirty-five years ago.

The EU could also help with the stability of African currencies which do not belong to the Franc Zone. New currencies could be linked right away to the Euro. This solution was mentioned in the Community memorandum on development policy which suggested that 'countries seeking to limit the fluctuations of their currency in relation to European currencies might choose to adopt the Ecu as a currency of reference' (Commission Européenne, 1982). Such a choice would facilitate currency stability at sub-regional level, and would foster the development of exchanges, on two conditions. First, a number of countries would need to do so, since this would maximise the benefits of such a venture; secondly, these countries would need to stabilise their currencies effectively in relation to the Euro, which would mean adopting margins of fluctuation that were not too wide and a parity that would not change too often.

The Maastricht Treaty is not incompatible with linking African currencies to the Ecu/Euro. Article 109.3 stipulates that the EU may negotiate an agreement concerning questions related to the monetary system or system of exchange with one or more states. This linking does not raise any technical difficulties, either. The African central banks will have to provide the importers with Euros and intervene on the market if transactions multiply. To do so, they will use 'private' Euros. They will, however, need to have enough of them, and they will need them all the more since they will be determined to maintain a more stable relationship with the European currency. Decisions will need to be made beforehand for the EU or any of its institutions to be able to provide assistance concerning the amount of the reserves granted and the conditions for drawing on such reserves.

The amount of the deficit allowed will have to be limited, unlike the situation with the operations accounts of the BCEAO and BEAC. Africa comprises a total of 53 states, some of which, like Nigeria or ex-Zaïre, would have considerable needs simply to stabilise their currencies. Could one imagine the EU agreeing to finance a French-style operations account for the benefit of the whole of Africa? The counterpart could be the initial deposit of a certain amount or a certain fraction of reserves from each country wishing to join such an association. The deposit could determine the drawing amount to which each country would be entitled. Finally, it would be advisable to clarify the conditionality that would be imposed when these withdrawals were made. The conditions would be economic and monetary policy measures, which the recipient country would be obliged to adopt so as to redress the external situation quickly and avoid the need for unlimited funds to stabilise its currency (Guillaumont and Guillaumont, 1989). This new institution would be a sort of Euro-African Monetary Fund, which in many ways would resemble the IMF with its quotas, drawing rights and stabilisation programmes, as they were called when the role of the Fund was indeed to help countries to stabilise their currencies. Guillaumont and Guillaumont (1989) once suggested the presence of an EU representative on the Board of Directors of the new institution.

A currency's stability cannot be protected indefinitely by its central bank. The help available from a specialised institution cannot go beyond certain limits. In the long term, the stability of a country's currency depends on the convergence of its economy and the co-ordination of its policy with those of its partners. In the developing countries, difficulties increase with the need to give such a policy longer-term objectives. This involves re-establishing the external balance by means of macroeconomic measures, but also ensuring durable growth of the economy and initiating a true development policy. The EU has introduced assistance for the balance of payments in the Lomé IV Convention and provides for a line of credit specifically designed to support structural adjustment (Chapter 3 of this volume). Its action thus appears to be complementary to that of the IMF or the World Bank, even if the economic policy conditions are not precisely the same (Petit, 1993).

One difference remains, however, which clearly indicates the originality of the EU concerns. Unlike the IMF, whose vocation is by definition international, the EU increasingly favours regional integration (Ntumba, 1990: 394–8; Robson, 1993a). The Lomé IV Convention is unambiguously in favour of economic regionalism in sub-Saharan Africa (Chapter 3 of this volume). The EU would be hard-pressed to choose since there are a host of regional agreements in Africa.

Hardly any of them have produced any concrete results (Bach, 1991), but these experiments are more likely to achieve their objectives if the participating countries demonstrate their will to take them seriously, as is notably the case with ECOWAS in West Africa and the PTA/COMESA in East Africa. The EU therefore has an important role to play in Africa. The global assistance granted under the Lomé Convention by the European Development Fund (EDF) or the European Investment Bank (EIB) could be increased, and at the same time put to better use for regional experiments that are doubtless among Africa's last chances.

The Franc Zone is already an area within which transactions are cleared, not because the member states participate in clearing houses but because intra-zone payments take place in CFA francs and their balances affect the operations accounts. The Franc Zone also guarantees the stability of currencies since the member countries share a common currency which is set in relation to the French franc. Finally, the Franc Zone should, in future, be able to facilitate regional integration, as long as the countries concerned define an 'open-door strategy' with regard to their neighbours, and co-operate in the implementation of their currency policy, notably with Nigeria, Ghana and the DRC (Bach, 1993).

This experiment could be extended with the establishment of an African monetary zone, in accordance with more flexible arrangements which could be made *ad hoc*. Although certain countries or groups of countries would join at the outset, the zone would remain open to those wishing to join later. The African monetary zone might also simply involve a set of arrangements designed to ensure the clearing of transactions; agreements might also be conceived so as to facilitate the stability of currencies. Finally, the objective of the African monetary zone might be the promotion of economic integration in certain regions. This may evolve gradually, beginning with bilateral agreements, then multilateral or regional ones, before becoming concerned with the whole of sub-Saharan Africa, or indeed all of Africa (L'Hériteau, 1993).

The hopes which European monetary integration raises in Africa are too high for the EU to run the risk of disappointing them. The first steps will no doubt be modest and tentative, but the objectives are ambitious. This constitutes a real challenge for the EU which remains aware of the multiplicity of ties binding it to the African continent. The crucial issue, however, is whether the Euro will eventually replace the Franc Zone in Africa, or whether the Franc Zone will remain an original link, built strong and firm on Franco-African co-operation. Everything will depend on the willingness and the ability of the Northern and Southern partners to manage a fixed relationship between the CFA franc and the Euro. The Maastricht Treaty may be the opportunity to strengthen the Franc Zone by encouraging it towards economic integration and thus justify the survival of an experiment that remains far too often misunderstood.

15 PETER TAKIRAMBUDDE
The Rival Strategies of SADC &
PTA/COMESA in Southern Africa

Although the Southern African Development Community (SADC) and the Preferential Trade Area for Eastern and Southern Africa (PTA) differ in several respects, certain notable similarities in their historical development so far have occasioned numerous attempts to compare the two organisations. Despite their substantial economic potential, their achievements have been limited. Each has been adversely affected by major shortcomings in spite of having undertaken ambitious initiatives towards regional co-operation and/or integration. Although both committed themselves to the achievement of economic liberalisation through regional integration, neither was able to develop and implement an effective strategy towards that lofty objective. Currently both organisations are engaged in restructuring exercises aimed at intensifying regional interaction with a view to overcoming their past and present developmental impasse. This restructuring was designed to transform the Southern African Development Co-ordinating Conference (SADCC) into the SADC and the PTA into the Common Market for Eastern and Southern Africa (COMESA) (see Table 3.3 for membership of the organisations).

This chapter reviews and discusses the achievements and difficulties of the SADCC and PTA strategies towards regional integration. It then examines the operational experiences and results of both organisations before concluding that the recent legal and structural changes are unlikely to produce significant results.

Objectives & Strategies

The adoption of the Declaration and Treaty establishing the Southern African Development Community (SADC) at Windhoek in August 1992 was preceded by the 1980 Lusaka Declaration that gave rise to the creation of the SADCC. The broad strategy for the achievement of the stated objectives was their translation into a programme of action that would be concerned primarily with infrastructure and production. SADCC eschewed trade and the movement of factors of production and placed emphasis on 'a joint search for solutions to shared

problems; co-ordination of economic policies as far as possible and without seriously abrogating national sovereignty' (Leistner, 1992b: 139). The institutional
structure for the pursuit of this developmental strategy was therefore characterised by 'low integration', consisting of a summit of Heads of State and
Government and meetings of ministers and senior officials.

The organisation of these gatherings was undertaken by a small Secretariat
based in Gaborone, Botswana. The Secretariat was, however, not unified since the
ministerial or sectoral units were co-ordinated by the relevant ministries within
the member states. Indeed, the Secretariat played no dominant role in setting
agendas, proposing projects or drafting resolutions. The net result of this institutional structure was that a European Community type model of regional integration was rejected, thus creating more room for involvement of the member
states in the programming process and commitment to the decisions taken
(Green, 1990: 123).

The Treaty of Windhoek, which transformed the SADCC into the SADC,
sought to change the previous style and structural design by the adoption of a
formal treaty instituting a more regionalised decision-making method so as to
strengthen links among the states; and establishing an administrative machinery
to monitor and carry out decisions more effectively. To that end, the 1992 SADC
Treaty sought to provide a more explicit definition of organisational principles,
functions of institutions and obligations of members (Weisfelder, 1991: 15).

The Treaty for the establishment of the Preferential Trade Area for Eastern and
Southern Africa was signed on 21 December 1981, as part of the 1980 Lagos Plan
of Action which sought to provide a conceptual framework for economic integration. The Plan divided sub-saharan Africa into three sub-regions: West Africa,
Central Africa and East and Southern Africa. According to the terms of the Plan,
each sub-region was to pass through three stages: free trade area, customs union,
and economic community. The Plan therefore envisaged that regional trade areas
such as the PTA would serve as building blocks for the larger Economic
Community for Africa whose target date was the year 2000.

Though the institutional structure of the PTA was similar to the SADCC
system, the PTA Treaty created a unified Secretariat without the SADCC type
sectoral co-ordinating units. Unlike the SADCC Secretariat, the PTA Secretariat
played a dominant role in setting agendas, proposing projects and drafting resolutions with the concurrent reduction of member state involvement in the
programming process and commitment to decisions taken (Green, 1990: 124).

While the focus of the SADCC was on production and infrastructure, the PTA
Treaty placed emphasis on the exchange of goods and services. Sectoral work with
respect to infrastructure (such as transport, communications, and joint planning
of agricultural and industrial development) clearly occupied a marginal position
in the PTA scheme. This made some authors conclude that the PTA was 'a
stopgap measure of neo-classical institutionalisation, according to the norms of
industrial economy markets, adopted with a view to obtaining short term gains on
productivity through competition, broadened complementarity (new products)
and marginal adjustments in national production structures' (Green, 1990: 124)

To facilitate the development of intra-community trade, the PTA, like the Latin
American Free Trade Association (LAFTA) and the Association of South East

Asian Nations (ASEAN), adopted a system of tariff reductions on distinct products in contrast to the earlier approach of the East African Community which wanted to abolish tariffs once and for all. Under the PTA's domestic market programme, member states agreed to reduce and eventually eliminate tariffs and non-tariff barriers on the basis of a negotiated list of products (styled the Common List) which would be limited to goods recognised as originating from the member states. In order to entice Botswana, Lesotho and Swaziland (BLS) from the South African-dominated Southern African Customs Union (SACU), the PTA adopted a special protocol under which the BLS countries would be granted tariff and non-tariff concessions on a non-reciprocal basis for a period of time while they remained parties to the SACU agreement. During the stipulated period, the BLS countries were to work towards a progressive reduction of their trade dependence on South Africa.

Achievements

An examination of the performance of the SADCC reveals a mixed pattern of limited achievements, innovations and regression. During its existence, the SADCC sought to reduce external dependence and to forge links that would promote regional integration and co-ordination and accelerate the mobilisation of resources to facilitate the implementation of national, inter-state and regional policies.

With respect to the reduction of dependence especially on South Africa, some progress has been recorded in a number of fields, particularly in transport and communications. Thus seven years after the founding of the SADCC, 75% of the dry cargo imports and exports of the landlocked member states were being shipped through the harbours of other SADCC members (Weimer, 1991: 80). The positive results in the transport and communications sector were realised thanks to SADCC's success in engaging the attention of major donors during its annual consultative meetings. As a result, SADCC was able to attract considerable amounts of aid commitments and disbursements (Green, 1990: 121).

Associated with the successful attraction of large amounts of external funds, especially in the transport and communications sector, there has been a discernible momentum towards a regional framework of co-ordinated indicative sectoral planning. The result has been an enhancement of institutional capacity in project preparation and operation.

On the debit side, signs of regression and stagnation have emerged. First, despite the avowed aim of reducing dependence, SADCC's dependence on foreign aid reached alarming levels; by the end of the 1980s, more than 90% of financial resources for SADCC projects came from external sources. Moreover, no significant increase in self-funding could be envisaged at the time (Green, 1990: 123). Secondly, intra-SADCC trade remained negligible, 'stagnating at some 5% of members' total trade – 80% of which is attributable to Zimbabwe alone' (Weimer, 1991: 118). Thirdly, full co-ordination of regional indicative planning was not achieved. Visible progress in this regard was limited to transport and communications (Green, 1990: 117 and 124).

But even in those instances where co-ordination was visible, there was 'evidence that SADCC operational structures yield less than optimal planning and implementation of many development projects' (Weisfelder, 1991), the explanation being 'that SADCC's strategy of sectoral decentralisation places civil servants of member governments in the dual roles of managing national programmes while coordinating SADCC projects. They are invariably ensnared in the red tape of their own centralised national bureaucracies' (ibid: 1991: 8). Green's prognosis of the prospects for SADCC over the period 1989–95 was, first, that overall prospects could be put at between 'moderate' and 'quite promising'; secondly, SADCC would continue at the same pace; and thirdly, it was unlikely to make a dramatic breakthrough in the full co-ordination of regional indicative planning or in a rise in inter-state trade's share of external trade or in the reduction of dependence on external finance (Green, 1990: 122–3) – quite a gloomy but nonetheless realistic prognosis that contrasts sharply with the rosy projections by SADCC's well-wishers.

In the case of the PTA, the available evidence in the form of accumulated trade statistics suggests that its achievements have been modest. Though the Treaty committed the member states to the reduction of tariffs within a period of 10 years, little progress has been achieved. Since the Treaty came into force on 30 September 1982, the programme for the elimination of tariffs should have been completed by the end of September 1992. But by the end of 1988 only Zimbabwe and Mauritius had fulfilled their obligations in this respect and at the beginning of 1992 only Mauritius, Uganda and Zimbabwe had implemented the second phase of tariff reductions. Moreover, ominous signs of defection from the PTA regime surfaced when the Burundi delegation informed the 1992 PTA summit that Burundi had just decided that it would not publish the second phase of tariffs and did not envisage doing so in the future. Furthermore, it had decided to make the necessary arrangements to cancel the first PTA tariffs and the first round of the new series of tariff reductions (PTA, 1992: paras 30–31).

In addition to marginal progress with respect to tariff reduction, the PTA's attempts to remove non-tariff barriers were ineffective and disappointing. The difficulties experienced in the programmes for the elimination of tariff and non-tariff barriers were exacerbated by the PTA rules of origin, especially with reference to local majority control of property and management. It was therefore not surprising that the PTA Council of Ministers at its Lusaka meeting in January 1992 decided that the provision on majority national equity holding and majority national management should be deleted from the Treaty (PTA, 1992: para. 33). The PTA's internal market programme was further bedevilled by the rules governing the composition of the Common List. Progress in expanding the List was therefore slow, and by 1993 it contained only approximately 700 products.

The establishment of the Clearing House in 1984, the creation of the Trade Development Bank, and the operationalisation of the PTA Unit of account (UAPTA) constituted notable steps in the implementation of the internal market programme, but their overall impact on regional trade was minimal, as emphasised by Chipeta (1992: 11) and Green (1990: 126). Efforts to entice Botswana, Lesotho and Swaziland away from SACU proved fruitless, despite their having been granted a further five-year period of derogation from the Treaty obligations.

Mulaisho (1992: 31) has thus aptly summed up the PTA record: the volume of intra-PTA trade as a proportion of the sub-region's total world trade actually decreased between 1982 and 1989, from 5.6 to 4.6%. There was a significant growth in total world exports by the PTA during this period, from US$11.7 billion in 1982 to US$14.2 billion in 1989, but exports within the group failed to increase, only just maintaining their level at US$579 million in 1989 against US$552 million in 1982.

Obstacles to Regional Integration

The basic documents in the SADCC and PTA are the 1980 Memorandum of Understanding, the 1992 Windhoek Declaration and Treaty and the 1981 Treaty for the Establishment of the Preferential Trade Area for Eastern and Southern Africa. Enforcement and application of decisions were left to the Secretariats, however, and were by no means assured since they were largely determined by external conditions and were particularly dependent on three variables: the political climate; the economic environment, and the judicial context.

Several aspects of the political climate have influenced the limited implementation of the SADC and PTA concepts. First, political will, which is a crucial ingredient in the process of regional integration, has been missing. In theory, member states of the SADCC and PTA/COMESA were obliged to implement commitments and decisions, but in practice there has been little willingness to do so. As a result, the ambitious aims embodied in the founding documents have not been matched by determination and capacity at the national level to implement joint decisions.

The lack of political will has been reinforced by the non-emergence of a regional identity. The building of a community requires the creation of a sense of solidarity among the people concerned. Though Weisfelder has asserted that one of the achievements of the SADCC has been the attainment of a Southern African mentality and identity, Van Staden's more cautious conclusion (1990: 27) would seem preferable, namely that the SADCC certainly succeeded in making its presence felt in most of the member states but that its image was either very general or very specialised and technical.

Given the strong nationalist tendencies of the Southern African states, a regional identity which operates above national concerns has yet to be created. To do this, the bureaucrats of any institution of economic co-operation in the region need to become servants of the region first, and then of their own particular countries. The lack of political will and the absence of a regional identity have been accentuated by the heterogeneity existing between the different members of the SADCC and PTA and by the effect of overlapping and exclusionary memberships in other competing groups which impose obligations that militate against the implementation of SADC and PTA objectives (Leistner, 1992a). The negative consequences of this situation could have been mitigated somewhat by the presence of a hegemonic leadership capable of using coercive measures to ensure compliance by member states. This has not been the case, however.

The difficulties faced by the SADC and PTA were also linked to an economic context that is inappropriate for the development of regional commitments. Virtually all member states have been afflicted by severe macroeconomic disequilibria: budget deficits; foreign debt-service burdens; low foreign reserves; over-valued currencies; lack of trade finance; and a narrow tax base, with customs duties a substantial source of revenue. Unable to resist external pressure, all the member states of SADCC and PTA, with the exception of Botswana, have embarked on Structural Adjustment Programmes (SAPs). Commitments made under these have invariably been at odds with regional integration commitments. For example, Rwanda informed the PTA Council of Ministers during its January 1992 meeting that it was facing problems of incompatibility between the principles stipulated in its Structural Adjustment Programme – and the fact that the PTA tariff consisted of rates ranging from zero to less than 10% (PTA, 1992: para. 40). It therefore asked for the application of the PTA tariffs to be suspended in its case until the end of its SAP in 1994 (Takirambudde, 1993: 153). The essence of the Rwandese plea was that economic problems stemming from macro-economic disequilibria are often country-specific, and therefore prove to be more crucial than the objectives designed to unite member states at the regional level. Member states focus their efforts on the adjustment of their domestic economies to the realities confronting them that at the national level; co-operation under SADCC and PTA therefore remains a distant dream.

Two additional factors underscore the irrelevance and ineffectiveness of the integrationist projects of the SADCC and PTA. First, both organisations have been faced with the issue of the equitable allocation of gains and losses from integration. Neither has established a mechanism to provide compensation for the sacrifices entailed in the pursuit of integration. Secondly, regional integration experiments, under both the SADCC and the PTA, have not been marked by circumstances of complementarity of production structures. The economies of the member states have been competitive rather than complementary. Regional integration has therefore been denied the material basis for the establishment of a genuine and sustainable framework for co-operation (Takirambudde, 1993: 153–4).

A last group of factors responsible for the difficulties of promoting regional integration concerns judicial structures which, in the case of SADC(C) and PTA/COMESA, have been largely ineffective. This failure can be attributed to an approach that has been lacking in strong international monitoring and enforcement machinery.

The 1980 SADCC Declaration was particularly lacking in institutional decision-making and effective enforcement procedures. The founders of SADCC deliberately created a structure that would not seriously abrogate national sovereignty, thus leading to the loss of initiative and control of the SADCC programme (Leistner, 1992a). As a result, national governments assumed a decision-making function as opposed to a mere legitimating function. And yet, implementation of the SADCC programme depended upon continued broad commitment and acceptance by national governments. Ten years on, there was a realisation that the body needed a more centralised, institutionalised and supranational machinery. This led to the adoption of the Treaty that transformed SADCC into SADC in 1992.

With respect to the perennial problem of the implementation of SADCC and PTA decisions, the Achilles heel of the founding texts is the unanimity rule and the requirement for domestic ratification and incorporation of regional instruments into the domestic laws of the member states. The implication is that each member state reserves the right to pursue an independent line of action if it does not agree with a particular measure (Agyemang, 1990: 70). Member states may have lost the initiative but not the control of the PTA/SADCC action programme. Both Secretariats remain hampered by the leeway enjoyed by member states in terms of honouring regional commitments, despite the trappings of supranationaiity which the founding treaties have conferred upon them.

The legal structure of the PTA and SADC therefore contrasts sharply with the EU Treaty. In the EU model, the Treaty takes precedence over domestic law and national governments cannot take measures which are liable to impair the effect of the Treaty. Moreover, unlike the unanimity rule under the SADC/PTA Treaties, the EU Treaty has been characterised by an increase in majority voting. Under the Single European Act, national governments surrendered both the initiative and control of the 1992 programme and its aftermath to the Commission. Once the concepts of a single market, with a date and timetable, and qualified majority voting were accepted, national governments were relegated to a mere legitimating as opposed to a decision-making function.

A fundamental problem under the SADC/COMESA dispensation is that member states subscribe to a dualistic approach to the status of international treaties. For a treaty to be applicable and to operate in the national or domestic legal order, there must be a translation of treaty provisions into national legislation. In contrast, under the monistic approach, a state's legal system is considered to encompass treaties to which the state is obligated (Jackson, 1993: 314).

The general trend under the legal systems of SADC/COMESA member states is the absence of direct application of international treaties within domestic legal systems. The general requirement is that more than mere ratification is demanded to render the Treaty applicable, invocable and operable within the domestic legal order. Moreover, even when a treaty becomes applicable within the legal systems of member states, its status would not necessarily be higher than that of other domestic laws including legislation enacted after the translation. The member states of both organisations have therefore adopted the dualistic approach of the United Kingdom whereby international treaties never have direct statute-like application (Jackson, 1993: 319).

From the point of view of regional integration, it could be argued that direct application and higher status for such treaties would have several beneficial effects. First it would increase the salience and importance of regional commitments; secondly, it would reduce the likelihood of national neglect and failure to effect translation; thirdly it would act as a check on national temptation to dilute or change agreed norms and mechanisms (Jackson, 1993: 322).

Since the early 1980s, the SADCC and the PTA have been used as the principal vehicles for the reduction of external dependence and the expansion of intra-regional trade exchanges. The two organisations have employed different strategies in the pursuit of their goals. While SADCC adopted a project-centred approach, the PTA pursued a common-market-centred strategy. Both entities have sought to evolve from their founding texts into working organisations. In doing so, both have recorded limited achievements and recently signs of regression and stagnation have emerged.

The reactions of both organisations have taken the form of an organisational restructuring, SADCC transforming itself into SADC in 1992 and the PTA launching the COMESA in 1993. The new structures have, however, been bedevilled by the same difficulties that constrained their predecessors. These include: an inappropriate political climate; a negative economic environment; and, thirdly, an ineffective legal structure. Full and effective implementation of a regional integration strategy is dependent upon these key variables. The rhetoric of co-operation may be eloquent and appealing, but the external variables must be appropriate for such integration to occur.

The setbacks suffered by the PTA have been particularly debilitating. The PTA's continued existence, or rather the absence of more acute signs of disintegration, can be explained mainly by the uncertainty associated with the consequences of such a breakdown and the comparatively low costs of its maintenance. The SADC, in comparison, has been able to generate some concrete benefits especially in the fields of transport and communications.

The old rivalry between the SADC and the PTA has not abated. Owing to the membership of South Africa and the past success of its public relations, the SADC probably has the edge over COMESA, which is handicapped by the organisational problems associated with multilateralism and a large membership. Lacking in common interest and failing to conform to current trade flows, formal integration under COMESA is unlikely to be more successful than it was under the PTA.

16

COLIN McCARTHY
SACU & the Rand Zone

South Africa crossed the political Rubicon in 1994 with the establishment of a pluralistic democracy (see Chapter 10 of this volume). Economic transformation, which will necessarily follow political change, is a more difficult and socially stressful process and will remain a major item on the South African agenda for many years to come. Bridging the welfare gap in society and establishing a process of rapid growth will be a formidable but necessary task. The political transition in South Africa has brought about fundamental changes in the Southern African region where the normalisation of political relationships allows South Africa to play a more significant role in the region's economy. I do not wish to dwell on the issue of whether South Africa can or will play the role of a regional economic locomotive or engine of growth. The point of departure is merely that the South African economy – accommodating 30.4% of Southern Africa's population and responsible for approximately 80% of the combined GNP of the region – is by far the largest and most developed economy in the region and from this dominant position, in a politically normalised situation, its enhanced role in the economic affairs of the sub-continent is bound to emerge.

In evaluating this role it is relevant to ask whether South Africa's contribution should be made through development-oriented market integration or through functional co-operation arrangements (Ostergaard, 1993: 29–42). It is not the intention at this point to become engrossed in this issue. What is important is that the sub-region has in place four integrative arrangements with considerable standing, namely, the Southern African Development Community (SADC); the Preferential Trade Area for Eastern and Southern Africa (PTA) which, in January 1993 approved the establishment of a Common Market of Eastern and Southern Africa (COMESA) by 2000; the Southern African Customs Union (SACU); and the Common Monetary Area (CMA). The CMA currently operates under the Multilateral Monetary Agreement (MMA) of 1992 that brought Namibia into the CMA.

This chapter focuses on SACU and the CMA, two institutions that are founded in the history of the member countries and reflect their close integration, to the point of dependency, with South Africa. The two organisations offer an advanced form of integration which is not matched by any other arrangement in Africa (De

159

la Torre and Kelly, 1992: 25). It has been claimed, with some justification, that SACU and the CMA 'are the envy of the region and ... far in advance of anything the PTA and SADC have to offer' so that they should constitute 'a core around which economic integration in the wider region needs to be built' (Maasdorp, 1993: 245).

The Southern African Customs Union

The Southern African Customs Union (SACU) must be understood within its politico-historical context. The first formal agreement was signed in 1910 between the Union of South Africa and the three British protectorates (which later became High Commission Territories) of Basutoland (Lesotho), Bechuanaland (Botswana) and Swaziland. This brought together four separate, although not sovereign, countries in a free trade arrangement with a common external tariff and a revenue-sharing mechanism. During 1966–8 Botswana, Lesotho and Swaziland (BLS) attained political independence and in December 1969 concluded a new customs union agreement with South Africa.

The 1969 Southern African Customs Union Agreement (SACUA), apart from providing for the free movement of goods and freedom of transit, has four important characteristics. First, the SACUA is development-oriented and thus contains specific provisions for the industrialisation of the smaller members, namely, the BLSN countries – Namibia having joined the agreement at independence in 1990. The primary means to achieve this is discrimination within the common customs area through infant industry protection against imports from South Africa. The common external tariff provides protection within the common customs area, while Article 6 of the SACUA provides for the protection of infant industries in BLSN domestic markets for a period not exceeding eight years.

Secondly, the revenue generated by import duties and surcharges, as well as excise duties, is paid into a central pool – administered by South Africa – and subsequently distributed. Distribution to the BLSN countries takes place by means of a formula (see Hudson, 1981) which leaves the residual of the revenue for South Africa. During the apartheid years South Africa used the same formula to transfer revenue from what remains in the pool to the former 'independent' homelands (Transkei, Bophuthatswana, Venda and Ciskei, the so-called TBVC states). The latter were never recognised internationally and the BLS countries consistently regarded this transfer as a domestic South African affair.

Thirdly, revenue distribution contains a substantial compensatory element in favour of BLSN, that is, revenue is distributed in excess of what is justified by the smaller SACU members' share in customs union imports and excisable production and consumption. The formula provides for a multiplier or enhancement factor of 42%. However, in 1976, the SACUA was revised to incorporate a stabilisation factor which in effect guarantees the BLSN a minimum revenue return of 17% and a maximum rate of 23% on imports and excisable consumption and production. The enhancement factor leads to an increase in the revenue rate for the BLSN above the revenue rate for SACU and in so doing represents indirect taxation of South African taxpayers to compensate BLSN citizens for certain disadvantages of SACU membership. Compensation for polarised development in a customs union of unequal partners is justified (McCarthy, 1992: 5–24), but BLSN have argued that compensation for the price-raising effects of trade diversion and for the loss of fiscal discretion is also legitimate (Luhndal and Petersson, 1991: 333–8).

Lastly, the depth of economic integration can conceivably be measured by the participating nations' sacrifice of sovereignty. In general, this sacrifice will apply equally to all participants. In the case of SACU, however, the forfeiture of sovereignty is not equally distributed, leaving South Africa effectively in the driving seat of the customs union. Article 10 of the SACUA determines that the BLSN governments shall apply customs and excise laws similar to those in force in South Africa. Also, the South African Board of Tariffs and Trade is the body that decides and advises on tariff duties and does so consistently on the basis of South African conditions and industrial needs. The custodian of SACU is a Customs Union Commission, comprising representatives of all the contracting parties, but it is an authority without a permanent secretariat. SACU is an institution without a fixed abode, address or telephone number. Much has been written about SACU, its operation, and the distribution of costs and benefits. The fact that no party to the Agreement is against maintaining SACU, albeit in a renegotiated form, indicates the success of the customs union. However, all parties to the agreement have experienced problems with it. On the one hand, South Africa used to emphasise the disproportionate distribution of SACU revenue which saw BLSN, responsible for approximately 6% of SACU GDP and less than 10% of the revenue, receiving nearly 32% of the revenue pool in 1991/2 (see Table 16.1). In a similar vein, South Africa has also complained about the inclusion of excise duties in the revenue pool, a practice which is not customary in customs union arrangements. For South Africa the problem is the fiscal dilemma of a heavy tax burden (Lachman and Bercuson, 1992: 26–31) and an escalating need to increase social expenditure in favour of the poor majority.

The BLSN countries, on the other hand, have never accepted the argument that South Africa is carrying an unfair revenue burden. From their point of view, South Africa does not take cognisance of the benefits which it derives from its free access to the captive and rapidly growing market of the four countries. This market absorbs approximately 40% of South Africa's manufactured exports in a

Table 16.1: Distribution of SACU revenue

	Revenue Pool R million	BLSN[a] share %	RSA share %
1969/70	640,7	2.6	97.4
1974/75	1,113,6	6.0	94.0
1979/80	2,122,6	10.8	89.2
1984/85	3,781,5	12.2	87.8
1991/92	8,017,0	31.8	68.2

[a]Namibia joined SACU at independence in 1990.
Source: Central Economic Advisory Service, Pretoria.

trade flow which is massively in South Africa's favour. In 1992 South Africa's trade surplus with the BLSN was over R8,000 million, that is, more than twice South Africa's overall current account surplus (Mogae, 1993). Furthermore, the BLSN correctly maintain that the increase in their revenue share is explained by the fact that they have been growing rapidly, while the South African economy has languished. Rapid BLSN growth fuelled growing imports from South Africa.

In addition to countering South Africa's complaint about excessive revenue transfers by emphasising the real benefits of job and income creation derived from a captive market, BLSN have also pointed to the price-raising effects of the common external tariff, administered by South Africa to meet the needs of South African industry. Other issues raised by BLSN include the loss of interest on revenue that results from the payments lag built into the revenue-sharing formula, the inadequacies of the provisions for infant industry protection, and basically the unsympathetic attitudes of South Africa to BLSN industrial development projects.

Towards the end of 1994, the members of SACU, organised into a Customs Union Task Team (CUTT), entered into a process of negotiations to reformulate the SACUA. The issues mentioned above are bound to feature prominently in the negotiations. All indications are that the negotiations are being conducted in a spirit which has the continuation of SACU as its primary concern. But the fact that the negotiations that were originally given months to produce a new agreement, are taking years to be concluded, seems to indicate that the accommodation of the diverse needs of South Africa and the BLNS countries is proving more difficult than expected.

The Common Monetary Area

With the exception of Botswana, all SACU members are also members of the CMA. Since the latter effectively represents monetary integration, this overlapping membership implies a deeper level of integration for the countries concerned. As is well-known, in the linear model of regional integration arrangements, monetary integration is one of the defining elements of an economic union, the highest form of regional integration. If one concentrates on intra-regional factor flows (labour and capital), and further notes that there is a close integration of the Lesotho labour market into that of South Africa,[1] all the constituent elements of a *de facto* common market between South Africa and Lesotho exist. These considerations all point to the simplicity of the view which regards the SACU/CMA integration arrangements as one-dimensional agreements between South Africa on the one hand and BLSN as a homogeneous group of smaller participants on the other. In several respects, the African Development Bank's advocacy of 'variable geometry' is alive and well in the SACU/CMA arrangement.

---

[1] In 1990, 127,330 migrant workers from Lesotho worked in the South African mines. This represents approximately 34% of Basotho males between the ages of 20 and 59. The border between Lesotho and South Africa is quite porous and the number of other Basotho working in South Africa must be substantial.

The CMA and the SACU share closely related historical backgrounds. When their economies became monetised in the second half of the nineteenth century, the BLS used South African currency. Namibia did the same after being occupied during World War I. South Africa formed part of the sterling area and the currency used was the South African pound, which since 1924 has been issued solely by the South African Reserve Bank (SARB). This monopoly was extended to Namibia in 1962 where until that date private banks could issue bank notes convertible at parity into South African currency. In 1960, South Africa decimalised its currency, while replacing the pound with the rand at a ratio of two rand to a pound.

In spite of their long history, these monetary arrangements were for the first time formalised in December 1974 when South Africa, Lesotho and Swaziland signed the Rand Monetary Area (RMA) agreement. Botswana refused to join and instead decided to establish its own fully-fledged central bank with an independent currency, the Pula, which was introduced in 1976.

Under the RMA agreement the smaller member countries were allowed to introduce their own currency. However, these currencies were convertible into rands which remained legal tender in Lesotho and Swaziland and were used for foreign-exchange transactions. The agreement also provided for a number of other conditions in support of monetary integration, such as the free movement of funds between member countries and access to South African money and capital markets. The RMA Agreement was superseded in 1986 by the Trilateral Monetary Agreement (TMA) which established the CMA. The TMA was accompanied by two bilateral agreements, one between South Africa and Swaziland, the other between South Africa and Lesotho. The TMA allowed both Lesotho and Swaziland to issue their own currencies but the bilateral agreement with Swaziland terminated the legal tender status of the rand in that country (the rand is still widely used in transactions); the agreement with Lesotho determined that both the rand and the maloti would be legal tender there.

Parity in the exchange rates between the currencies of these two countries and the rand is not required, and although Swaziland is entitled in terms of its bilateral agreement to modify its exchange rate unilaterally it has never exercised this right. The Lesotho and Swaziland currencies in circulation are fully backed by rand deposits at the SARB and holdings of RSA stock. Since the deposits earn interest the Central Banks of Lesotho and Swaziland earn seignorage. The SARB also pays compensation on rands that circulate in Lesotho. Common foreign-exchange controls apply in the countries but Lesotho and Swaziland are free to authorise foreign-exchange payments. Namibia joined the CMA in 1992 through a new agreement, now known as the Multilateral Monetary Agreement (MMA), which was consolidated by bilateral agreements between South Africa and all its partners. Namibia's decision to join was a mere formality, since prior to independence the country was *de facto* part of the RMA. In late 1993, the Namibian dollar was introduced as a national currency, with conditions similar to those that apply to the lilangeni in Swaziland.

In its 1993 report on regional integration in Southern Africa, the African Development Bank highlighted four features of the monetary arrangements in the region which are worth recalling here (African Development Bank, 1993: 238–40). First, the monetary arrangements have existed for over one hundred years, at first informally and then through formal arrangements. This suggests inherent viability and durability. Secondly, the economies of the sub-region are reasonably well adjusted as far as macroeconomic balances are concerned. Indeed, South Africa's inflation rate, the cornerstone of inflation rates in the CMA, has fallen to a steady level of below 10%. This demonstrates relatively good economic management, which is a prerequisite for closer monetary integration. Thirdly, there has been a high level of co-operation among CMA members since 1974, but there is still substantial room for closer co-ordination of monetary and fiscal policies. Lastly, the CMA operates through the co-existence of bilateral arrangements with a multilateral arrangement, the MMA. This has introduced a greater degree of flexibility than would have been possible under a multilateral arrangement alone.

Shifting the focus from formal monetary arrangements, it is perhaps worth noting that the rand has apparently grown in importance outside the CMA. Although highly anecdotal, there are signs that the rand is taking on the character of a hard currency in non-CMA countries with its growing acceptance in transactions in parallel markets. This development of a 'rand zone' beyond the borders of the CMA is a logical reflection of the regional dominance of the South African economy due to its size, level of development and supply of goods. Added to this is South Africa's relative economic stability and the increasing inflow of unskilled and skilled (brain drain) migrants from neighbouring states.

SACU/CMA in a Normalised Political Environment

Democratisation in South Africa has introduced new possibilities for regional economic co-operation within the SACU/CMA. An important feature of these institutions and their survival in the post-colonial era has always been the enigmatic relationship between South Africa – the apartheid pariah – and sovereign African states. The dominant position of the South African economy in the region and the dependence of the BLSN on South Africa largely account for the survival of the arrangements. It would also be unrealistic not to admit that political antipathy played a role in continuously straining relations between South Africa and the BLSN, thus giving rise to an unhappy but necessary marriage – a marriage of convenience. Now that the cause of the 'unhappiness' has been removed, the role and nature of SACU and the CMA may change significantly.

Democratisation in South Africa may also give rise to a regional option that SACU be eliminated. The rationale for such an option (African Development Bank, 1993: 268–9) would be the merger of SACU with SADC, the latter having been restructured to accommodate South Africa which became its eleventh member in September 1994. It is, of course, tempting to react to such an option by posing the following rhetorical question: why would one want to dissolve 'the only properly functioning Customs Union in Africa' (*ibid.*: 292) into an institution [SADC] which, according to the Secretary-general of the ACP group, 'has yet to prove itself' (*Cape Times*, 22 March 1994). An argument which deserves support is that SACU/CMA are in place and working. As the most advanced form of integration in the developing world, they should be improved through re-negotiation so as to remove sources of stress and strain.

In considering the proper role for SACU/CMA in the sub-region, it is helpful to evaluate market integration as a means to facilitate development. After all, in the Southern African context, integration and co-operation arrangements will in the end be judged by their contribution to the economic development of the participating countries. The structuralist approach to development, propagated and implemented in Latin America during the 1950s and 1960s (see Tussie, 1982: 399–413), and subsequently adopted in Africa and formalised in the Lagos Plan of Action, sees market integration as the ideal way of enlarging markets so as to enable extended import-substituting industrialisation. Whereas conventional market integration in the developed world seeks to increase efficiency within existing economic structures, development-oriented market integration is aimed at a transformation of economies through new opportunities for economies of scale and specialisation. Market integration becomes the paradigm for industriali-sation (Mytelka, 1973). In a somewhat paradoxical way, free trade is supposed to act as an instrument for inward-looking development through the build-up of the productive capacity which conventional market integration assumes to exist.

Unfortunately, this attractive theory does not work well in practice. Three observations are relevant. First, integration among developing countries usually means an integration of unequal partners, that is, the participating countries are unequal in size and levels of development. This, as is well-known, leads to polarised development if left to market forces, hence the need for mechanisms to reduce polarisation, or compensate for it as South Africa does in SACU (McCarthy, 1994). Since integration is properly regarded as a positive-sum game, and therefore expected to produce real net benefits for all participants, the diffi-culty, if not impossibility, of coping with the issue of polarisation (that is, equity in the distribution of the real costs and benefits of integration) creates tensions in integration arrangements. Unfulfilled expectations and diverging perceptions of costs and benefits have been the root cause of the failure of many integration arrangements (Vaitsos, 1978). Secondly, market integration of all varieties is driven by growth in intra-regional trade. However, in the experience of inte-gration among developing countries, intra-regional trade is, for structural reasons, conspicuously low (De la Torre and Kelly, 1992: 30). Also, to the best of my knowledge, there is no example of a rapidly growing developing (or newly indus-trialised country) that had based its growth on intra-regional trade; in all cases, insertion into the world economy had driven economic growth. Thirdly, successful market integration requires the political commitment of participants and a high level of institutional and technical capacity. These characteristics are all too often absent in developing countries. In these countries, especially those with a comparatively short history of independence, political commitment is in the first place to national sovereignty and not to integration exercises, which by defi-nition demand a sacrifice of national sovereignty. Institutional and technical capacities are also in their infancy and not sufficiently strong to support inte-gration arrangements.

These observations also explain why market integration does not have a proud record in the developing world, and why a more flexible, functional approach to regional co-operation could provide a more sustainable basis for regional devel-opment. Functional co-operation provides for an incrementalist approach to regional issues and avoids grandiose schemes of integration. The sacrifice of sovereignty is less than with market integration and it makes fewer demands on technical and institutional capacities. In fact, co-operative projects will, in an incrementalist way, foster the development of these capacities and the political commitment which in the long run will enable market integration arrangements to succeed.

Functional co-operation is also the most suitable strategy for regional development in Southern Africa. The South African economy, as noted earlier, is by far the largest and most industrialised economy in the region; the validity of market integration will inevitably result in polarised development. Also, the growing view that the former Southern African Development Co-ordination Conference has achieved only meagre results (Maasdorp, 1993: 242) can at least partly be attributed to the lack of institutional and technical capacities in the region, a situation which, for the SADC, may improve as a result of South Africa's membership. Another important element to consider is the mercantilist pattern of trade between South Africa and other African countries, as shown in Table 16.2. Within SACU, South Africa's exports exceeded imports by a multiple of 6.2 in 1990; for the rest of the SADC, the multiple was 4.3.

Although there is no real reason why a balance in regional trade must exist, the political and economic realities determine that regional integration and development cannot be built on a one-sided trade flow. For both South Africa and the rest of the sub-region, growth will require an expansion of exports from neighbouring countries to South Africa. The constraint the region faces in this respect is the incapacity of most countries to produce exportables for the South African market. However, if the trade focus is broadened to include not only primary products and manufactures, but also tourism and non-tradeables such as water and electricity, the scope for a profitable two-way trade is extended considerably.

Broadening the trade focus in this way brings functional co-operation to the fore as the most viable approach to regional co-operation and development. An example of such a co-operative project is the Lesotho Highlands Water Project which will supplement South Africa's water supply and substitute hydro-electric power generated in Lesotho for power currently being imported from South Africa. Furthermore, it can be envisaged that bilateral and multilateral co-operative arrangements, through the incorporation of private sector initiatives, could facilitate cross-border investment, with South African firms extending their considerable involvement in neighbouring countries to the advantage of capacity-building in export production.

If a more flexible functional approach to regional co-operation is to be considered as suitable for Southern Africa, where does this leave the SACU/CMA integration arrangements? One approach which has been advocated is that the SACU and CMA 'represent a core around which economic integration in the

Table 16.2: South Africa's trade with Southern Africa, 1990 (million rands)

	Imports	Exports	Exports/Imports
SACU	1,440	8,861	6.2
Rest of SADC	563	2,426	4.3

Source: Maasdorp and Whiteside (1993: 15).

wider region needs to be built' (Maasdorp, 1993: 245). Any attempt to use the SACU/CMA as a nucleus for broader integration will require that a new SACU Agreement addresses the strains and stresses referred to earlier; it will also be necessary to find a way for Botswana to join the CMA. But two specific dimensions of change will also have to be considered, namely the deepening and widening of the present SACU and CMA arrangements.

On the issue of deepening, changes toward a common market or even an economic union could be considered. It is important here to take the heterogeneity of the BLSN into consideration, with different levels of integration among present SACU members. The extreme case is that of Lesotho which could enter a fully-fledged economic union with South Africa. In academic circles in Lesotho, and in the National Union of Mineworkers in South Africa, the possibility of Lesotho's incorporation in democratic South Africa has been openly discussed for some time now (Weisfelder, 1992). The possibility of Botswana joining the CMA could also contribute significantly to a deepening of current arrangements. It is understood that changes to the exchange-rate and foreign-exchange regime in Botswana are being contemplated. However, it is not known what the outcome will be. Given Botswana's strong foreign reserve position, it would be understandable if this country decided to approach the issue of joining the CMA with circumspection or even scepticism. At the same time, the practices underlying the MMA create the ability to devise a bilateral agreement with South Africa that could accommodate Botswana's position and special requirements, while extending the position of the rand as a regional reserve currency.

It is difficult to envisage that the widening of the current arrangements, with other countries joining them, could be an immediate prospect. To bring neighbouring countries into the present customs union arrangement with its common external tariff will require unprecedented economic restructuring. Consider the example of Zimbabwe, perhaps the most appropriate candidate for joining the customs union. Its manufacturing industry would face major problems in competing with South African industries in a common customs area. However, the adjustment would not be one-sided. South African textile, clothing and footwear firms, as well as those in Lesotho and Swaziland, would face stiff competition from Zimbabwean producers. It is not the purpose of this chapter to speculate on the arrangements that could bring about the widening of SACU, which itself would face variations in integration in the spirit of variable geometry. However, concepts such as preferential trade agreements/areas, association agreements and free trade areas come to mind as instruments of incrementalism toward market integration organised in relation to the SACU core.

Maintaining the current structure of compensatory revenue transfers, based on a norm revenue rate, and leaving South Africa with the residual, cannot be a viable mechanism if an extension of the number of participating countries should be considered. The issue of polarisation will also remain an important, if not the most prominent, item on the agenda of SACU. Suffice it to note two points on this difficult problem. The first is of an indirect nature, namely, that regional co-operation is not a panacea for economic development problems. In fact, there is little evidence to support the contention that the region can play a decisive role in national development. The right domestic policies and international competitiveness appear to be more important. The second point is that compensation for polarisation through transfer payments does just that – it compensates without doing anything specific to counter polarisation. How the latter is to be undertaken is a complex question. The conventional approach (old orthodoxy) of co-ordinated regional industrial planning, supported, amongst others, by a regional development bank, is out of fashion in an era characterised by the effectiveness of planning being questioned. The focus in the 'second round of regionalism' (De Melo and Panagariya, 1992) has also changed towards an emphasis on regionalism as a means to support outward orientation and export-driven growth (McCarthy, 1994).

A sensible approach to the economy of Southern Africa would be a flexible, function-based co-operative strategy. This would enable the sub-region to exploit its growth potential in a way which is less demanding on institutional and technical capacities and in terms of sacrificing national sovereignty, yet is effective in building production capabilities in the smaller economies, while adequately coping with the disadvantages of polarisation and the extension of two-way trade. Co-operative arrangements can be bilateral or multilateral, with the SADC serving as the overarching institution for these arrangements. The Windhoek Treaty of 1992 has committed SADC to the establishment of a common market, and the acceptance in 1996 of a Trade Protocol that envisages a free trade area in eight years time has launched the region on a road of trade integration. But building on and extending SADC's proficiency as a co-operative arrangement would remain the ideal incrementalist way of moving towards integration.

The adoption of a free trade goal for SADC does not detract from the rationale of SACU/CMA being maintained as a core of intensive market integration in an overall two-track approach – the one track emphasising function-based co-operation and the other market integration. On the latter track the widening of the CMA and the deepening and widening of a renegotiated SACUA should be considered. The heterogeneity of the BLSN and consequently the advisability of adopting an approach of variable geometry, ranging from customs to economic union arrangements, should form an important factor in designing a new agreement. This two-track approach makes economic sense. It would also build on current institutional arrangements, while avoiding grandiose schemes. But regional affairs are highly politicised and in the end considerations of an overly political nature may decide future developments.

IV

NETWORKS

17

BRUNO STARY
Cross-Border Trade in West Africa
The Ghana–Côte d'Ivoire Frontier

African borders have often been criticised for the arbitrary way in which they delineate territories. As emphasised by Michel Foucher, a set of conventional arguments have come to be accepted without discussion. They picture 'Africa as being balkanised due to boundaries which result from colonisation [and are] arbitrary, absurd and artificial ...'. They are '... export products imposed without any base, regardless of the geography and the natural, ethnic or economic groupings; these straight-ruled lines appear to have divided and disunited a continent that was otherwise dedicated, either by its nature or the inborn wisdom of its leaders, to unity' (Foucher, 1988: 139). Beyond the separation of ethnic groups by these borders, some authors have seen in the political segmentation that resulted one of the causes for underdevelopment: 'It is clear that continents where homogeneous physical unities unfold over vast areas are not best suited to a political disaggregation that can only limit the possibilities of each State. And that is precisely the case of the African continent, notably in its inter-tropical area ...' (Seck, 1989: 378).

The reality is of course a lot more complex and nuanced. Thus the Ghana-Côte d'Ivoire border, except in its southern part where the Nzima population find themselves on both sides of the Tendo lagoon, is more of a secant border in relation to the major bordering ethnic groups (the Agni and Koulango on the Ivorian side, the Ashanti, Bron and Nafada on the Ghanaian side). On a larger scale, the distribution of ethnic groups and nationalities is more complex than this single juxtaposition. The populations in the border encampments are composed of native populations on to which alien populations have superimposed themselves (Burkinabe, Nigerians, amongst others), as well as populations that have traditionally been travelling over the whole of West Africa, like the Dyula. This interweaving of populations from diverse ethnic groups and nationalities results as much from the colonial partition of the continent as from the movements of population that came after it (the development of cocoa with its call for migrants, the arrival of the Ghanaian pioneering front on the eastern border of Côte d'Ivoire, and the creation of border encampments from the 1970s onwards). The arbitrary nature of the colonial division, as of the subsequent

169

ethnic redistribution, must here – as in other parts of West Africa – be nuanced and set in a more general context.

The distribution of the population is but one element in the development of cross-border trade. Agricultural and industrial products are two key factors in the intensification of relationships in the borderland. They take advantage of different monetary, customs and fiscal policies which create opportunities for those who can exploit them. The mid-1990s are particularly interesting to study because of the January 1994 devaluation of the CFA franc, which affected in a definite manner one of the driving forces behind these exchanges. Special attention will be given to the constitutive elements of this 'informal' trade as well as to some aspects of its consequences.

Agriculture as an Incentive to Cross-border Trade

The complementarity of systems of agricultural production is a structural element that often helps one to understand the development of exchanges between coastal countries and the Sahelian countries. It is not a pertinent explanation, however, for countries that belong to the same climatic zone. In Côte d'Ivoire and Ghana, the export of agricultural products was, and still is, one of the pillars of the national economy. Discrepancies between state policies offer opportunities to benefit from better prices across the border, and are at the root of the intense cross-border flow between the two countries. All export products are involved, whether it be coconut oil in the south or cocoa in the forestry area. After a first peak with over 850,000 tons of cocoa during the 1987–8 campaign, marketing in Côte d'Ivoire reached a new record in 1995–6, with a production of over 1 million tons. The production of Ghana, the world's third largest producer of cocoa, has over the last 10 years been around 250–350,000 tons, with a tendency to decline. A large part of the population of the two states is engaged in this sector.

The organisation of the marketing of agricultural products is not identical in the two countries. The state is, however, very active in both cases, fixing guaranteed prices for products at the beginning of each season. In the mid-1980s, the price guaranteed by the Stabilisation Office of Côte d'Ivoire was CFAF 400 per kg of cocoa. The fall in cocoa prices on the world market drove the Ivorian government to propose a price of CFAF 200 per kg during the 1989–90 campaign. Prices rose again only following the 1994 devaluation and successively settled at CFAF 250 and 350 during the 1994–5 season. As for the Ghana Cocoa Board, it has put forward a regular increase in its buying price, in cash, making it jump from 150 cedis per kg at the beginning of the 1980s to 700 cedis during the 1994–5 season. However, during this same period, changes in the exchange rate between the two currencies attenuated the differences between the guaranteed prices paid on each side of the border.

In spite of the fall in the Ivorian price and the rise of the Ghanaian price, the latter remained below the Ivorian price until the end of 1989. Following the devaluation, and for about one and a half years thereafter, the Ghana Cocoa Board's guaranteed price was higher than that offered in Côte d'Ivoire. The differences between the buying prices of cocoa, and also to a lesser extent of coffee, created attractive opportunities for Ivorian and Ghanaian traders. In the mid-1980s it was estimated that 10–15% of the cocoa exports from Côte d'Ivoire (60 to 65,000 tons) came from Ghana (Manshard and Schaaf, 1989: 9). These illegal transfers seem to have been reduced by the rise in the buying price of cocoa in Ghana and, mainly after Flt.-Lt. Rawling's coup d'etat in 1981, the rein-forcement of border controls carried out by the Militia and the Defence Committees of the Revolution. Nonetheless, several sources still suggest a trade amounting to several tens of thousands of tons per year. Despite the difficulty of counting these flows exactly, the illegal exportation of cocoa thus constitutes a significant source of income for the numerous intermediaries living in encamp-ments and small towns along the border.

The border town of Niable in Côte d'Ivoire belongs to one of the cocoa-producing areas and is located some 200 km from Abidjan. The study of its buyers' commercial networks enabled us to understand how the traffic operates. The buyers work with a number of farmers who have special knowledge of the paths across the border and who have settled in the four encampments that have developed on both sides of the border, about 5 to 15 km from the town. In the mid-1980s, there were about 50 of these border-trackers (*pisteurs*) in these encampments; roughly ten years later there were only about 20 left. In Mamploussi, one of the Ivorian encampments to the south of Niable, six of the ten frontier-trackers who had settled there in the second half of the 1980s worked exclusively with Ghanaian farmers. Further south, in the administrative region of Abengourou, the small village of Acatie has experienced the same phenomenon; most of the 12 border-trackers present in 1991–2 had settled there in the mid-1980s, with the objective of dealing directly with the Ghanaians. Mark K., who is one of these border-trackers, worked on a regular basis with nearly 25 Ghanaians until the beginning of the 1990s. Another element that emphasises the impor-tance of this traffic is that the status of the border-tracker working in the border encampments seems to be quite different from that encountered in other areas of production. Usually, the border-trackers are also farmers and this constitutes a guarantee for the buyer, who advances the money for the purchase before receiving the farmers' produce. The risk taken by the buyer thus seems to be in consonance with the scale of the financial rewards anticipated. However, it is also not unusual in the border encampments to find trackers who have no plantations whatsoever. Ghanaian cocoa sometimes constitutes the biggest portion of the volume that is actually handled by the Ivorian buyers. One of the buyers from Niable, in 1992, marketed more than 320 tons of cocoa, some 80% of which came from the six border-trackers he had regularly financed since 1985. Four of them were settled in two of the border encampments. According to this buyer, border-trackers from Mamploussi worked only with Ivorian farmers, whereas the trackers from Yalo Campe bought all of their 110 tons of products from Ghanaian farmers. This meant that at least 33% of the total volume handled by our buyer came from Ghana.

All of the actors involved in this traffic find it worthwhile for themselves. The Ghanaian farmers receive a price superior to that guaranteed by the Ghana Cocoa Board. The Ivorian border-tracker buys the products more cheaply from the Ghanaian farmer, and he does not pay out the commission he gets from his buyer unless he goes through the intermediary of a Ghanaian border-tracker. The Ivorian tracker also sells the goods on to his Ivorian buyer at the price guaranteed by the Ivorian Stabilisation Board. The Ivorian buyer can also afford to purchase smuggled cocoa at the same price as Ivorian cocoa since he will sell greater quantities to his exporter, and consequently will get a bigger commission than if he worked only with Ivorian farmers. The real conditions of the transactions in these products are sometimes far removed from the official rules, and the financial rewards are not always equally attractive for all the agents involved. The farmers cannot always control precisely the quantity of goods that they offer to the buyer or the border-tracker. Moreover, they are not always paid the price which would be guaranteed if they went through the 'official' channels: farmers often find themselves in an inferior position when they are in the midst of an 'illegal' transaction. The agreement is often based on the price of a bag, and the buyer is then unable to know exactly what it contains. However, this type of transaction allows the Ghanaian planter to be paid straightaway in cash for his production. Thus, even if the price differential appears to be the principal element in these exchanges, commercial policies and the immediacy of payment are elements that have to be taken into account. Consequently, even when the 1994 devaluation made the Ghanaian price superior to the Ivorian one, some Ghanaian farmers still carried on selling to the Ivorian border-trackers because they paid them straightaway.

Cross-border trade is stimulated by the organisation of the commercial networks, the prices proposed on each side of the border and the payment in cash to the farmers. Illegal trade in coffee and cocoa products is to be found over almost the whole of the forestry borderland. Changes in the organisation of marketing in Côte d'Ivoire or Ghana have an immediate impact on the intensity and direction of the traffic. Cross-border trade is directly affected by such factors as changes in the guaranteed producer prices or decisions to tie the guaranteed price to the quality of the product. In certain years, the Ivorian Stabilisation Board also refuses to buy cocoa during the shorter trading season of July–September in an attempt to support world market prices. The same Ivorian and Ghanaian agents can as readily traffic from Ghana to Côte d'Ivoire as in the opposite direction.

The Borderland Markets

The variation in prosperity between Côte d'Ivoire and Ghana is in several respects quite significant: GNP per capita in 1990 was $390 for Ghana and $750 for Côte d'Ivoire. Over the 1965–80 period, the annual rate of growth of GNP per capita was –0.8% for Ghana and +2.8% for Côte d'Ivoire. On the other hand, the crisis of the 1980s was more accentuated in Côte d'Ivoire: the rates of growth were respectively –0.6 and –3.7% over the decade. The difference in wealth is also seen in the prices that the inhabitants pay for common products; they are comparatively lower in Ghana than in Côte d'Ivoire. Accordingly, the border markets offer opportunities for increased incomes and they have multiplied since the end of the 1970s. They attract tradesmen from Abidjan who come to stock up on a diversity of goods, as do the inhabitants of the regions that are geographically close to the borderlands. Most of the Ghana-Côte d'Ivoire border markets developed in the second half of the 1970s and the beginning of the 1980s. This corresponded to a strong increase in the revenues of Côte d'Ivoire and a higher level of demand from its population. Commercial activity in small villages and in the encampments appears to have been complementary to the agricultural activity which led to the creation of these localities. In south-west Ghana, the two main markets along the border are those of Jewi Wharf and Elubo. Jewi Wharf is situated on the coast and faces the Tendo Lagoon, while Elubo is on the main road connecting the two countries, and faces the Ivorian border village of Noe. Jewi Wharf's market opened in 1981, at a time when the development of commercial activities across the border was hampered by the stricter border controls introduced after the arrival of the new Ghanaian government three years before. Following the official re-opening of borders in 1984, the people responsible for the market decided to advertise its existence to the Ivorian population of the villages situated north of the lagoon. Further north of the border, facing the town of Bondoukou, the market of Sampa was opened at the beginning of 1970. It was created on the initiative of the local government authorities in response to the needs of the population, and became one of the most important markets for Ivorian tradesmen.

Most Ghanaian border markets are weekly ones. The sellers are almost all Ghanaians who do not live in the border localities and only come in on market days; some traders go round all the border markets of the region. Thus many Jewi Wharf sellers travel to the markets of the small Ivorian villages, on the lagoon of Adiake, Mowa, Ngueme, Tiapoum, as well as to the Ghanaian markets of Elubo, Eyinase, Tikobo or Wharf. The two major Ghanaian cities of Accra and Kumasi maintain very strong ties with these border markets since this is where the wholesalers are to be found. Some sellers carry out tours lasting between two and three weeks in the Ivorian cities, as is the case when they travel around Bouna which is in the north-east of Côte d'Ivoire. These trips are facilitated by the Ghanaian communities established in the Ivorian cities, who accommodate the wholesalers for the duration of their trip. Consequently, a continuous string of border markets, which are sometimes 'twinned', has been established next to the paths and contact points across the frontier, from the lagoon to the savanna area. The Ghanaian markets are more important, however, and their influence often spreads beyond the nearby villages and encampments.

The principal customers of these markets are local Ivorian tradesmen seeking goods at a cheaper price so as to resell them in the larger Ivorian cities. In the Sampa market, we estimated that two-thirds to three-quarters of the buyers were from Côte d'Ivoire. In the Ghanaian markets, they benefit from prices that are less than half the prices charged by Ivorian wholesalers. The products bought are almost the same everywhere: enamelware, hardware, cloth, machetes, batteries, second-hand clothing, etc. It is illegal to import some of these products because they compete with national industries; this is the case for batteries and machetes. New products make their appearance from time to time: thus, since 1993, significant quantities of re-exported rice originating from Taiwan or Thailand have been purchased, in the first instance by Ghanaian wholesalers, and then resold in the border markets sometimes to Ivorian traders, who later resell it to Ivorian customers. In Jewi Wharf or Sampa, some of the traders saw their rice sales multiply four to five times within five years.

In January 1994, the devaluation of the CFA franc (Chapter 14 in this volume) changed its parity with the Cedi and contributed to a diminution in the market activity of the villages in the borderland. The differentials in prices on equivalent products narrowed sharply; sometimes they were even reversed, although overall purchasing in Ghana remained advantageous. The incentive to trade remained of primary significance only for the local population. The Ivorian sellers subsequently changed their strategy: they reduced their trips to the border markets and preferred to travel directly to Accra or Kumasi, where they could benefit from more advantageous prices (Stary, 1995). As a result, many shops in the small Ghanaian border towns ceased their activities during the 1984–6 period.

The border markets occupy an intermediary position in the marketing process. When price differentials are significant they can take advantage of their geographical proximity to attract Ivorian sellers. However, this can no longer be the case when price differentials are narrowed.

The Traffic in Manufactured Products

The majority of the buyers are regular customers and buy manufactured products in small quantities. The transport networks, mainly on the Ivorian side, have adapted to this commercial activity. Numerous taxis link Aboisso to the Ivorian lagoon localities on market days. In Niable, two locally-owned bus companies make the connection with Abidjan three to four times a day. Everywhere, a system for crossing the border has been organised. The lagoon, in the south, enables the buyers to move their goods directly to Abidjan within two to three days. In the other markets, groups of young people offer their services to the Ivorian tradesmen who want to cross the border without what they call 'administrative worries'. This is a tight-knit network, difficult to penetrate for newcomers and controlled by a few people in each city. The young people involved have no qualifications and operate on the fringes of modern economic activity; they may also be young farmers awaiting the result of their first harvest. They often belong to one of the ethnic groups of the borderland. In Niable, for instance, most of them are Agni, who work along with a few Burkinabe when carrying goods in the bush. Over time, these intermediaries have built up a list of regular customers on whose behalf the 'chef', namely the man in charge, organises and allocates work. Goods are purchased or sold indifferently in CFA francs or Cedis. This has not been affected by the August 1993 decision forbidding central banks to buy back CFA banknotes outside the Franc Zone, nor by the January 1994 devaluation.

The small cross-border networks are connected to more important merchant and ethnic-based networks (Malinke, Hausa, and Dyula) that cut across several states (Harding and Kipre, 1992; Grégoire and Labazée, 1993). These organise the long-distance flows which link the different coastal countries from Nigeria to Côte d'Ivoire. Due to its strategic location, the harbour of Lomé is one of the key staging-posts for the long-distance trade in manufactured goods sent to Côte d'Ivoire: the transactions involve hi-fi equipment, jewellery and many other products imported from Europe or Asia. From Nigeria, Ivorian tradesmen mainly bring back cloth, cosmetics and jewellery. This trans-state trade is very dynamic: in order to carry out their purchases in Lomé or Lagos, some tradesmen form a group of interested parties; they then rent a bus for a week and visit successively the markets of Accra, Lomé, Cotonou and Lagos.

The trade in manufactured products seems to be particularly diversified. Trans-state trade in manufactures implies the existence of commercial networks that extend across the whole of West Africa. Border markets are but one of the locations where the transactions take place. From the capillary network to the vast ethnic networks across the whole of West Africa, the borderlands connect together a vast sub-region and draw in a variety of specialised intermediaries. Schematically, each type of product (local agricultural products, cash crops, manufactured goods, etc) involves a specialised network of smugglers; these range from 'marginalised' youth to the 'merchant' ethnic groups, whose expertise relies on a long-standing practice of trade over vast areas and on a much larger scale. As a result, cross-border trade acquires a new and much broader dimension.

The Destructuring Effects of Trans-state Trade

The consequences of the border traffic are ambivalent. Igué emphasises that 'the agglomerations that have appeared on the main passage points are all twin cities. Their development took advantage of the attraction of migratory flows in the vicinity of cross-border points' (Igué, 1989a: 604). The related financial rewards, the demographic and urban growth, and the spill-over effects of border traffic on the local economies also involve perverse destructuring effects on the states.

Locally, the rewards appear to have positive effects for the agents and the markets where the transactions take place. Throughout West Africa, proximity to the boundary-line is a factor of urban growth. Border towns and encampments where agricultural and commercial activities are complementary have witnessed strong demographic growth within a few years. In 1955, Niable with its 300 inhabitants ranked ninth amongst the towns of the department of Abengourou; by 1975, it had become the second largest city in the department, a rank that it retained in 1988, when the census registered 11,200 inhabitants. A similar growth rate occurred in smaller centres like Jewi Wharf, which grew from a few inhabitants at the beginning of the 1970s to almost 4,000 twenty-five years later. Cross-border commercial activity can therefore reveal itself to be an important factor in urban growth. However, beyond a certain threshold, the size of the population requires a diversification of urban functions which cross-border trade cannot sustain.

Cross-border and trans-state trade in industrial products brings together a much larger number of intermediaries, all of whom attempt to take maximum advantage of their position in the transactions. Whether it be tradesmen, carriers or border-trackers, those involved are able to exploit their position directly; they can either buy goods cheaper, usually in Ghana, or get paid to take merchandise across the border. Government agents also take advantage of this traffic: they receive their own share of the takings from the different agents, and sometimes even participate directly in the traffic. Thus, it is not uncommon to see border-trackers and smugglers striking agreements directly with customs officials in order to ensure the safe arrival of goods. Similarly, government agents take advantage of road controls to negotiate their 'clemency' to the tradesmen in return for money.

The *laissez-faire* attitude of the national authorities vis-à-vis such behaviour says much for the notion of the 'rentier state', where each position in an adminis-tration is the occasion of a financial surplus for the agents. The contraction of government budgets in the context of structural adjustment programmes also means that government agents are faced with frozen salaries whilst prices keep on increasing. As a result of this, road blocks are sometimes perceived as a guarantee of social peace, even though the cost of these 'illegal capital gains' is borne by the local population. In 1988 and 1992, the Ivorian Government attempted to remove altogether, and later to limit to eighteen, the number of road blocks set up by the customs, the police, the border police and the constabulary, on the main highways to Burkina Faso and Ghana. In both cases, these attempts failed to withstand the pressure from the ground. In 1991, the deputy prefect of one of the borderland departments even attempted to mediate with the Ghanaian customs so that they would keep their demands to CFAF 500 per person!

The political and economic aspects of cross-border trade are particularly difficult to assess. The negative effect of the importation of external products on national industries is compensated for by the fact that these imports sustain and develop other sectors of activity, which would be unviable if the traders were to buy goods from the national industry or import them legally at higher cost. This is what happens specifically in the case of vehicle spare parts, which many garage mechanics from Abidjan buy directly from Ghana rather than from official car dealers who are subjected to prohibitive custom duties on such imports.

In spite of all the possibilities of 'informal arrangement', cross-border traffic remains an illegal activity which is susceptible to being heavily sanctioned. At the beginning of the 1980s, some Ghanaian farmers and border-trackers were said to have been killed by the CDRs. These dramatic events are exceptional, however, and suitable arrangements are usually found. Political, social and ethnic lobbying towards the continuation of cross-border trade is often vital in this respect.

Cross-border trade may be interpreted as an adjustment on the part of the borderland population to an economic crisis which invites them to maximise every source of profit. As such, the borderlands clearly follow a spatial logic which is different from that of the rest of the states and the inter-governmental organisa-tions (IGOs) for regional integration. Illegal trade has also been described as a form of bottom-up integration via the market; from this perspective it might seem able to achieve in an informal fashion what the authorities cannot manage to do within organisations like the ECOWAS or the UEMOA. Such analyses, however, overlook the fact that cross-border transactions also have a destruc-turing effect on the states from an economic and political point of view. Informal exchanges represent a loss of fiscal revenue of particular importance to the states concerned. As a result of the establishment of ties across several states, trans-state regionalism also calls the post-colonial state into question without favouring the emergence of broader territorial entities. Indeed, trans-state regionalism goes against the ambitions of the IGOs that wish to establish economic integration by means of the removal of the monetary and fiscal disparities between the states in the sub-region (see Chapter 1 in this volume).

The case of cross-border trade between Côte d'Ivoire and Ghana presents peculiarities that attenuate these destructuring effects. The boundary line corresponds to an inter-imperial border dating from colonial times, and brings into contact two states whose geopolitical projects were very different at independence. The subsequent political opposition between their leaderships (between Houphouet-Boigny and Nkrumah in the 1960s, then between the Ivorian president and Rawlings in the 1980s) may have helped to build up a national consciousness which is more marked here than in any other African state. The process of identification as a nation seems to have made progress in both cases. The political oppositions have reinforced these feelings. In this sense there is a specificity about the borderland where a common cross-border solidarity superimposes itself upon other territorial and national identification criteria. This is less attributable to the so-called ethnic factor (which is not always present) than to the nature of cross-border interactions.

The destructuring effects of cross-border trade also depend on their importance and impact on the economies of the countries concerned. The destructuring effects are limited in the cases of Côte d'Ivoire and Ghana because of the relative diversity of the economies. But other smaller countries are severely affected by these exchanges. The experience of two of West Africa's 'entrepot states' (Igué and Soulé, 1992) – Togo and Benin – illustrates the consequences of the extensive development of these trade networks. At the other end of the West African region, the failure of the Senegambian confederation in the late 1980s (Sall, 1992) exposed the influence of the Senegalo-Gambian cross-border trade lobbies: since their revenues were built upon the disparities between the two countries, they did not want to see them disappear once fiscal and customs tariff was harmonised.

It is always a delicate matter to draw a conclusion on the basis of one particular example. Cross-border trade between Côte d'Ivoire and Ghana, without being marginal, does not seem to question the territorial integrity of the two countries. Integration through the border markets and their related commercial activities seems to be quite limited; yet numerous participants clearly benefit from the financial rewards of these exchanges. However, looking at West Africa as a whole, spatial contradictions generated by the impact of trans-state trade are sometimes highly important. They also bring about a fundamental questioning of the role of the state.

18

JANET MacGAFFEY & RÉMY BAZENGUISSA-GANGA
Personal Networks & Trans-Frontier Trade
Zaïrean & Congolese Migrants

Ambitious schemes by national governments to achieve regional integration in Africa have generally failed dismally. At the same time, however, flows of commodities along autonomous trade networks have created what seems to be an unofficial integration over large areas of the continent. These trade flows, unrecorded in the national accounts of their countries of origin, take place on a huge scale all over Africa (Grégoire, 1993; 1991; MacGaffey *et al.*, 1991; Igué, 1983). The networks through which they operate are therefore highly significant politically, socially and economically, but we do not know very much about how they are organised, in what circumstances they arise, and why people use them. We present here some recent research findings on trade between the Democratic Republic of Congo (former Zaïre, henceforth DRC) and Congo and Europe in an attempt to answer some of these questions. Understanding how unofficial trade works may be useful in constructing new policies on local integration in an effort to counter the marginalisation of the continent in international trade.

Much of this trade and its associated activities are unrecorded and clandestine, or in some other way evade taxes and regulations imposed by the state. It represents a response to one or more of the following: the breakdown or absence of efficient marketing structures, the decline of infrastructure and of the effective functioning of the state, and the lack of opportunity for individuals to survive and better their lives in the official political and economic system of their own country.

The trade is organised through personal networks. Scholarly usage commonly employs 'network' as a general term, but does not precisely differentiate or compare various forms of networks and how precisely they function. In this chapter, we shall explore differences in two kinds of networks used in trade and their different cultural contexts, by presenting our data on traders from the DRC and Congo to Europe in a comparative framework of the organisation of trans-frontier trade within and from West Africa.[1]

[1] Our research is based on four months' fieldwork in Paris, and one month in Brussels and Holland, January-June 1994. The authors wish to express their gratitude for the assistance of a grant for this research from the Joint Committee on African Studies of the Social Science Research Council, UK and the American Council of Learned Societies with funds provided by the National Endowment for the Humanities and the Ford Foundation. We would also like to thank all our informants and to acknowledge our especial debt to Bitsindou Simplice.

The Nature of Networks

Personal networks are sets of linkages which exist simultaneously on the basis of specific interests and persist beyond the duration of a particular transaction: 'A network exists in the recognition by people of sets of obligations and rights in respect of certain other identified people. At times these recognised relationships may be utilised for a specific purpose' (Mitchell, 1969: 26). In long-distance trade, networks appeared historically where there were no effective central institutions to guarantee respect of contract, and where regular services for communication and transportation were lacking. When there is need for efficient, reliable information which is not readily available people put most trust in information that comes from someone they know well, and trust and mutual dependence result in the rapid communication of information (Powell, 1990: 304–5). Reciprocity is a key element in network organisation. Rather than involving a precise definition of equivalence in exchange, it tends to entail indebtedness and obligation.

We can contrast structured trade networks that are permanent, and which continue to operate over time for the trade of specific commodities, with instrumental networks, activated only sporadically to further the interests of individual traders from a latent set of relationships. We find both kinds of networks used in African long-distance trade. Networks based on ties of kinship or ethnicity across borders or transcontinentally have organised trade in Africa for centuries (see for example, Grégoire and Labazée, 1993; Curtin, 1984; Meillassoux, 1971; Cohen, 1969). Such structured networks continue to organise trans-frontier trade in West Africa. Our research shows that the trade between the DRC, Congo and Europe also depends on networks of personal connections but not on permanently structured ones: they are activated by individuals for particular needs and may or may not be reactivated for the same purpose. Such networks have been labelled 'instrumentally-activated personal networks' (Mitchell, 1969: 39). To investigate the differences between these forms of trading network, we shall first briefly examine some features of West African networks and their particular cultural context. In these networks, the biggest traders are Muslim men and they operate through structured, hierarchised and powerfully sanctioned networks. We shall then contrast and compare the networks used by men and women traders from Central Africa.

Long-distance Trade in West Africa

Traders between Mali, Burkina Faso and northern Côte d'Ivoire make strategic use of ties of kinship, locality, religion, politics and finance. They use networks stretching across frontiers and over several generations to circulate information, credit and goods. These traders invest in local politics, in marriage ties with important families, in financing of religious ceremonies, Koranic schools and mosques, and in pilgrimage to Mecca. All such investments constitute the means through which economic capital is converted into authority and position in the hierarchy of the religious community. Profits in the trade are in direct proportion to such social relations capital of the trader. These relations reduce the risks that are particularly high in clandestine forms of trade across these frontiers, in which agreements can be guaranteed only by the interdependence and recognition of reciprocal obligations between the parties concerned (Labazée, 1993: 144–70).

Islam also imposes and sanctions strict rules of conduct and ethics in the networks of big Hausa traders in their trade across the borders of northern Nigeria. Rich traders are closely linked to marabouts to whom they give money and substantial gifts for reciting the Koran and for healing. Breaking one's word means exclusion from the business world and betrayal of one's religious faith, both fundamental for membership of Hausa society. Confidence between the big traders and business partners who are also bound to them by religious ties, holds a guarantee more powerful than anything modern legislation can offer (Grégoire, 1993: 92–5).

From Senegal, diamond traders travel across a number of countries to reach the DRC and then to other continents. They are supported by local residents who themselves migrated earlier from the Senegal river valley, in a chain of links based on kinship, marriage and friendship, cemented by the bond of a common religion (Bredeloup, 1993). Senegalese trade widely in other commodities also: the Mouride Islamic brotherhood links large wholesalers in Dakar to networks of traders in New York, Paris, Brussels and Dubai. These Mouride emigrants form close religious, economic and hierarchically structured communities. The migrants who came first formed critical points of support for later comers; different networks specialised in organising trade in different commodities. Betrayal of trust inevitably brings grave consequences for an individual's whole existence, and such stringent controls promote commercial success (Ebin, 1992).[2]

Trade from Central Africa to Europe

Men and women from Congo and the DRC export and import goods. Women specialise particularly in importing to Africa wax-print cloth (*pagnes*), blouses and other clothes, shoes, jewellery, beauty products and food. Men specialise in importing second-hand cars, trucks, spare parts, office equipment (photocopiers, computers and printers), and pharmaceuticals. Both import televisions, VCRs, radios, and household appliances such as refrigerators and freezers. They export African foodstuffs to Europe for the large African communities in cities such as Paris and Brussels, where African migrants, who prefer to eat the same foods as they did at home, create a sizeable market. Traders sell these foods either directly themselves or to stores that serve these communities. In this chapter, for reasons of space, we shall focus particularly on trade by women.

The reasons DRC citizens and Congolese have come to Europe have differed according to historical periods. The first migrants were sent by the state for study or training programmes. They were supported by scholarships and came with the

---

[2] The scale of this trade boosts the wholesale business in New York, one Pakistani going so far as to claim that African customers account for the survival of many of his fellow New York wholesalers (Ebin, 1992: 95).

intention of returning. Some, however, got jobs in Europe and stayed permanently; this first wave formed a crucial support system for later arrivals. The SAPE (*Société des Ambianceurs et des Personnes Elégantes*) was a movement among young BaKongo who wanted to have luxury Parisian clothing. Soon they got the idea of going to Paris directly to get it, and the possibility arose for young people to go as adventurers. The *sapeur* movement made France accessible to uneducated people of small means, who had not previously gone there (Bazenguissa, 1992a ; 1992b). At the same time, women began to expand their economic role as traders, moving into trade across the borders of the DRC and Congo to West Africa and to Europe, and importing goods to supply their businesses at home. The 1980s was the peak period when women and men went back and forth in an extensive trade in commodities.

Recent political and economic events have diminished this trade. The DRC has been in a state of severe political and economic crisis since 1990; Congo recently went through the traumatising experience of a civil war; global and especially European recession adds to the crisis. Since 1988–9 it has become much more difficult to get a visa for Belgium, which used to be much easier to enter than France; now a 30-day visa often entails a wait of several months. The pillaging and riots in the DRC's major cities, intermittent since 1991, have resulted in the destruction of many businesses; people are afraid to invest in new ones for fear of losing them. The 1994 devaluation of the CFA franc has reduced the profitability of trade in this currency. Currently traders go back and forth to Europe much less, and trade consists of sending commodities in either direction rather than travelling to buy them in person. The flexibility and responsiveness of these traders to changing conditions are evident in the recent increase in trade to South Africa and the growth of a large DRC community in Johannesburg.[3]

Networks in the Trade from Congo & the DRC

This trade does not involve a continuing structured network of linkages between traders in particular commodities. Instead it involves mobilising other forms of networks on an individual basis according to circumstances. The basis of the linkages are ties of family and kinship, friendship from common locality, workplace or school, and ethnicity. Individuals activate them as they need shelter, assistance in establishing themselves in a new country, and help and advice with their enterprises. The most important of these links, and the ones most often called upon, are those based on family ties. Such family networks may not be organised for a specific purpose, but the relationships on which they depend can be activated by individuals as the need arises. These networks are also maintained by means of considerable material investment over time. They are networks in the sense defined above: 'a set of linkages which exist simultaneously on the basis of specific

---

[3] After the economic embargo by Western countries, South Africa turned increasingly to the rest of Africa for trading ties. Now with the dismantling of apartheid these connections are being developed. Visas are not necessary, only entry permits, and prices for European goods are often lower than in Europe.

interests and persist beyond the duration of a particular transaction.' They are an essential feature of the functioning and success of trade in all commodities.

Personal ties are mobilised at all stages of trade. They may be used in assembling venture capital, in getting to a foreign country and once there for finding lodging, for obtaining goods and credit, for transporting merchandise and getting it through customs, and finally for the process of finding customers and selling. In order to locate individuals and their activities in social processes (Bredeloup, 1991: 478), we shall give examples from our case histories of how people use personal ties in all these ways.

Venture capital is accumulated in various ways in this trade from Central Africa. Both men and women traders may purchase foreign exchange for importing from other countries on Kinshasa's parallel money market, where most foreign currencies are easily available. Foreign exchange is not available through the formal banking system. DRC citizens have to confront the problem that their national currency has collapsed and is without value beyond the border. They must find ways, legal or illegal, of obtaining currency or commodities that have value internationally. Illegal ways include smuggling diamonds or gold, trafficking in drugs or selling stolen goods. Gold and diamonds are not generally any good as trading capital: gold dust has to be refined and is not easily saleable on the open market; to buy diamonds, you have to be an expert in assessing their value so as not to be cheated, but traders who have access to the unofficial diamond trade networks obtain hard currency by this means. Some traders participate in the drug trade, reported on by Labrousse in Chapter 19 of this volume. In the early 1990s, Fottorino reported increased drug trafficking from both Congo and the DRC (1991: 31). Stolen goods are sold in Europe to finance trade by some male traders. Women in particular use the institution of rotating credit (*muziki* or *likelemba*) among a group of friends for start-up money. Some women have help from husbands, fathers or other family members, as in the following examples.

> Mme O. is from Congo. Her father gave his daughters 2,000 FF each to do their trade and further their education. She used this money as start-up capital to go into trade. Her father worked for *Air Afrique* which enabled her to travel free to West Africa and France. She went to Cotonou (Benin) and Côte d'Ivoire, bought sandals and sold them to the Senegalese traders in Brazzaville, becoming their wholesaler. If she needed further supplies, she had a 'frère' in Abidjan who bought them for her and sent them to her without paying (freight or customs) under the name of her father. After her father's death she went to France.
>
> Mme. E's father shared out the DRC government family allowance between his children. Her share served as her venture capital to trade in soap and cans of powdered milk in Brazzaville.

Goods are traded from Kinshasa and Brazzaville across the border between the DRC and Congo, and with West Africa, as well as Europe. Commonly DRC women will use trade with Congo as a stepping-stone to the more lucrative overseas trade. This practice enables them to accumulate money from the strength of the CFA franc compared with the zaïre.

> Mme. E. soon progressed to selling lingerie. By buying in Kinshasa and selling in Brazzaville she could return to Kinshasa and sell the CFA francs she earned for more

than the zaïres she had originally spent. She started at age 15 and in 5 years had accumulated enough capital to go to France and start trading back and forth to Kinshasa.

Arriving and trying to do business in a strange country presents plenty of problems that can be solved by having a personal contact who is already resident. All traders report having family members or friends who have helped them by offering hospitality, finding lodging, obtaining documents, and giving advice.

> Mme. M-R. was one of the first Congo women to go into this trade. She had a job as a nurse, but wanted to expand her earnings. Savings from her salary enabled her to trade to Kinshasa; a friend from work showed her how. After three years, she took leave of absence from her job to go to France to stay with a friend, also from work, who was on a training programme there. She asked for a loan from the bank in Brazzaville to buy goods in France to start trading, which she was granted because of her job as a state employee. She stayed a month, bought up 300,000 CFA francs worth of goods and took them back to Brazzaville to sell to friends and acquaintances. She continued to work as a nurse, made four more of these trips to France and in addition sold *pagnes* in Kinshasa. She was able to buy two taxis with the proceeds.[4]

In the first two cases given above, when Mme. O. went to France, she stayed with her sister.

> Mme. E. stayed with her brother when she arrived in 1990. She was pregnant, a circumstance she was able to use to her advantage: her son was born in France which meant that she automatically got a residence permit and had no further need of a visa to enter the country. She trades back and forth between Paris and Brazzaville, leaving the child in the care of a sister who also lives in France.

One of our male informants from the DRC went to Paris and stayed with friends from the neighbourhood in which he had grown up:

> When Mme. Y. from Congo went to France, she went to her sister who was in Paris, then used this sister's papers on a subsequent trading trip to England. In London, she stayed with friends living and working there, who were from the same locality as hers back home. One of them helped her find the goods she needed. On another trip to buy goods in Brussels, she stayed with her sister.

Some traders obtain credit from banks for buying their goods. Suppliers they know well will give them two to three months to pay, so that they have time to sell the goods. In such cases, a business relationship perceived to be reliable has built up over time. Traders who get goods sent from home need to have someone there to ship them and some means of sending money to this person.

> Mme. R. worked as a pavement seller of African foods in Paris for five years. This occupation is arduous not only because of standing out in all weathers, but also because it is illegal and police confiscate the goods and take the money of those they catch. Mme. R. sent money to her sister and brother in Kinshasa to pay for her orders of food, and for shipping them by freight to Paris, where she then paid customs duties. She now rents a store and sells a much wider range of goods which she obtains from wholesalers. But until the intensification of the crisis in former Zaïre, she continued to import foods directly with the help of her family. This source of supply helped to reduce her costs.

---

[4] An example from this early period from the DRC is that of a woman from Kisangani trading with Europe. She went three times a year to supply her business in the late 1970s: to Brussels for wax-prints and to Bologna for shoes bought directly from the factory. She had friends in both Brussels and Italy (MacGaffey, 1987: 176).

Confiding money to people to pay such suppliers was risky, however, as trust was sometimes betrayed. This flaw in the system has since been taken advantage of by airline flight attendants coming from Brazzaville. They bring sacks of manioc with them; having established relations with the pavement sellers; they telephone on arrival to announce how much manioc they have, and make a direct sale.

Our research continually reaffirmed De Soto's findings on the barriers to legality in Peru (De Soto, 1989). Mme. R. and her husband had to pay 70,000 FF down when she moved from illegal pavement selling to renting a store, and they pay 9,500 FF a month rent. They barely break even in this store but she desperately wanted to move out of pavement selling even though it incurs no overheads and no taxes and at least you keep what you make, whether or not it amounts to very much. Then again: 'If you have to pay full customs duties you operate at a loss', said one woman who traded between former Zaïre and Congo. To reduce customs duties, many people bribe officials or come to some arrangement with them, thus paying less than the due amount. If you have some relationship to such an official the amount you pay will be reduced.

> Mme. E. (above) imported her goods from France to Brazzaville under the name of a customs official (who is allowed to import for himself for free), paying him some money at a later date. In this way on one occasion, for example, she reduced her customs costs from 18,000 CFA francs to 7,500 francs.

Personal contacts increase the number of customers to whom goods are sold and make possible sales by telephone or direct conversation. These examples from Central African networks show that they do not constitute structured purposeful organisations, but are used instrumentally by individuals as the need arises. In between they are latent. But they operate by rules of reciprocity known to all, great importance is accorded to maintaining the relationships on which they are based, and sanctions of a sort exist to back up their values and modes of operation.

Reciprocity, Maintenance & Sanctions in Network Relations

Reciprocity in these relationships conforms to the pattern that people with strong personal relationships practise generalised reciprocity, while those with less strong personal relationships look for balanced reciprocity (Sahlins, 1965).[5] Among these traders and migrants, assistance and services rendered by family members are not directly repaid nor is their value calculated. A description of reciprocity within the urban middle class in Chile fits perfectly: 'the obligation is stored in a sort of savings account of future services to be rendered to various persons and drawn upon as the need arises' (Lomnitz, 1971: 94). Our informants speak of more direct and calculated returns when ties are not close.

---

[5] MacCormack provides a definition of this often ambiguously used concept, as a series of transactions which need not maintain a precise equivalence but which are directed towards securing it (1976: 90, 94).

Mme. R. (above) worked for her sister, a big trader, when she was a teenager but was not paid any wages. She says now that she can call on this sister and trust her to buy and ship the goods that she needs to sell in Paris in the context of family reciprocal obligations, to which she made her contribution as a young girl.

A male wholesaler from Congo with a business in Paris depends on his sister for purchasing and shipping foodstuffs from Brazzaville. He pays her no salary 'because she is family', but gives her presents of cloth, makeup, shoes, and financial help for her doughnut vending, from time to time. He comments: 'For her the idea is important that I work for the family; they will all benefit from it in the long run'.

This idea of working for the family is culturally specific to these traders and significant because it determines some of the ways in which they operate. The ability to be successful in trade is considered to be a gift that is inherited in the family. The money thereby accumulated, however, is family money and should be used to take care of the family, not for personal enrichment. The idea seems to explain the strong emphasis on family obligations which motivates people to help each other, even to working without regular wages. This help significantly reduces costs, not necessarily for maximising profits but more likely for making an enterprise viable and competitive. However, it should be noted that these generalised obligations can also give rise to disagreement on whether or not they are, or should be, fulfilled; our data include examples of such problems. As Powell observes, points of contact in networks can be sources of conflict as well as of harmony (Powell, 1990: 312).

These traders and migrants attach great importance to maintaining family relationships by sending money back home. They also attach great importance to giving their children a good education. One man noted specifically that such investment in the social capital of relationships was more important than the accumulation of wealth.

Mme. E. (above) invests her monthly profits in a muziki of 6 women. Every 6 months when she draws the money, she sends one third (as much as 10,000 FF) to her mother in Congo, puts one third in the bank, and spends one third on clothes. Mme. N., the owner of a nganda (an illegal bar run in her house which traders frequent to sell their goods) makes great efforts, despite an often precarious financial situation, to find means to send money at intervals to her parents in the DRC. Mme. Y. (above), sends money to the DRC to her sister with 8 children, to her younger brother and to her paternal uncle. She sends 500–1000 FF monthly, despite having great difficulty in finding profitable forms of trade.

Sanctions are weak but do exist. We found several examples where victims of breaches of trust and embezzlement were powerless to get their money back or bring any kind of retribution on the wrongdoer. Nevertheless, informants stated that trust was subject to sanctions: keeping it was motivated, first, by the possibility of a future need of assistance, secondly, by the need to preserve one's reputation in the milieu. The articulation between different networks (*sapeurs*, locality, workplace, etc.) helps to intensify this sanction, but traders do not belong to a close-knit community founded on a strong value system binding enough to constrain actions effectively. In the situation where credit was not repaid by a customer, traders said they would refuse to serve that person again. They had to absorb the loss, but said that their price margins were set to cover this contingency.

Conclusion

Several strong contrasts stand out between the networks from the two regions that we have considered. West African networks are much more highly structured; they organise trade in specific commodities; their mode of operation and the trust this demands are subject to powerful sanctions by the values of a close-knit religious community from which it is hard for individuals to distance themselves. In Central African networks, no such community organisation is brought to bear; networks of family and other ties are vital to the functioning of trading enterprise by individuals, but they must activate these networks themselves. Rules and values relating to the trust by which the personal relations of the networks operate are subject to sanctions but in a weak and diffuse way, which if ignored does not result in disastrous consequences for the wrongdoer.

Both forms of network show the effect of culture on economic organisation: the strong influence of Islam in the one case, of ideas about individual enterprise in relation to family obligations in the other. Both occur in response to particular political and economic conditions which give rise to forms of trade functioning in some way outside the official system and therefore requiring their own modes of organisation, of establishing trust and of an efficient means of communication. Another common element is the importance of migrants from an earlier historical phase who play an important supporting role for later arrivals in different circumstances. Networks from both regions make use of personal ties of kinship, friendship and locality.

Highly structured networks organising trade flows of particular commodities on a permanent basis are not unique to West Africa,[6] but represent one extreme in a range of possible forms of network along a continuum to the other extreme, of the instrumentally activated personal networks we have described from Central Africa. The latter form appears to be the most widespread for organising the cross-border trade that takes place all over the continent.

To conclude, understanding the functioning of these trade networks advances our knowledge of a significant phenomenon in Africa today: the flow of huge quantities of commodities across borders throughout the continent and beyond, that do not generally appear in the official statistics of national economies. The scale of this trade witnesses to its successful organisation and economic viability, in contrast to the dismal failure of so many official schemes for regional integration and development. Data on how the trade is done, for what reasons, and the systems of cultural values within which it operates, can perhaps be constructively incorporated and drawn upon in designs for projects by civil servants, policy planners and international aid organisations.

---

[6] Highly structured networks exist, for example, in the DRC among the Nande, who operated a trade diaspora between Kivu and Kinshasa, also among Asians dispersed throughout East Africa, the DRC, Canada, England and Pakistan (see MacGaffey, 1987: 74–7; 147–58).

19

ALAIN LABROUSSE
The Production & Distribution
of Illicit Drugs

According to the report of the United Nations International Narcotics Control Board (UNINCB) for 1992: 'The drug abuse and illicit trafficking situation has been worsening in Africa for a number of years and 1992 was no exception. If efficient steps are not taken, the illicit traffic and the abuse of drugs will get worse, adding to the poverty, the violence, the corruption and the destabilisation of communities' (INCB, 1993). Beyond the alarming tone of this warning, the precise information contained in various reports from international institutions – the US Bureau for International Narcotics Matters (BINM), INCB, Interpol and the Customs Co-operation Council – and the investigations carried out by the *Observatoire géopolitique des drogues* (OGD) since 1993 (OGD, 1993, 1996) have uncovered problems of thus far unsuspected scope.

International anti-narcotics institutions view sub-Saharan Africa as essentially a transit territory for narcotics. They view cannabis cultivation in Africa as traditional and subjected to social controls. This may have been true some twenty years ago. But today illicit cannabis crops are spreading rapidly, primarily to supply rapidly expanding domestic consumption markets and the international drug trade. At least since the early 1980s crops have been grown extensively in countries like Kenya, South Africa, Nigeria, Ghana, etc. In most other African countries, the transition is currently being made from cannabis grown in association with other crops, hidden among food crops, for instance, to cannabis grown on its own over surfaces that may stretch to several hectares. A number of clues indicate that experimental poppy and coca crops are being grown in Africa (Kenya, Tanzania, Nigeria, Benin, Togo, Côte d'Ivoire).

As far as the international drug trade is concerned, large quantities of all types of drugs transit through Africa: hashish from Southwest Asia and, in the coastal countries of West Africa, from Morocco; heroin from Southwest and Southeast Asia; cocaine from South America, most of which is bound for Europe. I shall make only passing mention of medicines diverted from Western and Eastern Europe as well as India, vast amounts of which are destined for African consumption markets, especially South Africa. While a large share of this trade is in the hands of smaller traffickers, most of it is organised and controlled by Nigerian, Kenyan and Tanzanian criminal organisations, among others, which are comparable to gangs from other parts of the world, ever since larger criminal organisations such as Cosa Nostra, Camorra and the Colombian cartels spread out their activities in order to elude law enforcement. The sheer scale of the African drug trade indicates that drug money is playing an increasingly large role in the funding of the various conflicts that are currently tearing Africa apart.

Economic & Political Causes

The birth and development of African international drug trafficking networks require a specific analytical framework allowing for a number of hypotheses, especially in the light of the better known phenomena which took place in Latin America. By contrast, phenomena such as drug consumption, drug production in rural areas and small-scale trafficking at the local level, or even small-scale cross-border trafficking, can be regarded as consequences of the social and economic crisis which Africa has experienced since the early 1980s. As a study undertaken for the French Ministry of Co-operation and Development emphasises: 'In twenty years, sub-Saharan Africa's share of world trade has thus been halved, its cereal imports trebled, and its total debt multiplied by more than twenty. Rural exodus, urban unemployment, repeated financial crises, bankruptcies of banking institutions, and the flight of capital are all indications of what must indeed be called an economic failure' (Michaïlof, 1993: 16). With a debt of $180 billion, the equivalent of its GNP, Africa is the most indebted continent per capita in the world. It accounts for no more than 1.5% of world trade. Of the 46 least-advanced countries, 32 are in Africa.

After the countries gained independence, a model of state-run development was prevalent, particularly with regard to industrialisation. On the one hand, this was undermined by corruption; and on the other hand, it was based on oversized, overbilled projects which were not, moreover, foreign to the business interests of Western countries. In order to remedy the situation and to permit a sustained renewal of growth, international financial institutions, mainly the International Monetary Fund and the World Bank, as well as industrialised countries, imposed structural adjustment programmes (SAPs) on Third World countries beginning in the 1980s. These consist of drastic reductions in public spending, notably by cutting social expenditures and downsizing the public sector, the opening up of industrial and agricultural production to international competition by removing trade barriers, the introduction of a policy of privatisation, etc.

As far as the drug situation is concerned, the consequences of the SAPs can be considered as either normal, given the nature of the programmes, or merely as 'unintended consequences'. Indeed, in urban areas, structural adjustment policies have rocked the social equilibrium. At a time when the urban population grew from 21 million in 1950 to 200 million in 1990 (and is projected to reach over 500 million in 2010), state investment in education, health and housing has, in practice, been drastically cut back.

The rise in unemployment provoked by the dismissal of tens of thousands of civil servants, to whom no real alternative for survival was offered, and the halt of public sector recruitment of graduates, have resulted in an explosion of the informal sector, which World Bank experts see as positive. But these experts feign ignorance of the fact that illicit or criminal activities, drug trafficking in particular, happen to be part of the informal sector, and its most profitable part at that. At first, drug couriers, or 'mules', were easily recruited in the back streets of African cities. For these couriers, one 'job' (a trip to Europe, for instance) could amount to the equivalent of up to five years' salary at a minimum. But today, the traffickers can afford to hire former civil servants or unemployed graduates: these educated people, who often speak foreign languages and know how to travel, constitute a far more efficient and inconspicuous work force.

As far as agriculture is concerned, the 'development model' which prevailed just after independence and the ultra-liberal philosophy which informed the implementation of the SAPs in the 1980s combined to accelerate the dismantling of subsistence farming in favour of cash cropping. But, during the last ten years or so the prices of coffee, cocoa, cotton and groundnuts have collapsed on the international market not only because of lower consumption in the countries of the North but also due to increased competition among the countries of the South. In this regard, Côte d'Ivoire provides one of the most striking examples. In 1988 the government stopped subsidising the price of cocoa paid to the farmers. The subsidy was aimed at offsetting the collapse of the price paid for cocoa on the international market, after a similar fall affected coffee prices. While a grower was paid CFAF 400 per kg (8 French francs, or about US$1.5),[1] following the devaluation of January 1994, he got a mere CFAF 320, while the prices of inputs rose sharply. According to a study carried out by the OGD in the cocoa-farming region of Sassandra, in south-western Côte d'Ivoire, in the summer of 1995:

> … Among the 36 farmers who put a precise date on the moment when they started growing cannabis, only three had started before the cocoa crisis of 1988/1989. By contrast, two-thirds launched into illicit cropping after 1990. The motivations expressed by the growers confirm this apparent correlation: the fall in cocoa and coffee prices is invoked as the main cause for starting cannabis in over one-third of cases while lack of access to land is given as a reason by 10% of growers. (OGD, 1995a)

The output of 0.1 hectare of cannabis, sold by the bag to a sponsor, makes for an annual income of CFAF 4–5 million (FF 5000, US $1000). This is the value of 13 to 16 tonnes of cocoa, the output of a plantation of about 30 hectares exploited by the owner himself along with 10 workers, or of about 40 hectares farmed by a tenant.

In the forest region of Guinea (Conakry), the same study established that the farm-gate price of a bag of cannabis of 22–5 kg, representing about 17 plants, or FF 2500 (US $500), is equivalent to the average annual income of a family of eight in a region where coffee, cocoa and kola nut are grown. For the moment, the only factor impeding a boom in illicit crops is the existing social prohibition against the appearance of economic differentiation among community members.

The development of cannabis crops fits perfectly into the logic that led to this situation and constitutes the response that is best adapted to the new market conditions. Indeed, a peasant made to specialise in cash crops by international

---

[1] Unless indicated otherwise, prices quoted here are in CFA francs at the 1993 rate, before the devaluation.

demand will naturally turn to those whose prices are attractive on the domestic or international market. It is not by chance that farmers all over Côte d'Ivoire plant cannabis among their cocoa trees.

At the level of national economies, illicit trading activities constitute a significant source of foreign currency. As a former adviser to the World Bank has noted: 'Once they have been laundered and recycled in the international banking system, narco-dollars can be used by the governments of developing countries in order to meet their obligations with their creditors' (Chossudowsky, 1993: 198). It could be added that dirty money also contributes to privatisation programmes in countries where foreign investors are reluctant to invest and where nationals lack capital. This is the reason why most currency-thirsty African countries cannot afford to be too demanding about the origin of the funds deposited in their banks. On the one hand, the international community, through the United Nations Drug Control Programme (UNDCP), is striving to get laws adopted in order to punish dirty money laundering, but on the other hand, as remarked by Chossudowski: 'as long as the service of the debt is assured, creditors do not make any difference between 'clean money' and 'dirty money'.' As long as there is no response to the contradictory demands of the rich countries, the steps taken in Africa in order to fight the drug trade may well remain fruitless.

Paradoxically, in the eyes of many observers, another phenomenon acts to worsen the drug production, trafficking and consuming situation – the democratisation process in which many countries have engaged. First, it has implied 'democratising corruption', a process which has been analysed quite well in the case of Guinea:

> the main effect of the bursting on the political scene of the military shortly after the funeral of the old leader (Sékou Touré) has been to put an end to the mafia-like monopoly of the gang which had been in power for twenty-five years. It ended up in the liberalisation and, one could say, the deregulation of the plundering of state resources … President Lansana Conté had no option but to meet the demands of all the groups, who previously had been repressed, with a view to gaining access to the resources and the positions offered by the state (Bayart, 1989: 290).

Secondly, in order to be able to compete on an equal footing with the former hegemonic parties that continue to monopolise state resources, the newly formed political parties must find alternative sources of funds and turn to trafficking in licit (timber, gold, precious stones, etc.) or illicit goods (drugs, arms, etc.).

The Emergence of Africa as a Drug Producer

As has already been said, the only 'classic' drug whose large-scale production is proven in Africa is cannabis. The sole cannabis derivative produced so far, marijuana (leaves), is first of all the object of domestic illicit trading in most of the countries which are both producers and consumers. There is also cross-border trafficking in the direction of other African countries. The latter is due to a variety of factors: first, domestic output in some countries may be less than domestic demand; secondly, some areas where consumption is high, especially cities, may be closer to production areas in neighbouring countries than to domestic sources.

Thirdly, the marijuana produced in some countries may be of a higher quality than domestic production and sought after by 'demanding' consumers.

But today a growing share of Africa's cannabis output is destined for export to Europe. The report of the Customs Co-operation Council covering the year 1992 thus notes: 'total quantities of the marijuana seized in Europe and in [sub-Saharan] Africa have grown 130% in comparison with last year, and reached 3,600 kilograms' (Customs Co-operation Council, 1993). It must be noted that, according to the same source, customs' seizures of African marijuana only represented 1.5% of world seizures and a diminutive share of the European consumer market. However, the following year customs worldwide seized 34,631 kg of marijuana from Nigeria alone (including a seizure of 7.72 metric tonnes hidden in containers bound for Amsterdam) and over one tonne from Ghana. In 1994, seizures of Nigerian marijuana made up 28.25% of total seizures worldwide.

In 1995, the South African authorities revealed that cannabis was grown on 83,000 hectares, producing 175,000 tonnes of marijuana, which makes their country the world's number one cannabis producer, far ahead of Mexico, the United States and Colombia. The main cannabis-producing region is Transkei, but the weed is also grown in Kwazulu/Natal, as well as in neighbouring countries such as Botswana, Lesotho and Swaziland. The marijuana is mainly destined for urban centres where it is widely consumed. According to the South African police, the annual turnover of the South African marijuana market amounts to several billion dollars. But the drug is also exported to Britain and the Netherlands. In March 1995, 2 tonnes of marijuana bound for Holland were seized in the port of Durban. Kenya is also a major producer, as suggested by the discovery of a 600-hectare cannabis plantation in the southwestern Rift Valley province in March 1996.

Let us take an example in order to illustrate the progressive passage from illicit cropping to activities which can be properly termed criminal. In Benin, cannabis, which is locally known as 'gué', is the only drug produced domestically over significant acreages. Benin's sub-equatorial climate is particularly suited to the crop, which can be found in each of the country's six provinces. In the Ouémé and Zou provinces, on the Nigerian border, cannabis plants are concealed among food crops. By contrast, in Mono province, especially in the villages of Idigni in the Ketou district, and Towé in the Pobé district, larger plantations where cannabis is grown on its own can be found. The crops fuel domestic consumption but are also for export.

In 1986, a seizure of 1,375 kg was carried out. In 1990, 9 tonnes were intercepted in Canada. The drugs had been embarked at Porto Novo, a port located on the border with Nigeria. Most of the drugs seized probably came from Nigeria, but it was not possible to assess how much of them had been grown in Benin itself. However, it can be noted that Yorubas live on both sides of the border and are known to grow cannabis. The figures of the seizures carried out inside Benin, which, since 1990, do not surpass 100 kg per year, paint only a hazy and underestimated picture of the drug production situation there.

According to the Beninois judiciary police, armed gangs – made up of Nigerian and other nationals – provide security at the plantations and protect trafficking activities in Benin. This information seems to be confirmed by an investigation made by the daily *La Nation* in the village of Kaboua, 45 kilometres away from Savé, in the south of Zou province, not far from the Nigerian border. Although the village's inhabitants do not grow cash crops and have never asked for help from a government agricultural expert, they enjoy a prosperity which can only be explained by the fact that they sow vast quantities of cannabis among their millet and maise crops. The police avoid the area as rumour has it that nosy people never come back. Officers posted in Kaboua are warned that if they tell the authorities about cannabis plantations, their families will be the target of reprisals.

An OGD correspondent maintained that he saw some opium-poppy plants hidden in a maise field in the Mono region, a cotton-growing area in Western Benin. Local informants told him that poppy was also grown in the neighbouring Atacora province, not far from the town of Djougou. This information seems to be confirmed by the discovery of poppy plants by a French diplomat, in the same geographic area, across the border in Togo.

Cannabis seizures operated in Europe suggest that the region's main producers are Nigeria and Ghana. As far as Nigeria is concerned, no detailed information is available on the location of crops or on the volumes produced. In Ghana, marijuana, which is known in the south and the centre of the country as 'Abonsam Tawa' ('the Devil's tobacco'), and more generally as 'wee', is grown throughout the country in a 'virtually uncontrolled manner', according to a customs official. Usually, cannabis plantations, or 'ganja farms' are no bigger than 3 hectares, but there are rumours, which could not be verified, that larger fields exist: an informant mentioned a plantation of 15 hectares under protection from the local police near Tamale, the regional capital of northern Ghana.

Nigerian Trafficking Networks

The above-quoted figures from the Customs Co-operation Council for cannabis trafficking go a long way to demonstrate that, in Africa, Nigerians play a part comparable to that assumed by Colombians in Latin America, and by ethnic Chinese in Southeast Asia. This can be verified by considering cocaine trafficking. According to international anti-drug agencies, African cocaine networks were allegedly established starting in 1984: 'the smuggling of cocaine from Brazil to Nigeria and Ghana has now become a significant trade. The main feature of this illicit trafficking is that it seems to a large extent to call on West Africans residing in Brazil' (Customs Co-operation Council, 1993). At the same time, relations with Brazil have become tighter. According to Interpol, between March 1992 and March 1993, the Brazilian authorities detained 15 Nigerians and 3 Ghanaians, mainly at the São Paulo and Rio airports, in possession of 270 kg of cocaine which they were preparing to transport or ship to Africa. Such traffickers buy 1 kg of cocaine for US $8,000–$10,000 in Brazil. In Europe, they can sell it for $50,000–$60,000. Over one hundred Africans were held in Brazilian prisons in 1996. In addition, some networks, mostly controlled by Nigerians, have been destroyed in Colombia, Ecuador and Brazil.

The professionalisation of these networks, which I alluded to earlier in the case of cannabis, is also verified for cocaine and heroine trafficking activities. On 20 November 1992, 350 kg of cocaine were seized in Hamburg on board a Russian cargo ship from Panama. The drugs, hidden in a shipment of fake 'Reebok' sports shoes and blue jeans, were to transit through Poland before being re-exported to Western Europe. Three Poles, who came to pick up the cocaine, were arrested. According to the German police, the mastermind behind the traffic was a Nigerian who was detained in Frankfurt.

Generally speaking, the Nigerians can count on important beachheads in Central Europe. They first appeared there following the demise of communism but were quickly wiped out by law enforcement. Since 1994, they have come back but they are now using much more sophisticated techniques. The Nigerians, who often are former recipients of scholarships from the communist regime, remain in the background and hire couriers from various Central European countries. Thus, Czechs working for Nigerians were arrested in 1995 and 1996 in Bangkok, Paris, Prague, the Netherlands and Finland. Two Nigerian bosses were arrested in Budapest during the summer of 1995. They had devised a simple but fairly efficient procedure. They recruited pairs of young Hungarian females. One girl travelled to Brazil or Venezuela to pick up from 2 to 5 kg of cocaine, which she carried to a West European city such as Paris, Zurich or Amsterdam. From Hungary, another young girl left for the chosen West European city. They exchanged suitcases in the transit area of the airport, for example in the toilet. The second girl, whose passport did not bear a Latin American visa, flew to London in order to deliver the drugs into the hands of Nigerian network members.

The networks function independently of one another, even though they may be strengthened by ethnic, clan or family links. Thus, in Lagos, the vertical networks in charge of recruiting the 'mules', setting up travelling arrangements, transferring money or recycling profits, are made up of Ibos and Yorubas. They are Hausas in Kano, Fulanis elsewhere. Recent investigations suggest that Nigerian networks are more strongly structured than was previously thought and it is no exaggeration to call them criminal organisations. 'Drug barons' allegedly command 'under-barons', who in turn monitor a team of smugglers. Within this scheme, 3 bosses allegedly supervise 85 cells of about 40 members each. Within each cell, a Nigerian 'lieutenant' allegedly leads from 6 to 20 'soldiers'.

Possible favours between groups must be paid for. While Nigerians make up the majority, they work with representatives of other nationalities, especially Lebanese, Indians, Pakistanis, Filipinos and, perhaps, even Hong Kong Chinese. Gang members are equipped with modern weaponry which they do not hesitate to use. These networks can only function with accomplices within official circles. Two former Nigerian Presidents, as well as their wives, have been accused, not only in the press but also by the secret services of Western embassies, of being directly involved in the drug trade.

The Anglican bishop of Nigeria, the Right Reverend Abiodun Adetiloye, declared in 1992: 'Nigeria is one of the countries in the world with the largest number of young millionaires without any known source of income'. The ostentatious displays of unexplainable wealth by new millionaires alone would suffice to suggest the existence of money laundering activities in Nigeria. They drive flashy, brand-new Japanese or German cars along Allen Avenue – nicknamed 'Cocaine Avenue' – in Ikeja (a Lagos district), live in exclusive and architecturally baroque mansions in the newly-developed residential districts of Victoria Island and Maroko, and use one of the hundred newly opened privately owned banks that have mushroomed in Lagos. Laundering activities are made easier by the fact that Nigerian banks have branches throughout the world and that Nigeria does not have anti-laundering laws. Furthermore, Nigerians use the same techniques as Indians and Pakistanis in order to repatriate their money from abroad – the 'hundi system'. Suppose a Nigerian trader based in Lagos needs British pounds in order to buy goods in England. He can make a call to an office – consisting of a secretary and a telephone – in Lagos specialising in this kind of service. Suppose that around the same time, a Nigerian drug trafficker located in England wants to bring home the profits of his latest heroin operation. He rings the Lagos office looking for help. The secretary contacts the trader who wires money in naira, the Nigerian currency, to a Lagos bank account, while the trafficker wires pounds on an account in London, which the Lagos trader opened in a no-questions-asked Nigerian or Pakistani bank.

Until 1 August 1993, selling CFA banknotes to the Bank of France was an easy way of laundering drug money. The introduction of restrictions on the free convertibility of CFA banknotes (see Chapter 14 of this volume) was quickly bypassed by Nigerian speculators. They set up, in Togo and Benin in particular, shops which they use as fronts in order to recycle CFA francs collected in Nigeria and other countries in West Africa. Bank deposits on behalf of these shops, which are officially recorded as earnings from sales, are none other than the CFA francs imported from the countries such as Nigeria where the currency is now no longer convertible. Import and export activities in Nigeria also serve to cover laundering operations. High-fi equipment and exclusive Japanese cars are sold in Lagos at prices less than their cost in their country of origin.

The same technique of over-invoicing (in US dollars, since there are no narco-naira) and selling at a loss is used by some privately owned airlines whose sole reason for existence is precisely these laundering operations. These small companies buy Bac 111, Trident III, Tupolev 134, Yakolev 40 and Boeing 727 aircraft at a high price. The planes, of venerable age, are flown commercially until their first major breakdown.

Funding Conflicts by Taxing Cannabis Crops & Trafficking Drugs

Similarly to what has been established in other parts of the world, West Africa shows that armed conflicts create a favourable context for drug production, trafficking and consumption. Some analyses, which could be viewed as prospective a few years ago, have already become facts: 'the recent spread of modern light weaponry represents a new qualitative phase in the history of land conflicts and it fosters the development of social gangsterism with a high return on investment' (Michaelof, 1993). Thus, in Casamance, a region of southern Senegal where a guerrilla movement is active, an investigation carried out by OGD shed light on the part played by the cannabis trade in bankrolling the rebels.

The Role of Yamba in the Funding of the Casamance Rebels. While practically nothing had been done in the previous ten years against the cannabis, or *yamba*, crops developing in Casamance, the Senegalese gendarmerie and Drug Squad carried out large-scale eradication campaigns in 1995. In fact, the campaigns were part of an attempt to regain control over the territory where the Movement of the Democratic Forces of Casamance (MFDC) operates. The MFDC has been fighting for over a decade for the independence of Casamance. Although it has lost most of its credibility with the population, the movement continues to fight government forces with unabated rage in the departments of Ziguinchor and Oussouye, bordering on Guinea Bissau. A police operation, carried out in the Kafoutine sector of the Drouloubou district, in November 1995 resulted in the seizure of 77 tonnes of *yamba*. The OGD correspondent in the area estimated that this amount represented only one-fifth of the crops he was able to observe himself. In June and July 1996, close to 80 tonnes of cannabis were destroyed in the Karones islands. A month later, 27 tonnes of marijuana were seized in the Sindia district. At an average price of US $80 per kg when sold at the farm gate, the cannabis destroyed represents just under $15 million. Even if the MFDC had deducted only a 10% tax on these profits, the resulting amount would have meant a lot to a small guerrilla movement.

Cannabis crops started to assume a truly commercial outlook in Senegal at the end of the 1960s when Ghanaian traders offered seeds to farmers in the Niayes, a region close to Dakar, the capital, and promised to buy the crops. Law enforcement campaigns in that region in the late 1970s fostered the development of crops in Casamance, which became Senegal's top cannabis producer. This is precisely the region where, in 1982, Attika, the armed branch of the MFDC, was founded. In 1989, a crisis situation in Dakar forced the armed forces to concentrate on the capital and helped the spread of cannabis in a region escaping from the control of the state. When the military did intervene, they concentrated on urban centres and made only occasional incursions into the villages where their brutal behaviour sent the population on the run. Vacant lands were farmed by non-village people who, among other things, planted cannabis. Some observers estimate that the rebels started collecting a tax on cannabis in the late 1980s. At the beginning, *yamba* was grown, above all, by the families of the fighters as a means of supporting the rebellion financially. The rebels endeavoured to protect the families and assist them in the marketing of their crops. But now reports increasingly state that the rebels force the growers to pay.

This phenomenon not only affects the inhabitants of Casamance. Support is also demanded from natives of Casamance living in other parts of Senegal, sometimes under threat of reprisals against their families. The tax takes the form of contributions to cultural associations. It is probable that the involvement of the rebels goes beyond merely taxing growers, especially as their armament has considerably improved over the last few years. Involvement in cannabis trafficking allegedly represents 60 to 70% of MFDC revenue. Exchanges of marijuana for guns, with the involvement of Senegalese traffickers as well as Liberians, Ghanaians and Nigerians, allegedly took place at the limit of Senegal's territorial waters. The former Gambian president, Dawda Jawara, who was toppled on 23 July 1994, revealed that drugs and precious stones from Liberia cross Guinea,

Sierra Leone and Guinea Bissau to transit Casamance before being finally shipped from The Gambia. Here, too, taxes are collected by the rebels

But these phenomena take place on a much larger scale in Liberia, Sierra Leone, Chad, the former Zaïre and Congo (militias), and confirm the most pessimistic prognosis. Warlords on all sides, like their Asian counterparts, engage in large-scale trafficking. When they are able to operate on a territory for a period of time, they first control the cannabis plantations. They encourage the consumption of various drugs by their soldiers in order to stimulate their eagerness for combat. This state of affairs helps to explain the atrocities that have been perpetrated during the wars in Liberia and Sierra Leone. The officers themselves are drug users. Problems continue when soldiers are demobilised, since they often do not hesitate to use any means available to obtain the drugs they now cannot do without. A number of child-soldiers, aged 8 to 15, are also the victims of such practices. In contrast to Senegal and Chad, where France exerts supervision and influence, both Liberia and Sierra Leone meet the criteria of the so-called 'new conflicts' which now escape the control of the major powers.

Drugs in the Liberian Conflict. In order to bankroll the war waged by the National Patriotic Front of Liberia, Charles Taylor first engaged in gold and diamond trafficking in Lofa County, on the border with Sierra Leone in north-eastern Liberia. When he was ousted from Lofa County by the United Liberation Movement for Democracy in Liberia (ULIMO), following the failed invasion of Sierra Leone in 1991, he had to look elsewhere for funds and turned to drugs. He used the port of Buchanan, south of Monrovia, a hub for all kinds of illicit trading activities which he controlled from 1990 to 1992, for his trafficking operations. Taylor also controlled the port of San Pedro, 100 kilometres away from the border with Côte d'Ivoire. His partners were Greek and Lebanese smuggler-traders. Cargo ships unloaded guns and loaded up with valuable tropical timber and containers in which, according to local rumours, were concealed significant quantities of cannabis. The cannabis came from producing areas under NPFL control, stretching from Mount Nimba, on the border with Guinea, up to central Liberia. Journalists reported that they had seen vast cannabis fields in swampy areas where rice was grown before the war.

Since it took part in the offensive against the Taylor-supported rebels from Sierra Leone, ULIMO also controls plantations stretching along the border between both countries. The ECOWAS Monitoring Group (ECOMOG), however, is far from appearing as a guarantee of stability and a shield against corruption. According to the Nigerian press itself, which is normally not inclined to criticise the intervention of Nigerian soldiers in Liberia, cases of plunder, rape and murder by troops of the 'peace force' are rife.

Journalists were able to verify that the ECOMOG force, especially the Nigerian and Guinean soldiers, cashed in on the opportunities available in the port of Monrovia and on their connections with Lebanese and Pakistani traders – who came back in 1991, after they had fled Liberia in the early stages of the war – to act as protectors of the contraband goods that pass in and out of the port. Drugs probably use the same route. Trafficking in licit goods alone is not enough to explain how some people became so rapidly and vastly wealthy in Monrovia. There is also intense air traffic between Nigeria and Liberia. Since Roberts

International Airport is no longer fit for use, planes use Spriggsfield Airport in downtown Monrovia. According to accounts by various journalists, every time a plane lands the airport is cleared of civilian staff and cordoned off by two lines of armed Nigerian soldiers. Since no control by international drug agencies is possible in Liberia, it is likely that those Nigerian soldiers who actively engage in drug trafficking and money laundering in their own country have decided to turn Liberia into a hub for the time being. Moreover, it is well known that, in spite of the dangers implied, a posting in Liberia is actively sought after by Nigerian military officers.

Many of the remarks made about West Africa can be applied to the rest of sub-Saharan Africa, as suggested by the information available on the former Zaïre, Rwanda and Burundi. The case of Congo, where a situation of civil war exists, is further confirmation. By 1996, the majority of cannabis fields found in numerous villages were allegedly run on behalf of politicians. According to the Central Office for the Fight Against Narcotics, several neighbourhoods in Brazzaville were used as rear bases for private militias collectively known as 'chanvrés' (marijuana junkies). Bacongo and Makelekele, neighbourhoods in southern Brazzaville, were controlled by the 'Ninjas', a private militia of Brazzaville's mayor and head of the opposition, Bernard Kolelas. Talagai, Mpila, and Poto Poto, in the north, were the fiefdoms of the 'Cobras' of former President Denis Sassou Nguesso. Mflilou, in western Brazzaville, was controlled by the 'Zulus', a government militia. The situation was identical in Dolisie, some 360 kilometres west of Brazzaville, the fiefdom of Congo's Head of State, Pascal Lissouba, which was held by the 'Aubervillois' militia, a presidential division trained by Israeli mercenaries.

The rise in drug-related violence in Dolisie surprised observers. On 2 November 1995 the government decided to dismiss 77 'deserters', including a general, four colonels and four lieutenant-colonels, charged with not having taken up their new posts. It should be noted that at least half of the dismissed soldiers were from the north of the country and supported former president David Sassou Nguesso. Nonetheless, criminals arrested by the police claimed that some of the 77 'deserters' were their main suppliers in arms and drugs. Several of the soldiers, as well as some retired military, directly took part in the operations of two of the most famous gangs from the north of Brazzaville – 'The Ambassadors' and 'The Dirty 25 from America', the latter gang led by a former policeman, Albert Tsika, who was later jailed for the murder of a teenager. In early November 1995, a senior policeman declared that numerous arrested criminals, as well as others who remain at large, were linked to 'foreigners who are involved in the drug trade'.

Discussing what the drug situation will be in Africa during the forthcoming decade depends on one's diagnosis of the continent's future. Various scenarios exist in this respect. Those of the World Bank (1994b) are based on the assumption that the reforms implemented, such as the structural adjustment programmes, the devaluation of the CFA franc, administrative reform, etc. will allow a restructuring of African economies, their insertion into the world economy and renewed sustained development. There is another scenario, however, a far less optimistic one: Africa, with the exception of South Africa, will plunge deeper into chaos, famine, ethnic wars, slaughtering of whole populations, the ravages of AIDS, etc. It is obvious that in such a context, drugs and 'predatory economics' would play a major part. The truth probably lies halfway between these two extreme hypotheses. Those who have observed the development of the drug phenomenon on other continents, cannot help remarking that Africa is currently in a situation comparable to that of Latin America in the mid-1970s, and Nigerian criminal organisations have already become capable of assuming the role of the 'Colombian cartels'.

Bibliography

Abbink, Jon, 1997, 'Ethnicity and constitutionalism in contemporary Ethiopia', *Journal of African Law*, Vol. 41, No. 2, pp. 159–74.

Abbink, Jon, 1995, 'Breaking and making the state: the dynamics of ethnic democracy in Ethiopia', *Journal of Contemporary African Studies*, Vol. 13, No. 2, pp. 149–63.

Abel, R.L., 1995, *Politics by Other Means: Law in the Struggle Against Apartheid, 1980–1994*, London: Routledge.

ACMS, 1991, *Towards Monetary Integration in Africa: Option and Issues*, Dakar: ACMS.

Adibe, Clement Emenike, 1994, 'ECOWAS in Comparative Perspective', in: Shaw, Timothy M. & Okolo, Julius Emeka (eds), *The Political Economy of Foreign Policy in ECOWAS*, New York: St Martin's Press, pp. 187–217.

Adji, Souley, 1992, 'Conférence-débat sur la démocratisation en Afrique', Niamey, 12 February.

Africa South of the Sahara 1994, 1993, London: Europa.

African Development Bank, 1993, *Economic Integration in Southern Africa*, Abidjan: African Development Bank.

Aggarwal, Vinod, 1993, 'APEC and NAFTA: Commonalities and Differences', paper presented at the conference on Economic and Security Cooperation in the Asia-Pacific, Canberra.

Agyemang, A.S., 1990, 'Trade Liberalisation Under the Treaty of the Economic Community of West African States', *The Journal of World Trade*, Vol. 24, No. 6, pp. 37–89.

Aikhomu, Augustus, 1993, 'Federal-State Relations Under Military Government, 1985–93', *The Guardian* (Lagos), 20 January, pp. 1–2.

Aka Ebah, 1980, 'L'intensification des échanges commerciaux entre les États de l'Afrique de l'Ouest: les motivations et les supports socio-économiques', *Annales de l'Université d'Abidjan. Série K-Sciences économiques*, III, pp. 241–67.

Almond, Gabriel & Verba, Sidney, 1963, *The Civic Culture*, Princeton, NJ: Princeton University Press.

Almond, Gabriel & Verba, Sidney, 1980, *The Civic Culture Revisited,* Boston, MA: Little Brown.

Aron, Raymond, 1967, *Les désillusions du progrès: essai sur la dialectique de la modernité*, Paris: Agora.

Asante, S.K.B., 1986, *The Political Economy of Regionalism in Africa: a Decade of Economic Community of West African States*, New York: Praeger.

Asiwaju, A.I. (ed.), 1985, *Partitioned Africans: Ethnic Relations Accross Africa's International Boundaries, 1884–1984*, London & Lagos: Christopher Hurst & Lagos University Press.

Asiwaju, A.I., 1976, *Western Yorubaland under European Rule, 1889–1945,* London: Longman.

Assidon, E. & Jacquemot, P., 1988, *Politique de change et ajustement en Afrique*, Paris: Ministère de la Coopération et de Développement-CCCE.

Atelier sur la promotion de la coopération et de l'intégration régionales en Afrique subsaharienne, 1992, Florence: European University Institute & Global Coalition for Africa.

Axline, Andrew W., 1980, 'The Economic Community of West African States (ECOWAS) in Comparative Perspective: the Lessons of Asia, Caribbean and Latin American Integration', Paper presented at the Conference on the Economic Community of West African States, Washington, DC: State Department.

Azam, J.P., 1991, 'Marchés parallèles et convertibilité. Analyse théorique avec référence aux économies africaines', *Revue Economique*, No. 1, January, pp. 75–93.

Bach, Daniel, 1997a, 'Federalism, Indigeneity and Ethnicity in Nigeria' in: Diamond, Larry, Kirk-Greene, Anthony & Oyediran, Oyeleye (eds), *Democratic Transition in Nigeria: Politics, Governance and Civil Society, 1986–92*, Boulder: Lynne Rienner, pp. 333–50.

Bach, Daniel, 1997b, 'Institutional Crisis and the Search of New Models' in: Lavergne, Réal (ed.), *Regional Integration and Cooperation in West Africa,* Trenton, NJ: Africa World Press, pp. 77–102.

Bach, Daniel, 1995, 'Les dynamiques paradoxales de l'intégration en Afrique sub-saharienne: le mythe du hors-jeu', *Revue française de science politique,* Vol. 45, No. 6, December, pp. 1023–38.

Bach, Daniel, 1994, 'Organisations régionales, espaces nationaux et régionalisme transétatique: les leçons d'un mythe ouest-africain' in: CEAN, *L'Année politique 1993,* Paris: Karthala, pp. 93–118.

Bach, Daniel, 1993, 'Un ancrage à la dérive, la convention de Lomé', *Revue Tiers Monde*, Vol. XXXIV, No. 136, October–December, pp. 749–58.

Bach, Daniel, 1992, 'Europe-Afrique: des acteurs en quête de scénarios', in: Léonard, Yves (ed.), *L'Europe dans le monde*, Paris: La Documentation française (*Cahiers français*, No. 257), pp. 118–31.

Bach, Daniel, 1991a, 'Fédéralisme et modèle consociatif; l'expérience nigériane', in: Médard, Jean-François (ed.), *Etats d'Afrique noire, formations, mécanismes et crise*, Paris; Karthala, pp. 117–40.

Bach, Daniel, 1991b, 'L'intégration économique régionale en Afrique', *Economie. Prospective Internationale*, (No. 48), pp. 33–49.

Bach, Daniel, 1989a, 'Managing a Plural Society: the Boomerang Effects of Nigerian Federalism', *The Journal of Commonwealth and Comparative Politics,* Vol. XXVII, No. 2 (July), pp. 218–45.

Bach, Daniel, 1989b, 'Francophone Regional Organisation and ECOWAS, or What is Economic Cooperation about in West Africa?', in: Wright, S. & Okolo, J. (eds), *West African Regional Integration and Development*, Boulder, CO: Westview Press, pp. 53–65.

Bach, Daniel, 1983, 'The Politics of West African Economic Cooperation: CEAO and ECOWAS', *Journal of Modern African Studies*, Vol. 24, No. 4, pp. 605–13.

Bach, Daniel & Kirk-Greene, Anthony H.M. (eds), 1993, *Etats et Sociétés en Afrique francophone*, Paris: Economica.

Bach, Daniel & Vallée, Olivier, 1990, 'L'intégration régionale: espaces politiques et marchés parallèles', *Politique Africaine*, No. 40, pp. 68–78.

Badie, Bertrand, 1995, *La fin des territoires: Essai sur le désordre international et sur l'utilité sociale du respect*, Paris: Fayard.

Badie, Bertrand, 1992, *L'Etat importé, l'occidentalisation de l'ordre politique*, Paris: Fayard.

Bakary, Tessy, 1993, 'Société civile et modes de transition politique en Afrique', Gorée (mimeo).

Balassa, Bela 1992, 'Europe and Its Implications for non-member countries', in: Schott, Jeffrey (ed.), *Free Trade Areas and US Trade Policy*, Washington, DC: Institute for International Economics, pp. 301–35.

Bayart, Jean-François, 1993, *The State in Africa*, London: Longman.

Bayart, Jean-François, 1989, *L'Etat en Afrique: la politique du ventre*, Paris: Fayard.

Bayart, Jean-François, 1984, *La politique africaine de François Mitterrand*, Paris: Karthala.

Bayart, Jean-François, Ellis, Stephen & Hibou, Béatrice, 1999, *The Criminalization of the State in Africa*. Oxford: James Currey.

Bayili, E., 1976, 'Les rivalités franco-britanniques et la zone frontière Haute-Volta-Ghana, 1896–1914', Mémoire de Maîtrise, Université de Paris I.

Bazenguissa, Rémy, 1992a, "Belles maisons' contre S.A.P.E.: pratique de valorisation symbolique au Congo', in: Haubert, Maxime *et al.* (ed.), *Etat et société dans le-tiers-monde: de la modernisation à la démocratisation?*, Paris: Publications de la Sorbonne, pp. 247–55.

Bazenguissa, Rémy, 1992b, 'La Sape et la politique au Congo', *Journal des Africanistes,* Vol. 62, No. 1, pp. 151–7.

Bekker, S., Buthelezi S., Manona, C.W., Mlambo, B., & van Zyl, A., 1997, 'Local Government Transition in Five Eastern Seaboard South African Towns', *Politikon*, Vol. 24, No. 1, pp. 38–56.

Bekker, Simon, 1996, 'La nouvelle nation sud-africaine et la restructuration de la société civile', *Hérodote,* No. 82–3, pp. 141–60.

Bekker, Simon, 1993, *Ethnicity in Focus: the South African case,* Durban, Indicator Press.

Belaoune-Gherari, S. & Gherari, H., 1988, *Les organisations régionales africaines, recueil de textes et documents*, Paris: Ministère de la Coopération et du Développement, la Documentation Française.

Berelson, B., Lazarsfeld, Paul & MacPhee, W., 1954, *Voting, A Study of Opinion in a Presidential Campaign,* Chicago: Chicago University Press.

Berger, Mark T., 1994, 'The end of the 'Third World?', *Third World Quarterly*, Vol. 15, No. 2, pp. 257–76.

204   Bibliography

Bergsten, Fred, 1997: *Open Regionalism,* Washington, DC: Institute for International Economics.

Bergsten, Fred, 1996: *Competitive Liberalisation and Global Free Trade: A Vision for the Early 21st Century*, Washington, DC: Institute for International Economics (APEC Working Paper 96–15).

Blaauw, L.C., 1988, 'The Constitutional Tenability of Group Rights', LLD-Thesis, Pretoria: UNISA, mimeo.

Boas, Morten & Hveem, Helge, 1997, 'Regionalism Compared: The African and the Southeast Asian Experience', Oslo (mimeo).

Bollard, Alan & Mayes, David, 1992, 'Regionalism and the Pacific Rim', *Journal of Common Market Studies*, Vol. 30, No. 2, pp. 195–209.

Bomsel, Olivier, 1991, *'Instruction Sysmin III. Gécamines'*, Paris: Centre d'économie des ressources naturelles, Ecole Nationale Supérieure des Mines, July.

Braeckman, Colette, 1997, 'Comment le Zaïre fut libéré', *Le Monde Diplomatique*, July, p. 12–13.

Braeckman, Colette, 1993, 'La nouvelle société civile est déjà là', *Le Monde diplomatique*, May, p. 18.

Bratton, Michael, 1989, 'Beyond the State: Civil Society and Associational Life in Africa', *World Politics*, Vol. 41, No. 3, April, pp. 407–31.

Bredeloup, Sylvie, 1993, 'Les migrants du fleuve Sénégal: A quand la 'Diams'pora'?', *Revue Européenne des Migrations Internationales,* Vol. 9, No. 1, pp. 67–93.

Bredeloup, Sylvie, 1991, 'Des négociants au long cours s'arrêtent à Dimbokro (Côte-d'Ivoire)', *Cahiers d'Etudes africaines*, Vol. 31, No. 4, pp. 475–86.

Brinkerhoff, D., Kulibaba, N. & Monga, Célestin, 1994, *Participation in Economic Policy Reform in Africa: A Review of the Literature*, Washington, DC: USAID.

Bustin, Edouard, 1975, *Lunda Under Belgian Rule: The Politics of Ethnicity,* Cambridge, MA: Harvard University Press.

Buzan, Barry, Morten, Kelstrup, Tromer, Elzbieta & Waever, Ole, 1992, *The European Security Order Recast,* London: Centre for Peace and Conflict Research & Pinter Publishers.

Callaghy, Thomas M., 1984, *The State-Society Struggle: Zaïre in Comparative Perspective,* New York: Columbia University Press.

CCCE, 1992, *Intégration et coopération régionale en Afrique Sub-Saharienne*, Florence: Institut Universitaire Européen.

CCCE, 1991, *Eléments sur la compétitivité de l'économie du Nigeria*, Paris: CCCE.

CEDEAO, 1979, 'Protocole sur la libre circulation des personnes, le droit de résidence et d'établissement', *Journal officiel*, No. 1, June, pp. 3–5.

CEPII, 1992, *Economie (L') mondiale à l'horizon 2000,* Paris: Economica.

CERED/Forum; Coussy, J., Hugon, Ph., Richard, C. & Sindzingre, A., 1994, 'Etude macro-économique sur le Bénin après la dévaluation: rapport', Paris: Ministère de la Coopération (mimeo).

CERGEP, *L'intégration régionale en Afrique Centrale: une mise en perspective*, Libreville: Centre d'Etudes et de Recherches en Géopolitique et Prospective.

Cerruti, Patrick, 1991, 'Systèmes de compensation et convertibilité régionale', in: Coussy, Jean & Hugon, Philippe (eds), *Intégration régionale et ajustement structurel en*

Afrique sub-saharienne, Paris: Ministère de la Coopération et du Développement, pp. 161–91.

Cerruti, P., Hugon, Ph. & Collignon, S., 1992, *La coopération monétaire en Afrique sub-saharienne. Le rôle des Arrangements Régionaux de Paiements,* Brussels: European Commission.

Ceylan, A., 1993, 'Le communautarisme et la question de la reconnaissance', *Conflits et cultures,* No. 12, pp. 169–84.

Chipeta, C., 1992, *Strengthening of Regional Dimensions of Policy Reforms and Coordination,* Gaborone: Institute of Development Management.

Chossudowsky, M., 1993, 'Le FMI et l'argent de la drogue' in: Labrousse, A. & Wallon, A. (eds), *La Planète des drogues*, Paris: Editions du Seuil, pp. 198–206.

Christianson, D., 1994, 'Local Government, the Loser', *Indicator SA,* Vol. 11, No. 4, pp. 27–32.

Clapham, Christopher, 1996a, *Africa and the International System: the Politics of State Survival*, Cambridge: Cambridge University Press.

Clapham, Christopher,1996b, 'The Developmental State: Governance, Comparison and Culture in the Third World', in: McKinlay, R.D. (ed.), *Comparing Government Performance*, London: Macmillan, pp. 159–78.

Clapham, Christopher, 1996c, 'Boundary and Territory in the Horn of Africa', in: Nugent, Paul & Aswaju, A.I. (eds), *African Boundaries and Borderlands*, London & Edinburgh: Pinter & Centre for African Studies, pp. 237–50.

Clapham, Christopher, 1994, 'Ethnicity and the National Question in Ethiopia', in: Woodward, P. & Forsyth, M. (eds), *Conflict and Peace in the Horn of Africa: Federalism and its Alternatives*, Aldershot: Dartmouth Press, pp. 27–40.

Claval, Paul, 1991, 'Quelques variations sur le thème: État, contrôle, territoire', in: Théry, Hervé (ed.), *L'État et les stratégies du territoire*, Paris: Editions du CNRS, pp. 11–26.

Cloete, F., 1995, *Local Government transformation in South Africa*, Pretoria: J.L. Van Schaik.

Cloete, F., 1990, 'Cultural and Religious Safeguards for Minorities in Public International Law and Comparative Constitutional Law', Johannesburg: University of Witwatersrand (Centre for Policies Studies Research Report, No. 8).

Cohen, A., 1969, *Custom and Politics in Urban Africa: a Study of Hausa Migrants in Yoruba Towns,* London: Routledge and Kegan Paul.

Cole, Bernadette, 1993, 'The Changing Face of WACH', *West Africa*, 1–7 March, pp. 331–2.

Collectif 'Changer le Cameroun', 1992, *Le Cameroun éclaté? Une anthologie commentée des revendications ethniques,* Yaoundé: Collectif Changer le Cameroun.

Collier, Paul, 1991, 'Africa's External Economic Relations: 1960–1990', *African Affairs*, Vol. 90, No. 360, pp. 339–56.

Collier, Paul & Gunning, Jan Willem, 1993, *Linkages Between Trade Policy and Regional Integration,* Nairobi: AERC.

Commission Européenne, 1982, 'La politique communantaire de developpement – memo de la commission transmis au Conseil, le 4 Octobre 1982', *Bulletin CE,* Supplément V/82.

Commission Européenne, 1993, 'Les leçons du processus européen', in: 'L'intégration régionale', *Le Courrier ACP-CEE,* No. 142, November–December, pp. 48–90.

Conac, Gérard & Gaudusson, Jean de (eds), 1990, 'La justice en Afrique', *Afrique contemporaine*, No. 156 (special issue).

Constantin, François, 1991, 'Les relations internationales', in: Martin, D. & Coulon, C. (eds), *Les Afriques politiques*, Paris: La Découverte, pp. 231–50.

Coquet, Bruno & Daniel, Jean-Marc, 1992, 'Quel avenir pour la Zone Franc?', *Observations et diagnostics économiques* (OFCE), No. 41, July, pp. 241–91.

Cornevin, Marianne, 1978, *Histoire de l'Afrique contemporaine*, Paris: Payot.

Cornia, A., 1991, *Is Adjustment Conducive to Long-Term Development? The Case of Africa,* Innocenti Occasional Papers, Florence: Unicef Child Development Centre, Economic Policy Series.

Coset, L., 1964, *The Functions of Social Conflict*, New York: The Free Press.

Coste, Jérôme, Egg, Johny & Igué, John, 1988, 'Echanges régionaux, commerce frontalier et sécurité alimentaire en Afrique de l'Ouest: méthodologie et premiers résultats', in: *Echanges régionaux, commerce frontalier et sécurité alimentaire en Afrique de l'Ouest*, Cotonou-Montpellier-Paris: UNB-INRA-IRAM.

Coughlan, R. & Samarasinghe, S.W.R. de A., 1991, 'Introduction' in: Samarasinghe, S.W.R. de A. & Coughlan, R. (eds), *Economic Dimensions of Ethnic Conflict,* London: Pinter.

Coussy, Jean, 1993, 'La Zone Franc: logique initiale, infléchissements ultérieurs et crise actuelle', in: Bach, Daniel & Kirk-Greene, Anthony H.M. (eds), *Etats et Sociétés en Afrique francophone*, Paris : Economica., pp. 177–98.

Coussy, Jean & Hugon, Philippe (eds), 1991, *Intégration régionale et ajustement structurel en Afrique sub-saharienne,* Paris: CERED-LAREA & Ministère de la Coopération.

Curtin, P.D., 1984, *Cross-Cultural Trade in World History,* Cambridge: Cambridge University Press.

Customs Co-operation Council (CCC), 1993, *Customs and Drugs 1992*, Brussels: CCC.

Dahl, Robert, 1992, 'The Problem of Civic Competence', *Journal of Democracy*, Vol. 3, No. 4, October, pp. 45–59.

Danjuma, T.Y., 1993, 'Revenue Sharing and the Political Economy of Federalism', a paper presented at the National Conference on Federalism and Nation-Building in Nigeria, Abuja (mimeo).

Darbon, Dominique, 1995, 'Les enjeux du droit des groupes dans la négociation constitutionnelle en Afrique du Sud', in: Conac, Gérard (ed.), *L'Afrique du Sud en transition*, Paris: Economica, pp. 133–50.

Darbon, Dominique, 1994, 'Les logiques différenciées du droit des groupes sur l'intégration: retour sur la dépendance', Talence: CEAN (mimeo).

Darbon, Dominique, 1992, 'Fluctuat Nec Mergitur: Keeping Afloat', in: Baynham, Simon (ed.), *Zimbabwe in Transition*, Stockholm: Almqvist & Wiksell, pp. 1–23.

Das, Dilip, 1990, *International Trade Policy: Developing Countries in Perspective*, London: Macmillan.

Davies, Arthur, 1983, 'Cost-Benefit Analysis Within ECOWAS', *The World Today*, No. 39, May.

De Boeck, Filip, 1996, 'Identité, résistance et 'effervescence' sociale: perspectives locales et globales au Zaïre', in: de Villers, Gauthier (ed.), 1996, *Phénomènes informels et dynamiques culturelles en Afrique,* Brussels & Paris: Institut Africain-CEDAF & Editions L'Harmattan, pp. 184–218.

De la Torre, Augusto & Kelly, Margaret, 1992, *Regional Trade Arrangements,* Washington, DC: IMF Occasional Paper No. 93.

De Melo, Jaime and Panagariya, Arvind, 1992, *The New Regionalism in Trade Policy,* Washington, DC: World Bank and London: Centre for Economic Policy Research.

De Soto, H., 1989, *The Other Path: the Invisible Revolution in the Third World,* New York: Harper and Rowe.

De Villers, Gauthier (ed.), 1992, *Economie populaire et phénomènes informels au Zaïre et en Afrique,* Brussels: Institut Africain (Cahiers du CEDAF No. 3–4).

Delancey, M.W. & Mays, T.M., 1994, *Historical Dictionary of International Organisations in Sub-Saharan Africa,* Trenton, NJ & London: the Scarecrow Press.

Desneuf, Paul, 1980, 'Problèmes monétaires en Afrique de l'Ouest', *Revue d'Etudes Politiques et Economiques Africaines,* February–March, pp. 20–49.

Deutsch, Karl, 1961, 'Social Mobilisation and Political Development', *American Political Science Association,* Vol. 55 (September), pp. 493–514.

Diamond, Larry, 1993, 'Civil Society and Democratic Consolidation: Building a Culture of Democracy in a New South Africa', paper presented at the colloquium on Consolidating Democracy in South Africa, July 22–23, Johannesburg (mimeo).

Dollfus, Olivier, 1994, 'Mondialisme et particularisme' in: GEMDEV (ed.), *L'intégration régionale dans le monde, innovations et ruptures,* Paris: Karthala, pp. 35–44.

Dreux-Brézé, J. de, 1968, *Le problème du regroupement en Afrique Equatoriale,* Paris: LGDJ.

du Pisanie, J.A., 1991, 'Intergovernmental Flows of Funds', paper delivered at a Workshop on Financing Local Government, Stellenbosch: Centre for Contextual Hermeneutics.

Dudley, Billy J., 1966, 'Federalism and the Balance of Political Power in Nigeria', *Journal of Commonwealth Political Studies,* Vol. 4, No. 1, pp. 16–29.

Durand, M.-F., Levy, J. & Retaillé, D., 1992, *Le monde; espaces et systèmes,* Paris: Presse de la Fondation Nationale des Sciences Politiques, pp. 394–6.

Ebin, V., 1992, 'A la recherche de nouveaux 'poissons': stratégies commerciales mourides par temps de crise', *Politique Africaine,* No. 45, pp. 86–99.

ECOWAS, 1994, *Annual Report of the Executive Secretary, Mr. Edouard Benjamin, 1993/1994,* Lagos: ECOWAS Secretariat.

ECOWAS, 1987, *Creation of a Single Ecowas Monetary Zone,* Lagos: ECOWAS Secretariat.

ECOWAS, 1984, *Report of the Executive Secretary Covering the Period of His Tenure of Office (1977–1984),* Lagos: ECOWAS Secretariat.

ECOWAS, 1981, 'Protocol Relating to the Definition of the Concept of Originating Products of the Member States of the ECOWAS', *Journal officiel,* Vol. 3, June.

ECOWAS, 1979, *Unrecorded Trade Flows Within ECOWAS,* prepared by the ECA, Lagos: ECOWAS Secretariat.

ECOWAS, 1976a, *Treaty of the Economic Community of West African States (ECOWAS)*, Lagos: Roacraft Adv. Associates.

ECOWAS, 1976, *Protocols Annexed to the Treaty of ECOWAS*, Lagos: Roacraft Adv. Associates.

Egg, Johnny, 1989, *Disparités des politiques économiques et échanges agricoles régionaux en Afrique de l'Ouest*, Ouagadougou-Paris: CILSS-Club du Sahel (OCDE)-Ministère de la Coopération.

Egg, Johnny & Igué, John, 1993, *L'intégration par les marchés dans le sous-espace est: l'impact du Nigeria sur ses voisins immédiats*, Paris : OCDE, Club du Sahel.

Egg, Johnny & Igué, John, 1987a, 'Commerçants sans frontières', *Inter-Tropiques*, No. 21, pp. 15–17.

Egg, Johnny & Igué, John, 1987b, 'Echanges invisibles et clandestins', *Inter-Tropiques*, No. 22, pp. 4–7.

Ekwueme, Alex, 1992, 'More Than a Government of National Consensus', *The Guardian* (Lagos), 21 March, p. 9.

Elbaz, M., Murbach, R. & Olazabal, M., 1993, 'Minorités visibles et action positive au Canada: une affaire de générations?', *Revue européenne des migrations internationales*, Vol. 9, No. 3, pp. 119–46.

Engola Oyep, J. & Harre, D., 1992, *Le Cameroun sous l'emprise commerciale du Nigeria?* Paris: OCDE, Club du Sahel; Ministère de la Coopération.

Faroutan, F., 1993, 'Regional Integration in Sub-Saharan Africa: Past Experience and Future Prospects', in: de Melo, J. and Panagarya, A. (eds), *New Dimensions of Regional Integration*, Cambridge: Cambridge University Press, pp. 253–71.

Federal Republic of Nigeria, 1982, 'Allocation of Revenue Act 1981', *Supplement of the Official Gazette*, Vol. 69, No. 8, pp. A1–5.

Federal Republic of Nigeria, 1976, *Federal Military Government Views on the Report of the Panel on Creation of States*, Lagos: Federal Ministry of Information.

Ferguson, James, 1995, 'How Is Africa Ruled? Beyond 'the Local' and 'the National' in the Study of African Politics', mimeo.

Fernandez, Raquel, 1997, *Returns to Regionalism: An Evaluation of Non-traditional Gains from Regional Trade Arrangements*, Washington, DC: World Bank.

Fidani, G., 1993, 'Afrique du Sud, le géant d'en bas', *Jeune Afrique*, Vol. 34, No. 1716, 25 November, pp. 26–7.

Fieleke, Norman S., 1992, 'One Trading World or Many: The Issue of Regional Trading Blocs', *New England Economic Review,* Vol. 3, No. 3, pp. 169–95.

Filipek, Jon G., 1989, 'Agriculture in a World of Comparative Advantage. The Prospects for Farm Trade Liberalisation in the Uruguay Round of GATT Negotiations', *Harvard International Law Journal*, Vol. 30, No. 1, pp. 123–70.

Fottorino, Eric, 1993, 'L'Afrique, nouvelle 'élue' des drogues', in: Labrousse, A. & Wallon, A. (eds), *La planète des drogues,* Paris: Seuil, pp. 207–17.

Fottorino, Eric, 1991, *La Piste blanche. L'Afrique sous l'emprise de la drogue*. Paris: Balland.

Foucher, Michel, 1988, *Fronts et frontières. Un tour du monde géopolitique*, Paris: Fayard.

Fried, Jonathan T., 1990, 'Squaring the Circle: Unilateralism, Bilateralism and Multilateralism in US Trade Policy', *Boston University International Law Journal*, Vol. 8, No. 23, pp. 232–3.

Friedman, Steven, 1996, 'Sarafina 2 Affair has Taken Our Democracy Just a Tiny Bit Forward', *Business Day*, 10 June 1996.

Gallais, Jean, 1982, 'Pôles d'États et frontières en Afrique contemporaine', *Cahiers d'Outre-Mer*, No. 138, pp. 103–22.

Gamble, Andrew & Payne, Anthony (eds), 1996, *Regionalism and World Order*, London: Macmillan.

GATT, 1993, *Activités du GATT en 1992*, Geneva: GATT.

Gautron, Jean-Claude, 1981, 'Pactes économiques et projets supra-nationaux', *Débat*, No. 30, pp. 51–8.

Gbabendu Engunduka, A. & Efolo Ngobaasu, E., 1991, Volonté de changement au Zaïre, Paris: L'Harmattan, Vol. 1.

Gboyega, Alex, 1987, *Political Values and Local Government in Nigeria*, Lagos: Malthouse Press.

Gérardin, Hubert, 1989, *La Zone Franc; Tome 1: Histoire et Institutions*, Paris: L'Harmattan.

Gerstin, Michael and Rugman, Alan, 1994, 'NAFTA's Treatment of Foreign Investment', in: Rugman, Alan (ed.), *Foreign Investments and NAFTA*, Columbia, SC: University of South Carolina Press, pp. 183–99.

Global Witness, 1998, *A Rough Trade: The Rôle of Companies and Governments in the Angolan Conflict,* London: Global Witness.

Gluckman, M., 1967, *Politics, Law and Ritual in Tribal Society*, Oxford: Basil Blackwell.

Götz, G., 1995, 'Cracks in the Edifice: Local Government Elections 1995', *Indicator SA,* Vol. 12, No. 3, pp. 11–17.

Gould, David, 1980, *Bureaucratic Corruption and Underdevelopment in the Third World: The Case of Zaïre,* New York: Pergamon.

Govender, C., 1996, 'Shifting the Balance: Local Elections in KwaZulu-Natal', *Indicator SA,* Vol. 13, No. 3, p. 36–40.

Graf, William D., 1988, *The Nigerian State: Political Economy, State Class and Political System in The Post-Colonial Era*, London: James Currey.

Grawitz, Madeleine & Leca, Jean (eds), 1985, *Traité de science politique*, Paris: Thémis.

Green, Reginald H., 1990, 'Economic Integration Coordination in Africa: The Dream Drives But How Long Can It Be Lived?', in Pickett, James and Singer, Hans, eds, *Towards Economic Recovery in Sub-Saharan Africa*, London & New York, Routledge.

Greenwald, Joseph, 1992, 'Negotiating Strategy' in: Hufbauer, Gary (ed.), *Europe 1992, An American Perspective*, Washington, DC: The Brookings Institution, pp. 345–88.

Grégoire, Emmanuel, 1993, 'La Trilogie des réseaux marchands haoussas: un clientélisme social, religieux et étatique', in: Emmanuel, Grégoire & Labazée Pascal, (eds), *Grands commerçants d'Afrique de l'Ouest: Logiques et pratiques d'un groupe d'hommes d'affaires contemporains*. Paris: Karthala, pp. 71–101.

Grégoire, Emmanuel, 1991, 'Les Chemins de la contrebande: étude des réseaux commerciaux en pays haoussa', *Cahiers d'Etudes africaines,* Vol. 31, No. 124, pp. 509–32.

Grégoire, Emmanuel, 1986, *Les Alhazai de Maradi*, Paris: Editions de l'ORSTOM.

Grégoire, Emmanuel & Labazée, Pascal (eds), 1993, *Grands commerçants d'Afrique de l'Ouest. Logiques et pratiques d'un groupe d'hommes d'affaires contemporains*, Paris: Karthala-Orstom.

Griggs, R.A., 1995, 'Cultural Faultlines: South Africa's New Provincial Boundaries', *Indicator SA*, Vol. 13, No. 1, pp. 7–12.

Grofman, B., & Davidson, C. (eds), 1992, *Controversies in Minority Voting: the Voting Rights Act in Perspective*, Washington, DC: The Brooking Institution.

Guillaumont, Patrick & Guillaumont, Sylviane, 1994, 'Franc CFA: restaurer la confiance', *Marchés tropicaux et méditerranéens*, No. 2522, 11 March, pp. 468–9.

Guillaumont, Patrick & Guillaumont, Sylviane, 1993a, 'L'intégration économique: un nouvel enjeu pour la Zone Franc', *Revue Economique du Développement*, No. 2., pp. 83–111.

Guillaumont, Patrick & Guillaumont, Sylviane, 1993b, 'La Zone Franc à un tournant vers l'intégration régionale', in: Michaelof. pp. 411–30.

Guillaumont, Patrick, Guillaumont, Sylviane, & Plane, P., 1991, *Comparaison de l'efficacité des politiques d'ajustement en Afrique, Zone Franc et hors Zone Franc*, Paris : CCCE (*Notes et Etudes* No. 41).

Guillaumont, Patrick & Guillaumont, Sylviane, 1989, 'Monnaie européenne et monnaies africaines', *Revue Française d'Economie*, Vol. 4, No. 1, Winter, pp. 97–115.

Hallaire, A., 1989, 'L'intérêt d'une frontière: l'exemple des Monts Mandara (Cameroun/Nigeria)' in: Antheaume, B. *et al.* (eds), *Tropiques, lieux et liens*, Paris: ORSTOM, pp. 589–93.

Halliday, Fred, 1986, *The Coming of the Second Cold War*, London: Verso.

Harding, Leonhard & Kipré, Pierre (eds), 1992, *Commerce et commerçants en Afrique de l'Ouest; vol 1, la Côte-d'Ivoire*, Paris: L'Harmattan.

Hargreaves, J.D., 1985, 'The Making of the Boundaries: Focus on West Africa', in: Asiwaju, pp. 19–26.

Haudeville, Bernard, 1993, *La Zone Franc: Mécanisme et perspectives*, Orléans: Institut Orléanais de Finance.

Hawes, Gary & Hong Liu, 1993, 'Explaining the Dynamics of the Southeast Asian Political Economy, State, Society, and the Search for Economic Growth', *World Politics*, Vol. 45, No. 4, pp. 629–60.

Henry de Frahan, Bruno, 1993, 'Les enjeux de la libéralisation mondiale de l'agriculture', *Politique étrangère*, Vol. 2, No. 1, pp. 89–105.

Herbst, Jeffrey, 1992, 'The Potential for Conflict in Africa', *Africa Insight*, Vol. 22, No. 2, pp. 105–10.

Hess, Richard, 1994, 'Rationalisation and Strengthening of Regional Integration Institutions in Africa', paper presented at the meeting of the Global Coalition for Africa, Dakar.

Hibou, Béatrice, 1996, *L'Afrique est-elle protectionniste?*, Paris: Karthala.

Hibou, Béatrice, 1993, 'La réforme de l'UDEAC', Paris: Ministère de la Coopération (mimeo).

Hine, Robert C., 1992, 'Regionalism and the Integration of the World Economy', *Journal of Common Market Studies*, Vol. 30, No. 2, pp. 115–23.

Hudson, J., 1981, 'Bostwana's Membership of the Southern African Customs Union', in: Harvey, Charles (ed.), *Papers on the Economy of Botswana*, London: Heineman, pp. 131–58.

Hufbauer, Gary, 1992, *Europe 1992, An American Perspective*, Washington, DC: The Brookings Institution.

Hufbauer, Gary C., & Schott, Jeffrey, 1992, *NAFTA, An Assessment*, Washington, DC: Institute for International Economics.

Hufbauer, Gary, & Schmitt, Claudia, 1992, 'The North American Argument about a "Fortress Europe"', in: Schott, Jeffrey (ed.), *Free Trade Areas and US Trade Policy*, Washington, DC: Institute for International Economics, pp. 159–84.

Hughes, Arnold & Lewis, Janet, 1993, 'L'expérience de la Confédération Sénégambienne', in: Bach, Daniel & Kirk-Greene, Anthony H.M. (eds), *Etats et Sociétés en Afrique Francophone*, Paris: Karthala, pp. 252–62.

Hugon, Philippe, 1994a, 'Franc CFA – Opportunités et risques', *Afrique contemporaine*, No. 169, January-March, pp. 18–26.

Hugon, Philippe, 1994b, 'Intégration régionale, Zone Franc et Zone Ecu', in: Dolfuss, O. *et al., Intégration et désintégration régionale*, Paris: Karthala.

Hugon, Philippe, 1994c, 'Passer de la zone franc à la zone Ecu', *Le Monde*, 4 January.

Hugon, Philippe, 1993a, 'L'Europe et le Tiers Monde: entre la mondialisation et la régionalisation', *Revue Tiers Monde*, Vol. XXXIV, No. 136, October-December, pp. 725–48.

Hugon, Philippe, 1993b, *L'économie de l'Afrique*, Paris: La Découverte.

Hugon, Philippe, 1993c, 'Modèles et performances économiques' in Bach, Daniel & Kirk-Greene, Anthony (eds), *Etats et societés en Afrique francophone*, Paris: Economica, pp. 139–58.

Hugon, Philippe & Robson, Peter, 1991, *La dimension régionale de l'ajustement dans les ACP*, Brussels: European Commission.

Humphries, Richard, 1995, 'The Provincial Power Struggle', *Indicator SA*, Vol. 12, No. 3, pp. 7–10.

Humphries, Richard, & Meierhenrich, J., 1996, 'South Africa's New Upper House: the National Council of Provinces', *Indicator SA*, Vol. 13, No. 4, pp. 21–4.

Hurrell, Andrew, 1992, 'Latin America in the New World Order : A Regional Bloc of the Americas?', *International Affairs*, Vol. 68, No. 1, pp. 121–39.

Ibrahim, Jibrin, 1991, 'Le développement de l'Etat nigérian', in: Médard, J.F. (ed.), *Etats d'Afrique noire: formations, mécanismes et crises*, Paris: Karthala, pp. 141–72.

Igué, John, 1995, *Le territoire et l'État en Afrique. Les dimensions spatiales du développement*, Paris: Karthala.

Igué, John, 1993, 'Echanges et espaces de développement: cas de l'Afrique de l'Ouest', *Travaux de l'Institut de Géographie de Reims*, No. 83/84, pp. 19–39.

Igué, John, 1989a, 'Le développement des périphéries nationales en Afrique', in: B. Antheaume *et al.* (eds), *Tropiques. Lieux et liens*, Paris: ed. Orstom, pp. 594–605.

Igué, John, 1989b, *Les périphéries nationales, support des échanges régionaux*, Ouagadougou-Paris: CILSS-Club du Sahel (OCDE).

Igué, John, 1983, 'L'officiel, le parallèle et le clandestin: commerces et intégration en Afrique occidentale', *Politique Africaine*, No. 9, pp. 29–51.

Igué, John & Soulé, Bio, 1992, *L'État-entrepôt au Bénin. Commerce informel ou solution à la crise?*, Paris: Karthala.

International Monetary Fund (IMF), 1991, *IMF Survey 1991*, Washington, DC: IMF.

International Narcotics Control Board (INCB), 1993, *Report of the International Narcotics Control Board 1992*, Vienna: INCB.

Jackson, B.S., & McGoldrick, D. (eds), 1993, *Legal Visions of the New Europe*, London: Graham & Trotman.

Jackson, John H., 1993, 'Status of Treaties in Domestic Legal Systems: A Policy Analysis', *American Journal of International Law*, 86 (2), pp. 310–40.

Jackson, John H., 1987, 'Multilateral and Bilateral Negotiating Approaches for the Conduct of U.S. Trade Policies', in: Stern, Robert (ed.), *U.S. Trade Policies in a Changing World Economy*, Cambridge, MA: MIT Press.

Jackson, Robert, H., & Rosberg, Carl, 1986, 'Sovereignty and Under-development: Juridical Statehood in the African Crisis', *Journal of Modern African Studies*, Vol. 24, No. 1, pp. 1–31.

Jackson, Robert. H., & Rosberg, Carl, 1982, 'Why Africa's weak states persist', *World Politics*, Vol. 35, No. 1, pp. 1–24.

Jacquemot, Pierre & Raffinot, Marc, 1993, *La nouvelle politique économique en Afrique*, Vanves: Edicef; Aupelf.

Jewsiewicki, Bogumil, 1992, 'Jeux d'argent et de pouvoir au Zaïre: la bindomanie et le crépuscule de la 2ème République', *Politique Africaine*, No. 46 (June), pp. 55–70.

Johnson, A., 1996, 'Peace and Alignment? Post-election Prospects' *KwaZulu-Natal Briefing* No. *3*, Johannesburg: The Helen Suzman Foundation.

Johnson, R.W., 1996, 'Understanding the Elections', *KwaZulu-Natal Briefing No. 3,* Johannesburg: The Helen Suzman Foundation.

Joseph, Richard, 1987, *Democracy and Prebendal Politics in Nigeria, the Rise and Fall of the Second Republic*, Cambridge: Cambridge University Press.

Kahler, Miles, 1992, 'Multilateralism with Small and Large Numbers', *International Organisation*, Vol. 46, No. 3, pp. 681–708.

Kaiser, David, 1980: *Economic Diplomacy and the Origins of the Second World War, Germany, Britain, France and Eastern Europe, 1930–1939*, Princeton, NJ: Princeton University Press.

Kaptinde, F., 1994, 'Bénin. L'Esprit de famille', *Jeune Afrique,* No. 1730, 9 March, pp. 24–7.

Kelly, Margaret & McGuirk, Anne Kenny, 1992, *Issues and Developments in International Trade Policy*, (World Economic and Financial Surveys), Washington: IMF, 1992.

Kennes, Erik, 1998, 'Du Zaïre à la République démocratique du Congo: une analyse de la guerre de l'Est', in: CEAN (ed.), *L'Afrique politique 1998,* Paris: Karthala, pp. 175–204.

Klug H., 1994, 'Rethinking Affirmative Actions in a Non-Racial Democracy', *South African Journal of Human Rights,* Vol. 7, pp. 317–33.

Knopf, R., 1990, *Human Rights and Social Technology: a New War on Discrimination*, Ottawa: Carleton University Press.

Kodjo, Edem, 1986, ... *Et demain l'Afrique,* Paris: Stock.

Kondo, S., 1994, [Interview in], *Jeune Afrique*, 31 March, pp. 52–3.

Kostrzewa, Wojciech & Schmiedling, Holger, 1989, 'EFTA Option for the Reform States of Eastern Europe', *World Economy*, Vol. 12, No. 4, pp. 481–500.

Krueger, A., 1985, *La détermination des taux de change*, Paris: Economica.

Krugman, Paul, 1988, *EFTA and 1992*, Geneva: EFTA (Occasional Paper No. 23).

Labazée, Pascal, 1993, 'Les Echanges entre le Mali, le Burkina Faso et le nord de la Côte-d'Ivoire', in: Grégoire & Labazée, pp. 125–74.

Lachman, D. & Bercuson, K., 1992, *Economic Policy for a New South Africa*, Washington, DC: IMF Occasional Paper No. 91.

Lafay, Gérard & Unal-Kesenci, Deniz, 1991, 'Les trois pôles géographiques des échanges internationaux', *Economie prospective internationale*, No. 45 (1er quarter), pp. 47–74.

Lallement, B., 1960, 'Le Dahomey, voisin de la Nigeria', mémoire de l'ENFOM, Paris: ENFOM.

Lambert, Agnès, 1989, *La dynamique des réseaux marchands en Afrique de l'Ouest*, Ouagadougou-Paris: CILSS- Club du Sahel (OCDE).

Landau, Alice, 1996, *L'Uruguay Round: conflit et coopération dans les relations économiques internationales*, Brussels: Bruylant.

Landau, Alice, 1995a, 'L'Union Européenne face à ses périphéries, de la nécessité d'une recomposition', *Revue internationale de politique comparée*, Vol. 2, No. 3, pp. 467–85.

Landau, Alice, 1995b, 'The External Dimensions and Geo-political Determinants of European Construction', in: *European Union-Southern African Development Community, Regional Integration Process*, Bordeaux: CEAN, pp. 85–111.

Landau, Alice, 1994, 'L'espace économique européene', in: *Encyclopédie Universalis*, Paris: Encyclopédie Universalis.

Landau, Alice, 1991, 'Les pays africains dans les négociations économiques internationales: éléments d'un paradoxe', In: CEAN, *Année africaine, 1990–1991*, Bordeaux: Centre d'étude d'Afrique noire, pp. 21–42.

Landau, Alice, 1983, *La Convention de Lomé, un défi à l'inégalité*, Lausanne: Editions LEP.

Lapierre, J.W, 1977, *Vivre sans Etat? Essai sur le pouvoir politique et l'innovation sociale*, Paris: Seuil.

Lavergne, Réal (ed.), 1996, *Intégration régionale et coopération en Afrique de l'Ouest*, Paris: Karthala.

Lawrence, Robert, 1996: *Regionalism, Multilateralism, and Deeper Integration*, Washington, DC: The Brookings Institution.

Lawrence, Robert Z. & Litan, Robert E.,1990, 'The World Trading System After the Uruguay Round', *Boston University International Law Journal*, Vol. 8, No. 3, pp. 303–31.

Lazarsfeld, Paul F., Berelson, B. & Gaudet, H., 1944, *The People's Choice*, New York: Columbia University Press.

Leenhardt, B. & L'Hériteau, M.F., 1993, *Les effets de l'inconvertibilité des billets F CFA*, Paris: CFD.

Leistner, Erich, 1997, 'Regional Cooperation in sub-Saharan Africa', *Africa Insight*, Vol. 27, No. 2, pp. 112–23.

Leistner Erich, 1992a, 'Post-Apartheid South Africa's Economic Ties With Neighbouring Countries', *Development Southern Africa,* Vol. 9, No. 2, 1992, pp. 169–86.

Leistner, Erich, 1992b, 'Designing the Framework for a Southern African Development Community', *Africa Insight,* Vol. 22, No. 1, pp. 4–13.

Lelart, Michel, 1998, *Le système monétaire international,* Paris: La Découverte, 3rd edn.

Lelart, Michel, 1997, 'Un exemple d'intégration institutionnelle: le cas de la Zone Franc', *Revue Tiers Monde,* Vol. 38, No. 152, pp. 897–918.

Lelart, Michel, 1994a, *La construction monétaire européenne,* Paris: Dunod.

Lelart, Michel, 1994b, 'La Zone Franc face à Maastricht', in: Sandretto, R. (ed.), *Zone Franc; Du Franc CFA à la monnaie européenne,* Paris: Editions de l'Epargne, pp. 271–89.

Lelart, Michel, 1989, 'L'avenir de la Zone Franc dans la perspective de la construction monétaire européenne', *Revue d'Economie Financière,* No. 8/9, March–June, pp. 195–204.

Lelart, Michel, 1986, 'Zone monétaire et convertibilité: l'expérience africaine', *Economies et Sociétés,* série F, No. 30, pp. 135–67.

Lelart, Michel, 1985, 'Le Système Monétaire Européen et le Système Monétaire Franco-Africain', *Eurépargne,* November, pp. 9–14 & December, pp. 21–6.

Lemarchand, René, 1991, 'African Transitions to Democracy: an Interim (and Mostly Pessimistic) Assessment', *Africa Insight,* Vol. 22, No. 3, pp. 178–85.

Lemarchand, René, 1992, 'Uncivil States and Civil Societies: How Illusion Became Reality', *Journal of Modern African Studies,* Vol. 30, No. 2, June, pp. 177–92.

Leroy, Etienne (ed.), 1996, 'Besoin d'Etat', *Politique africaine,* No. 61 (special issue).

Leroy-Ladurie, Emmanuel, 1973, *Le territoire de l'historien,* Paris: Gallimard.

Lévi-Strauss, C. & Eribon, D., 1990, *De près et de loin,* Paris: Odile Jacob.

Lewis, I. M., 1989, 'The Ogaden and the Fragility of Somali Segmentary Nationalism', *African Affairs,* Vol. 88, No. 353, pp. 573–79.

Lewis, P. M., 1992, 'Political Transition and the Dilemma of Civil Society in Africa', *Journal of International Affairs,* Vol. 46, No. 1, Summer, pp. 31–54.

L'Hériteau, M.-F., 1993, 'Intégration régionale en Afrique et coopération monétaire euro-africaine', in: Michaelof, pp. 449–58.

L'Hériteau, M.F., 1989, *Comparaison des performances des pays de la Zone Franc et des pays hors Zone Franc, Note,* Paris: CCCE.

Lloyd, Peter J., 1992, 'Régionalisation et commerce mondial', *Revue économique de l'OCDE,* No. 18, pp. 7–49.

Lochak, D., 1989, 'Les minorités et le droit public français: du refus des différences à la gestion des différences', in: Soulier, Gérard, & Fenet, Alain (eds), *Les minorités et leurs droits depuis 1789,* Paris : L'Harmattan, pp. 111–85.

Lodge, T., 1995, 'The South African General Election, April 1994: Results, Analysis and Implications', *African Affairs,* Vol. 94, No. 377, pp. 471–500.

Lomnitz, L., 1971, 'Reciprocity of Favors in the Urban Middle Class of Chile', *Studies in Economic Anthropology,* Washington, DC, American Anthropological Association.

Lunhdal, M. & Petersson, L., 1991, *The Dependent Economy: Lesotho and the Southern African Customs Union,* Boulder, CO: Westview Press.

M'Bokolo, Elikia (ed.), 1993, *Développement; de l'aide au partenariat*, Paris: Commissariat général au Plan- La Documentation française.

Maasdorp, Gavin, 1993, 'The Advantages and Disadvantages of Current Regional Institutions for Integration', in: Baker, Pauline, Boraine, Alex & Krafchik, Warren (eds), *South Africa and the World Economy in the 1990s*, Cape Town: David Philip, pp. 239–46.

Maasdorp, Gavin, & Whiteside, Alan, 1993, *Rethinking Economic Cooperation in Southern Africa: Trade and Investment*. Johannesburg: Konrad Adenauer Foundation,

Mabandla, B., 1996, 'Government must unite a fragmented art community', *Business Day*, 19 July.

MacCormack, G., 1976, 'Reciprocity', *Man*, No. 11, pp. 89–103.

MacGaffey, Janet, 1987, *Entrepreneurs and Parasites*. Cambridge: Cambridge University Press.

MacGaffey, Janet *et al.*, 1991, *The Real Economy of Zaïre*. London & Philadelphia: James Currey & University of Pennsylvania Press.

Mafikiri, Tsongo, 1996, 'Pratiques informelles, phénomènes informels et problèmes ethniques au Kivu (Zaïre)', in: de Villers, Gauthier (ed.), 1996, *Phénomènes informels et dynamiques culturelles en Afrique*, Brussels & Paris: Institut Africain-CEDAF & Editions L'Harmattan, pp. 43–63.

Makau wa Mutua, 1994, 'Redrawing the Map Along African Lines', *The Boston Globe*, 22 September.

Maliyamkono, T. & Bagachwa, M., 1990, *The Second Economy of Tanzania*, London: James Currey.

Manshard, Walther & Schaaf, Thomas, 1989, 'The growth of spontaneous agricultural colonisation in the border area of Ghana and Ivory Coast', *Applied Geography and Development*, Vol. 17, No. 34, pp. 7–22.

Marceau, Gabrielle, 1997, 'NAFTA and WTO Dispute Settlement Rules, A Thematic Comparison', *Journal of World Trade*, Vol. 31, No. 2, pp. 25–81.

Martin, Denis-Constant, 1991, 'Le multipartisme pour quoi faire? Les limites du débat politique: Kenya, Ouganda, Tanzanie, Zimbabwe', *Politique Africaine*, No. 43, October, pp. 21–30.

Mayer, Nona & Perrineau, Pascal, 1992, *Les comportements politiques*, Paris: Armand Colin.

Mazrui, Ali, 1993, 'The Bondage of Boundaries', *The Economist*, No. 150, p. 34.

Mbembe, Achille, 1992a, 'Provisional Notes on the Post-colony', *Africa*, Vol. 62, No. 1, pp. 3–37.

Mbembe, Achille, 1992b, 'De l'idée de 'société civile' en Afrique au Sud du Sahara, histoire, méthodes et interprétations' (mimeo).

Mbembe, Achille, 1992c, 'Pouvoir et économie politique en Afrique contemporaine: une réflexion', *Afrique 2000*, No. 8, pp. 51–71.

McCarthy, Colin L., 1994, 'Regional Integration of Developing Countries at Different Levels of Economic Development', *Transnational Law and Contemporary Problems*, April, Vol. 4, No. 1, pp. 1–20.

McCarthy, Colin L., 1992, 'The Southern African Customs Union', *Journal of World Trade*, Vol. 26, No. 4, pp. 5–24.

Meagher, Kate, 1997, 'Informal Integration or Economic Subvention: the Development and Organisation of Parallel Trade in Sub-Saharan Africa', in

Lavergne, Real (ed.), *Regional Integration and Cooperation in West Africa*, Ottawa & Trenton, NJ: IDRC & Africa World Press, pp.165–88.

Meagher, Kate, 1990, 'The Hidden Economy: Informal and Parallel Trade in Northwestern Uganda', *Review of African Political Economy*, No. 47, p. 64–83.

Médard, Jean-François (ed.), 1991a, *États d'Afrique noire. Formations, mécanismes et crises*, Paris: Karthala.

Médard, Jean-François, 1991b, 'Autoritarismes et Démocraties en Afrique Noire', *Politique Africaine*, No. 43, pp. 92–104.

Médard, Jean-François, 1990, 'L'Etat Patrimonialisé', *Politique Africaine*, No. 39, pp. 25–36.

Meillassoux, Claude (ed.), 1971, *The Development of Indigenous Trade and Markets in West Africa*, Oxford: Oxford University Press.

Michaclof, Serge (ed.), 1993, *La France et l'Afrique: vade-mecum pour un nouveau voyage*, Paris: Karthala.

Milner, Helen, 1992, 'Commerce mondial, une nouvelle logique des blocs', in: Laïdi, Zaki (ed.), *L'ordre mondial relâché, sens et puissance aprés la guerre froide*, Paris: Presses de la FNSP, pp. 132–53.

Ministry of Finance, 1995, *Restructuring the Development Finance System in South Africa*, Pretoria: Government Printers.

Mitchell, J. C. (ed.), 1969, *Social Networks in Urban Situations*. Manchester: Manchester University Press.

Mogae, F. G., 1993, 'Remarks by the Honourable F. G. Mogae, Vice President and Minister of Finance and Development Planning of the Republic of Botswana', Meeting of Ministers of Finance of Member States of the Southern African Customs Union, 17 August (mimeo).

Momoh, John, 1991, 'Monetary Cooperation: the West African Clearing House Experiment', *West Africa*, 1–7 July, p. 1087.

Mondjannagni, Albert, 1963, 'Quelques aspects économiques, politiques, sociaux de la frontière Dahomey-Nigeria', *Etudes dahoméennes,* Vol. I, 3rd quarter, pp. 17–57.

Monga, Célestin, 1997, *L'Argent des Autres; Banques et Petites Entreprises en Afrique: le Cas du Cameroun*, Paris: LGDJ.

Monga, Célestin, 1994a, 'Elements for an Anthropology of Anger: Civil Society and Democracy in Sub-Saharan Africa', in: Brüne, Stefan, Betz, Joachim & Kühne, Winrich (eds): *Africa and Europe: Relations of Two Continents in Transition*, Münster: Lit. Verlag, pp. 205–24.

Monga, Célestin, 1994b, 'Social Responses to Trade Liberalisation in Cameroon, Time-Inconsistency and Compatibility Issues in the Franc Zone', Walter Rodney Seminar paper, Boston, MA: Boston University.

Monga, Célestin, 1986, *Cameroun: quel avenir?*, Paris: Silex.

Monnier, Laurent, 1973, *Ethnie et intégration régionale au Congo: le Kongo Central, 1962–1965*. Paris: EDICEF.

Moseley, K.P., 1992, 'West African Industry and the Debt Crisis', *Journal of International Development*, Vol. 4, No. 1, pp. 1–27.

Moundoumba, P., 1992, 'Coopération régionale et spécificité gabonaise', *L' Union*, 7 April, p. 8.

Movement for National Reformation, 1993, 'Position Paper', *The Guardian* (Lagos), 29 January, p. 18.

Mulaisho, D., 1992, *Post-Apartheid Implications for SADCC and the Drive Towards Economic Integration*, Gaborone: Institute of Development Management.

Mytelka, Lynn K., 1973, 'The Salience of Gains in Third-World Integrative Systems', *World Politics*, Vol. 25, No. 2, pp. 236–50.

National Democratic Institute for International Affairs, 1992, *Cameroon Presidential Elections of October 11, 1992: An NDI Interim Report of the International Observer Mission*, Washington, DC: NDI.

Neveu, C., 1993, *Communauté, nationalité et citoyenneté: de l'autre côté du miroir: les Bangladeshis de Londres*, Paris: Karthala.

Ngayap, P.F., 1982, *Cameroun: qui gouverne? De Ahidjo à Biya, l'héritage et l'enjeu*, Paris: L'Harmattan.

Niandou Souley, Abdoulaye, 1992, 'Crise des autoritarismes militaires et renouveau politiques en Afrique de l'Ouest. Etude comparative Bénin, Mali, Niger, Togo', Thèse de doctorat en Science Politique, Talence: Université de Bordeaux I (mimeo).

Niandou Souley, Abdoulaye, 1991, 'Ajustement Structurel et Effondrement des Modèles Idéologiques: Crise et Renouveau de l'Etat Africain', *Etudes Internationales*, Vol. 22, No. 2, June, pp. 253–65.

Ntumba Luaba Lumu, 1990, *La Communauté Economique Européenne et les intégrations régionales des pays en développement*, Brussels: Bruylant.

Nugent, Paul & Aswaju, A.I., 1996, 'Introduction: the Paradox of African Boundaries', in Nugent, Paul & Aswaju, A. I (eds), *African Boundaries; Barriers, Conduits and Opportunities*, London & Edinburgh: Pinter & African Studies Centre, pp. 1–17.

Nuttall, Simon, 1990, 'The Commission: Protagonists of Inter-Regional Cooperation', in: Edwards, Geoffrey and Regelsberger, Elfriede (eds), *Europe's Global Links, the European Community and Inter-Regional Cooperation*, London: Pinter Publishers,

Obasanjo, Olusegun, 1992, 'A Government of Consensus', *The Guardian* (Lagos), 8 January, p. 15.

Observatoire géopolitique des drogues, 1996, *Atlas mondial des drogues*, Paris: PUF.

Observatoire géopolitique des drogues, 1995a, *Afrique de l'Ouest: étude de la production de drogues et du trafic local, en particulier de la culture de cannabis*, Paris & Brussels: DGVIII (D-AFR/94/01).

Observatoire géopolitique des drogues, 1995b, *Géopolitique des drogues 1995*, Paris: La Découverte.

Observatoire géopolitique des drogues, 1994a, *Etat des drogues, drogues des Etats*, Paris: Hachette.

Observatoire géopolitique des drogues, 1994b, *Etude régionale sur le trafic, la production et la consommation des drogues en Afrique de l'Ouest*, Paris & Brussels: DGI/DGVIII, (Doc. D-AFR/93/07).

Observatoire géopolitique des drogues, 1993, *La drogue. Le nouveau désordre mondial*, Paris: Hachette.

OECD, 1993, *Regional Integration and Developing Countries*, Paris: OECD.

Ogoula, Serge P., 1992, 'La nouvelle politique sud-africaine et l'intégration économique de la RSA en Afrique noire', Mémoire de DEA, Institut de Géographie et d'Aménagement Régional de l'Université de Nantes.

Okolo, Julius Emeka, 1985, 'Integrative and Cooperative Regionalism: the Economic Community of West African States', *International Organisation*, Vol. 39, No. 1, pp. 121–53.

Oman, Charles, 1996, *Les défis politiques de la globalisation et de la régionalisation*, Paris: Centre de développement de l'OCDE.

Osaghae, Eghosa E., 1992, 'The Status of State Governments in Nigerian Federalism', *Publius: The Journal of Federalism*, Vol. 22, No. 3, pp. 181–200.

Ostergaard, Clemens Stubbe, 1993, 'The European Community in World Politics', in: Noorgaad, Thomas Pedersen & Petersen, Nicolaj (eds), *From Strategic Triangle to Economic Tripolarity: Japan's Responses to European Integration*, London: Pinter Publishers, pp. 157–89.

OUA, 1991, *Traité instituant la Communauté africaine*, Addis Ababa: OUA.

OUA, 1990, *Déclaration de l'Assemblée des Chefs d'Etats et de Gouvernements à l'occasion du XXVI ème sommet de l'Organisation de l'Unité Africaine*, Addis Ababa: OUA.

Oyovbaire, S. Egite, 1979, 'The Theory of Federalism: A Critical Appraisal', *Nigerian Journal of Political Science*, Vol. 1, No. 1.

Oyovbaire, S. Egite, 1985, *Federalism In Nigeria: A Study in the Development of the Nigerian State,* London: Macmillan.

Perrot, Claude-Hélène, 1974, 'Les Anyi-Ndenye et les Ashanti', in: *Les populations communes de la Côte-d'Ivoire et du Ghana*, (Colloque interuniversitaire Ghana-Côte-d'Ivoire. Bondoukou), Abidjan-Accra: Universities of Abidjan & Legon, pp. 306–29.

Petit, Bernard, 1993, 'L'ajustement structurel et la position de la Communauté Européenne', *Revue Tiers Monde*, Vol. XXXIV, No. 136, October–December, pp. 827–50.

Pomfret, Richard, 1986, 'The Trade-Diverting Bias of Preferential Trading Arrangements', *Journal of Common Market Studies*, Vol. 25, No. 2, pp. 105–17.

Pool, David, 1993, 'Eritrean Independence', *African Affairs*, Vol. 92, No. 368, pp. 389–402.

Pourtier, Roland (ed.), 1998, 'Le Congo Brazzaville entre guerre et paix', *Afrique contemporaine*, April–June (special issue).

Pourtier, Roland, (ed.), 1997, 'Congo-Zaïre-Congo: un itinéraire géopolitique au coeur de l'Afrique' *Hérodote*, No. 86–7 (special issue).

Pourtier, Roland, 1994, *Atlas de l'UDEAC*, Paris: Ministère de la Coopération.

Pourtier, Roland, 1992, 'Zaïre: l'unité compromise d'un 'sous-continent' à la dérive', *Hérodote,* No. 65–6, pp. 264–88.

Pourtier, Roland, 1991, 'L'Afrique dans tous ses États', in: Lévy, Jacques (ed.), *Géographies du politique*, Paris: Presses de la Fondation Nationale des Sciences Politiques.

Powell, W. W., 1990, 'Neither Market nor Hierarchy; Network Forms of Organisation', *Research in Organisational Behavior*, No. 12, pp. 295–336.

Preeg, Ernest H., 1970, *Traders and Diplomats*, Washington, DC: The Brookings Institution.

Prkic, François, 1995, 'Libéria: de Cotonou à Akossombo: espoirs et déceptions sur le chemin de la paix', in CEAN (ed.), *L' Afrique Politique 1995*, Paris: Karthala, 1995, pp. 163–80.

PTA, 1992, *Report of the Seventeenth Meeting of the Council of Ministers* PTA/CM/ XXII/3, Lusaka: PTA.

PTA, 1990, *The Monetary Harmonisation Program of the PTA for Eastern and Southern African States*, Lusaka: PTA.

Putnam, Robert D., 1988, 'Diplomacy and Domestic Politics: The Logic of Two-Level Games', *International Organisation,* Vol. 42, No. 3, pp. 427–60.

Putnam, Robert D., 1993, *Making Democracy Work, Civic Traditions in Modern Italy*, Princeton, NJ: Princeton University Press.

Pycroft, C., 1998, 'Integrated Development Planning or Strategic Paralysis? Municipal Development during the Local Government Transition and Beyond', *Development Southern Africa*, Vol. 15, No. 2, pp. 151–63.

Raffestin, Claude, 1974, 'Eléments pour une problématique des régions frontalières', *L' Espace Géographique*, No. 1, pp. 12–18.

Rapoo, T., 1995, *A System in Dispute: Provincial Government in Practice,* Johannesburg: Centre for Policy Studies.

Renner, F.A., 1985, 'Partition and Political Integration in Senegambia', in Asiwaju, 1985, pp. 79–80.

Reno, William, 1998, *Warlord Politics and African States*, Boulder, CO: Lynne Rienner.

Reno, William, 1997, 'Sovereignty and Personal Rule in Zaïre', *African Studies Quarterly*, Vol. 1, No. 3 (Fall) [http: //web.africa.ufl.edu/asq/v1/3/4.html].

Reno, William, 1995, *Corruption and State Politics in Sierra Leone*, Cambridge: Cambridge University Press.

Republic of South Africa, 1998a, *Ministry of Provincial Affairs and Constitutional Development, the White Paper on Local Government*, Pretoria: CTP Book Printers.

Republic of South Africa, 1998b, *Department of Trade and Industry, Financial Access for SMME's: Towards a Comprehensive Strategy – a Draft Discussion Document,* Pretoria: Government Printer.

Republic of South Africa, 1997, *Department of Trade and Industry, Local Government in a System of Intergovernmental Fiscal Relations in South Africa: A Discussion Document*, Pretoria: Government Printer.

Republic of South Africa, 1996, *Constitution of the Republic of South Africa*, Act 108 of 1996, Pretoria: Government Printer.

Republic of South Africa, 1995, *Ministry of Finance, Restructuring the Development Finance System in South Africa*, Pretoria: Government Printer.

Republic of South Africa, 1994, *White Paper on the Reconstruction and Development Programme*, Pretoria: Government Printer.

Republic of South Africa, nd., *Growth, Employment and Redistribution: a Macroeconomic Strategy*, Pretoria: Department of Finance, Government Printer.

Revel, Jean-François, 1992, *Le regain démocratique*, Paris: Fayard.

Ricupero, Rubens, 1993, *O Rodada Uruguai e o futuro do sistema multilateral de comércio*, Rio de Janeiro.

Robson, Peter, 1993a, 'La Communauté Européenne et l'intégration économique régionale dans le Tiers Monde', *Revue Tiers Monde*, Vol. 34, No. 136, October–December, pp. 859–79.

Robson, Peter, 1993b, 'The New Regionalism and Developping Countries', *Journal of Common Market Studies*, Vol. 31, No. 3, pp. 329–46.

Rochebrune, Renaud de, 1994, 'Afrique an 2000: pas de miracle à l'asiatique, mais
   …', in: Jeune Afrique, *L'annuaire Jeune Afrique 94, Rapport sur l'Etat de l'Afrique,*
   Paris: Jeune Afrique, pp. 17–27.
Ropivia, Marc-Louis, 1994, *Géopolitique de l'Intégration en Afrique Noire,* Paris:
   l'Harmattan.
Ruggie, John Gerard, 1985, *'Beyond the Crisis of Multilateralism: The Economic and
   Social Sectors of the United Nations',* New York: United Nations.
Ruggie, John Gerard, 1992, 'Multilateralism: the Anatomy of an Institution',
   International Organisation, Vol. 46, No. 3, pp. 561–98.
Saclier, Pierre, 1988, 'Pour une zone monétaire Nord-Sud basée sur l'Ecu', *Le
   Courier ACP/CEE,* July–August, pp. 85–8.
Sahlins, M.D., 1965, 'On the Sociology of Primitive Exchange', in: *The Relevance
   of Models for Social Anthropology.* London: Tavistock, pp. 148–58. Saldago, I.,
   1996, 'Language Testing in Schools Thrown Out' *Business Day,* 9 April.
Salgado, I., 1966, 'Language Testing in Schools Thrown Out', *Business Day,* 9 April.
Sall, Ebrima, 1992, 'Sénégambie: territoires, frontières, espaces et réseaux
   sociaux', Talence: CEAN (*Travaux et documents* No. 36).
Sall, Ebrima & Sallah, Halifa, 1994, 'Senegal and Gambia: the Politics of
   Integration', in: Diop, Momar-Coumba (ed.), *Le Sénégal et ses voisins,* Dakar:
   Sociétés-Espaces-Temps, pp. 117–41.
Samatar, S., 1985, 'The Somali Dilemma; Nation in Search of a State' in Asiwaju,
   pp. 155–94.
Sandretto, René, 1988, 'Zone franc, Système monétaire européen, Système
   monétaire international'. *Problèmes Economiques,* No. 2065, 9 March, pp. 9–15.
Saro-Wiwa, Ken, 1993, 'Address at the Open Meeting of Oil-Bearing Areas with
   The Secretary to The Federal Government, 4 March 1993', *The Guardian*
   (Lagos) 17 March, p. 9.
Schatzberg, Michael, 1988, *The Dialectics of Oppression in Zaïre,* Bloomington, IN:
   University of Indiana Press.
Schlesinger, Arthur M., 1991, *The Disuniting of America: Reflections on a Multicultural
   Society,* New York: W.W. Norton & Co.
Schott, Jeffrey, 1991, 'Trading Blocs and the World Trading System', *World
   Economy,* Vol. 14, No. 1, pp. 1–17.
Schott, Jeffrey, 1989, 'More Free Trade Areas', in: Schott, Jeffrey (ed.), *Free Trade
   Areas and US Trade Policy,* Washington, DC: Institute for International
   Economics, pp. 1–59.
Schulders, Guy, 1990, *S'unir. Le défi des Etats d'Afrique centrale,* Paris: L'Harmattan.
Seck, Assana, 1989, 'Découpage territorial et mal développement en Afrique', in:
   Antheaume, B. *et al.,* (eds), *Tropiques. Lieux et liens,* Paris: ed. Orstom, pp. 377–84.
Seekings, Jeremy, 1996, 'Anticlimax – Cape Town's Local Elections', *Indicator SA,*
   Vol. 13, No. 3, pp. 41–5.
Seekings, Jeremy, 1995, 'What swing? Local government elections in the Western
   Cape', *Indicator SA,* Vol. 13, No. 1, pp. 29–32.
Sjolander, Claire Turenne, 1991, 'Managing International Trade: The United
   States, Trade Protection, and the GATT', Kingston (Ontario) (mimeo).
Sklar, Richard, 1997, 'An Elusive Target; Nigeria Fends Off Sanctions', in *Polis,
   Cameroonian Journal of Political Science,* Vol. 4, No. 2, November, pp. 19–38.

Smouts, Marie-Claude, 1995, *Les organisations internationales*, Paris: Armand Colin.

South Africa Law Commission, 1991, Human Rights and Group Rights, Pretoria (mimeo).

Southall, Aiden, 1985, 'Partitioned Alur' in Asiwaju, 1985, pp. 87–105.

'Special Forum on the Local Government White Paper', 1998, *Development Southern Africa*, Vol. 15, No. 2.

Srinivasan, T.N., Whalley, John, Wootton, Ian, 1995, 'Measuring the Effects of Regionalism on Trade and Welfare', in Anderson, Kym and Blackhurst, Richard (eds), *Regional Integration and the Global Trading System*, New York: Harvester Wheatsheaf, pp. 52–79.

Stary, Bruno, 1996, 'Réseaux marchands et espaces transfrontaliers en Afrique de l'Ouest', *Afrique Contemporaine*, No. 177, pp. 45–53.

Stary, Bruno, 1995, *Dévaluation du CFA et flux transétatiques en Afrique de l'Ouest. Exemple de la frontière entre la Côte-d'Ivoire et le Ghana*, Talence: CEAN (*Travaux et documents* No. 47).

Suberu, Rotimi T., 1994, *The 1991 State and Local Government Reorganisations in Nigeria*, Talence: CEAN (*Travaux et Documents* No. 41).

Svensson, F., 1979, 'Liberal Democracy and Group Rights: the Legacy of Individualism and its Impact on American Indian Tribes', *Political Studies*, No. 3, pp. 421–40.

Takirambudde, Peter, 1993, 'Rethinking Regional Integration Structures and Strategies in Eastern and Southern Africa', *Africa Insight*, Vol. 23, No. 3, pp. 149–58.

Toulabor, Comi, 1994, 'Les Etats Africains face à la problématique démocratique', paper presented at Delphes forum, 30 October–2 November, Talence: CEAN.

Tredano, A. Benmessaoud, 1989, *Intangibilité des frontières coloniales et espace étatique en Afrique*, Paris: LGDJ.

Turner, Thomas, 1997, 'Kabila Returns in a Cloud of Uncertainty', *African Studies Quarterly*, Vol. 1, No. 3 (Fall). [http://web.africa.ufl.edu/asq/v1/3/3.html].

Tussie, D., 1982, 'Latin American Integration: From LAFTA to LAIA', *Journal of World Trade*, Vol. 16, No. 5, p. 399–413.

Vaitsos, C.V., 1978, 'Crisis in Regional Economic Cooperation (Integration) Among Developing Countries: A Survey', *World Development*, Vol. 6, pp. 719–69.

Vallée, Olivier, 1989, *Le prix de l'argent CFA. Heurs et malheurs de la Zone Franc*, Paris: Karthala.

Van Dantzig, Alfred, 1974, 'The demarcation of the southern section of the border between the Gold Coast and Ivory Coast', in: *Les populations communes de la Côte-d'Ivoire et du Ghana* (Colloque inter-universitaire Ghana-Côte-d'Ivoire, Bondoukou), Abidjan & Accra: Universities of Abidjan & Legon, pp. 629–46.

Van Staden, G., 1990, 'Beyond 2000: South and Southern Africa into the Next Century', *Focus on Africa*, 1 (3).

Vengroff, Richard, 1993, 'Governance and the Transition to Democracy: Political Parties and the Party System in Mali', *The Journal of Modern African Studies*, Vol. 31, No. 4, pp. 541–62.

Verlaeten, 1991, *Les échanges frontaliers du Nigéria: une dynamique régionale d'intégration en cours*, Paris: DIAL.

Verlaque, Christian, 1993, 'Du déterminisme géographique aux réseaux organisés: clefs pour une intégration régionale en Afrique centrale' in: CERGEP, *L'intégration régionale en Afrique Centrale: une mise en perspective*, Libreville: CERGEP, pp. 22–5.

Villiers, B. de, 1989, Die Staatsregtelike beskerming van outonome besluitneming van minderheidsgroepe, LLD-Thesis, Rand-Afrikaans University, Johannesburg (mimeo).

Viner, Jacob, 1975, *The Customs Union Issues*, New York: Carnegie Endowment in International Peace.

Weimer, Bernard, 1991, 'The Southern African Development Coordination Conference: Past and Future', *Africa Insight*, Vol. 21, No. 2, pp. 78–89.

Weinstein, Brian, 1966, *Gabon: Nation-Building on the Ogooué*, Cambridge, MA: MIT Press.

Weisfelder, R.F., 1992, 'Lesotho and the Inner Periphery in the New South Africa', *The Journal of Modern African Studies*, Vol. 30, No. 4, pp. 643–68.

Weisfelder, R.F., 1991, 'Collective Foreign Policy Decision-Making Within SADCC: Do Regional Objectives Alter National Policies?', *Africa Today*, Vol. 38, No. 1, pp. 5–17.

Whalley, John, 1993, 'Expanding NAFTA: Who Benefits?', *Options politiques* (Ottawa), January–February, pp. 8–11.

Wiechers, M., 1994, 'Le droit et l'ethnie', in: Darbon, Dominique (ed.), *Ethnicité et nation en Afrique du Sud: imageries identitaires,* Paris : Karthala, pp. 211–21.

Willame, Jean-Claude, 1994, *Gouvernance et pouvoir : Essai sur trois trajectoires africaines*, Brussels & Paris: CEDAF/ASDOC & L'Harmattan.

Willame, Jean-Claude, 1986, *L' Epopée d'Inga: Chronique d'une prédation industrielle,* Paris: L'Harmattan.

Willame, Jean-Claude, 1980, *Patrimonialism and Political Change in the Congo,* Stanford, CA: Stanford University Press.

Winham, Gilber R., *International Trade and the Tokyo Round Negotiation*, Princeton, NJ: Princeton University Press.

Woods, Dwayne, 1992, 'Civil Society in Europe and Africa: Limiting State Power Through a Public Sphere', *African Studies Review,* Vol. 35, No. 2, September, pp. 77–101.

World Bank, 1997: *The State in a Changing World*, *World Development Report*, No. 2. New York: Oxford University Press.

World Bank, 1994a, *Adjustment in Africa*, New York: Oxford University Press.

World Bank, 1994b, *Adjustment in Africa: Lessons from Country Case Studies*, Washington, DC: World Bank.

World Bank, 1994c, *L'ajustement en Afrique. Réformes, résultats et chemins à parcourir*, Washington, DC: World Bank

World Bank, 1994d, *The Economic Crisis in the CFA Zone. The Need for a Comprehensive Reform Program and a New Development Strategy*, Washington, DC: World Bank.

World Bank, 1990, *A Proposed Program for the Promotion of Intra-African Trade and Investment*, Washington, DC: World Bank.

World Bank, 1989a, *Intra Regional Trade in Sub Saharan Africa*, Washington, DC: World Bank.

World Bank, 1989b, *Sub-Saharan Africa: From Crisis to Sustainable Growth*, Washington, DC: World Bank.

World Bank, 1988, *Proceedings of the Workshop on Regional Integration and Cooperation in Sub-Saharan Africa*, Washington, DC: World Bank.

Wright, Stephen, 1998, 'The Changing Context of African Foreign Policies' in: Wright, Stephen (ed.), *African Foreign Policies*, Boulder, CO: Westview, pp. 1–22.

Wright, Stephen, 1992, 'Africa in the Post-Cold War World', *Trans Africa Forum*, Vol. 9, No. 2, p. 26–37.

Yalden, M., 1993, 'Collective Claims on the Human Rights Landscape: a Canadian View', *International Journal of Group Rights*, Vol. 1, No. 1, pp. 17–25.

Yondo, Marcel, 1970, *Dimension nationale et développement économique (Théorie et application dans l'UDEAC)*, Paris: LGDJ.

Young, Crawford, 1994, *Ethnic Diversity and Public Policy: An Overview*, Geneva: UNRISD Occasional Paper No. 8.

Young, Crawford, 1978, 'Zaïre: The Unending Crisis', *Foreign Affairs*, Vol. 57, No. 1, pp. 169–85.

Young, Crawford & Turner, Thomas, 1985, *The Rise and Decline of the Zaïrean State*, Madison, WI: University of Wisconsin Press.

Zartman, William (ed.), 1995, *Collapsed States; the Disintegration and Restoration of Legitimate Authority*, Boulder, CO: Lynne Rienner.

Zolberg, Aristide, 1966, *Creating Political Order*, Chicago: Rand McNally.

Index

Abacha, Gen. Sani, 97
Abbink, Jon, 63
Abel, R.L., 103
Abiola, M.K.O., 70
Aboyade Commission, 94–5
Abuja Plan, 5
accountability, 58, 105
ADB, 33, 36, 121, 162–4 *passim*
Adetiloye, Rt Rev. Abiodun, 195
Adibe, Clement Emenike, 122
Adji, Souley, 70
adjustment, structural, 1, 7, 8, 12, 26, 33–7
    passim, 57, 77, 121, 123, 133, 148, 156,
    176, 190, 191, 199
AEC, 2, 27, 31, 124, 125, 152
AEF, 3, 130, 131
AERC, 37
Affirmative Action, 43
Afristat, 144
AFTA, 22
Aggarwal, Vinod, 22, 23, 25
agreements, free trade, 15, 17; monetary,
    159, 163, 164, 167; preferential, 17–19;
    regional, 1, 15–26, 32, 37, 148–9, 167; *see
    also individual headings*
agriculture, 9, 10, 21–2, 27, 34, 117, 120,
    144, 170–4, 191–2; CAP, 21, 22, 25
agro-industry, 120, 133
Agyemang, A.S., 157
Ahidjo, President Ahmadou, 75
aid, xvii, 6, 18, 63–5 *passim*, 69, 70, 153 *see
    also* donors
Aikhomu, Augustus, 92

Alexander, Dr Neville, 116
Algeria, 40, 71
Almond, Gabriel, 78
Americas, 2, 12; Central, 22, 23; Latin, 3, 19,
    22, 23, 38, 58, 165, 190, 194, 200, ECLA,
    19, LAFTA, 152; North, 1, 2, 20, 108,
    NAFTA, 2, 16, 19, 20, 22–4 *passim*; *see also
    individual countries*
Andean Pact, 19, 22
Angola, 5, 40, 47, 57, 59, 60, 65, 82, 84, 85,
    90, 126, 127, 131
AOF, 3, 5
Argentina, 19, 22, 23
arms trade, 12, 59, 60, 196
Aron, Raymond, 41
arrears, of contributions, 123–4
Asante, S.K.B., 123
Asia, 2, 8, 12, 22–4, 58; AFTA, 22; ASEAN,
    2, 22, 153
Asia-Pacific, 1, 20; APEC, 2, 22–3
associations, civic, 73, 75–80 *passim*, 97, 106
Aswaju, A.I., 8, 9, 59
Australia, 24
Austria, 20, 61
authoritarian regimes, 3, 58, 68–71 *see also*
    single-party regimes
authority, 62–3
autonomy, 3, 50, 63, 98–101 *passim*, 109
Axline, Andrew W., 119

Babangida, Gen. Ibrahim, 70, 96
Bach, Daniel C., 1–13, 19, 49, 100, 122, 135,
    144, 149

Badie, Bertrand, 3, 41, 47, 50
Bakary, Tessy, 73
Baker, James, 25
balance of payments, 37, 148
Balassa, Bela, 21
bargaining power, 15–1, 20, 22, 26
Barre, Siyad, 60
Bayart, Jean-François, 12, 42, 63–4, 69–70
Bayili, E., 9
Bazenguissa-Ganga, Rémy, 12, 179–87
BCEAO, 139, 141, 142, 146–8 passim
BEAC, 28, 132, 134, 139, 141–3, 146–8
  passim
Bekker, Simon, 43, 103–18
Belgium, 9, 44, 46, 56, 82, 83, 89, 126, 182
Benelux, 32
Benin, 5, 9, 11, 12, 86, 121, 177, 189, 193–4,
  196
Bercuson, K., 161
Berelson, B., 78
Berenson, K., 161
Berger, Mark T., 58–2
Bergsten, Fred, 16
Biafra, 3, 55, 56
Birindwa, Faustin, 86
Biya, President Paul, 75, 80
Blaauw, L.C., 50
Boas, Morten, 12
Boganda, Barthélémy, 131
Bomsel, Olivier, 87
Botswana, 6, 7, 153, 154, 156, 160–4 passim,
  167, 168, 193
boundaries/borders, xviii, 3–5, 7–12 passim,
  30, 41–2, 47–8, 53–66, 72, 82, 84, 110,
  127, 134, 135, 169–77; challenge to 56–61;
  cross-transactions see trade; redefinition
  of, 61–6; -trackers, 171–2, 175–6
Braekman, Colette, 77, 89 n7
Bratton, Michael, 77
Brazil, 19, 22, 23, 194
Bredeloup, Sylvie, 181, 183
Bretton Woods institutions, 38, 89, 133 see
  also individual headings
Brinkerhoff, D., 77
Britain, 4, 9, 17, 43, 55, 92, 126, 140, 193;
  London Rainforest Action Group, 99;
  Parliamentary Human Rights Group, 99
budgetary factors, 32, 37, 156
Burkina Faso, 72, 77, 180

Burundi, 45, 48, 55, 59, 72, 82, 84, 126, 131,
  154, 199
Bustin, Edouard, 81–90
Buzan, Barry, 18

Callaghy, Thomas M., 85
Cameroon, 4, 47, 54, 71, 75–80 passim, 82,
  127, 130, 133, 135, 136
Canada, 19, 20, 23, 42, 45–6, 48
cannabis, 189, 191–9 passim
capacity building, 37, 108, 166; utilisation,
  122
Cape Verde, 124
capital, 18, 31, 38, 141, 183, 184; flight,
  141–3 passim, 190
CAR, 84, 127, 131, 133, 135, 136
Caribbean, 19, 34, 35; – Basin Initiative, 22;
  CARICOM, 19
Casamance, 4, 45, 196–8
CEAO, 5, 7, 31, 122, 123, 126
CEDEAO, 119
CEEAC, 7, 28, 29, 40, 125, 126, 131, 131–1
CEMAC, 7, 8, 31, 36, 40, 127, 134–7 passim,
  144, 146
Central Africa, 6, 7, 28, 31, 34–6, 65, 85,
  125–37, 147, 181–7 passim; Federation, 3;
  see also CEEAC
centralisation, 91–7 passim, 100
CEPGL, 28, 29, 40, 125, 131
CEPII, 24
Cerruti, Patrick, 147
Ceylan, A., 42, 43
CFA franc, 7, 8, 31, 129–30, 133–5 passim,
  139–49, 170, 174, 182, 183, 196;
  devaluation of, 7, 31, 129–30, 133–5,
  140–3 passim, 145, 146, 170, 172, 174, 182,
  191, 199
Chad, 5, 11, 47, 59, 60, 131, 133, 135, 136,
  146, 198
Chile, 23, 185
Chipeta, C., 154
Chossudowsky, M., 192
Christianson, D., 111
CIMA, 7
CILSS, 28
CIPRES, 7
civil society, 30, 38, 39, 48, 74–80, 87, 106
civilisation, 73–80
Clapham, Christopher, 53–66

clearing house system, 147–9; WACH, 123
Cloete, F., 50, 111
CMA/Rand Zone, 28, 33, 40, 159, 162–8
cocaine, 194, 195
cocoa, 169–72 *passim*, 191
coffee, 83, 84, 171, 172, 191
Cohen, A., 180
Cole, Bernardette, 123
Collectif Changer le Cameroon, 79
Collier, Paul, 38, 76–5
colonialism, 1–6 *passim*, 9, 10, 41, 54–6, 61,
  62, 82, 83, 92, 130–1, 137, 169; pre-, 3,
  8–9, 47, 56, 60, 61, 63, 65, 82
COMESA, 7, 19, 28, 29, 31, 33, 36, 40, 147,
  149, 151, 158, 159
COMILOG, 132–2
Commonwealth, 17
communalism, 42–51
communications, 9, 27, 30, 34, 36, 80, 127,
  134, 136, 137, 152, 153, 158
Comoros, 139
compensation, 11, 121, 122, 134, 156, 160–1,
  163, 165, 168
Conac, Gérard, 46
conflict/civil strife, 16, 30, 45–6, 48, 59, 65,
  80, 84, 100, 190, 196, 198–9 *see also* war,
  civil
Congo-Brazzaville, 3, 76, 82, 84, 86, 126,
  127, 131, 133, 179, 182–5, 198, 199
Congo/Zaire, 3–5 *passim*, 8, 10, 47, 56–60
  passim, 65, 81–90, 126, 127, 131, 133, 135,
  136, 147, 148, 198, 199; Democratic
  Republic of, 28, 85, 131, 133, 149, 179,
  181–5
CONSAS, 6
Constantin, François, 51
co-operative programmes, 5, 6, 34, 166–8
copper, 83, 85, 87
Coquet, Bruno, 145, 146
Cornevin, Marianne, 41
Cornia, A., 122
corruption, 190, 192, 193
Coset, L., 45
Côte d'Ivoire, 5, 54, 62, 72, 75, 121, 122,
  169–77, 180, 189, 191, 192
Coughlan, R., 115
Coussy, Jean, 133
credit, 65, 77, 141, 148, 183, 184
CSCE, 50

Cuba, 60
culture, 61, 80, 82, 92, 100, 107–8, 114–17,
  137, 187; political, 77–8, 106
currencies, 8, 9, 55, 57, 65, 132, 146–9 *passim*
  see also CMA; Franc Zone; convertibility,
  8, 36, 57, 65, 146, 163, 196
Curtin, P.D., 180
customs and excise, 6, 10, 11, 17, 29, 55, 83,
  93, 119, 121, 126, 134, 141, 144, 156,
  160–1, 176; Customs Co-operation
  Council, 189, 193, 194; unions, 17, 35,
  119, 136 *see also* SACU
Czechoslovakia, 58

Dahl, Robert, 78
Dahomey, 9, 10
Daniel, Jean-Marc, 145, 146
Danjuma, T.Y., 93–5 *passim*
Darbon, Dominique, 41–51
Das, Dilip, 19
Davidson, C., 43, 45
Davies, Arthur, 121
Davey, William, 16
debt, 19, 68, 69, 142, 143, 145, 146, 190;
  service, 142, 156, 192
decentralisation, 91, 92, 97, 101, 112
decolonisation, xvii, 54, 60
deficits, expenditure, 144, 145, 148, 156;
  legitimacy, 85–9; territorial, 41, 46–8, 50
de la Torre, Augusto, 19, 159–60, 165
De Melo, Jaime, 168
democracy/democratisation, 58, 67–80, 86,
  106, 164, 192
deregulation, 1, 36, 126 *see also* liberalisation
De Soto, H., 185
destructuring, 175–7
Deutsch, Karl, 82
devaluation, 57, 122, 140 *see also* CFA franc
development, 11, 30, 34, 58, 108, 112–14,
  117, 121, 165–6, 191; associations, 76
Diaka, Mungul, 86
Diamond, Larry, 73
diamonds, 12, 59, 64, 84, 87, 181, 183, 198
discrimination, 17, 25–9, 43, 100, 160
disintegration, 74–80, 98–101, 126, 127, 132
disobedience, civil, 3, 71
dispute settlement, 16, 24
Djibouti, 57, 59, 65
donors, 6, 27, 31, 38–9, 69–71, 153

Dreux-Brézé, J. de, 125
drugs, 8, 12, 183, 189–200
Dudley, Billy J., 92
du Pisanie, J.A., 113

EAMA, 125–6
East Africa, 5, 28, 34–6 passim, 65, 149;
　Community, 3, 5, 28, 33, 153
Ebin, V., 181
ECDPM, 37
ECOMOG, 64, 120, 198, 199
economy, 57–8, 64–6, 72, 76–7, 87, 92, 107;
　parallel, 10
ECOWAS, 7, 19, 28, 29, 31, 33, 35, 40, 64,
　65, 119–24, 126, 149, 176, 198; problems,
　121–4
education, 10, 34, 68, 77, 107, 116, 117, 132,
　144, 190; FESAC, 132
EFTA, 17, 20, 21, 23, 24
Egg, Johnny, 11, 135
Egypt, 28
EIPA, 37
Ekwueme, Alex, 97
Elbaz, M., 45
elections, 49, 58, 68–70 passim, 76, 80, 89, 90
elites, 44, 48, 55, 57, 64, 65, 69, 75–7 passim,
　126, 127
employers, 75, 76; employment, 11, 68, 100
Enahoro, Chief Anthony, 93
energy, 120, 135, 166
Engola Oyep, J., 135
environment, 24, 27, 30, 144
equality/equity, 43, 45, 68, 94
Equatorial Guinea, 126, 127, 130, 135, 139
Eribon, D., 74–2
Eritrea, 3, 4, 54, 59, 60, 62
Estonia, 62
Ethiopia, 4, 54, 55, 57, 59–61 passim, 63, 65
ethnic factors, 4, 46, 49, 55, 56, 61, 62, 72,
　75–6, 79, 84, 87–92 passim, 95, 96, 99, 100,
　135, 169, 175, 180, 182, 195
Etolo Ngobaasu, E., 86
Etzioni, Amitai, 43
Eurafrique, 125–6
Europe, 1–3 passim, 12, 18, 41, 43, 60, 179,
　184, 194, 195; Court of Justice, 46; East/
　Central, 21, 50, 67, 142, 146, 195;
　Economic Area, 2, 21
European Community/Union, 1, 15–26, 29,

32–8 passim, 48, 108, 125, 126, 134, 140,
　142–9 passim, 157; ECSC, 32, 130; ECB,
　146; EDF, 149; EIB, 149; EMS, 140–4;
　EMU, 33, 142–6 passim; enlargement, 20,
　33, 126; Single Market, 7, 21, 24, 140,
　141, 157
exchange rate, 36, 47, 140, 145, 163, 167,
　170
expenditure, public, 32, 190
exports, 18, 21, 23, 24, 26, 27, 57, 59, 63, 83,
　92, 127, 146, 155, 166, 170, 171;
　re-exports, 9, 11, 12, 122
Eyadéma, 69

Faroutan, F., 28
federations/federalism, 3, 5, 10, 11, 32, 63,
　81, 91–3, 101, 130
Fernandez, Raquel, 16
Fieleke, Norman S., 19
financial factors, 8, 10, 12, 26, 30, 36, 133,
　143
Finland, 20
fiscal factors, xviii, 8, 10–12 passim, 30, 114,
　126, 133, 134, 164
foreign exchange, 8, 36, 87, 163, 167, 183
forum movement, 106–7
Fottorino, Eric, 183
Foucher, Michel, 3, 169
fragmentation, xvii, xviii, 4, 27, 64, 81, 96,
　100, 111
Franc Zone, 6–8 passim, 10, 28, 31, 32, 130,
　139–49
France, 1, 5, 6, 9, 18, 25, 32, 35, 54, 56, 60,
　79–6, 89, 125–6, 129–34, 139–46 passim,
　182, 184
free trade areas/agreements, 16, 17, 21, 23,
　119, 167, 168 see also individual headings
Fried, Jonathan T., 25–7
Friedman, Steven, 106

Gabon, 76, 78, 127, 133, 135
Gambia, The, 5, 9, 11, 47, 77, 197–8
Gamble, Andrew, 1
GATT, 1, 15–19, 22–6 passim; Rounds,
　Kennedy, 25, Tokyo, 26, Uruguay, 1, 15,
　16, 22, 25, 26, 31
Gaudusson, Jean de, 46
Gautron, Jean-Claude, 47
Gbadendu Engunduka, A., 86

Gboyega, Alex, 96
Gérardin, Hubert, 139
Germany, 1, 18, 25, 141, 142
Gerstin, Michael, 23
Ghana, 8, 9, 54, 57, 62, 72, 141, 149, 169–77, 193, 194; and ECOWAS, 121–3 *passim*
Global Coalition for Africa, 36
Global Witness, 84–1
globalisation, xvii, 2, 12, 13, 15, 26, 43, 64
Gluckman, M., 45
gold, 12, 63, 84, 87, 183, 198
Götz, G., 111
Gould, David, 85
Govender, C., 111
governance, 32, 63, 80, 103, 105–8 *see also* democracy
Graf, William D., 92, 96
Gramsci, Antonio, 74
Grawitz, Madeleine, 41
Green, Reginald H., 152–4 *passim*
Grégoire, Emmanuel, 8, 9, 174, 179–81 *passim*
Griggs, R.A., 110
Grofman, B., 43, 45
groups, 12, 42–51 *passim*, 78–9, 106 *see also* civil society
growth, economic, 19, 37, 38, 107, 108, 129, 162, 165, 168, 172
Guillaumont, P.& S., 143, 148
Guinea, 6, 11, 65, 9191, 192, 197
Guinea Bissau, 28, 77, 139, 198
Gunning, Jan Willem, 38

Hallaire, A., 135
Halliday, Fred, 61
Harding, Leonhard, 174
Hargreaves, J.D., 41
Harre, D., 135
Hawes, Gary, 23
Helsinki Act, 50
Herbst, Jeffrey, 3
Hess, Richard, 28
Hine, Robert C., 2, 15–1
Hong Liu, 23
Horn, 4, 34, 57
Houphouct-Boigny, President, 177
Hudson, J., 160
Hufbauer, Gary C., 18, 20, 21, 25
Hughes, Arnold, 11

Hugon, Philippe, 133, 142
Humphries, Richard, 110
'hundi system', 196
Hurrell, Andrew, 22
Hutu, 45, 90
Hveem, Helge, 12
Ibrahim, Jibrin, 41

ideology, 1, 42–51, 53, 56, 115
Ignacu, declaration of, 19
Igué, John, 5, 11, 12, 135, 175, 177
Igué Ogunsola, J., 179
IMF, 19, 24, 35, 36, 133, 142, 146, 148, 190
implementation, of agreements, 30, 32, 33, 121–2, 124, 134, 155, 157
imports, 9, 12, 20–2 *passim*, 24, 36, 122, 162, 176; substitution, 2, 15, 18, 30, 108, 165
identity, 2, 4, 45, 62, 81, 89–90, 115, 117–18, 137, 155
INCB, 189
India, 44
Indian Ocean, 28, 34–6 *passim*; Commission, 28, 33, 36, 40
indigenisation, 122
industrialisation/industry, 103, 121–3 *passim*, 144, 160, 162, 165, 167, 190
inequality, 107, 108, 111
inflation, 57, 141, 164
informal sector, 65, 75, 87, 136, 191
infrastructure, 6, 11, 27, 30, 34, 36, 82–5, 121, 132, 136, 151, 152, 179
institutions, 1, 2, 5–7, 10–13, 30, 38–40, 44, 48, 49, 51, 53, 64, 73, 76, 82, 84, 87, 104–6, 112–17, 124, 143, 144 *see also individual headings*
insurance, 7, 143
insurgency, 57–60 *passim*
integration, market, 30, 31, 165, 168; national, 6, 41, 45, 75–80, 91, 132, 135; regional 6, 16–40 *passim*, 64–5, 119–68 *passim*
intellectual property, 18, 25–9
intergovernmentalism, 32, 102–3, 108–12 *passim*, 114; IGOs, xviii, 2, 5–7 *passim*, 11, 13, 176, 177
International Court of Justice, 50
investment, xvii, 2, 18, 24, 29, 30, 36, 38, 108, 119, 141, 166
irredentism, 3–4, 49, 81, 84

Islam, 60, 92, 180, 181, 187
Italy, 1, 4, 25, 44, 55, 62
ivory, 12, 63, 83

Jackson, B.S., 45
Jackson, John H., 18, 157
Jackson, Robert H., 3, 56
Japan, 20, 23, 24, 25–9
Jawara, Dawda, 197
Jewsiewicki, Bogumil, 87
Johnson, A., 111
Johnson, R.W., 111
Joseph, Richard, 69
judicial factors, 45, 46, 49, 103, 156

Kabila, Laurent Désiré, 81, 84–6 *passim*,
    89–90
Kagame, 89
Kahler, Miles, 25–8
Kaiser, David, 17
Kaptinde, F., 71
Kasai, Southern, 81, 85
Katanga, 3, 55, 56, 81, 83, 85
Kelly, Margaret, 19, 160, 165
Kengo wa Dondo, 88–9
Kennes, Erik, 89–7
Kennes, Walter, 27–40
Kenya, 6, 33, 48, 55, 71, 189, 193
Kérékou, 69
kinship, xviii, 4, 180–7 *passim*
Kipré, Pierre, 174
Kivu, 88n4
Klerk, F.W. de, 105
Klug, A., 43
Knopf, R., 43, 45
Kodjo, Edem, 3
Konaré, President Alphar Oumar, 71, 79–80
Kondo, S., 76
Kostrzewa, Wojciech, 21
Krugman, Paul, 21

Labazée, Pascal, 8, 174, 180, 181
labour, 123, 144, 162
Labrousse, Alain, 12, 183, 189–200
Lachman, D., 161
Lacroix, 41
Lafay, Gérard, 1
Lagos Plan of Action, 152, 165
Lallement, B., 10

land tenure/reform, 107, 117
Landau, Alice, 1, 15–26
language factors, 46, 62, 82, 107, 115–17,
    137; LANTAG, 115–16
Lapierre, J.W., 48
Latvia, 62
laundering, money, 196
law, 32, 42, 46, 80, 135, 143; business, 7,
    143; customary, 116; international, 41, 50
Lawrence, Robert Z., 18, 25
Lazarsfeld, Paul F., 79
League of Nations, 53
Lebanon, 44, 139
Leca, Jean, 41
Leistner, Erich, 7, 152, 155, 156
legal factors, 7, 32, 44, 46, 49, 57
legitimacy/legitimation, 2, 4, 43, 44, 50, 72,
    76, 77, 81, 85–90
Lelart, Michel, 139–49
Lemarchand, René, 77
Leroy, Etienne, 3
Leroy-Ladurie, Emmanuel, 79–6
Lesotho, 6, 7, 28, 55, 153, 154, 160–4 *passim*,
    167, 168, 193; Highlands Water Project, 166
Lévi-Strauss, Charles, 74 n2
Lewis, I.M., 5
Lewis, Janet, 11
Lewis, P.M., 77
L'Hériteau, M.-F., 149
liberalisation, financial, 141; political, 10;
    see also trade
liberation movements, 48, 58
Liberia, 57, 59, 64, 65, 72, 120, 121, 198–9
Libya, 59, 60
Litan, Robert E., 25
Lithuania, 62
Lloyd, Peter J., 20
local government, 94, 96–7, 100, 103, 109,
    111–12, 114, 116
Lochack, D., 45
Lomé Conventions, 18, 21, 34, 35, 148–9
Lomnitz, L., 185
Luhndal, M., 161
Lumumba, Patrice, 85; Lumumbists, 81, 85
Lusaka Declaration, 151, 156

Maasdorp, Gavin, 160, 166, 167
Mabandla, B., 116
MacCormack, G., 185–5

MacGaffey, Janet, 4, 10, 12, 179–87
MacIntyre, Alasdair, 43
Madagascar, 139
Maghreb, 7, 139; UMA, 7, 28, 29, 40
Makau wa Mutua, 3
Mali, 4, 71, 72, 77–80 passim, 139, 180
Malraux, André, 88
Mandela, President Nelson, 105, 107
Mann, Thomas E., 45
Manshard, Walther, 171
manufacturing, 16, 18, 127; products, 174–5
Marceau, Gabrielle, 16
marketing, 10, 170, 179
markets, 9, 13, 16, 19, 21, 23, 30, 34, 39, 55,
    65, 108, 161–3, 165, 167, 168; border,
    172–5, 177; parallel, 141, 164, 183
Marsile of Padua, 43
Martin, Denis-Constant, 68
Matabeleland, 45
Mauritania, 4, 124, 139
Mauritius, 28, 154
Mauss, Marcel, 74–2
Mayer, Nona, 78
Mazrui, Ali, 3
Mba, Léon, 132
Mbembe, Achille, 10, 70, 73, 76–4
McCarthy, Colin, 159–68
McGoldrick, D., 45
Meagher, Kate, 10
Médard, Jean-François, 12, 48, 67, 68, 71
media, 137
Mediterranean countries, 21
Meierhenrich, J., 110
Meillassouux, Claude, 180
MERCOSUR, 2, 19, 22, 23
Mexico, 19, 20, 22, 23
MFN 17, 23
Michaelof, Serge, 190, 196
migration, 9, 47, 61, 72, 82, 164, 169, 181–2
military rule/militarisation, 58, 60, 92–3
Mill, Stuart, 78
Millns, Susan, 43
Milner, Helen, 20
minilateralism, 25, 25n8
mining, 84–5, 134
minorities, 43–6, 48–50 passim, 96, 98, 100
Mitchell, J.C., 180
MNR, 97
Mobutu, 4, 59, 69, 81, 83–8 passim, 90, 131

Mogae, F.G., 162
Momoh, John, 123
Mondjannagni, Albert, 9, 10
monetary factors/policy, xviii, 6, 9, 10, 30,
    32, 114, 123, 146, 162–4 see also CMA;
    Franc Zone
Monga, Célestin, 73–80
Monnier, Laurent, 81
Montesquieu, 78
Moseley, K.P., 122
Moundoumba, P., 127
movement of persons, 29, 31, 36, 119, 123,
    124
Mozambique, 28, 47, 59, 60, 63, 64, 90
Mulaisho, D., 155
Multi-Fibre Arrangements, 26
multilateralism, 1, 2, 15–26
Museveni, President, 89
Myrdal, Gunnar, 42
Mytelka, Lynn K., 165

Naam groups, 77
Namibia, 3, 49–50, 84, 159–68 passim
nation-building, 81–3, 88, 107, 115
national conferences, 86, 87, 97–8
National Democratic Institute for Internal
    Affairs, 80
nationalism, 4, 5, 56, 155
Netherlands, 44, 193
networks, 10, 12, 13, 53, 65, 76, 83, 130,
    135–6, 169–200 passim; drug, 190, 194–6;
    personal, 179–87
Neveu, C., 43, 45
New Zealand, 24
Ngayap, P.F., 75
Nguesso, President Denis Sassou, 199
Nguz Karl-i-bond, 86, 87
Niandou Souley, Abdoulaye, 67–72
Niger, 4, 5, 11, 47, 48, 69, 71, 72, 77, 146
Nigeria, 3–5, 8–12, 47–9 passim, 54, 58, 65,
    69–72 passim, 79, 82, 91–102, 135, 141,
    148, 149, 174, 175, 181, 189; and drugs,
    193–6, 198, 200; in ECOWAS, 121–3
    passim, 64
Nkrumah, Kwami, 58, 177
non-tariff barriers, 25, 29, 119, 153, 154
Ntumba, Luaba Lumu, 148
Nugent, Paul, 8, 59
Nuttall, Simon, 18

OAU, 2, 3, 5, 36, 53, 55, 58, 125
Obasanjo, Olusegun, 97
OECD, 28
OEEC, 18
OGD, 189, 191, 194, 196–8 passim
Ogoni, 98–9
OHADA, 7
oil, 10, 12, 92, 98, 134; companies, 98, 99;
    OMPADEC, 98
Ojo, Olatunde B.J., 119–24
Okolo, Julius Emeka, 121, 123
Oman, Charles, 2
Osaghae, Eghosa E., 95
Ostergaard, Clemens Stubbe, 24, 159
Ottoman Empire, 44, 61
Oyovbaire, S. Egite, 92, 94, 95

Pacific region, 22, 23, 34, 35, 108; PCTD,
    22; PECC, 22, PREC, 22
Panagariya, Arvind, 168
parastatals, 112–13, 123
Paraguay, 19
participation, 74, 74–1, 76, 78, 106
patronage/patrimonialism, 10, 48, 55, 57, 60,
    63, 71
Payne, Anthony, 1
Perrineau, Pascal, 78
Peru, 185
Petersson, L., 161
Petit, Bernard, 148
Pisani, Edgar, 133
planning, 153, 168
pluralism, cultural, 115; political, 45, 46, 49,
    86; social, 44, 45
polarisation, 1, 45, 165, 167–8
political factors, xviii, 1, 31, 43, 46, 48, 49,
    58–80, 86–90, 105–6, 126, 140, 168;
    parties, 70–4, 104–6 passim, 110, 192; will,
    30, 37, 38, 127, 135, 155
Pomfret, Richard, 21
Pool, David, 62
population growth, 112, 175, 190
Portugal, 4, 21–3, 83
Pourtier, Roland, 5, 82, 129–37
poverty, 107, 108, 112
Powell, W.W., 180, 186
Prebisch, Raul, 19
Preeg, Ernest H., 19
preferences, 9, 18–21 passim, 122, 134

press, 71, 79
prices, 9, 21, 47, 92, 141, 170–4 passim, 191
private sector, 30, 36, 37, 77, 80, 166
privatisation, 12, 123, 190, 192
Prkic, François, 120
protectionism, 1, 19, 21, 22, 24–6, 39, 160,
    162
PTA, 7, 147, 149, 151–60 passim
Putnam, Robert D., 73
Pycroft, C., 112, 113

quantitative restricition, 21, 144
quotas, 75, 148; trade, 18, 21; voting, 49

racial factors, 107, 109, 111, 115
railways, 83; Trans-Gabon, 132
Rapoo, T., 110
Rawlings, President, 177
rebellion, 3, 81, 84–6 passim, 90, 197 see also
    insurgency
reciprocity, 15, 17, 21, 22, 180, 181, 185–6
refugees, 47, 59, 90
regulation, 36, 64, 65, 121
religious factors, 60, 62, 78, 79, 92, 100, 107,
    116, 180, 181, 187
Renner, F.A., 10
Reno, William, 59
rents, 92–4 passim, 98; rent-seeking, 8, 11
Reoboth community, 49–50
restructuring, 37, 58, 75, 117, 151, 158, 167
retrenchment, 123, 190
Revel, Jean-François, 73
revenue, 5, 11, 12, 32, 55, 56, 92–5, 114,
    122, 134, 176; sharing, 6, 92–5, 97, 103,
    160–2, 167
Rhodesia, 49, 83
Ricupero, Rubens, 26
rights, 42, 45–6, 50, 117; of establishment/
    residence, 123, 124, 144; group, 3, 43–6
    passim, 49; human, 45, 49, 50, 69
roads, 83, 84, 120, 121, 136; blocks, 29, 176
Robson, Peter, 19, 148
Rochebrune, Renaud de, 125
Ropivia, Marc-Louis, 125–7
Rosberg, Carl, 3, 56
Rouland, Norbert, 43
Rousseau, Jean-Jacques, 43
royalties, 92–4 passim, 98
Ruggie, John Gerard, 15–1

Rugman, Alan, 23
rules of origin, 120, 122, 154
Rwanda, 45, 48, 55, 57, 59, 72, 82, 84, 85, 89, 126, 131, 156, 199

Saharawi movement, 4
Sahlins, M.D., 185
salaries, 10, 57, 176
Salgado, I., 116
Sall, Ebrima, 11, 177
Sallah, Halifa, 11
Samarasinghe, S.W.R. de A., 115
Samatar, S., 4
sanctions, 70, 176, 186, 187
Sandretto, René, 140
Sao Tomé & Principe, 126
SAPE, 182
Saro-Wiwa, Ken, 98, 99
Savimbi, Jonas, 59, 62, 84
savings, 77, 141–3 passim
Schaef, Thomas, 171
Schatzberg, Michael, 85
Schlesinger, Arthur M., 43, 45
Schmiedling, Holger, 21
Schmitt, Claudia, 21
Schott, Jeffrey, 15–1, 17
Schulders, Guy, 133
secession, 3, 50, 55, 56, 58, 60, 81, 99, 116
Seck, Assana, 169
security factors, 16, 31, 58, 85, 126, 131, 134
Seekings, Jeremy, 111
self-determination, 107, 115, 116
Senegal, 3–5 passim, 9, 11, 47, 48, 77, 79, 122, 181, 196–8; Senegambian Confederation, 11, 177
services, 16, 18, 24, 25–7, 30; government, 57, 114
Seychelles, 28
Shaba, 59, 81, 83, 87, 88–4
Shaka, 61
Sierra Leone, 5, 57, 59, 65, 120, 123, 198
single-party regimes, xviii, 68–71 passim
Sjolander, Claire Turenne, 25–9
Sklar, Richard, 70
smuggling, xviii, 8–12 passim, 65, 72, 84, 122, 135, 169–77, 183, 189–200
Smouts, Marie-Claude, 1
Somalia, 3–5 passim, 47, 54, 55, 57–60 passim, 62, 64, 65, 72

Soulé, Bio, 5, 11, 12, 177
South Africa, xvii, 4, 6, 7, 28, 45, 46, 49, 64–5, 84–5, 103–18, 153, 158–68 passim, 182, 189, 193; Constitution, 104, 109–11 passim; economy, 107, 108, 159; elections, 104, 111; homelands, 109, 110, 112, 160; institutions, 104–6, 112–17, FFC, 114; Law Commission, 44–5, 49; RDP, 107, 108, 113, 117
South Korea, 25–9
Southall, Aiden, 9
Southern Africa, 3, 5, 7, 27, 28, 33–6 passim, 64, 85, 151–68 see also COMESA; SACU, 6–7, 10, 28,, 33, 40, 153, 154, 159–68; SADC, 6, 7, 19, 28, 29, 31, 33, 36, 40, 84, 85, 151, 155–60, 164, 166, 168; SADCC, 6, 31, 151–8 passim, 166
sovereignty, 1, 2, 4, 6, 32, 47, 51, 53, 56, 60, 72, 103, 156, 161, 165, 166, 168
Soviet Union, 1, 18, 56, 58, 60, 62
Spain, 21–3, 126
Special Forum, 112
Srinivasan, P.N., 16
Stary, Bruno, 169–77
state, 4, 5, 41–80, 136, 166, 176; creation, 95–6, 99–100; -society relations, 2–5, 41–51; see also integration, national
Suberu, Rotimi, 91–102
subsidies, 21, 22, 25, 112, 191
Sudan, 3, 47, 48, 55, 57, 59, 60, 65, 83, 84
superpowers, 3, 56, 60
supranationalism, 6, 31, 32, 48, 134, 157
surveillance, 17, 35, 143, 144
Survival International, 50
Svennson, F., 50
Swaziland, 6, 7, 55, 153, 154, 160–4 passim, 167, 168, 193
Sweden, 20
Syria, 139

Takirambudde, Peter, 151–8
Tanzania, 4, 6, 33, 55, 189
tariffs, xviii, 6, 8–12, 18–22 passim, 25, 26, 30, 36, 39, 119, 133, 134, 136, 153, 154, 156, 160, 161; common external, 17, 20, 35, 36, 144, 160, 162
taxation, 35, 36, 47, 92, 93, 113, 114, 134, 136, 156, 161
Taylor, Charles, 43, 59, 62, 65, 198

technical assistance, 34, 37, 38
technology, 19, 44
telecommunications, 6, 26, 120, 121, 127, 137
territoriality, xviii, 3–5 passim, 9, 41–2, 47–8, 50, 51, 103–4, 109–10
timber, 59, 64
Tocqueville, Alexis de, 78
Togo, 5, 11, 47, 71, 77, 171, 189, 196
'toll-points', 136
Toulabor, Comi, 72
tourism, 166
trade, xvii, xviii, 1, 2, 8–12, 15–24 passim, 29, 30, 36, 47, 63, 65, 83, 84, 108, 119, 122–2, 127, 133, 141, 143, 144, 146, 152–5 passim, 161–2, 166, 181–7, 190; creation, 16, 20; cross-border, 7–12 passim, 47, 65, 72, 84, 122, 132, 135–6, 169–87, 192; diversion, 16, 17, 20, 161; intra-regional, 20, 21, 28–30, 65, 127, 143, 165; liberalisation, xviii, 7, 11, 13, 15, 16, 19–23 passim, 25, 30, 36, 38, 120–2 passim, 151,190; unofficial/illicit, xviii, 9, 11, 12, 29, 79–87, 122, 170–2, 189–200
trade unions, 75–9 passim
traditional authorities, 107, 109, 116
training, 34, 37–9 passim, 77, 143, 144; retraining, 77
transit, 133, 134, 189; TIPAC, 134
transport, 8–10 passim, 27, 30, 34, 36, 82, 83, 121, 132–4 passim, 144, 152, 153, 158, 174
Traoré, Moussa, 80
treaties, 157; Abuja, 2, 5, 27, 31, 125, 129; Brazzaville, 130; CEMAC, 7, 36, 134, 144, 146; ECOWAS, 121, 124; Libreville, 126, 131; Maastricht, 7, 140, 142, 144–9 passim, 157; PTA, 152, 154, 155; Rome, 17, 125, 141; UEMOA, 7, 34–5, 144; UMAC, 134; Windhoek, 6, 151, 152, 155, 157, 168
Tredano, A. Benmessaoud, 41
tribalism, 49, 50, 76, 79, 88, 99–100
Triffin Report, 147
tripolarity, 1, 15, 20
Tshisekedi, Etienne, 86, 88–4
Turner, Thomas, 85, 89–7
Tussie, D., 165
Tutsi, 45, 85, 90

UDEAC, 7, 28, 29, 35, 125–7 passim, 129–37; reform of, 129, 130, 133–5
UEAC, 131

UEMOA, 7, 8, 19, 28, 29, 31, 33–5 passim, 40, 122–4 passim, 144, 146, 176
Uganda, 6, 33, 55, 57, 59, 84, 85, 154
UMAC, 134
UMOA, 123, 142, 143
Unal-Kesenci, Deniz, 1
unemployment, 10, 112, 190
United Nations, 50, 53, 61, 99; UNCTAD, 18; UNDCP, 192; UNECA, 36; UNINCB, 189
United States, 15, 17–25, 42–5 passim, 48, 56, 60, 78, 89; BINM, 189; Section 301, 25, 25–9
Unrepresented Nations and Peoples Organisation, 99
URAC, 130
urbanisation, 82, 103, 109, 112
Uruguay, 19

Vaitsos, C.V., 165
Van Staden, G., 155
variable geometry/speed, 32–3, 162, 167, 168
Venezuela, 22
Vengroff, Richard, 80
Verber, Sidney, 78
Verlaque, Christian, 127
Viner, Jacob, 20, 22
violence, 3–5 passim, 45, 71, 74, 99

WAMA, 123
war, civil, 57, 58, 65, 84, 91, 126, 133, 135, 182, 199; Cold, xviii, 1, 3, 15, 23, 26, 53, 60, 62–4 passim, 108; World I, 163, II, 17
water supply, 120–1, 166
Weber, Max, 5
Weimer, Bernard, 153
Weinstein, Brian, 82
Weisfelder, R.F., 152, 154, 155, 167
West Africa, 3, 5–7 passim, 9, 28, 33–5 passim, 62, 119–24, 126, 139–49, 169–81, 187 see also ECOWAS
Western Sahara, 50
Whalley, John, 22
Wiechers, Marinus, 45
Willame, Jean-Claude, 83, 85, 87
women, 10, 122, 181–7
Woods, Dwayne, 77
World Bank, 16, 19, 29, 35, 36, 48, 129, 133, 134, 142, 148, 190, 191, 199

World Trade Organisation, 15, 16, 25, 26, 37
Wright, Stephen, xvii, 3

Yalden, M., 46
Yaoundé Convention, 125
Young, Crawford, 85, 115
young people, 9, 68, 77, 174, 182
Yugoslavia, ex-, 48

Zaïre *see* Congo/Zaïre
Zambia, 58, 78, 82, 84, 85
Zanzibar, 4
Zartman, William, 3
Zimbabwe, 45, 48, 49, 84, 153, 154, 167
Zolberg, Aristide, 82
'zonalisation'/zoning, 97, 100
Zululand, 61
Zysman, John, 24